PRIVATE AND COMMERCIAL RECREATION

PRIVATE AND COMMERCIAL RECREATION:

ARLIN F. EPPERSON
UNIVERSITY OF MISSOURI—COLUMBIA

JOHN WILEY & SONS
NEW YORK □ SANTA BARBARA
LONDON □ SYDNEY □ TORONTO

Copyright © 1977, by John Wiley & Sons, Inc.

All rights reserved. Published simultaneously in Canada.

No part of this book may be reproduced by any means, nor transmitted, nor translated into a machine language without the written permission of the publisher.

Library of Congress Cataloging in Publication Data:

Epperson, Arlin.
 Private and commercial recreation.

 Includes bibliographical references and index.
  1. Tourist trade. 2. Recreation-Economic aspects. I. Title.
G155.A1E6   338.4'7'91   76-56453
ISBN 0-471-24335-3

Printed in the United States of America

10 9 8 7 6 5 4 3 2 1

PREFACE

The field of private and commercial recreation has achieved its own identity only in the past few years. For sometime it had been overshadowed by the tourism and travel industries or associated with the image of the lighted, smoked-filled pool halls of years past.

In the last 10 to 15 years with the advent of the family bowling centers, outdoor recreation attractions such as Disney World and Six Flags, ski resorts, and other enterprises, private and commercial recreation has gained the respect and the attention that it deserves. It is now considered a legitimate form of business for anyone interested in combining the skills and tools of business with the philosophy of leisure.

University recreation education curriculums have not previously considered this sleeping giant. Only recently have they realized that most of the education and training in the municipal, therapeutic, and outdoor sectors (all public supported) account for only two percent of the total expenditures spent for the leisure pursuits of the American public. Many courses and even a few curriculums are beginning to appear in park and recreation departments across the country. Some of these have been the result of graduates in recreation and park studies taking positions in private and commercial recreation establishments, as well as of the influence of the traditional state recreation extension specialist whose responsibility in years past was to work with and assist private recreation enterprises to increase their income. The United States Department of Agriculture has helped farmers increase their incomes for many years through the development of private recreation enterprises. The Soil Conservation Service has also had a secondary purpose of assisting landowners and farmers to develop private and for-profit recreation facilities to supplement their incomes.

The first major efforts to draw together representatives of several private recreation enterprises, and national representatives of the municipal recreation and park agencies and organizations took place in the fall of 1976 as an adjunct to the National Recreation and Park Congress at Boston. This is expected to be the forerunner of closer cooperation and joint efforts between these groups.

The purpose of this book is to help to draw together and cement the relationship between public and private sectors, and to remove the observable lines of difference between the two. It is also intended to introduce prospective students to private and commercial recreation, particularly those who may be considering careers in these types of leisure industries, as well as to expose students who are now majoring in one of the traditional options of municipal, therapeutic, or outdoor recreation to the private recreation and commercial leisure service delivery system, in order to promote future cooperation between groups.

Throughout the book the pronouns he, him, and his refer to the enterprise operator. This has been done only for style, accepted English usage, and convenience. Since both men and women work in leisure-related enterprises or are enterprise managers, whenever the words he or his are read, my intent is to mean also the words she and her.

This book could not have been written without the assistance of the following individuals.

Dr. Karl Munson, Program Leader in Recreation, U.S.D.A., Washington D.C., who provided me with both the atmosphere for learning about this field and motivation to pursue it as an interest and as a Recreation Specialist at the University of Missouri, and with the suggestion and motivation to write this book.

Robert Blundred, Executive Vice-President of the International Association of Amusement Parks and Attraction, Oak Park, Illinois, for his encouragement, insights, and information concerning the amusement parks and attraction's sector of private and commercial recreation, his selected reading "Why the Increase in Travel, Tourism and Outdoor Recreation," as well as his editorial assistance and ideas for materials.

Larry Blundred, for assistance in preparing Chapter 7, "Planning the Recreation Enterprise," and in editing other portions of the manuscript; also, for his teaching of the course in private and commercial recreation at the University of Missouri and for implementing a number of his own ideas.

Dr. Robert Langman, previously President of American Range and Recreation Association, Salt Lake City, Utah currently, assistant professor Department of Recreation and Parks, California State College at Northridge California, who provided inspiration, information concerning the management and operation of resort and hotels, and his selected reading "Challenging Professions Available in Commercial Recreation" as well as information in Chapter 9 concerning competencies for private and commercial recreation education.

John Bullaro, Assistant Professor of the Department of Recreation and Parks, California State College at Northridge, California, who has reviewed this manuscript and provided a wealth of valuable suggestions for improvement. John also wrote the "Questions for Discussion" that follow each chapter, the selected reading "Commercial Recreation Salaried Employment Versus Entreprenurship," and prepared material in the Appendix for the Guide to the Instructor.

The members of the first class in "Introduction of Private and Commercial Recreation, "who helped to gather and write sections on various types of enterprises in Chapter 4.

Sandra Sue Brose	Randall S. Kurtz
Nancy Dee Conde	Parricia L. Marshall
Harlie Major Frankel	Craig Stephen Meltz
Scott Jay Gitel	Alison Parchman
Catherine E. Grant	James Lee Russell
Evelyn Ann Ice	Amy Maria Schmidt
Christine Ann Johnson	Joan Renee Thoenes
Wendy Ann Kriesky	

Arlin F. Epperson

CONTENTS

LIST OF TABLES

INTRODUCTION

CHAPTER 1   TOURISM AND TRAVEL

Scope of Industry   4
Components of Tourism and Travel   4
Transportation   6
Food and Lodging   6
Entertainment and/or Recreation   6

HISTORY OF TRAVEL AND TOURISM   7
Early American Travel   8
Automobile Travel   8
Hotel and Motel Development   10

THE TRAVEL AGENT   10

REASONS FOR INCREASED TRAVEL AND RECREATION   11
Increased Income   11
Mobility   13
Urbanization   13
Education   13
More Leisure Time   14
Technology   14
Cultural Objectives   14
Television Advertising   14
Larger Number of Young Adults   15
An Attitude of Luxury Now A Need   16

THE PROBLEM OF DEFINITION   16

TRADE ASSOCIATIONS   21

TRADE JOURNALS   23

ADDITIONAL REFERENCES   24

CHAPTER 2   WHY PEOPLE TRAVEL FOR RECREATION

PSYCHOLOGY OF TRAVEL   26

TRAVEL MOTIVATION STUDIES   34
Effect of Industrialization   36
Effects of Distance   37
Effect of Cost   39
Effect of Age   40
Effect of Education   40
Effect of Urbanization   41

SOCIAL SIGNIFICANCE OF TRAVEL   41

BARRIERS TO TRAVEL   42

ADDITIONAL REFERENCES   44

SELECTED READING "Why the Increase in Travel, Tourism and
Outdoor Recreation"   44

CHAPTER 3   THE DEMAND FOR RECREATION

PUBLIC VERSUS PRIVATE RECREATION   54

ORRRC STUDIES   58

PROBLEMS WITH DEFINITION AND MEASUREMENT   63
Outdoor Recreation Demand   65

INDOOR RECREATION DEMAND   70

RECREATION DEMAND AS MEASURED BY EXPENDITURES   72

ADDITIONAL REFERENCES   83

CHAPTER 4   THE SUPPLY

PUBLIC AREAS AND FACILITIES   85

PRIVATE AREAS AND FACILITIES   88

PRIVATE NON-PROFIT RECREATION EFFORTS   89

BUREAU OF OUTDOOR RECREATION 1965 PRIVATE OUTDOOR
RECREATION ENTERPRISES STUDY   91

BUREAU OF OUTDOOR RECREATION 1973 PRIVATE ENTERPRISE
STUDY   93

THE SUPPLY AS MEASURED BY THE GOVERNMENT'S STANDARD
INDUSTRIAL CLASSIFICATION (SIC) SYSTEM   96

PRIVATE AND COMMERCIAL ENTERPRISES   96
Problems of Categorization   97

SPECTATOR SPORT FACILITIES   110
Cultural-Historical-Educational Attractions   110
Sports, Convention and Entertainment Facilities   113

OUTDOOR AMUSEMENT PARKS AND ATTRACTIONS   117

INDIVIDUAL SPORTS AND SMALL GROUP ACTIVITIES   125
Bicycling   125
Bowling Centers   130
Commercial Wilderness Outfitters   134
Canoe Liveries   138
Ice Skating Rinks   140

Roller Skating Rinks   141
Snow Skiing   144
Resident Camps   149
Travel Camps   153
Tennis   157

MECHANIZED SPORTS   **161**
Marinas-Boat Yards   161
Motorcycles and off-the-Road Vehicles   164
Recreation Vehicles   167
Snowmobiling   171

CLUBS-RESORTS-SECOND HOMES   **173**
Country Clubs   173
Destination Resorts and Hotels   175
Health and Sports Clubs   178
Homes Associations   180
Second Home Developments   181

ADDITIONAL REFERENCES   **183**

CHAPTER 5   MANAGEMENT OF THE RECREATION ENTERPRISE

Organizational Theory   185

FACILITY MANAGEMENT   **188**

PROGRAM OR SERVICES MANAGEMENT   **190**

PERSONNEL MANAGEMENT   **190**
Recruitment   192
Selection   194
Orientation   195
Inservice Training   196
Supervision or Consultation   196
The Probationary Period   196
Evaluation   197
Staff Morale and Work Incentives   197

FINANCIAL MANAGEMENT   **199**
Functions of Records   201
Daily Income Receipts   201
Daily Expense Record   201
Profit and Loss Statement or Summary   202
Tax Records   202
Payroll Records   204
Mortgage and Debt Records   204
Balance Sheet   204
Bookkeeping Procedures   206

Wisconsin's One-Write System 206
Procedures for Reducing Theft 208
Accrued Accounting 208
Break Even Concept 209
Set Prices 209
Tax Considerations 210

CHARACTERISTICS OF GOOD BUSINESS MANAGEMENT 211

HOW TO ANALYZE THE BUSINESS 211

LIABILITY-INSURANCE-VANDALISM 212
Liability Limitations 213
Fire 215
Vandalism 215

GOVERNMENTAL AGENCIES INVOLVED WITH COMMERCIAL
RECREATION 215

SUMMARY 216

ADDITIONAL REFERENCES 218

CHAPTER 6 PLANNING AND DEVELOPMENT OF THE RECREATION ENTERPRISE

THE FEASIBILITY ANALYSIS 222
Description, Goals, and Objectives 222

MARKET ANALYSIS 224
Description of the Market, Past, Present, and Future 224
General Characteristics of the Market 224
Location and Accessibility 225
Evaluate the Attitude of the Community 229
Evaluate the Attractiveness of the Locality 229
Consideration of Supply and Demand 229
Availability of Utilities 231
Accessibility 231
Highway Travel Data 232
Information and Directions 233
Attendance 233

MANAGEMENT ANALYSIS 242
Operating Expenses 243
Estimating Net Income 248

SUMMARY 251

ADDITIONAL REFERENCES 252

CHAPTER 7   MARKETING THE PRODUCT

Current Conditions   256
Three Marketing Sins   256
The Problem   256
Why People Travel for Recreation   257

MARKET ANALYSIS   257
Market Segmentation   260
User Behavior   262
Sources of Data for Market Segmentation   263

PRODUCT ANALYSIS   265

COMPETITOR ANALYSIS   266

MARKETING CYCLES   266
Expanding the Model   268

THE MARKETING PLAN AND PROGRAM   270

PROMOTION   271
Promotion Through Sales   272
Promotional Sales through Printed Matter and Other Materials   272
Printed Literature   272
Brochures   273
Direct Mail   273
Distribution   274
The Promotion Target   275

ADVERTISING   275
Word of Mouth Advertising   276
Hospitality Training   276
Using An Advertising Agency   278
Outdoor Display Advertising   278
Newspaper Advertising   279
Magazine Advertising   279
Radio   279
Awareness Advertising   279
Package Plans   280

PUBLICITY   280

MARKETING BUDGET   281

TOURISM ASSOCIATIONS   281
Chambers of Commerce   283
Travel Agencies   283
State Tourism Departments   284

COMMUNITY AWARENESS   284

ADDITIONAL REFERENCES   286

CHAPTER 8   IMPLICATIONS FOR THE FUTURE

FORCASTING   288

EXTERNAL IMPLICATIONS   289

The Attitude of the Public   289

Spending Implications   292

Income Implications   294

Time Implications   295

Mobility Implications   297

Urbanization Implications   298

Education Implications   298

Implications of Social Factors   298

Conflicting Examples   299

Changing Activity Interests   302

Summary-External Implications   304

Americans Will Stay Closer To Home   305

What to Look For in 1975   306

INTERNAL IMPLICATIONS   307

SUMMARY   309

CHAPTER 9   IMPLICATIONS FOR COMMERCIAL RECREATION EDUCATION

TYPES OF JOBS FOUND IN PRIVATE AND COMMERCIAL RECREATION   312

Recreation Services   313

Recreation Resources   313

Tourism   314

Amusement and Entertainment   314

Follow-up Study by Contract Research   315

Common Environments of Hospitality and Recreation   316

Hospitality and Recreation   316

Lodging   317

Recreation   317

Entertainment Services   318

Cultural   318

Sports   319

Food and Beverage Services   319

Travel Services and Promotion   319

Information Systems and Services Incorporated   320

NRPA Employ   322
Summary   324
COMPETENCIES NEEDED FOR POSITIONS IN PRIVATE AND COMMERCIAL
RECREATION   324
CURRICULUM IMPLICATIONS   326
PROBLEMS CONFRONTING FACULTY AND STUDENTS INTERESTED IN
PURSUING PRIVATE AND COMMERCIAL RECREATION EDUCATION   328
PROJECTED 1980 EMPLOYMENT LEVELS FOR PRIVATE, FOR-PROFIT
RECREATION BUSINESSES   332
PROJECTED 1980 NEW RECREATION POSITIONS   332
SUMMARY   333
SELECTED READING "Challenging Professions Available in Commercial
Recreation"   335
SELECTED READING "Commercial Recreation Salaried Employment Versus
Entrepreneurship"   341
APPENDIX A "Key Terms in Recreation"   353
APPENDIX B "Standard Industrial Classification Index Definitions"   356
APPENDIX C "Glossary of Accounting Language"   361
APPENDIX D "Instructors Guide to Commercial Recreation   364
INDEX   381

LIST OF TABLES

	Chapter
Most Popular Outdoor Recreation Activities by Number of Participants	3
Most Popular Outdoor Recreation Activities	3
Most Popular Private Recreation Activities	3
Most Popular Indoor Recreation Activities	3
Recreation Expenditures	3
Number Acreage and Attendance of Public and Private Outdoor Recreation Areas	4
Private Outdoor Recreation Enterprises	4
Private Outdoor Recreation Enterprise Employees	4
National Association of Conservation Districts Private Sector Recreation Inventory Primary Facilities	4
National Association of Conservation Districts Private Recreation Inventory-Type of Activity	4
Number of Recreation Establishments	4
Payroll and Number of Employees of Recreation Establishments	4
Total Receipts-Recreation Establishments	4
Projected Attendance Attraction A	6
Attraction A Capacity Requirements	6
Attraction A Attendance/Gate Receipts	6
Attraction A Auxiliary Revenues	6
Attraction A Total Revenues	6
Campground-Anticipated Revenues	6
Attraction A Pre-Opening Expenses	6
Campground Pre-Opening Expenses	6
Attraction A Estimated Operating Expenses	6
Campground Estimated Operating Expenses	6
Attraction A Estimated Net Income 1976	6
Campground Estimated Net Income	6
Safari Systems Campground Profit and Loss Statement	6
National Time Budget and Time Division of Leisure	8

INTRODUCTION

A little over 130 years ago, a wagon train of over 1000 men, women, and children traveled a distance of more than 2000 miles from the Mississippi River to the Pacific Ocean, in a trip across our land that lasted more than 6½ months, and which was accomplished with much sickness, death, physical hunger, hardship, and cold.

Less than 10 years ago, in just under ten minutes Astronaut Edward H. White crossed the 3000 miles of the American Continent in the famous Gemini 4 spacecraft. During these past 130 years, our nation has experienced the most fantastic economic, social, and technological growth and advancement of a nation in the history of mankind. In these few short years, we have come from a people struggling for food, warmth, and shelter to a leisure and luxury oriented society. Today we are the most affluent and mobile people on the earth. An increasing population, new prosperity, longer vacations, shorter work weeks, longer life expectancy, labor saving devices, and other factors have indeed produced a leisure society unequaled in any previous generation. Although, to some extent, Greek and Roman societies may have approached that which we know today, theirs was to some degree available because of slavery, rather than technology. In every generation, leisure and financial affluence has been the ultimate goal of each and every person.

It can be said that man's pursuit and use of leisure underly predominantly all of the social, economic, and political forces by which he lives as an individual and as a member of society. It is through leisure that we have developed our cultural heritage, and increased our education. It is through leisure that we attain the quality of life that we all seek. It is through leisure that we attain the self satisfactions from our own creations, and the self esteem and self actualization, that comes from acceptance of our peers, and our desire to convey our thoughts and personalities through various forms of creative leisure pursuits.

In the 1880s, most of the people in our nation knew little leisure, working 70 and 80 hours a week, from dawn to dusk, in agricultural and industrial pursuits to provide the necessities of food and shelter. In the 1930s, leisure had increased while work encompassed a six-day work week and a 40- to 50-hour week. In the 1950s, the work week had reduced to 5½ days or 44 hours. In 1970, over 2000 companies have been experimenting with the four-day work week, and the United States Government moved five legal holidays to Mondays, creating five additional three-day long weekends. In 1973, there is more discretionary time or leisure time than work time for the average American, with over 3030 leisure hours per year.

By the year 2000, the work week is expected to be reduced to at least 35 hours per week or less, and will produce over 5000 hours of leisure per year.

Some recreation and sociological experts predict that by the year 2000 it will be possible for one-third of the population to support the other two-thirds.

We have indeed moved from a society of work to a society of leisure. As viewed in the words of Herbert Hoover, "a nation is known better by what it does during its leisure, than what it does during its work."

The additional leisure, is not necessarily a blessing to all. To the 20 million over the age of 65, or the 26.7 million who are handicapped or disabled, or the nine percent of our population which is unemployed, leisure is indeed a curse.

Nevertheless, because of the increase in leisure time for whatever the reasons, the demand for recreation has increased at an unbelievable rate. If the 1930s is to be any example, the demand for recreation will increase again, regardless of the status of the economy. As the economy falls, people will turn to recreation to fulfill their leisure hours, as they will do when the economy is on the increase. Indeed the demand for the types of recreation will fluctuate. However, it is a certainty that the demand for additional leisure opportunities and services will continue to increase, although it may not be possible to predict the diversity or the types of demand in particular areas.

The Private Recreation industry has a large part to play in providing these opportunities now and in the future, probably a much larger part than does the public sector.

It is for students who may be interested in learning more about these private recreation providers that this book is written.

As most students of tourism and private recreation know, the literature on the subject is very limited, if it exists at all. Although there are several books on tourism— there is none directed to the totality of the private and commercial recreation providers. A book on tourism this is not. A book on private recreation enterprises it may be, realizing that any first attempt is just that. Many will find subjects covered inadequately or not at all. By the very nature of the private and commercial recreation field it is anyone's choice what is included and what is not. There are no agreed upon definitions or classifications.

It is hoped, however, that this material will provide the student with an awareness of the field of private and commercial recreation, sufficient to assist them to decide if this is the area in which they would like to find career employment. It is only an introduction. Certainly others, perhaps more knowledgeable and qualified, will contribute to this body of knowledge so that in the future recreation and park curriculums in cooperation with Departments of Business and others on the campus can field other courses, emphasis, or curriculums in this area. As a result—hopefully—those that have provided such good preparation for public recreation programs can also do as well, for those interested in the private field.

CHAPTER 1

TOURISM
AND
TRAVEL

Since humanity's first existence, we have sought opportunities to play, to recreate, to relax, to travel, to adventure, and to be entertained. We have sought the opportunity to learn of other lands, other cultures, to see new places, and visit areas of outstanding natural beauty. We have always enjoyed many of the forms of what we today would call recreation experiences, even though some of these opportunities may have been limited in years past. Among the recreation experiences enjoyed by human beings a favorite has been that of travel. Although travel for pleasure and recreation has developed only recently, the urge and desire has always existed since our beginning. Today it is both a necessity of life, and a recreation pursuit enjoyed by more people than ever before. It is difficult to live one day without being involved in some form of travel, whether for work, necessities of life, or leisure.

The Discover America Travel Association indicates that the travel industry encompasses a very wide variety of businesses and enterprises amounting to over 61 billion dollars a year in sales today and is second only to grocery store sales. Tourism and travel sustains the employment of more than four million Americans and one out of every 20 in the civilian labor force is an employee in a tourism or travel related enterprise. In 46 of the 50 states, tourism ranks as one of the top three leading industries.[1]

This is a considerable change from the days of long ago when human beings traveled primarily to search for food, water, shelter, and security.

As the travel industry is one of the biggest and most comprehensive in our world today, it is also one of the most complex, and cuts across many aspects of our economic society. The majority of the goods and services that we consume daily would be impossible without a transportation system. Unfortunately it is extremely difficult to isolate that portion of the travel industry that relates to tourism and recreation. The problems of definition continue to exist within the tourism industry, which makes it even more difficult for the student to gain an adequate and clear understanding of what is represented in the travel and tourism industry.

---

[1] Discover America Organizations, Inc., *Why Discover America . . . A Letter About Membership,* Washington, D.C. 1975.

SCOPE OF INDUSTRY

Although there is estimated to be over 135,000 private and commercial recreation enterprises, and an additional 5000 or more attractions that play a significant role in the travel and tourism industry, the amount of money spent and the number of jobs in the private and commercial recreation sector of the travel and tourism industry is relatively small compared to those other industries encompassed in the travel and tourism industry as a whole.[2]

COMPONENTS OF TOURISM AND TRAVEL

Providing tourism services and opportunities is indeed a complex business, crossing the lines of many kinds of industries. Although different authorities classify the components differently, the following distribution gives an example of the proportion of each dollar spent by the average traveler or tourist.[3]

Lodging	$0.23
Food and Drink	0.27
Recreation and Amusement	0.12
Gasoline and Automobile Expense	0.09
Clothing and Footwear	0.11
Jewelry and Souvenir	0.07
Drugs, Cosmetics, Tobacco	0.07
Miscellaneous	0.04
	$1.00

It can be readily seen that the travel and tourism industry is comprised of a number of different kinds of business enterprises. Even though a "traveler" or "visitor" as they may be called may go camping, boating, picnicking, sightseeing, or visit a historical area, he must also have a way to get there, a place to stay, and a place to eat.

Other authorities in the field break the components of tourism into different categories.[4]

1. Eating and drinking establishments.
2. Hotel and motels.
3. Trailer parks and camps.
4. Sports and miscellaneous amusements.

[2] Bureau of Outdoor Recreation, *The 1965 Nationwide Inventory of Publicly Owned Recreation Areas and Assessment of Private Enterprises,* Department of Interior, Superintendent of Documents, Washington, D.C., 1965, p. 211.

[3] From TOURISM: PRACTICES, PHILOSOPHIES, by Robert McIntosh. Copyright © 1972 by Grid, Inc., Columbus, Ohio. Reprinted by permission of Grid, Inc.

[4] From THE TOURIST BUSINESS, by Donald E. Lundberg. Copyright © 1972 by Donald E. Lundberg. Reprinted by permission of Donald E. Lundberg.

5. Laundries and dry cleaning establishments.
6. Gasoline and service stations.
7. Retail trades, souvenirs, and gifts.
8. Rooming and boarding houses.
9. Motion picture theaters and theatrical productions.

Dr. Robert McIntosh, a recognized expert and authority in the field of tourism for many years, breaks the tourism components and supply into five main categories of slightly different figuration in his book, "Tourism: Principles, Practices and Philosophies."[5]

1. *Natural Resources.* The water, climate, mountains, beaches, and other features natural or man-made that attract tourists for beauty and aesthetic purposes.
2. *Interest Structure.* All those necessary parts of a tourism enterprise that can be thought of as on the ground or under it, such as water supplies, sanitation systems, utilities, transportation modes such as highways, roads, drives, parking lots, and so on.
3. *Transportation and Transportation Equipment.* Including automobiles, trains, buses, limousines, and other related facilities.
4. *Super Structure.* The above ground facilities such as hotels, motels, terminals, restaurants, shopping centers, museums, stores, and similar structures.
5. *Hospitality Resources.* All of the social and cultural backgrounds and traditions of a given area and its residents. These in many cases are enhanced, and other cases can be developed, as in efforts to educate those in direct contact with the traveler and pleasant and helpful attitudes to make the visitors stay as pleasant as possible. These would also include such things as special events, social activities, spectator sports, festivals, pageants, and so on.

It can readily be seen that all will not agree that each component or portion thereof should be included. The areas are indeed not mutually exclusive, and include the expenses of many "locals," as well as tourists. They are however included in the total for reasons discussed previously to give as broad a picture of the impact of the traveler on the economy as possible.

The makeup of various tourism and travel associations both regional, state, and national, give some idea as to the varied interests and backgrounds of those who feel they have a share in the travel and tourism business. Many of these components whether as "transient facilities," or "destination facilities," must rely on one another, and together provide all of the services and activities needed by a tourist. It is travel however, that is the common denominator in all of the various industries concerned.

It is not the purpose of this book to discuss the components of tourism other than the recreation business. They will however be mentioned in relation to their effect on

---

[5] From TOURISM: PRACTICES, PHILOSOPHIES, by Robert McIntosh. Copyright © 1972 by Grid, Inc., Columbus, Ohio. Reprinted by permission of Grid, Inc.

Figure 1 Hotels and resorts have a variety of facilities for children and adults such as these at the Grand Bahama Hotel and Country Club, West End Grand Bahama. Courtesy: American Hotel and Motel Association, New York, New York.

the recreation business even though they may be either primary or secondary in nature. For our purposes, we will consider basically three general component areas.

TRANSPORTATION

Eighty percent of tourism and travel occurs in private automobiles; airlines, buses, and trains also are prime organizations interested in the travel and tourism market.

FOOD AND LODGING

The restaurant and motel accommodations industries are indeed a major segment of the tourism and travel economy, with such giants as Hilton Inn, Holiday Inn, Ramada Inn, and others bidding for the traveler and promising to make their stay more attractive.

ENTERTAINMENT AND/OR RECREATION

Even though the reason for the trip may have been to visit a particular place or participate in a certain form of recreation, the amount of money spent in this area is much smaller than that spent for transportation, food, and lodging.

HISTORY OF TRAVEL AND TOURISM[6]

Although travel as we know it had its beginning many centuries ago, traveling for pleasure is a relatively recent phenomena. The first "travelers" were probably groups or bands of nomads in search of food, water, and shelter. Centuries ago, early Phoenicians toured in caravans throughout the Middle East and Mediterranean and participated in trade with a number of countries in Southeast Asia. The purpose for this early travel was almost 100 percent business. The invention of money by Southeast Asian countries at approximately 4000 B.C. allowed a much more highly developed system of trading. As both writing and the wheel were invented in this era, a means of trade through money or barter was one of the aspects that created an opportunity for travel for business purposes. Much of the earlier travel was by water, because of the possibility of carrying of wares, and the difficulties with foot-and-cart travel over mountains with no roads, thus resulting in travel primarily between areas lying near water and waterways. Some of the early vessels apparently were no more than 40 feet in length. How travel, to any significant extent, was accomplished with such primitive means is almost beyond imagination.

Some have said that tourism had its beginning about this time, with Noah and the Ark being the first cruise operator. It is fairly well agreed that the Romans were among the first travelers for pleasure, or for reasons other than business or physiological needs. Because of the high development of the Roman Empire, including paved roads, road maintenance, chariots and fast horses, Romans were able to travel as much as 100 or more miles in a day by using relays of horses at regularly established rest posts or change stations. One report indicates that Romans may have traveled as much as 1300 miles in nine days using this method.

China and Japan also were said to have rather sophisticated travel and were traveling for pleasure by the time of the birth of Christ.

It is the Romans, however, that began to combine travel, tourism, and recreation. Because of the leisure society created by wealth and slavery, Romans were free to travel to distant places to see famous temples, monuments, or mountains, and travel to selected places on the Mediterranian for vacations, or to popular destinations for holiday travel for Olympic games and activities, as well as to health spas for health purposes.

Tourism attractions were in evidence as early as 334 B.C. when Alexander the Great, through entertainment by acrobats, circus performers, animal acts, magicians, and other large-group entertainment attracted as many as 700,000 tourists to Ephesus, which is now Turkey.

After the fall of the Roman Empire, travel was much reduced or nonexistent. It was filled with danger because of roving groups of nomads or thieves, and other than

[6] Robert W. McIntosh, Ibid, pp. 7-22: Donald Lundberg, The Tourist Business, Institutions/Volume Feeding Management Magazine, Chicago, 1973, pp. 9-12: *Travel Trade,* Lickorish and Kershaw, Practical Press, London, 1958, and "A Short History of Tourism" *Travel and Tourism Encyclopedia,* Travel World, London, 1959: "The History of Tourism," Giblert Sigaux, Edito-Service, Ltd, Geneva, Taken from the *Dictionaire Universal du XIXe,* Siecle of 1876.

the religious crusades to the Holy Land from England and other European countries, little travel for pleasure took place.

The health spas surprisingly lead the way for expanded travel in the late 18th century. Supported by a strong work ethic and the philosophy of "re-creation" to refresh and prepare one for additional work, spas became popular attractions, and included not only the health aspects but also other recreation opportunities such as games, dancing, gambling, special events, and so on. Russia and Europe as well as Switzerland all participated in the spa and health club attractions, with Switzerland having over 100 at one time. A similar progression was seen consistently throughout Europe. First the sick came to be healed, and then the tourists came for pleasure and recreation.

It was not until the advent of the railroad in England in the 1830s that travel was available to the masses. The development at that time of a railroad system that would allow the British to travel for a penny a mile brought tremendous demand for travel by rail.

EARLY AMERICAN TRAVEL[7]

America was founded primarily by people traveling for either exploration purposes, including the Spaniards and Norwegians, or for religious purposes, such as the settlements at Cape Cod in 1602 and Plymouth in 1629. Travel was almost entirely by horseback or small boat along trails that connected major settlements or were along waterways. The advent of the stagecoach and wagon came later, but even this method was very slow and uncomfortable over long periods of time. As travel continued to develop, taverns or inns were built at convenient distances along major routes, to provide refreshment, relaxation, and rest. The primary purpose of the inn-tavern in those days was to provide food, drink, and sleeping accommodations.

Rapid development of the railroad in the late 1800s and early 1900s through 1920 had a pronounced effect on travel. Large hotels with comforts and accommodations unknown previous to that time were built along the railroad lines near railroad stations. They provided almost all of the needed services and accommodations for the traveler that day. The trains themselves, with sleeping and dining cars, provided comforts and pleasures that would rival the private trains of Napoleon III and Queen Victoria of many years previous in European history. In the 1920s a private railroad or railroad car was indeed the mark of wealth and the ultimate in traveling comfort.

AUTOMOBILE TRAVEL

The tourism business as we know it today had its beginning in the early 1920s with the advent of the automobile and the construction of roads and highways. Although primary use of these "machines" was for pleasure, because they were not dependable

[7] Rev. Andrew Burnaby, *Travels Through the Middle Settlements in North America,* Cornell University Press, 1960.

Figure 2 Recreation travel has improved and grown considerably since the days of early travel.
Courtesy: Recreation Vehicle Industry Association-Chantilly, Virginia.

over long distances or long periods of time, and persons with abilities to work on them were even more scarce, many of the resorts and tourist homes were constructed in that era to accommodate the automobile traveler. Travel increased rapidly in the late 1920s as people were beginning to be able to travel "when and where they pleased."

The depression of the 1930s saw less travel and less development in all aspects of the economy as well as the tourism and travel industry. Travel during the war years was primarily by rail, because of gasoline and rubber shortages. Today with the advent of a 41,000 mile network of inter-state highways linking all cities of 50,000 or more, there are more than 83 million automobiles in the U.S. and the number is growing. It is estimated that over 85 percent of the travel today is by automobile and the "average family" drives approximately 20,000 miles per year.[8]

Automobile	86.8
Air	9.8
Bus	2.3
Rail	1.1
Water	0.3

[8] Transportation Association of America, *Annual Report,* Washington, D.C., 1970.

It is difficult at this point to estimate the impact of energy shortages and the declining economy in relation to the modes of transportation used, and the extent to which each is a means of transportation.

HOTEL AND MOTEL DEVELOPMENT [9]

The early 1950s and 1960s saw many new hotels and convention centers built. These hotels had an occupancy rate of approximately 65 percent prior to World War II. During World War II the occupancy rate was up to 93 percent. The early 1950s and 1960s also saw a number of tourist courts and motels develop all along major highways, at entrances into notable tourist attractions in the West, and outside the large cities in the Midwest and East.

During the 1960s, additional hotels were constructed in an effort to gain back much of the tourism accommodation business that had been lost during the 1950s and 1960s to the tourist courts and motels. This has been coupled with a desire and an effort on the part of cities to develop themselves as tourist attractions. The completion of the freeway systems into the city centers again provided the hotels with the much needed opportunities to provide accommodations. This system of freeways however has caused the train revenues to drop by 90 percent since the war.

THE TRAVEL AGENT [10]

The rise and development of travel and tourism has resulted in a similar increase in persons who have decided to make their livelihood by arranging trips for others. Thomas Cook of England is credited with being the first bona fide travel agent to work as a full-time professional when he chartered a train in 1841 to take over 500 persons to a "temperance" convention. He later became a full-time excursion organizer and tour retailer and published the "Handbook of the Trip." The business grew and now has over 625 offices and 10,000 employees around the world.

In America, the American Express Company, which grew out of the old Wells-Fargo Company, had a well-established travel business by 1920. By 1945 business was estimated at $75 million annually, which included the sales and distribution of the well-known travelers checks. The company also sold casualty, life, and property insurance which made up a good portion of its earnings.

Following World War II the travel business began to increase at an unprecedented pace. Today there are over 17,000 travel agencies that employ over 100,000 persons in the world. The over 6000 travel agencies in this country produce an annual sales volume in excess of 4 billion dollars, over one-half of which is in domestic air sales.

---

[9] George Podd & John D. Lesure, *Planning and Operating Motels and Motor Hotels,* Ahrens, New York, 1964, pp. 4-12.

[10] Donald Lundbert, op. cit. pp. 87-106.

The travel agent is a person who "acts for" other transportation carriers, hotels, and agencies selling travel services.

The Association of Retail Travel Agents, Croton-on-Hudson, New York, and the American Society of Travel Agents, 360 Lexington Avenue, New York, New York, 10017 are organizations that are continually attempting to upgrade and professionalize the jobs of travel agents.

While the financial requirements are high, however, the rewards are many, including inexpensive travel to many parts of the world and involvement in a number of areas, geography, peoples, political conditions, foods, history, and recreation. An excellent reference on the responsibilities of the travel agent can be found in the Tourist Business, pages 87 to 106.

REASONS FOR INCREASED TRAVEL AND RECREATION _____

Tourism, travel, and recreation is the fastest growing aspect of our economy. During the past 20 years, while world exports showed an annual growth rate of approximately 7.7 percent, world tourism grew at a rate of over 12 percent. Airlines, for an example, have enjoyed fantastic increases primarily because less than three percent of the population has never been in an airplane.

Primary reasons for increased travel and tourism are many and extensive efforts will not be made here to describe these factors other than to mention them briefly. The same factors that have been working to produce increased leisure time, also influence increases in travel and tourism. Although increases in leisure and increases in travel and tourism are not directly proportional, their relationship is highly related.

INCREASED INCOME

Personal income has been increasing every year, even though current inflation has slowed this rate of growth.

Disposable income, which is one of the keys to travel growth, has also increased each year. In 1963 the disposable income was over 2100 dollars and by 1971 it had increased to almost 3600 dollars. The median family income now is estimated above 10,000 dollars. Disposable income increases at approximately a rate of 4.4 percent per year. In 1950 it was approximately ten percent of personal income. The discretionary income as a percent of personal income averages approximately 22 percent in 1975, and is projected to approach 30 percent by 1980.[11]

Real family income has doubled in a generation. The number of people living in poverty is less than ten percent—one-half of what it was in 1959. In 1955, 202,000 households earned incomes over 25,000 dollars. Twenty years later, these were 4,225,000.

[11] "A Marketing Managers Guide to High Risk Strategy in the '70's", Special Report, Business Management Magazine, **38**, Number 5, August 1970.

Figure 3 The thrill and excitement of rides such as the mine train at Six Flags over Mid-Missouri is one reason why people travel for recreation.
Courtesy: International Association of Amusement Parks and Attractions. Oak Park, Illinois.

Family spending has increased fastest on education, health, recreation, and housing.[12]

Other factors to be discussed later, such as education, family size, ages of children, and age of travelers, all affect travel and tourism. However few will travel without the means to do so. The disposable income is increasing at a faster rate than the economy itself. Although many people in todays society complain of high taxes, increased inflation, and other things the average family still has more discretionary or disposable income today than they did five or ten years ago.

MOBILITY

Americans have placed a high priority on the development of excellent streets and highways. This is illustrated by the 41,000 miles of interstate freeways which connect all cities of over 50,000. The average family now owns two automobiles or more, and drives over 20,000 miles per year. Driving for pleasure is enjoyed by more Americans than any other single outdoor recreation activity. The availability of streets, highways, freeways, and the comforts of the modern automobile have all contributed to the increased travel and tourism that we see today. Accessibility plays a large part in the popularity of the tourist areas. Indeed, the automobile and the freeway have put many remote vacation and recreation areas within the reach of most of the nation's population.

URBANIZATION

The desire by many who live in urban areas to escape to the country has contributed to the increase. Over 80 percent of the population within the United States now lives in what the federal government considers urbanized areas. This percentage has continued to increase every year until 1974. It appears now to be stabilized. However as millions of people continue to live in cities and metropolitan areas, the pressure and the desire to escape, even for a day, when combined with a means and the funds to do so produces strong motivations for tourism and travel.

EDUCATION

Travel has traditionally been a middle- and upper-class phenomena. Studies have shown that as education of the head of the family increases, the desire to see new things and new places also increases almost proportionately. The level of education is increasing each year in the country. Likewise a proportional increase in the amount of travel can be expected by persons in these categories also.

In 1960, college enrollment stood at 3.5 million. In 1973, it reached 8.6 million, and is expected to exceed 10 million by 1980.

[12] Howard Flieger, "A Case Against Gloom," U.S. News and World Report, March 17, 1975.

Sixty percent of todays college students come from facilities in which the head of the household never completed one year of college.[13]

MORE LEISURE TIME

Although the 40-hour work week has been standard for 10 or 15 years, many companies are experimenting with four-day weeks, 35-hour work weeks, extended vacations, more three day weekends, and other work schedules which have produced considerable additional leisure time. Many of the marketing techniques today center on the amount of time that can be saved, rather than on the job that the product will do or its' low cost. Increases in leisure time contribute significantly to increases in travel and tourism.

TECHNOLOGY

The Rand Corporation indicates that with present technology by the year 2000, one quarter of the population could be producing all the goods and services required by the other three quarters. Many examples are evident of unions and other groups forcing the continuation of jobs no longer needed. Although in some quarters it is suggested that individuals must work to have good mental health, the industrialization and technology has indeed produced a leisure society, and probably will continue to do so in the future. Most homes are full of luxuries that are labor saving or time saving devices.

CULTURAL OBJECTIVES

With travel drawing localities, states, and nations closer together, there is more demand and more opportunity to view the cultural and social aspects of other groups of people. Because of this exchange of ideas and ways of life, and because of our inter-changing relationships, with one out of five families moving every year, travel has both helped to knit us closer together as a group and as a nation, as well as give us the desire to see many of the things, people, and places that others have described.

TELEVISION ADVERTISING

Television and advertising may have contributed more to travel and tourism than any other single factor. Prior to the advent of tv, travelers shared their sights and experiences to others with whom they worked and lived, and the images were only in the minds of the traveler. Television has brought into every home, the heights of the Rockies, the rippling streams, the seashores, and when coupled with advertising which says "you owe it to yourself," "get away for the weekend," and other slogans suggesting time and again the attractiveness and advantage of travel, it is no wonder that large numbers of persons are now traveling who have not traveled before.

[13] Ibid.

Figure 4 People travel for cultural and historical reasons to visit places of historical significance.
Courtesy: National Trust for Historical Preservation, Washington, D.C.

LARGER NUMBER OF YOUNG ADULTS

Both the affluent society and the emancipation of our young people at an earlier age has produced many adults who include travel in their plans regularly. It was not long ago that only the most adventurous spent the college break at Fort Lauderdale. Now college students expect to travel at Christmas, Spring Break, and at the end of their summer employment. Because of better transportation opportunities, more mature attitudes, and larger discretionary incomes, this group has contributed significantly to the increase in the numbers of people traveling.

Married couples are putting off the raising of a family longer. They are getting married later, and as a result are doing considerably more traveling before they "settle down." The number of automobiles on vacation trips containing only two people has increased dramatically in recent years.

Our changing life styles from rural to urban has contributed also to the increase in travel and tourism. Fewer people are afraid to get out and travel, and more and more are doing so because of the pleasure involved as well as the status, prestige, and "keeping up with the Joneses."

The status symbol no longer is to have a cabin on the lake but rather to have traveled to the Bahamas, the seashore, to Europe, or Hawaii.

AN ATTITUDE OF LUXURY NOW A NEED

Recreators as well as industrial psychologists have long been attempting to promote the philosophy that recreation, travel, and vacations are necessary if one is to have good mental health and be able to perform his job, duties, and responsibilities to the best of his ability. To some extent these authorities along with the marketing experts of recreation businesses and other components of tourism have succeeded in convincing most of todays society that they indeed deserve a vacation, and should plan for one soon. The college students are expecting a week or two for travel and vacation after their summers work, and many refuse to sign contracts that will not allow for this. Unions in many instances are negotiating longer vacations rather than increased wages; thus creating in the minds of society the motivation to travel as well as the desire. A prime example of this new attitude was illustrated during the recession of 1974-1975 in the Detroit area when many of the employees in the automobile manufacturing industry who were laid off took vacations to Florida nevertheless.

THE PROBLEM OF DEFINITION _____

In addition to the problems encountered in the study of travel and tourism with the breadth and scope of industry that relates to the travel market, is the problem of definition. This has been a significant roadblock when attempting to gather statistical information concerning the traveler, the tourist, the recreator, and others.

The National Resources Review Commission defines a tourist as "one who travels away from his home for a distance of at least 50 miles (one way) for business, pleasure, personal affairs, or for any other purpose except to commute to work whether he stays over night or returns the same day."[14]

The International Union of Official Travel Organization uses as a definition persons traveling for business, family, mission, or fun, which would appear to be all encompassing. "Traveling for fun; persons traveling for business, family mission or meeting purposes."[15]

Each state also appears to have their own definitions.

The Virginia definition is "anyone residing outside the state who visits Virginia for vacation or pleasure." Persons coming for business only or who are merely passing

---

[14] National Tourism Resources Review Commission, *Destination, U.S.A.*, Superintendent of Documents, Washington, D.C., June 1973, **2**, page 5.

[15] United Nations Conference on International Travel and Tourism, 1963.

through are not classified as visitors. If they combine business with pleasure or pause to enjoy an attraction or visit a friend however, they appear to be included.[16]

The Nevada definition an out-of-state visitor is defined as those "residents of states other than Nevada who visit the state or stop somewhere in the state while en route through and without regard for trip purpose. Commonly referred to as a tourist."[17]

New Hampshire *defines* "A tourist or pleasure traveler is anyone who has traveled away from home *for pleasure purposes.*" Expenditures for recreational and leisure activities that are not connected with pleasure traveling or vacationing are excluded. Spending for sports, movies, reading, television, and occasional dining out are thus excluded. It must be admitted that tourists and especially seasonal residents spend money on these items. The reason for excluding such expenditures is that the bulk of them are made by persons who are not engaged in vacationing or pleasure traveling. Also excluded are expenditures made in New Hampshire by residents of border states unless made in the course of a vacation or pleasure trip.[18]

The Vermont definition is "The tourist and recreation industry . . . includes, business activity generated by out-of-state travelers and seasonal residents visiting Vermont regardless of length of stay, for vacation and recreation purposes, including other seasonal reasons in which *an element of recreation* is involved, but excluding visits for business purposes unless the primary reason Vermont was chosen for the visit was its recreational attraction, as is frequently the case with business conventions or conferences."[19]

Because of the adverse reaction to the term "tourist," many areas refer to those who travel to participate in recreation, business or pleasure as "travelers," "visitors," or "guests."

Students of travel, tourism, and recreation business must understand that there is indeed no commonality of definitions; that statistics, research, and findings must all be interpreted in terms of the definitions on which they were based, and what one terms tourism another may not.

Even though the definitions seem to have consistencies, most differ mainly on the following points.

1. The distance traveled.
2. The length of time stayed.
3. The purpose for the visit, whether business, recreation, visit relatives, or other.

---

[16] *Virginia Travel Study,* Commonwealth of Virginia, 1968.

[17] State Highway Department Staff, *Nevada Out-of-State Visitor Survey,* 1963, Nevada State Highway Department, Carson City, Nevada, 1964, p. vi.

[18] P. Hendrick, R. L. Pfister, and M. Segal, *Vacation Travel Business in New Hampshire*—A Survey and Analysis, New Hampshire Department of Resources and Economic Development, Concord, New Hampshire, 1962, p. 4.

[19] John M. Thompson, *The Tourist and Recreation Industry in Vermont,* Vermont Development Department, Montpelier, Vermont, 1963, p. 2.

Because of the commonality of many of the enterprises in the travel and tourism industry, it indeed makes a strange collection of "bedfellows."

It can be readily seen that all businesses do not fit equally well into any category. Therefore in an effort to get some idea of the magnitude of the industry, and the fact that most of the available figures are in terms of gross receipts or sales-tax receipts, which are also probably the most accurate, the whole industry must be included as one entity thus eating and drinking establishments may indeed include all of the restaurants, bars, cocktail lounges, and other establishments within a given state.

Additional difficulties surround the inability to identify and distinguish businesses that are solely in the recreation or tourism industry from those that derive only a portion of their income from such source. These would include many restaurants, service stations, motels, and other business. Another problem exists in businesses that operate only a few months out of the year, while others operate year round.

Also significant are those that operate for profit and those that are nonprofit such as youth serving camps, church activities, industrial firms, and membership clubs.

Some agencies, such as the National Tourism Resources Review Commission, apparently avoid the question by saying "in terms of resources evaluation a distinction between tourism and recreation is useful. However, for purposes of analysis it is not productive to separate tourism from recreation conceptually or technically."[20]

Another reason why an all encompassing definition may be used is that it tends to show a market that is exceedingly high in comparisons with other means of figuring, and thus state departments of tourism can justify higher budgets for their departments on the basis of income to the state, jobs supported by the industry, sales tax receipts generated, and so on.

The variety of definitions of "recreation" also add to the problem. Agencies such as the Bureau of Outdoor Recreation are apparently only concerned with that portion of travel, tourism, and recreation that occurs outdoors. They define outdoor recreation as active and passive leisure time activities which normally occur outdoors, whether in urban, rural, man-made, or natural environments. Activities would be of a pleasurable nature excluding work and life- or home-supported activities.

Smith, Partain, and Champlin in their book, *Rural Recreation for Profit,* define outdoor recreation simply as doing activities out of doors for wholesome exercise, enjoyment, and relaxation.[21] Others, such as Kenneth McIntosh, generally describe recreation as relating to the type of use man makes of his leisure time.[22] McIntosh indicates there is a wide array of uses that man can choose among to absorb his leisure time; outdoor recreational activities are only part of these uses.

---

[20] National Tourism Resources Review Commission, op. cit.

[21] Clodus R. Smith, Lloyd E. Partain and James R. Champlin, *Rural Recreation for Profit,* Interstate Printers & Publishers, Inc. Danville, Illinois, 1968, p. 3.

[22] Kenneth Dale McIntosh, *Privately Owned Hunting Lands in West Virginia Supply Quality and Access Arrangements* (unpublished dissertation) Department of Agriculture and Economics, University of Wisconsin, 1966, p. 10.

Clausen and Knetsch states that "recreation means activity (or planned inactivity) undertaken because one wants to do it.[23] In a deeper psychological sense, they imply that recreation refers to the human emotional and inspirational experience rising out of the recreation act. The most significant contribution of their discussion is that the distinguishing characteristic of recreation is not the activity but the attitude with which it is undertaken. The same activity may be work at sometime to some and recreation at other times to others.

There are also major differences of opinion on what constitutes recreation among "recreation professionals" who readily accept as recreation, participation in one of the recognized outdoor recreation activities such as tennis, baseball, or swimming but tend to regard attendance at an outdoor attraction facility such as Disney Land, Disney World, or one of the six parks* as entertainment.

It is important to realize that one cannot provide "recreation." It is possible to provide opportunities for it, or the resources and facilities for it, but it is not possible to provide recreation as such, all neatly packaged and digested.

Although there is wide variety in definitions of tourist, traveler, and recreation participant, there is some degree of commonality among terms used to measure these activities. The "outing" is defined by the Bureau of Outdoor Recreation in its National Recreation Survey as outdoor recreation occasions during which persons will stay away from home for the major part of the day, eight hours on the average, with little variation but not overnight. The "trip" is defined as an overnight recreation occasion during which persons are away from home at least overnight. "Vacation," on the other hand, was defined as an outdoor recreation occasion lasting four or more days. Other agencies include additional criteria such as distance traveled, expenditures made, and so on. The above definitions give rise to the "visitor day," "camper day," or "occasion day," that has long been used to measure attendance and usage levels at state and national parks. Since the main objective of this book is to discuss various aspects of the recreational business, less attention will be paid to whether or not the participant traveled to participate in the recreation activity or not, and more concerning the various aspects of operation and management of various recreation businesses.

Some definitions relating to recreation however are somewhat consistent among federal agencies. Examples of these can be found in Appendix A. Many travel and tourism agencies, including most state departments of tourism, are accepting the definitions used by the Bureau of Census for such terms as duration of trip, person miles, person trip, trip purpose, trip, traveler, and other terms used extensively in the travel industries.[24]

---

[23] Marian Clawson and Jack L. Knetsch, *Economics of Outdoor Recreation,* John Hopkins Press, 1966, Baltimore, Maryland, pp. 6-7.

[24] *National Travel Survey, Travel During 1972,* Department of Transportation, U.S. Bureau of the Census, Superintendent of Documents, Washington, D.C. pp. A1-A4.

*Six Flags Corporation opened its first amusement park in Arlington, Texas (Fort Worth-Dallas) in 1961, and now operates parks in Atlanta, St. Louis, Houston, the movieland wax museum in Buena Park, California, and the Stars Hall of Fame in Orlando, Florida.

For the purposes of this text, "travel" will be used as the broader term including travel to any place for any purpose, for any length of time, or for any distance. "Tourism" will be used as a broader term than recreation, and will be thought of as including significant travel, for purposes primarily for pleasure, recreation, or leisure.

Recreation however may be the primary purpose of either travel, tourism, or both, but may not encompass either, such as playing ball in the back yard. Thus the participants or visitors to a private or commercial recreation enterprise may or may not be tourists, depending on the distance traveled, length of time stayed, and so on.

Therefore, the recreator, the traveler, and the tourist differ somewhat, primarily in that the recreator's main interest is in participation in the recreation activity of his choice, for which he may or may not need to travel to do so. The tourist on the other hand may have less interest in recreation activities per se, but may indeed achieve, receive, or participate in his "re-creation" during his travel, which provides pleasure and which he does for pleasurable purposes. It does not normally involve a large measure of physical activity or exertion, nor the use of any particular leisure recreation skills.

It may not be possible, nor even desirable, to attempt to separate tourist activities from recreation activities. Many travelers travel for both reasons. It should be noted however that tourism in general requires a number of tourist "attractions" that may or may not already be in existence, such as natural areas, aesthetic or scenic places, historic or educational sites, and supporting facilities such as hotels, motels, restaurants, and gas stations. Other recreation facilities, such as boat lodging ramps, campgrounds, ski areas, hunting preserves, picnic tables, or swimming pools might also be required.

Travel, tourism, and recreation by whatever name has grown in recent years. It is now the number one item of international trade and is the result of over 100 billion dollars of business. Every town has some kind of Chamber of Commerce that attempts to attract people to the community either to visit or to initiate a business. All fifty states have departments of tourism whose primary purpose is to attract visitors to the state for travel and tourism purposes, to spend their money and to leave their taxes. Many of these are small businesses as defined by the Small Business Administration with gross receipts of less than a million dollars. A great many, particularly in the recreation business, have gross receipts of less than 100 thousand dollars. But regardless of their size or their location, the one overriding purpose for being is to attract the tourist and attempt to sell him an opportunity for relaxation, recreation, food, or lodging, send him home satisfied in hopes that he will tell his friends about his good experience and return again. There is little doubt that the primary overriding concern of the tourist business is one of economics, and the final proof as to the success of his operation will be told in the bottom-line figure on his profit and loss statement. As difficult as it is for a traveler to understand in some instances why things are the way they are, there is no mistake that few businesses catering to tourism and travel can remain in business without showing a profit.

Summary

Travel, tourism, and private and commercial recreation encompasses a speculum of agencies, organizations, and corporations. Those identified in this area range from TWA Airlines to float guides taking groups down the Colorado River, from the manufacturer of motorcycle parts to nightly entertainment in supper clubs. The common thread that knits all of these agencies and organizations together is the interest and desire of the American public for satisfying travel, recreation, and entertainment. The components of tourism and travel industry fall into three basic categories: transportation; food and lodging; and entertainment and/or recreation.

The history of travel and tourism is as old as travel itself, although most of the travel before the mid-nineteenth century was for business and trade. Travel and tourism increased almost.in direçt portion to the availability of low cost transportation available to the masses. In the United States, the advent of the automobile probably had more to do with the increase in travel than any other single factor. This caused a direct increase in hotel and motel development across the country following major highways. As travel increased so did those who supplied, organized, and sold travel in the form of travel agencies.

There has been a number of reasons for increased travel and recreation including increased income, mobility, organization, education, leisure time, technology, cultural objectives, television advertising, a larger number of younger adults, and an attitude that travel, tourism, and recreation is now a luxury.

This continues to be a serious problem in the industry in terms of definitions. The industry does not speak with a common voice nor use common units of measurement in researching, reporting, or discussing an aspect of the industry. Whatever the beginning and whatever the problems, the era of private and commercial recreation is in full swing.

Trade Associations

American Sightseeing Institute
1270 Avenue of the Americas
New York, New York 10020

American Society of Travel Agents
360 Lexington Avenue
New York, New York

Association of Group Travel Executives
c/o WDI Mundy, Ind.
Empire State Building, Suite 540
New York, New York 10001

National Tourism Resources Review Commission
2110 Wisconsin Avenue, N.W.
Washington D.C.

Organization of American States
Division of Tourism Development
1725 Eye Street, N.W., Suite 301
Washington, D.C. 20006

American Hotel and Motel Association
888 Seventh Avenue
New York, New York 10019

The Educational Institute of American Hotel & Motel Association
1407 South Harrison Road
East Lansing, Michigan 48823

American Motor Hotel Association
1025 Vermont Ave., N.W.
Washington, D.C. 20005

Council of Hotel, Restaurant, and Institutional Education
Statler Hall
Cornell University
Ithaca, New York 14850

Discover America Travel Organizations, Inc.
100 Connecticut Ave. N.W.
Washington, D.C. 20036

Hotel-Motel Greeters International
166 East Superior Street, Suite 501
Chicago, Illinois 60611

Hotel Sales Management Association
55 East 43rd Street
New York, New York 10017

National Association of Hotel-Motel Accountants
Essex House, 100 Central Park South
New York, New York 10019

National Executive Housekeepers Association
Business and Professional Building
Second Avenue
Callipolis, Ohio 45631

National Institute of Foodservice Industry
120 South Riverside Plaza
Chicago, Illinois 60606

National Restaurant Association
One IBM Plaza
Suite 2600
Chicago, Illinois 60601

Trade Journals

Hotel Management Review
Hayden Publishing Company Inc.
Ahrens Division
850 Third Avenue
New York 22, New York

Tourist Court Journal
306 E. Adams Avenue
Temple, Texas
Ed.-Publ. Bob Gresham

Budget Travel
Maco Publishing Company
800 2nd Avenue,
New York, New York 10001

Hotel & Travel Index
Ziff-Davis Publishing Company
3850 Hollywood Blvd.
Hollywood, California 90028

Student Travel In America
United States National Student Association
Educational Travel, Inc.
265 Madison Avenue
New York, New York 10016

Travel
Travel Magazine, Inc.
Travel Building
Floral Park, New York 11001
Ed. Malcom Davis

Travel & Leisure
U.S. Camera Publ. Corp.
132 W. 31 St.,
New York, New York 10001
Ed. Caskie Stinnett

Vacation Land
Marketing Division of Disneyland, Div. of Walt Disney Prod. At Disneyland
133 Harbor Blvd.
Anaheim, California 92802
Ed. Richard Smith

Ms. Joan Black Bakos, Editor
Restaurant Business
633 Third Avenue
New York, New York 10017

Ms. Jane Wallace, Editor
Institutions/Volume Feeding Management
5 South Wabash Avenue
Chicago, Illinois 60603

Adventures
Club Adventures, Inc.
Suite 455, Edifice G-L, Place Laval,
Ville-De-Laval, Quebec, Canada

Additional References

Books, Bulletins, and Reports

Burkart, A. J. and S. Medlik, *Tourism: Past, Present, and Future,* Sir Issac Pitman and Sons, The British Hotel and Catering Industry, Heinemann: London, 1974.

Cuebro, *Tourism as a Medium of Human Communication,* Mexican Government Tourism Department, 1967.

Dickerman, Pat, Editor and Publisher, *Country Vacations USA,* Farm and Ranch Vacations, Inc. New York, New York 1976.

Checchi and Company, *Tourism in the South Texas Triangle: An Analytical Framework and Action Program,* U.S. Department of Commerce, Superintendent of Documents, Washington, D.C. 1969.

Clement, Harry G., *The Future of Tourism in the Pacific and Far East,* Checchi and Company, U.S. Department of Commerce, Superintendent of Documents, Washington, D.C. 1961.

Holway, C. P., *How To Profit From The Tourist Business,* Milwaukee, Wisconsin 1949.

Little, Arthur D. Inc., *Tourism and Recreation,* U.S. Department of Commerce, Superintendent of Documents, Washington, D.C. 1967.

Norval, A. J., *The Tourist Industry,* London: Sir Issac Pitman and Sons, 1936.

Ogilvie, F. W., *The Tourist Movement, An Economic Study,* P. S. King and Sons, London, 1933.

Revell, Jack, *The Impact of Domestic Tourism,* University of Wales Press, Bangor, 1973.

Urban Land Institute, *Land: Recreation & Leisure,* Washington, D.C. 1970.

Wilder, Robert L., *Selected Recreation References for Recreation and Tourism,* Extension Service, Oregon State University, Corvallis, Special Report 295, June 1970.

Young, George, *Tourism: Blessing or Blight,* Penguin Books, Harmondsworth, Middlesex, England, 1973.

Zehnder, Leonard E., *Florida's Disney World: Promises and Problems,* Peninsular Publishing Company, Tallahassee, Florida, 1975.
Zwicker, Ted and Paul Todd, *Unusual Vacations for Particular People,* Travel News, Los Angeles, California 1974.

Periodicals
American Hotel & Motel Association, "Motivation in a Changing Environment" Operations Bulletin, September 1970, New York, New York.
ASTA Travel News, "What Makes People Travel", American Society of Travel Agents, New York, New York, August 1964, pp. 64 & 65.
Business Research Division, *Bibliography of Tourism and Travel Research Studies, Reports, and Articles,* University of Colorado in cooperation with the Travel Research Association, **I**, National and Regional; **II**, State; **III**, Foreign.

Discussion Questions

1. What factors suggest that travel and tourism as a business will continue to flourish?
2. What evidence is there that tourism and travel activities were popular in earlier civilization?
3. What events occurred during the early 1900s that launched tourism as we know it today?
4. Is there any logical reason for the numerous different definitions of a tourist?
5. What historical factors made travel available to the masses?
6. What factors make travel popular in the United States today?

CHAPTER 2

WHY PEOPLE TRAVEL FOR RECREATION

PSYCHOLOGY OF TRAVEL

The attitude one has about travel, and the factors that motivate us to travel, are paramount to the successful operation of the recreation business. If the recreation business manager, or employees of the business, do not understand why that particular location or facility was selected, or why it was selected instead of another, or what the traveler expects to receive in terms of satisfaction and personal benefit, they may well be shooting at a target that they cannot see and do not understand. The reason people travel, has changed down through history. As mentioned previously, early efforts were primarily for food, water, and economic gain, and later efforts were for religious reasons, war, migration, and so on. Some of these reasons probably are more easily identifiable and easily understood than travel for pleasure. The fact that a large portion of the traveling public travel for more than one reason, gives rise to the complications of the understanding. Why people travel is related very closely to their personalities, as well as their expectations.

It is true that pleasure travel and recreation is considered in the minds of most only after other more basic needs have been satisfied. Most students are familiar with Maslow's theory concerning the hierarchy of needs of individuals.[1] The first of these needs and most important are those associated with their physiological needs of the individual such as hunger, thirst, and the need for air, or those needs for "personal survival." Until these needs are satisifed, the individual will not consider any others. Second in magnitude are the needs for safety and security, food, water, and warmth. The fact that an individual will steal to satisfy his hunger if he becomes hungry indicates to some extent the relationship of these needs. Only after the individual has satisfied the previous two levels will he be concerned about his social needs or that of belonging to a group and being accepted.

The benefits of travel, tourism, and recreation begin to play a part in ones highest level of needs, which are self-actualization or the realization of self needs in developing ones own personality and ones own potential. The need for creativity, for adventure,

[1] A. H. Maslow, *Motivation and Personality,* Harper, New York, 1954.

Figure 5 Special recreation programs and events such as this balloon race are among a myriad of activities arranged for children at such resort hotels as the Arizon Biltmore in Phoenix. The hotel provides swimming instructors, tennis instructors, cowboy guides, horse ranglers, and recreation directors to serve its pre-adult quests.
Courtesy: American Hotel and Motel Association, New York, New York.

for new challenges, for aesthetic appreciation, for praise from ones peers concerning accomplishments, or for joy of individual accomplishment and fulfillment are all a part of these higher level needs.

Therefore these have strong implications in the marketing aspects of travel, as well as understanding the motivational aspects of why people travel. Those groups in society that are still struggling to meet their lower-level needs, will be less interested in recreation, vacation, and travel opportunities than those who have fulfilled them.

Because of the individual nature of each ones needs, the kinds of opportunities and activities that will fulfill these needs are as diverse as society itself. The fact that some people enjoy active recreation, while others enjoy the creative arts or enjoy working on the farm on weekends, gives rise to the philosophy that "recreation is by definition in the eyes of the recreator," to borrow a phrase. What, in affect, is one person's food is another person's poison, and likewise, what is one person's recreation is another person's work.

A number of authors have listed motivations for travel. The following were listed by John A. Thomas in his article "What Makes People Travel."[2]

Education and Cultural Motives:

1. To see how people in other countries live, work, and play.
2. To see particular sites.
3. To gain understanding of what goes on in the news.
4. To attend special events.

Relaxation and Pleasure:

1. To get away from everyday routine.
2. To have a good time.
3. To achieve some sort of sexual or romantic experience.

Ethic:

1. To visit places your family came from.
2. To visit places your family or friends have gone to.

Other:

1. Weather (to avoid cold).
2. Health (sun, dry climate, etc.).
3. Sports (to swim, ski, fish, or sail).
4. Economy (inexpensive living).
5. Adventure (new areas, people, experiences).
6. One-upmanship (status, relation to ones neighbors and friends).
7. Conformity (keeping up with the Joneses).
8. To participate in history (ancient temples in ruins, current history).
9. Sociological motives (get to know the world).

Other researchers classify the motivators into four areas.

1. Physical (relaxation, sports).
2. Cultural, education, historic.
3. Interpersonal, escape from boredom, prestige.
4. Status and prestige, esteem and personal development.

Authors and researchers disagree concerning the main reasons for traveling; however some groups would tend to imply that the desire to escape ranks high in the magnitude of motivating factors. They would indicate that traveling is a pleasant form of temporary insanity, which has some psychological relationship to the use of drugs or alcohol,

[2] From ASTA TRAVEL NEWS, by John Thomas. Copyright © 1964.

*Figure 6 Physical recreation and sports is one of the motivators for travel.
Courtesy: Photo by Peter Miller, courtesy Ski Industries America.*

in being able to forget their trials and troubles of the world in which one lives for a time which is much more socially acceptable, pleasurable, and contributes significantly greater to ones self-esteem.

The relationship of personal values and expectations to the motivation for travel is considerable. Many travelers have difficulty in indicating why they travel other than in broad general terms, but are much more able to choose or to classify reasons for travel in terms of experiences enjoyed or disliked. This would give weight to the importance of "expectation" of the traveler in determining his travel mode, destination, and so on, and is of particular interest to the recreation business manager concerning his relationship to repeat business.

A number of studies consistently show the following reasons for travel, probably in descending order of importance.

-Beautiful scenery -Good sports or recreation facilities
-Natural surroundings -Reasonable prices
-Natural attractions -Good climate
-Meet congenial people -Historical or family ties
-Outstanding food

The fact that significantly increasing numbers of travelers have multiple reasons for travel makes the evaluation and research process much more difficult. The fact that choices of vacation spots and activities are indeed an extension of ones values and personality is born out of several studies.

According to the Travel Research Study, the four principle determinants of vacation plans were:[3]

1. *Financial.* Recreation and vacations are determined to a large extent by the amount of money a person has or is willing to spend.
2. *Obligation to visit.* The nearness of relatives to a given recreation area contributes greatly to these decisions.
3. *Advertising.* Advertising affects the final selection of vacation spot when not excluded for other reasons.
4. *Family Status.* The number of people in the family and their ages had a great affect on the final destination, in many cases the needs of the children being the overriding factor.

The case study tends to support the philosophy that vacationers tend to picture in their minds eye what they expect the vacation area and the related experiences, opportunities, and services to be. When he is well satisfied, he feels the opportunity has been a success. When he is not satisfied, he will tend to seek other areas or other types of opportunities. The advertising and marketing specialist then tries to create visions of sunny beaches and warm air, or sites of grandeur and natural beauty, and the recreation business manager and other managers of travel and tourism components try to make the individuals stay meet the expectations which he brings with him.

Lundberg lists the following reasons for most of which relate to personality and values of the traveler.[4]

[3] "Travel Research International Vacation Attitude Survey", New York, 1967.

[4] From THE TOURIST BUSINESS, by Donald E. Lundberg. Copyright © 1972 by Donald E. Lundberg. Reprinted by permission of Donald E. Lundberg.

Reasons for Travel.

1. Travel for business.
2. Travel for pleasure.
3. The need for a change.
4. The search for the exotic.
5. Travel for learning.
6. Travel to experience power, beauty, and wonder.
7. Travel for ego enhancement and sensual indulgence.
8. Travel for rest and relaxation or excitement.
9. Travel for recreation and sports.
10. Travel to shop.
11. Travel for travel's sake.
12. Travel for fun.
13. Traveling to plan and recapitulate or recollect.
14. Travel for vacation homes.
15. Travel to gamble.
16. Travel as a challenge.
17. Travel for acceptance.
18. Travel for culture.
19. Travel to sharpen perspective.
20. Travel for spiritual values.

Attraction indices have been attempted by a number of researchers including VanDoren, Tiedmann and Milstein, Cesario and Ellis, and O'Rourke[5] in an effort to overcome the difficulties inherent in measuring the qualities of recreation areas. Attraction indices as related to preference as a factor for motivation for travel has not been widely used. Researchers are not satisfactorily measuring levels of preference attached to individuals to various experiences. Such factors as park size, aesthetic qualities, distance, type of facility, crowding, and alternative recreation opportunities must be considered.

Thus no relative weight can be established for motivating factors because of the difference in values to the individuals to which the definition of recreation is equally appropriate. Distribution of recreational resource facilities relative to the population exert a strong influence on travel behavior; however, the individual's motivation and perception relative to those resources ultimately determines trip direction, distance, frequency, and benefits.

The fact that a number of writers and experts including Johnson and Plog tend to believe that travelers can basically be classified into two groups. On the one hand are

[5] From TRAVEL IN THE RECREATIONAL EXPERIENCE, Journal of Leisure Research, **6**, #2, pp. 140-156. Copyright © 1974 by National Recreation & Parks Association. Reprinted by permission of Robert M. Artz, Director, Technical Publications, NRPA.

Figure 7 Beautiful scenery, natural surroundings, and natural attractions such as the mountains are one of the top reasons for travel.
Courtesy: American Hotel and Motel Association, New York, New York.

what Johnson[6] terms "locals" as opposed to the "cosmopolitans" Plog[7] classifies in terms of "psychocentric" and "allocentric," psycho meaning self and centric meaning centered, or self-centered, allo meaning outside or broadly centered. Characteristics of these two are listed below.

Allocentric/cosmopolitans are active, work hard, play hard, more secure, self-confident, adventurous, go without guilt, less anxious, more practical, realistic, plan their own trips, is in higher income bracket, travels more, and reads more.

The allocentric prefers non-tourist areas, enjoys a sense of discovery and delights in new experiences before others have visited the area. They prefer novel and different destinations, have a high activity level, prefer flying to destinations. Tour accommodations should include adequate hotels and food not necessarily modern or chain type hotels. They enjoy meeting and dealing with people from a strange or foreign culture. Tour arrangements should include basics (transportation and hotels) and allow consid-

---

[6] Russ Johnston, "Motivation in a Changing Environment", Marketing, September 1970.

[7] Stanley G. Plog, "Why Destination Areas Rise and Fall in Popularity", Speech before the Travel Research Association, Southern California Chapter, October 10, 1972.

Gp of people who go for vacation ✓

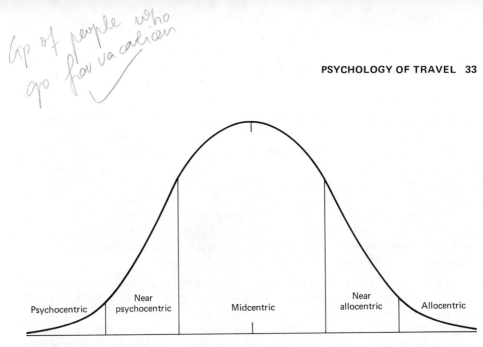

Figure 8 Psychographic groups fall into the above categories and their number approximate the shape of the bell shape.
Courtesy: From speech before Travel Research Association, Southern California Chapter, October 10, 1972. Reprinted by permission of Stanley Plog.

erable freedom and flexibility.

Psychocentric/locals-passives have lower incomes, are less active, watch more TV, are a repeat visitor, hotel residents, have more fear, live a more restricted life, use automobile travel, spend less per capita per day, participate in group tours, and probably are older. They prefer the familiar in travel destinations, like common place activities and travel destinations, prefer fun and sun spots including considerable relaxation and a low activity level. They prefer destinations that they can drive to, prefer heavy tourist accommodations such as heavy hotel development, family-type restaurants, and tourist shops. They prefer a familiar atmosphere, hamburger stands, familiar type entertainment and absence of foreign atmosphere.

Part of the differences between the allocentric and psychocentric are related to sex. Males tend to be more allocentric, and females tend to be more psychocentric. Males tend to have a continual struggle between the values of business and the values of home. Males seek excitement, novelty, visual exploration, while although not always true, females tend to find satisfaction through affiliate needs, warmth of experiences in preserving their images of beauty. Thus the final destination choice may be a compromise between these two, rather than the utmost desire of either.

It should be stated that the distribution of psychocentrics and allocentrics in the normal population appropriates a normal curve, with a few of each at either extreme, and a great many in the midcentric area with qualities of both.

The implications for the recreation business are significant. The first people to "discover new areas" are the cosmopolitans or allocentrics. They prefer new experiences, fending for themselves, the natural, the new, and the exciting. As the allocentric begins to convey his new-found areas to his friends, their allocentric friends begin visiting the area in greater numbers, and are closely followed by increased numbers of travelers who are midcentric. Thus additional development of supporting facilities including motels, restaurants, and other normal tourist facilities are added. Thus the curve begins to move toward the midcentric to the near psychocentric who then find the area more familiar with more comforts and more nearly what they have at home and prefer away from home. Because of the development, the allocentrics are turned off by the destination because it has lost its sense of naturalness and they begin to seek other areas that are less developed and more natural and new.

Thus the appeal of the area reaches its magic high point of the population curve and then as the destination moves toward the psychocentric end of the curve in terms of its appeal and popularity, it begins to draw smaller numbers of travelers as it approaches the descending point of the curve. More important, these travelers because of their psychocentric characteristics and expectations make them very difficult to attract. They are more comfortable (or less-motivated) at home.

Thus it becomes extremely important that those involved with planning, developing, and operating facilities in tourism areas try to keep them new, creative, attractive, and interesting, so as not to lose their appeal to the unsophisticated traveler, in order that the above phenomena will not take place.

TRAVEL MOTIVATION STUDIES[8]

The desires of tourists are consistently changing. Many of the factors previously mentioned contribute to these changes. As one looks at the long-term motivating factors for travel, there tends to be some patterns that emerge; from relaxation to activity to relaxation; from familiarity to novelty to familiarity; from dependence to autonomy to dependence; from order to disorder to order.

To say the least, an understanding of the motivation and perception of why people travel will be achieved only through analytical studies in human behavior in several of the disciplines. Four broad categories of studies of recreational travel have been made but their categories can certainly not be construed to be mutually exclusive and may, in fact, be rather arbitrary. However, they do serve a purpose, to get a summary or generalized view of the phenomena.

A. *Inventory and descriptive studies.* Many of these are general in nature, and may not be concerned solely with travel. They may include car counts in specific areas, characteristics of travel, relative loads of traffic for various purposes, and relative traffic on different days and times in relationship to the distance traveled to recreation activities.

[8] Barry O'Rourke, "Travel in the Recreational Experience", Literature Review, Journal of Leisure Research, **6**, Number 2, pp. 140-156. A major portion of section on Travel and Motivation studies was adapted from this article.

B. *Behavioral studies.* The perception of the recreation experience in the mind of the traveler has always been considered important and a large factor in the satisfaction the traveler achieves from his trip. There is little doubt that travel affects the character of the individual recreation experience although satisfactory methods in measuring these effects remain elusive. Research into user satisfaction preferences is always difficult and their recreation experience is broadly defined as it is in some people's minds can be difficult to qualify. Researchers have only scratched the surface in this area and research of this nature will probably occupy a predominant position of discipline for at least the next decade.

C. *Economic studies of travel.* Efforts to place quanitative measure and economic values on recreation resources rightly extend beyond the travel phase of the recreational experience. Efforts in this area to compare economics as a factor in distance traveled or motivation have met with limited success. The common theme in these studies is the evaluation of the costs of license fees, tolls, accommodations, and equipment costs together with a measure of travel cost and plotting the total cost against the participation rates.

D. *Studies based on travel models.*

1. By far the most research into travel and travel models has been based on the gravity model, which utilizes a concept borrowed from the physical sciences. It is based on the formation of the law of gravity, which states that "two bodies attract each other in proportion to their masses and inversely to the square of the distance between them." This model is used in many cases to measure the attractiveness of the given area to a given population, and the relatedness of such items as park size, attractiveness, distance, population, and capacity to participation. These and other models used by researchers will not be described here because of their sophisticated nature.

2. There are, however, many researchers who question the adaptability of the gravity model to the human behavior, which they say involves more complex senses of forces than a mere physical law will bring into play, and most behavioral geographers would probably agree.

3. Other models using frictional effects of distance suggest that the effective distance is not constant and in fact the further the distance the greater the reluctance to travel in accordance with some unknown increasing proportion.

   Systems analysis and computerized models are also being used for some studies. It works in such a manner that the number of visitors at any given site is determined by the resistence of all localities and all lengths and strengths of the source of origin.

4. Multiple regression techniques have also been used to integrate location factors in addition to the attractiveness and social economic variables. These however are rather sophisticated statistical techniques and cannot prove a causal relationship but merely signify that statistical relationships exist.

5. A variety of models have attempted to explain and predict travel behavior with varying degrees of success. The behavioral model appears to offer the best

potential of success but three obstacles have yet to be overcome.
1. The complex structure of the decision-making process.
2. Relative importance of the diversity of factors influencing recreation travel that have to be ascertained.
3. The sophisticated measures of human and other values will need to be established.
4. Obviously the resolution of these problems is outside the bounds of a single discipline.

Even though people travel for a variety of reasons, and many of these reasons vary from person to person because of personal values, likes, dislikes, previous experience, and other psychological factors. Research, over the years, has been able to document a number of reasons why people travel which apply to large segments of the population as a whole. The "effect" of certain factors on the desire to travel can be predicted with some degree of accuracy. Travel agents, marketing specialists, or recreation enterprise managers consider these factors carefully in planning their programs to attract the traveler or tourist.

EFFECT OF INDUSTRIALIZATION

Many of the factors listed previously as reasons for increased leisure time and demand for recreation are also factors that have produced an increased demand for travel and tourism. There is little doubt that increased income, particularly discretionary income, improved transportation, longer vacations, television and advertising, industrialization, and technology have all contributed significantly to the increase in travel and tourism. The increase in technology or industrialization however, has probably contributed as much or more to this increase as any other single item. It has provided people a vehicle with which to travel, and time in which to do so.

Henry Ford many years ago indicated "I will build a motor car for the great multitude . . . so low in price that no man . . . will be unable to own one . . . and enjoy with his family the blessings of hours of pleasure in God's great open spaces."[9]

The automobile indeed contributed significantly to the development and increase in travel and tourism. Toffler,[10] in his book, "Future Shock" says "the automobile is a technological incarnation of spacial freedom." It should be remembered that prior to the development of the automobile, there was very little recreational travel, as most trips were primarily for business or other similar reasons. Lovelace[11] recalls that the automobile was originally developed for recreational purposes and only later did it acquire other uses.

[9] R. Arvill, *Man and Environment,* 1967, London, Penguin Press.

[10] Alvin Toffler, *Future Shock,* 1972, London, p. 84.

[11] E. Lovelace, The Automobile and Recreation Travel Quarterly, 1966, pp. 525-540.

Duffell and Peters[12] indicates that recreation travel has increased at a faster rate than any other trip purposes.

The Outdoor Recreation Resources Review report of 1962[13] indicates that driving for pleasure is the most popular form of outdoor recreation. At that time 18 percent of all trips had a social or recreation purpose and accounted for 34 percent of the vehicle's 15 miles. Other studies indicate this percentage varies considerably with reports as high as 75 percent on certain highways in countries such as Canada,[14] and from 61 percent to 95 percent in other locations.[15]

The motor vehicle has indeed exerted a strong influence on outdoor recreation and tourism primarily because of the flexibility in journey time, choice of route, privacy, comfort, convenience, and relative cheapness, thus allowing distant places to become accessible to large numbers of people. As might be expected, traffic attached to a recreational area is not a function of the size of the population. It may more nearly be considered a function of the traffic flow. Two recent studies in Missouri[16] indicate that on any given weekday, approximately 23 percent to 25 percent of the travel is for vacation and recreational purposes. Other studies have found that recreational traffic is heavier in the beginning and ending of the weekend. A number of researchers have found that Sunday afternoon traffic is heavier even than comparable times on weekdays.

Houghten, Evans, and Mild[17] have found that "recreational motorists use their cars primarily for one of two reasons, either to get to a particular place for recreation or as a means of recreation, that is, more or less on aimless drives through which they hope to be pleasant roads and views in order that they may picnic and enjoy the countryside."

EFFECTS OF DISTANCE

Distance indeed begins to play a significant part in the reasons why people travel or why they do not travel, and can usually be viewed as having a negative or inverse

[12] J. R. Duffell and C. M. Peters, *Recreational Travel in Urban and Rural Areas,* 1971, Traffic Engineering and Control, pp. 31-35.

[13] Outdoor Recreation Resources Review Report, 1962, *Outdoor Recreation for America,* Washington, D.C.

[14] G. D. Boggs, and R. McDaniel, *Characteristics of Commercial Resorts and Recreational Travel Patterns in Southern Ontario,* Ontario, Department of Highways, Report RR133.

[15] W. Houghton-Evans, and J. C. Miles, 1970, "Weekend Recreational Motoring in the Countryside", Journal of the Town Planning Institute, pp. 392-397.

[16] Arlin Epperson, *Southwest Missouri Tourism Information Center Study I & II and 144 Rest Stop Study,* University of Missouri, Recreation Department 1974.

[17] W. Houghton-Evans, and J. C. Miles, op. cit.

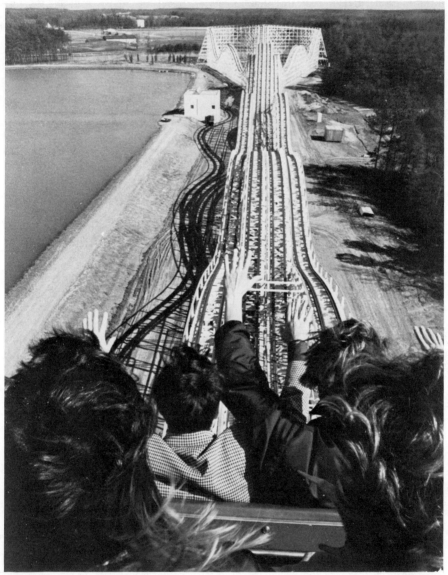

Figure 9 Amusement parks and attractions provide a variety of recreation experiences close to home, one factor which has contributed to the increase in attendance at parks is to ride roller-coasters such as this one at King's Dominion in Ashlen, Virginia.
Courtesy: International Association of Amusement Parks and Attractions, Oak Park, Illinois.

proportional relationship to the recreational experience. Thus as the distance grows larger, the desire for the trip or the recreational experience decreases. A number of researchers including Wagner, Burton, Coppock, Law, Duffell and Peters, Sessoms, and others have investigated the relationship of distance to recreation, tourism, and travel and the distance may, in fact, effect the choice of recreation opportunities as significantly as any other factor.

A study by Keogh[18] in 1969 found that 86 percent of the drivers enjoy the time spent traveling, 64 percent chose the route they took because it was the fastest, 13 percent because there was less traffic, 8 percent because it was the most scenic, 6 percent because it was the cheapest, and 3 percent because it was the safest. The study also concludes that travel cost was of the most concern by only 4 percent of the persons studied, while travel time was of the most or highest concern by 25 percent of the surveyed travelers, and 21 percent indicated that cost and time were of equal concern. Fifty percent, however, suggested that neither travel cost nor time were a particular concern. The inference here is drawn that the majority of drivers accept travel as a necessary part of the recreational experience and probably a means to a satisfying end. Keogh's study reconfirms many others that time is a most significant element in determining the distance the driver would travel on a day trip, rather than cost or other factors.[19]

EFFECT OF COST

Recreation costs do play an important part in why people travel, where they choose to go, and include such costs as (a) the purchase cost; (b) background cost such as license fees, prior investments; and (c) travel and transportation costs. Usually an inverse relationship exists between travel and other costs for a given purchase cost, thus the higher the cost the less travel. Some researchers have found that the average maximum trip point is probably in the area of 400 miles, up to which accommodations contribute the major proportion of total trip cost, beyond which cost of gasoline, vehicle maintenance, transient meals, and so on increase more rapidly. Therefore, lower rates of accommodation were sought in an effort to offset other expenses.

The effect of the shortage of gasoline and the reduction of discretionary income caused by recent rapid inflation will be addressed in a later chapter; however, the full impact of these factors have not yet been determined in relation to the use of the automobile for travel purposes.

[18] B. M. Keogh, *The Role of Travel in the Recreational Day Trip,* Unpublished Master's Thesis, University of Western Ontario, 1969.

[19] Ibid.

EFFECT OF AGE

Sessoms, Masser,[20] and others have long since found that recreation patterns are related very closely with the age of children in the family unit. The number of occupants in automobiles of vacation travelers have been consistently decreasing for many years, and several studies, including the two in Missouri, indicate that the average number of occupants in the vehicle is getting closer and closer to two. It now is somewhere between two and three occupants per vehicle on the average. Some studies indicate that automobiles with two people or less, comprise almost 50 percent of the recreational travel. As the age of retirement decreases and the birthrate continues to decline, people are beginning to travel (due to their retirement) at an earlier age, and young people are having less children and having them later, allowing them much more time to travel in their young adult years. In the future these factors will produce even larger numbers of two person automobile travelers.

During the time of child rearing, time and income are more heavily committed, and recreation becomes more informal, trips are of shorter distance and duration, and the car becomes more a tool for family living than for recreation. With increasing age, additional leisure time is experienced, and more thought and specific consideration is then given to recreation activities.

The young traveler has a high tolerance for new ideas and new experiences, and is less concerned about inconvenience and discomforts. The middle-aged traveler is more concerned about the comforts of the trip, the status, and others he will be traveling with. The old traveler tends to turn inward and be more immobile. They travel in groups, or lean toward those experiences that appear to be more secure which do not cause him concern for his safety.

EFFECT OF EDUCATION

It has long been known that there is a high correlation between travel and education. The higher the level of education, the longer the vacation trips, and the more money spent. It should be understood however, that normally increased education is accompanied by increased income, more and better automobile travel capabilities, and other related characteristics all of which contribute to the significant differences in the travel patterns of those with more education. Those in the professions for instance, tend to take fewer shorter trips but more trips of both longer duration and to locations farther from home. There are types of activities that seem to be participated in by a high percentage of persons with higher education such as boating, snowmobiling, and skiing, perhaps because of the investments required. Those with higher levels of education use air travel much more than those with less. Education affects the type

[20] H. D. Sessoms 1963, *An Analysis of Selected Variables Affecting Outdoor Recreation Patterns,* Social Forces 42: 112-115.

of new or novel experience an individual is willing to accept. The better educated person is more apt to seek a new experience or a change, and feels more secure in new surroundings.

There are recent changes in the high school graduate that may change this trend. The high school graduate, through unions, has perhaps as high a standard of living as the professional; their income has risen to equal that of a college graduate or more, but their status and interests are still those of a blue collar worker. This has significant impact on the marketing aspects of the recreation business, and will be discussed in more detail in the chapter on marketing.

EFFECT OF URBANIZATION

The urbanized life that surrounds 80 percent of the population in the United States, even though having many disadvantages is associated with all the social problems that come with living close together and the problems of transportation, pollution, and others, nevertheless has given rise to increased leisure. Because of technology, we are now experiencing more discretionary time in our life than the time that is required on our jobs at work. As vacations tend to increase, long weekends continue to increase, and we will indeed have more leisure time than ever before. Many advertisers are now advertising products on the basis of the time they save, rather than on the low cost or the amount of labor they save. It does, however, give motivation for us to get away from it all and get out of the asphalt jungle and go to the green and living sights of the countryside. Thus the magnitude and the percent of travel increase as one moves toward the urbanized centers of our geography.

SOCIAL SIGNIFICANCE OF TRAVEL _____

Travel is increasingly becoming a social phenomena. The history of travel and tourism as well as recreation in general have indicated that it's primary purpose in previous eras was "re-creation," to prepare and renew one for more work. The amount of travel and tourism in the present day is probably inversely proportioned to the attitude of society toward the work ethic. Even though in many quarters, it is expected that people will vacation and recreate, in others it is still looked on as a less honorable use of time than work. The number of people who moonlite or take second jobs may do so more to fill the time than to provide additional income. Although the attitude of "year-round leisure" has indeed become a reality in the attitudes and minds of certain classes of people, it is still not equated equally with year-round work. Although the summer vacation is now an expected fringe benefit by almost all employees as well as college students and others, the attitudes of recreation or travel as a necessity at regular points throughout the remaining portions of the year has still not received complete acceptance.

Our schools continue to spend 99 percent of their time preparing students for a life of work, and perhaps one percent of their time educating them for a life of leisure. The problem is compounded as the unemployment rate continues to rise and the numbers of people required in industry is reduced because of technology. The individual finds himself with more leisure, whether it is "enforced" or not. At the same time, he is equipped only to work and does not know how to use his leisure satisfactorily. The agonizing result is "time-filling" leisure, consisting mostly of mass entertainment, from television to sports watching to other kinds of boredom-oriented or boredom-motivated activities.

The advent of additional leisure time, additional income, and the other factors that contribute toward increased participation in recreation, tourism, and travel, has indeed influenced our society to become more accustomed to travel. What used to be a phenomena reserved for the wealthy and higher social classes is now available to all of the middle class and to some in the lower class. Travel clubs, airline group rates and arrangements, company incentive tours, and special interest groups, have all contributed to motivating society toward travel.

It has, however, probably produced a "work alienation" phenomena where leisure has been more of a time-filling process than a conscious effort to locate and participate in those activities that will bring satisfaction to the individual. Television, mass entertainment, and some of the other aspects of travel and tourism continue to supply opportunities for escape from boredom. Pleasure travel is indeed a learned behavior, and is usually the product of one or more of the following reasons.

1. Business
2. Friends
3. Health
4. Recreation
5. Education
6. Historic
7. Cultural
8. Boredom

The impact of television has probably contributed more to this change than most people would realize. With slogans such as "get away," "You owe it to yourself," and other advertising campaigns as well as the visual response of seeing the best sides of these distant locations portrayed or paraded on the television screen, has done much to motivate individuals to participate.

BARRIERS TO TRAVEL

Large numbers of people do not travel significantly or do not travel at all. The reasons for this are deeply rooted and very complex. A limited number of basic psychological studies have given some light to these reasons. Most of these studies support the fact that barriers to travel fall into five broad categories.[21]

1. *Expense.* In one particular study 62 percent of the respondents indicated the cost as the primary reason for not taking a vacation. Costs may be the principle reason for some people staying home.
2. *Lack of time.* Many business executives and professional persons use this as their primary reason for not traveling or vacationing because they are not able to leave their job.
3. *Physical limitations.* These include poor health, children, oldsters, and other reasons.
4. *Family stage.* When the children in the family are young, families are less likely to travel because of family obligations and the inconvenience.
5. *Lack of interest.* Unfamiliarity with travel destinations and other lack of information contribute to a lack of interest.

Even though the desire for travel may be strong, the magnitude of these barriers may in the end overcome those desires and influence the would-be traveler to remain at home. It is evident by several studies that there are some people who do have a desire to travel, but it is overbalanced by nervousness or fear of what the experience may be. Thus because of fear, anxiety, or erroneous expectations, there is a large segment of the population that does not travel. The struggle continues on the hierarchy of needs between desires for self-realization and self-esteem, and the needs for safety and security.

All would surely agree that the urge and desire to travel and vacation is rooted in the basic desires of everyone. These desires, whether learned or culturally derived, are inherent in the society in which we live. The answers then to the question of why people travel are both psychological and sociological and is a process of matching physical promises with more important mental and psychological expectations. In many instances recollections or memories may be more important than the miles driven or the places visited.

Summary

The reasons people travel for recreation has been questioned since travel and tourism began. In the early days of travel, the reasons were known, 99 percent of travel was for business purposes and for life's necessities as travel was too uncomfortable and unpleasant to be done for any other reason. The remaining 1 percent of travel was done by the rich who could afford special accommodations, special modes of travel, and special amenities not affordable by the masses.

Since those days, travel has become a very desirable and pleasurable leisure activity. While previously it was a status symbol for the rich, now it is participated in by all

---

[21] J. B. Lansing, and D. M. Blood, *The Changing Travel Market,* Braun-Brumfield, Inc., Ann Arbor, Michigan 1964, p.11.

socioeconomic groups, although not equally.

A number of studies and research efforts have been made to determine exactly why people travel. Those who sell travel and recreation want to supply those things anticipated and expected by the traveler in order to produce more travelers or the same travelers more frequently. These studies, in large part, have been done by transportation carriers and travel research groups. These studies have been grouped into categories according to their effect on travel; industrialization, distance, cost, age, education, and urbanization.

Even though travel is something very much sought after by the majority of the American public, there are still large segments of the population who do not travel and who apparently would not do so if they had the opportunity. The barriers to travel for this group are significant, and need additional research.

A number of studies seem to indicate that the destination to which many people travel, and the mode of transportation they select as well as the accommodations they prefer is based to some degree on the type of personality that the individual has. Some experts categorize the reasons people travel into as many as 20 categories that would seem to encompass most all of the reasons that have been suggested. These might be grouped into the following seven categories; scenery, people, food, sports or recreation, climate, family ties, and educational and historical purpose.

Most researchers agree that people travel for a number of reasons, and these reasons have different priorities among different people. A great deal of additional research will need to be done to isolate many of these reasons why people travel.

Additional References

Books, Bulletins, and Reports

Dice, Eugene F., *Impact of Travel Stress on the Tourist Trade in Michigan* Bulletin E-794, Cooperative Extension Service, Michigan State University, East Lansing, September 1974.

Risk, Paul H., *Resource Interpretation-An Unexplored Asset,* Department of Park & Recreation Resources, Cooperative Extension Service, March 24, 1971 Michigan State University, East Lansing. Selected papers.

Discussion Questions

1. What motivates people to travel?
2. In what ways do the researchers differ in their reasons why people travel?
3. Discuss the principle determinants of vacation plans as outlined by the Travel Research Study. Can you think of additional concerns of the vacation planner?
4. What value do Attraction Indexes have in measuring the qualities of recreation areas?
5. How does the understanding of "allocentric" and "psychocentric" definitions help the student of commercial recreation understand facility needs of the traveler?
6. What effect has industrialization had on the demand for travel and tourism?

7. A businessperson in the travel/tourism industry should understand the forces working against his success. What factors tend to keep people from traveling? What can you suggest to meet these challenges?

SELECTED READING

WHY THE INCREASE IN TRAVEL, TOURISM AND OUTDOOR RECREATION

by Robert Blundred*

There is one universal problem in discussing why the increase in relating people and entertainment. That is the lack of agreement on what is meant by entertainment. Its impact is magnified when the discussion narrows down to relating people to types of outdoor entertainment activities.

Is barbecuing for the immediate family entertainment or satisfying a basic human need? Is the role of the spectator at a baseball game versus participating entertainment or a vicarious thrill? Is the annual Thanksgiving visit to the homestead entertainment, or an obligation? Is a visit to an amusement park entertainment because it is a commercial activity?

We shall not try to define terminology. Rather, let us just say there are various forms of entertainment and my major goal is to discuss the many reasons why their use is on the increase. A secondary goal is to prompt thinking so that the subject of people and entertainment can be better understood.

Most of the thinkers on "people and entertainment" agree on certain basic reasons why the increase. These reasons are what the marketeers call the feasibility factors. The proportional weight of these factors has a direct bearing on the increase, i.e., the greater the weight, the greater the increase.

These include the following:

1. Increase in the leisure time of the working person due to shorter work week and longer periods.
2. Increase in the amount of disposable income, particularly in the segment of the population that historically never had the opportunity to spend money for various forms of entertainment.
3. More older, retired people on an independent income.
4. Earlier retirement, again with an income source.
5. Better health standards, particularly among the elderly, thereby permitting people to be more active.
6. Greater life span.
7. Changes in the form of mobility, more opportunity for people to move from one place to another. The expanded federal highway system, group travel plans, better bus service, increase in automobile ownerships, AMTRACK, incentive travel plans.
8. More group participation in entertainment activities.

* Executive Vice President International Association of Amusement Parks and Attractions, Oak Park, Illinois.

9. More and better advertising, publicity, and promotional efforts. Reams have been written on the use of T.V. in relation to such devices to motivate people to participate in forms of entertainment.
10. Less physical labor exerted on the job, more people less tired at the end of the work day, more energy to expend for entertainment reasons.
11. The higher level of education and the resultant broader interests of people.
12. More things to "see," more things to "do."
13. More and more business, union, and fraternal meetings being held in recreational areas and environments, with planned entertainment activities part of the program, thereby creating more interest in using such facilities and programs on a personal basis.
14. More people due to the population growth.

In addition to these universal reasons, there are others that bear on the increased use of entertainment.

These reasons are utilized by the business executives associations with all forms of the entertainment industries. They have been refined and utilized even further by the

Figure 10 Amusement parks provide recreation for more people than all other the professional sports.
Courtesy: International Association of Amusement Parks and Attraction, Oak Park, Illinois.

personalities in the outdoor amusement industry. These reasons are presented here to illustrate the art of (stimulating) people to entertain themselves, and be entertained by visiting outdoor amusement activities and facilities. By listing the impact of these specialized reasons for the increase in entertainment it is hoped the second goal of this paper, to prompt additional thinking, will also be achieved. The following are reasons for the increased participation in the outdoor amusement park and attractions industry and ways owners/operators of these facilities have utilized factors listed above in making this the most participated in recreation activity of them all.

First, todays outdoor amusement industry is offering greater diversification by appealing to people's emotions. The start of the themed attractions in the outdoor amusement industry broadened this diversification concept. The result was increased attendance.

Some of their facilities have turned their calendar back a century. Visitors can watch authentic blacksmiths, candle makers, glass blowers, wood carvers and other period craftsmen plying their trades exactly as they did 100 years ago. In "Santa's village" and "Mother Goose" facilities, story book characters come alive to delight adults as well as wide-eyed children. "Frontier Towns" and entertainment activities in other types of facilities across the United States recreate the Old West, complete with steam trains, stage coach rides, mail order brides, bank robberies and Indian attacks, all convincingly realistic. In tune with the current nostalgia craze, you can step into a mining town of the 1980s, a typical 1910 county fair . . . or the naive gaiety of a band concert in the town square, because a depression and two world wars made us a global village. Or, you can depart for Egypt, or the moon, or some other part of the world and be back in time for dinner.

Complementing the diversification on trend is the effect the improved highway system has had on expanding the primary market of each facility. Today, people find it much easier to travel longer distances to visit the facilities than 20, 10, or even 5 years ago. The result is an increasing number of bodies passing through the front gates each year.

The facilities in the industry today are prepared to receive their visitors with every convenience. There are vast parking areas, if they are situated at any distance from the grounds, scuttles whisk passengers to the main gate. Fun food stands offer every specialty from hot dogs to egg rolls, or the diner can enjoy a full-course dinner in comfort at a sit-down restaurant. At the larger amusement-recreation complex, the traveler is likely to find hotel-motel facilities, campgrounds and even swimming pools and golf courses to make the stay even more enjoyable.

Once inside, visitors find the modern facility offers much more than just straw hats and merry-go-rounds. There is diversified entertainment for all family members, regardless of age. Miniature rides for tots, up and down, or turn them around rides for the teen agers and adventurous adults, rides the family can enjoy as a unit, lots of shade trees, benches, and picnic areas where Mom and Dad, Grandma and Grandpa can relax while their more spirited youngsters seek out the thrill rides. Free big name concert type acts, roving bands of cartoon or storybook characters come to life, circus type acts, magicians and puppet performances and other forms of entertainment pleasing young and old alike.

Numerous drinking fountains and restrooms are easily accessible. One of the more salient features of the modern outdoor amusement facility is cleanliness. A uniformed employee is likely to swoop down, broom and dustpan in hand, and remove the carelessly dropped cigarette butt.

Studies of the hospitality and recreation-amusement industries all report the same thing: The quality of the food, the speed of service and the cleanliness of the facility have a lot to do with why business is good. The owners-managers are well aware of the importance of such practices.

These facilities offer a unique blend of excitement, thrills, recreation, and relaxation. There are the thrilling rides such as the giant roller coasters that appeal to the young and the young in heart. There are picnic and recreation facilities for rest and relaxation adjacent to the entertainment areas. Special areas for small children featuring different forms of entertainment are available. They can be enjoyed for an hour, or a day, without losing their basic appeal. Like the supermarket, the visitor can spend as little or as much as is desired, since individual attractions, products and services can be purchased or used separately, and at will.

An oddity about the facilities in the industry is that while they are essentially the same in terms of family fun offerings, no two are exactly alike. All have the traditional type rides, and one or several thrill rides are usually a must. Many other types of rides are also duplicated but that is about where the similarity ends. Some operate within the concentrated area of a city, others are laid out over vast acreage with groves, lakes and extensive landscaping. Since the advent of·the themed attraction, the differences have become greater . . . because such facilities have different themes. These differences are just another reason why the increase in visits to such facilities . . . people go to different facilities becasue of the differences in character and personality of the facilities.

Second, outdoor amusement facilities, by and large, have excellent safety records when compared to other forms of entertainment offered the general public. Rigid inspection by qualified safety engineers hired by the insurance companies, government inspections during the operating season, the tests and inspections imposed on the equipment used in the facility during the manufacturing, and the daily inspection by qualified personnel employed by the facility, are some of the reasons for this excellent record. The great majority of any incidences relating to injuries incurred are either induced by the visitors themselves, and are of the minor variety such as a scraped knee that they are of little consequence.

Third, more and more family units are becoming aware of a simple truth: The modern outdoor amusement facility is a place where families come together, not just some families, but family. This fact tells why there has been such an increase in the customer load, when doubt and despair seem to abound in other segments of our society. The things families see and do when visiting a facility are the things that hold them together, things they all can do together, and talk about with each other. About the only things we all have in common are the things our children really enjoy, and they are found in every outdoor amusement facility. And, because more people are becoming more aware of these simple truths, increased business is the result.

Fourth, all of the senses are appealed to during the visit to the typical outdoor amusement facility. The tunes of the merry-go-round, the texture of the cotton candy, the swaying of the bright colored balloon, the taste of the barbecue rib, the odor of freshly popped buttered corn—all of these are examples of why the visitor can pick and choose among an array of delights.

Fifth, the down right thrill and competitiveness of the big ride and other units of entertainment, such as the flume ride, the bumper car ride and shooting gallery, the roller coaster. As Isaac Asimov, the science fiction writer says, "It would be hard to improve on the old roller coaster for scaring you out of your wits without hurting you." Read about the amusement park he envisages for the future, including the on the moon in which patrons would flap about like Icarus under domes.

An amusement facility is full of challenge for everyone. Can Dad put a dart in the balloon and win a stuffed animal? Does Mom dare to try to ride? Will there be screams in the dark ride? Can Junior stay on the kiddie merry-go-round without falling off? How about the ability to play skee ball, or the arcade games? Everywhere there is a test, a test that looks just a little harder than it is. Upon entering the facility, we leave a world where we meet some measure of frustration and failure every day and we enter a world of challenge where we can win, and enjoy it.

Sixth, the profile, personality and character of the people in the industry are conducive to people enjoying themselves while visiting the facility. The industry is basically people oriented and to service his visitors, the owner-manager of the facility has to like people, and know what people want. Consequently, the owner-manager is an extroverted, easy-going type interested in seeing that people have a good time. He realizes he is an important member of his community, and that he has a reputation to uphold at his facility. This personality, soul, fibre, intestinal fortitude, mentality, outlook, attitude of the owner-manager means they are warm hearted, friendly, and cooperative.

Seventh, who cannot remember his or her first visit to an outdoor amusement facility? There was cotton candy, a pinwheel, and maybe a monkey that climbed the stick. Remember the red balloon that was tied to your wrist, and how it came loose and you, heartbroken watched it soar heavenward until it was lost in the summer sky?

These memories of the merry-go-round tunes, the texture of the cotton candy and the red balloon, belong to the fanciful world of childhood. But what adult really outgrows those first magical memories? These memories become indelibly printed in our lives, including the tears that followed when we let go of the string of our souvenir helium balloon.

What is the typical outdoor amusement facility? It is color, it is motion, it's musical. It's a sea of happy faces. It's light flashing and rides whirling. It's the sound of giggles and the shrieks of delight. It's the smell of hot dogs, hamburgers, and fresh buttered popcorn. It's the feel of excitement in the air. It's laughter bridging the generation gap.

Figure 11 Amusement parks provide a combination of clean natural outdoor surroundings, water, fun, and thrills.
Courtesy: International Association of Amusement Parks and Attraction, Oak Park, Illinois.

Eighth, the outdoor amusement industry caters to more people, as members of a group, than any other form of outdoor entertainment or recreation in the United States. This in itself, is one reason for the increase in attendance and business. But, just as important, when visiting the facility, as a member of the group, the visitor is becoming conditioned to something so enjoyable he returns time after time on his own, or with his family or friends.

Ninth, the majority of the employees are young adults, between 16 and 21. Highly-trained, efficient, courteous and safety-conscious, they have a rapport with the visitors. Whether ride operators, game attendees, food service employees, souvenir-novelty retail store clerks or members of the clean up brigade, their aim is to make the visitors stay a pleasant one. As a result, people are more willing to return for another visit. Visitors know they will be well received, and well handled, despite their age, sex or race.

Tenth, the vast majority of the owner-managers of outdoor amusement facilities have added another factor to the leisure, income, mobility and people factors mentioned earlier in this chapter. They have added showmanship, or flair. Showmanship begins where design, planning and construction end. It is the combined result of many things, including live shows and attractions, event timing, background and live music, wardrobe, sound effects, crowd control techniques, guest relations, host and hostess training, to name a few. A perfect example is that personnel are rarely called employees, but hosts and hostesses.

Eleventh, the outdoor amusement industry is more non-competitive than most industries. It possesses this characteristic for two reasons. First, the facilities service their own local market areas. The California and Florida Disney facilities are not too concerned over the amount of business done by Opryland in Nashville, Tennessee or one of the Six Flags facilities. Likewise, the amusement park within a radius of where you are located does not worry too much about the facility that is located 300 miles away. Second, as mentioned earlier, although the ride concept is common to the vast majority of the facilities, after this commonality is considered, the specific and different personalities of the facilities become obvious. As a result, people who wish to be entertained, and amused by these different characteristics or personalities will visit these facilities for this reason.

Now, due to the non-competitive nature of the industry, by and large, the vast majority of the people in the industry are more willing to exchange viewpoints and information than in many other industries. As a result, people within the industry learn from each other to a far greater extent than in other industries. Thus, the industry is becoming stronger, and with this increased strength, management is becoming more efficient and sophisticated.

Twelfth, are employees techniques practiced by the better operated facilities that are conducive to increasing patronage. Because of these practices the employees are better trained, more service minded, and they do a better job treating the customer right. A happy customer is more likely to return, and does. The following list of such techniques is based both on material developed by the facilities for their personnel program and on ground observations while visiting operating facilities.

1. Get the employees involved. Make them feel they are important, that their views and suggestions are desired, valuable, and needed. How do these successful facilities get them involved, obtain their views? The employees elect spokesmen to periodically sit down with top management to discuss matters of mutual concern. Rap sessions are held in the evenings after the facility has closed for the day.

2. Several different types of competitive and motivational programs are maintained by the facility. Scholarships are awarded to deserving employees and payment of cash awards for suggestions to save money in the operation of the facility. Programs of this second type are usually under the exclusive direction of a committee consisting entirely of employees. Owners and top level management personnel are not involved. The winning suggestions are rated and selected by fellow employees.

3. Everything else being equal, the successful facility will hire that employee standing in the top 25 percent of their class. This class standing is usually found out during

the course of a personal interview.

4. The sharpest employees are placed in the guest relations department, and they are given the authority to over-ride and cut through red tape. If they need a wheel chair in a hurry they can command one without going through the entire organizational procedure. Most of these successful facilities make sure their best looking, "bright" young ladies are employed in the guest relations department.

5. At the end of the operating season, the "better," first year employees who are students are told they have a job for the next season.

6. In their printed material the successful facility does not use the word "employee." Instead, they use the words ambassadors, host and hostesses.

7. Most parks rotate the job assignments of their seasonal personnel to eliminate monotony. Someone will be the roller coaster operator for one or two weeks, he may be operating a game. A girl may be selling hot dogs one week, and be selling gifts next week.

8. Some facilities try to reduce customer waiting line times. To do this, some facilities use the time stamp method. Namely, a customer is given a specific reserved time for the ride, the game, the restaurant seating. Other facilities make waiting in line more interesting. Live musicians entertain in the area. Strolling actors perform where the customers are waiting in line.

9. They hire professional and experienced people for security and admission positions. People who know how to handle people.

10. A successful facility makes sure there is smooth handling of all accidents and arguments.

11. Above all, they hire enthusiastic and happy people.

12. They also print, publish and distribute rules and regulations for the ambassadors, hosts and hostesses. They hold orientation sessions to make sure they understand the seriousness of following the rules and regulations.

13. Successful facilities all emphasize they are in the pleasure business, and that their ambassadors should realize they are dispensing pleasure in their day to day activities.

14. The handling of lost kids. Today, the kids are not lost, their parents are. The kids are not put into a first aid room while waiting for their "lost" parents. Instead, they are entertained in a nursery school type environment. Also directional and informational signs are in strategic locations throughout the facility telling parents where to go and what to do, when and if there is a need to be classified as lost parents.

15. Finally, good hospitality starts in the successful facility when the customer enters the parking lot. Soft music, adequate lighting, ambassadors to help you with information and when you take a trackless train, there are announcements on what to expect when you arrive. In addition, there will be live musicians, strolling actors and characters performing near the entrance, when people are arriving.

Thirteenth, the development of large, themed attractions in regions of the country has concentrated amusement park attendance among fewer facilities. In addition, the gasoline crisis of the last two seasons has been a benefit to the majority of the facilities in the industry ... because people had to travel shorter distances in order to enjoy these attractions.

Fourteenth, the changes in the living habits and desires of the American public, coupled with the changes in the relationships of the American family unit, have caused shifts in the marketing and advertising techniques to get more people to visit outdoor amusement facilities. The more sophisticated marketers are taking advantages of these changes by doing the following:

1. The advertising and promotions utilized by the facility stress the "fun" that can be expected during the visit to the facility.
2. Restore adventure to the otherwise jaded or monotonous day-to-day routine resulting from today's jobs.
3. A return to the natural, both in terms of physical settings, and "doing what comes naturally," emphasizing that both can be found when visiting an outdoor amusement park.
4. To emphasize the simple, uncomplicated pleasures in visiting an outdoor amusement facility. A psychological study could be made on why patrons visit a facility to let off steam. An experienced owner-manager will emphasize this in his sales presentations to groups considering the facility for a group outing.
5. To emphasize that when visiting an outdoor amusement facility, you can extend yourself as an individual, to be a little different from others. This is reflected in the craft operations at certain facilities and the volume of such sales to people who want to be able to express their individuality by owning these craft items. And, don't forget the competitiveness of the shooting gallery, the game arcade, the bumper car ride.
6. The changing role of women today, the fact that they can and do say what they want in entertainment more so than in the past. For example, the entertainment they prefer have to be advertised and directed at them, because they have great influence over family entertainment decisions.

The first part of this paper outlines the reasons why there has been an increase in the travel, tourism and outdoor recreation and entertainment. The second part explains how the owner-manager of outdoor amusement facilities has utilized these basic reasons in making the amusement park/attraction industry one of the fastest growing entertainment forms in the country. It represents virtually the only form of entertainment/recreation that has not been adversely affected by various technological and entertainment developments such as motion pictures, radio, and television. Indeed, it has prospered despite these onslaughts, and projections are that it will continue to do so. Because the remembered childhood and teenage fun of the facility carries over to new families and generations in visiting this healthy and wholesome form of recreation and the outdoor amusement industry appeals to young and old alike. It packages many enjoyable experiences and activities under one roof. The present, as well as the future status of this industry looks bright.

CHAPTER 3

THE DEMAND FOR RECREATION

The recreation enterprise manager, for obvious reasons, should be concerned with the kinds and types of recreation activities and opportunities in which the American public enjoys participating. To some extent, the types of recreation opportunities and services that his enterprise offers will determine how large a potential clientele he may have. The relationship between the *demand,* as determined by participation, and the *supply* as measured in terms of the number of facilities, programs, or services, has always been confusing. This chapter will attempt to indicate the kinds of leisure and recreation opportunities that the American public enjoys and the magnitude of these activities in relation to one another. The following chapter on supply will attempt to categorize those enterprises of various kinds that offer recreation and leisure opportunities.

Most experts have agreed that, in general, the demand is usually always greater than the supply, particularly because of the regionalized nature of the present population along the Eastern and Western seaboards, creating extremely high demand in those areas, with the supply centralized in the Middle West and West, a significant distance away from the population. It would be an incompetent recreation enterprise manager who did not look at the types of recreation in which most people participate as he plans his facility and his services. However a word of caution should be noted; it is very difficult to determine the difference between the *demand* (measured in terms of participation normally by activity days), and the *need,* (determined by studies or research which would ask people what they would enjoy doing if they had the opportunity).

PUBLIC VERSUS PRIVATE RECREATION

Unfortunately, many public recreation managers in days past have looked at the private enterprise operator with less than equal respect, and have held the attitude that to accept money for providing leisure services is something less than honorable. Other early authorities in leisure and recreation have indicated that in the end, all of the

Figure 12 Bicycling is one of the activities for which the demand is measured by the Bureau of Outdoor Recreation.
Courtesy: Bicycle Manufacturers of America, Washington, D.C.

recreation that any individual needs can and should be provided by public tax supported services.

On the other hand, the private recreation operator although perhaps not a professional recreator in the strict sense of the word, is indeed selling a product which happens to be a recreation service, in exchange for a fee. In most cases (as will be determined later) he is doing a more efficient job of providing his service than the public recreator, because of the immediate built-in evaluation mechanism involved; that is, if sufficient people do not patronize his establishment, he goes out of business. The governmental agency may provide a large number of services for a small number of people at a relatively high cost, because of this tax supported nature, and there may not be an easy method of determining at what point the program should be continued or discontinued.

Public and private recreation services had their beginnings independently. As has been indicated previously, private recreation opportunities preceded public supported recreation services by many years. Many of the public governmental services in existence today began as a program of social welfare organizations such as settlement houses, or playgrounds, park areas, or gardens for the residents in high density low income areas. These were later assumed to a greater and greater degree by public agencies and have come now to be accepted as a necessary part of life which should be available to all residents in a community regardless of income level or residents location or other factors. As a result of this early philosophy, many of the recreation services in large cities are concentrated in the inner city areas, and consist primarily of playground programs, summer recreation opportunities, and community center programs with highly developed sports activities.

For some time, the public has apparently accepted the providing of parks and recreation facilities and services as a necessary governmental function, because of the significance to the health and welfare of the residents, as well as the part it plays in the quality of life. Thus the public philosophy has continued to progress toward providing free public recreation services, as has been seen in providing free education, free health service, and free "all the other city services" which many community residents now enjoy.

Private recreation in its infancy was conceived as a result of one or more of the following reasons. Individuals with high incomes could afford to pay for the kinds of recreation experiences they desired, and did so rather than be associated with those of low income and the crowded recreation facilities of the inner city, and thus be associated with a "social welfare program." Other reasons included the desire for travel and a combination of lodging, meals, and recreation services that could be provided by recreation complexes, which the public agency was not in a financial position to develop.

The attitude and philosophy of public recreation professionals and city officials has changed down through the years, and because of increased leisure, and related increases in the demand for recreation opportunities and services, most public leaders as well as those in the private sector have come to realize that local governments can never provide all the opportunities needed or desired by the residents, nor can they provide the diversity required because of the difference in individual interests.

Although the philosophy is changing rather slowly in many quarters, more progressive communities are indeed coming to realize that the public agencies should provide several functions.

1. Take the leadership in providing recreation areas, facilities, and services, and to initiate studies and research projects to determine what these needs are, and how they can best be provided.
2. Determine which recreation opportunities and services desired by the residents, can best be provided by the public sector, and which can best be provided by the private sector or through a combination of the two.
3. Take the initiative in acquiring open space for parks and recreation in cases where condemnation or urban renewal are involved.
4. Act as a monitoring agent and safeguard for the natural resources in the area, to see that they are used wisely, and that the resource is not destroyed or depleted by other groups with special interests, whether they be economic or otherwise.

The extent and the level to which this has been accomplished in various areas depends on a number of factors, including finances, state legislation, nearness to federal lands and recreation areas, and many other factors too numerous to categorize.

The private sector has continued to grow by leaps and bounds far beyond the imagination of even the most futuristic thinker, and now is considered to be a 100 billion dollar a year industry. Fortunately a great many people are able to choose from a wide variety of privately provided recreation opportunities. Should the total number of participants all demand public services, the demand would far outstrip the supply, perhaps by a hundred-fold. The range of private recreation would stagger the imagination and range from opportunities in one's own backyard to vacation homes, to weekend educational seminars and a host of social profit and nonprofit business concerns.

The public sector cannot fail to recognize the contribution made by the more than one million nonprofit organizations, agencies or enterprises, providing some recreation opportunities such as Boy Scouts, Girl Scouts, YMCA, Campfire Girls, religious groups, or those of special interest groups such as horse clubs, card clubs, and so on. These are the organizations which in the beginning fostered the recreation movement and they continue to provide significant recreation opportunities although they may do so as a secondary objective, rather than a primary one, as is the case with the public and private concerns. The public agency has a responsibility, to assist and work with these agencies when and wherever possible primarily in providing of facilities, so that these agencies can continue to provide their services. Should they cease to do so, the demand on the public sector would be increased many times. Thus the public sector philosophy should be to assist both nonprofit and private organizations to provide whatever recreation opportunities they are able, so that the public sector can attempt to fill those special needs that are not economically feasible from a private sector point of view or which require special areas, facilities, and so on, which cannot be obtained through private means or are of sufficient magnitude that the private sector is not willing to provide the kind of investment required because of the lack of investment return which is expected. Any of these opportunities or services that are provided by these nonprofit organizations or private business concerns are then opportunities that do not need to be provided by the public sector. Many of these organizations by the nature of their goals and purposes serve special interest groups such as handicapped, the elderly, or the underprivileged, which are normally high cost per participant programs, and require leadership from those knowledgeable and experienced in working with these groups. Public assistance in use of public resources, planning, design, management, and information concerning present recreation services being provided, needs for recreation, and other services should be provided by the public sector. While individually small in scale, the efforts of these agencies and groups can fill significant needs, especially when providing opportunities close to the homes of those served. These agencies should indeed expect this kind of assistance from federal, state, and local governmental agencies.

The need for the public and private sectors to lower the barrier that has been between them is obvious. As many have known for sometime, the only hope of providing sufficient recreation and park areas, facilities, and services to meet the ever increasing demand must come from new and innovative cooperative efforts between public and private enterprise toward the common goal.

It is unfortunate that many public and nonprofit recreation agencies consider the commercial recreation business with some lesser degree of acceptance; even though in many cases the only visible difference between them is that the commercial business provides leisure services for profit, where the others do not. Many public agencies have comparable schedules of fees and charges, particularly for golf courses, ice rinks, and swimming pools, and to the user they appear for all intents and purposes to be commercial recreation ventures except for the ownership. Many public facilities of this kind are in fact planned and developed through the use of revenue bonds, which allows the cost of development and construction to be paid from fees collected rather than from taxes as is the case with general obligation bonds. It is therefore difficult to understand why the lower degree of acceptance for privately organized recreation opportunities and services for profit when many facilities of this nature already exist in the public sector. And if the truth were known, the public probably cares little who provides the services as long as their needs can be met. Many leaders in the recreation field feel that the trend is toward more "pay as you go" services and facilities in the public sector because of the reluctance of the public to increase taxes to support such facilities. The public sector, while providing public measure to protect, enhance and interpret areas of national, historic, or cultural significance, may produce a demand for allied services such as food, lodging, fuel, rental of equipment such as boats, bicycles, horses, and so on; and, in fact, both the public and private sector will come to rely on the other to provide either accompanying attractions or accompanying accommodations.

ORRRC STUDIES

The Outdoor Recreation Resources Review Commission (ORRRC) will probably be known in history as the turning point or beginning of federal interest in private recreation. Established originally by executive order—the purposes of the commission were: (1) To determine the outdoor recreation wants and needs of the American people now, and estimate what they will be in the years 1976 and 2000. (2) To determine the recreation resources of the nation available to satisfy those needs now and in the years 1976 and 2000. (3) To determine what policies and programs should be recommended to insure that the needs of the present and future are adequately and efficiently met.

In 1962, the Outdoor Recreation Resources Review Commission made its initial report to the President and the Congress after a three-year study headed by Mr. Laurence Rockefeller and recommended that "our national policy should encourage private enterprise to provide outdoor recreation opportunities and sevices wherever feasible. Profit making enterprises already satisfy a significant part of the total needs, but they could do much more to complement, diversify, and augment government efforts."[1]

The five major recommendations of the commission sought to provide a framework for continual assessment of recreation needs, and a method of providing recreation requirements.

1. A national outdoor recreation policy.
2. Guidelines for the management of outdoor recreation resources.
3. Expansion, modification, and intensification of present programs to meet increasing needs.
4. Establishment of the Bureau of Outdoor Recreation in the federal government.
5. A federal grants and aids program to the states.

In reponse to these recommendations, President Kennedy in his March 1, 1962 presidential message on conservation announced that the Bureau of Outdoor Recreation (BOR) would be established in the Department of the Interior. The Congress, by the act of May 28, 1963, set forth the principle duties that were delegated to the new bureau.

1. Prepare and maintain a continuing inventory of the outdoor recreation needs and resources of the United States.
2. Prepare a system for classification of outdoor recreation resources.
3. Formulate and maintain a nationwide outdoor recreation plan.
4. Give technical assistance and cooperate with the states, their political subdivisions, and private interests.
5. Encourage interstate and regional cooperation in planning acquisition and development for outdoor recreation.
6. Sponsor, engage in, and assist research and education programs.
7. Encourage interdepartmental cooperation and promote coordination of federal lands and activities generally relating to outdoor recreation.
8. Accept and use donations for outdoor recreation purposes.

At the first national conference on Outdoor Recreation Research held at the University of Michigan in the Spring of 1963, Secretary of Agriculture Orville L. Freeman[2] said "Let me begin with this prediction. The outdoor recreation needs of the American people cannot now be met . . . nor will they ever be met . . . by the combined efforts of local state and federal governments alone. These needs . . . the unsatisfied appetite for open spaces and green areas which grows more rapidly than

[1] Outdoor Recreation Resources Review Commission, *Outdoor Recreation for America* Supt of Documents, Washington, D.C. Summary & Volume 1-27. 1965.

[2] Orville, L. Freeman, *Proceedings of Outdoor Recreation Research Workshop,* Bureau of Outdoor Recreation, University of Michigan, Spring 1963.

our population increases . . . will be met only as we turn to the three-fourths of our land area which is in private hands."

The results of this report, which surveyed 17,342 households concerning their recreation participation, has been the most widely used and quoted resource in the recreation and park field concerning recreation participation and demand.

Information of interest from the report included the following: Participating in outdoor recreation is increasing at the rate of ten percent per year, and rising income and more leisure time will cause participation to increase four-fold by the year 2000. The study found that most recreation (75 percent) occurred close to home in after-school, after-work hours, and on short one-day outings. Overnight recreation trips accounted for 12 percent of the time spent, and 13 percent of the recreation was done away from home, but not on overnight trips. Four fifths of the participation in outdoor recreation was by persons 45 years of age or younger.

The study also indicated that the higher a family's income, the more days per year they took part in water activities, active sports, and backwoods activities. Those with incomes under $5000 annually, for example, spent only 17.1 days per year attending outdoor-sports events or concerts. But higher income groups spent more time at these two activities. It is interesting to note that participation in television decreases with the level of education, for example 29 percent of persons with a college background say watching TV is their favorite way of spending an evening compared to 62 percent of those whose formal education has been limited to grade school. The percent apparently has changed a little since 1966.

As a part of the outdoor recreation planning process, and a part of the commission of the Bureau of Outdoor Recreation, later surveys were taken to update the demand data obtained in the 1965 study. In 1972, the Bureau made personal interview surveys with 4029 randomly selected households throughout the United States. Results of this most recent survey are shown in Table 1.

Some of the major changes in outdoor recreation participation were the following:

1. The simple pleasures were the most favored. Activities with the most participants and the greatest participation in the summer of 1972 were swimming, picnicking, sightseeing, driving for pleasure, and walking for pleasure.
2. Vacation participation and outdoor recreation activities have risen significantly since the 1965 report for most of the activities reported. Camping in a remote or wilderness area showed the most market increase, while other activities that more than doubled including camping and developed campgrounds, picnicking, canoeing, nature walks, swimming, and fishing. Substantial increases, although not to the same extent, were reported in sailing, sightseeing, and hiking.
3. A lower rate of increase was noted for overnight trips.
4. As was noted in the 1965 study, most recreation took place on the weekends, and the 1972 study verified that in every case more than one half of the total participation took place on weekends. The increased number of three-day holiday weekends probably has contributed significantly to this figure.

Table I Most popular outdoor recreation activities by number of participants [a]

Activity	Percent of Survey Respondents Who Participated	Average Number of Hours of Participation Per Activity Day
Picnicking	47	2.7
Sightseeing	37	3.1
Driving for pleasure	34	1
Walking for pleasure	34	1.9
Other swimming outdoors	34	2.6
Visiting zoos, fairs, amusements parks	24	4.5
Other activities	24	1
Fishing	24	4.4
Playing outdoor games or sports	22	2.6
Outdoor pool swimming	18	2.8
Nature walks	17	2.0
Other boating	15	2.8
Going to outdoor sports events	12	4.2
Camping in developed campgrounds	11	2
Bicycling	10	2.0
Going to outdoor concerts, plays	7	3.6
Horseback riding	5	2.7
Hiking with a pack/mount/rock/climb	5	3.0
Tennis	5	2.1
Water skiing	5	2.6
Golf	5	4.9
Camping in remote or wilderness areas	5	2
Riding motorcycles off the road	5	4.0
Bird watching	4	2.1
Canoeing	3	2.3
Sailing	3	4.4
Hunting	3	4.4
Wildlife and bird photography	2	1.6
Driving 4-wheel vehicles off the road	2	3.1

[a]Bureau of Outdoor Recreation, *Outdoor Recreation, A Legacy For America*, U.S. Department of the Interior, Superintendent of Documents, Washington D.C., 1973, Page 23.

Figure 13 Boating is one of the outdoor recreations which continues to require a sizable investment.
Courtesy: Bonair Boats, Lenexa, Kansas

In 1965, when a nationwide study was completed for the Bureau of Outdoor Recreation[3], it was found that recreation areas and facilities provided by private individuals, nonprofit organizations, and businesses attracted some two billion visits annually. Three-fifths of these visits were made to commercial profit making enterprises. It is apparent that these figures give only a slight indication as to the magnitude of the potential. It does not include those individuals who might have made additional stops or stayed longer if other choices were offered at the destination area. Neither do the figures include the numbers of individuals who may have patronized private recreation facilities and satellite services if located close enough to their homes to be available and which were geared to their income levels.

In 1968 a plan had been formulated in accordance with the duties set forth of the Bureau. In 1970, after an expenditure of approximately 7 million dollars, Secretary Henkel had prepared a final draft of the plan which by then was two years overdue. The version was, however, never transmitted to Congress or made public but was subsequently revised and released in 1973 as the final plan "A Legacy for America."

[3] Chilton Research Services for the Bureau of Outdoor Recreation, *Private Sector Study of Outdoor Recreation Enterprises,* 1966, Supt. of Documents. Washington, D.C.

The final plan was a result of increased interest and demand among those in the public and private sector and the increased emphasis by the administration in 1972 and 1973.

Although the ORRRC Report of recreation participation has been most noteworthy and will be the focal point for which the agency will be remembered, the Bureau has been very active in assisting each state in producing a state recreation plan, and in distributing land and water conservation funds, which have been made available to local municipalities and state agencies on a matching basis to purchase and develop recreation lands and facilities.

Only recently has the Bureau taken significant steps to fulfilling their commission to be of assistance to the private recreation industry.

PROBLEMS WITH DEFINITION AND MEASUREMENT _____

Although many of the studies and research efforts have produced varying statistics on the leisure interests and participation for the American public, there has been little concensus on the exact figures primarily due to several reasons.

Differences in definition, which have been discussed previously, account for a large portion of the variance. Studies have used varying definitions of participation, tourism, and recreation, and have studied different segments of populations as well as used different study methods.

Another reason suggested for the differences in figures is the amount of weight given to the lack of participation because of limiting factors, such as distance, types, and kinds of activities available or not available, numbers of participants at a particular facility, the individuals skill, and other reasons. These can be seen through a review of a number of these studies that have made an attempt to discern the participation characteristics in recreation and leisure of the American public.

A third, major reason that statistics differ is inherent in the policies of the agencies who are primarily involved. An obvious problem of significant impact is the fact that the Bureau of Outdoor Recreation studies only recreation in the out of doors.

It is unfortunate that such a differentiation must be made by a governmental agency which should be concerned about all of the recreation needs of the American public, not just the outdoor ones which would take place predominantly during the summer months. It is understood that such policy was probably originated because of the need of the federal government for policies, planning, and development concerning its many public land holdings, most of which would be categorized as outdoor recreation areas and facilities. Perhaps some day the Bureau of Outdoor Recreation will be called the Bureau of Recreation, and the dichotomy will no longer exist.

A further problem concerns the definition of recreation itself, which plays no small part in the reliability of the figures. Only the more generally accepted activities are most often listed. Such items as "working on the farm," "gardening," or "volunteer service," which may be recreation for some because it gives them personal satisfaction and is derived from leisure opportunities which they engage in by choice, are reflected in most studies in only the more generally accepted classifications and categories.

One of the biggest problems with measuring demand are the peaks and valleys of the participation in recreation. The summer months usually show very high participation whereas winter months are low.

Another problem surrounds the many ways that demand is measured today. These include:

1. Participation.
2. Number of visitors.
3. Amount of money spent.
4. Number of visitor days.
5. Number of contact days.
6. Number of activity days.
7. Amount of tax collections.
8. Amount of gasoline sales.

Some park and recreation master planners are now beginning to base their recommendations for public facilities and services on studies within the community, based on how many days per year a composite of all of the individuals in the community say they would participate if the facilities were available. These are then projected in terms of a total number of activity days of need for the community. The number of activity days that one tennis court, for example, will provide is determined by multiplying the number of people that can play on a tennis court by the number of normal playing hours per day, by the number of potential playing days per year. If it is determined that an average of three people per hour will play, a balance between singles and doubles, and that the average tennis court will be used for eight hours per day, for 180 days, thus the tennis court will provide some 4320 activity days of participation per year. Through study and research in the community, individuals are asked how many hours per day or per week they would play tennis if facilities were available, and these hours per day are added to obtain a summary. Thus, if 2000 people indicate they would play one hour per week for 15 weeks, a need is determined for facilities that will provide 30,000 hours of participation. This is divided by the number of participation hours that a tennis court can provide—4320, as previously determined, and thus a need for eight tennis courts is determined.

Today, many governmental recreation facilities, particularly large flat-water recreation areas are planned on this basis.

There are other experts that point to a number of falacies in this type of reasoning, one problem being the location of the supply. It is known that people will travel only so far to participate in certain kinds of recreation. Others indicate that attempting to supply the demand is similar to building a new highway, it cannot be accurately foreseen how many people will use a new highway from point A to point B, until after it is built, at which time it seems that the highway normally will become of immediate use until it is full, then others begin to find alternate routes once again. Thus a supply can create its own demand.

And there is always disparity between what people say they would like to participate in, and what they would actually participate in if they had the opportunity.

Another problem involved in investigating the demand relates to how participation is measured. Care should be taken in reviewing any particular demand data as to whether the participation refers to total activity days of participation (usually eight hours of participation per day) or whether the data refers to the percentage of the population that participate in the activity, with no relation or no attempt to measure the amount of participation, only the fact that they do participate, which may mean only once per year.

Differences in figures may also result from what they represent. Some statistics reflect the percent of the population participating in a particular activity while others reflect the aggregate activity or total number of activity days. Thus driving for pleasure is the most participated in, but in terms of aggregate activity days, playing outdoor games including golf, tennis, teen sports, and so on moved from third place to first between 1960 and 1970.

The above concerns should be taken into consideration when evaluating the demand data which follows.

OUTDOOR RECREATION DEMAND

In terms of total number of participants, bicycling and camping showed the highest percentage rates of growth between 1960 and 1970 followed by attending outdoor events and playing outdoor games. Numbers of participants in hunting, fishing, and boating grew relatively slowly over the 1960s. The total-activity days grew considerably more rapidly. This pattern is characteristic of activities that are relatively mature. By now, most people have decided which of these activities they enjoy and which they do not, so that these well-established activities attract new participants rather slowly. Because of increases in leisure time and disposable income however, individuals interested in these activities pursue them considerably more frequently.

As might be expected, we are a nation of spectators. The following statistics will indicate that over 97 percent of the population participate in some kind of spectator activity, with this category receiving 89 percent of the time spent in leisure activities.

To some extent, travel can be categorized in this classification because it provides many of the same types of spectator benefits as does television watching or watching of sports events. It is a passive, nonparticipatory, nonconsumptive type of activity, which seems in many cases to fit here rather than in other categories. Travel is not mutually exclusive because many people combine traveling with educational and historical purposes or other types of participative recreation endeavors.

Table II Most popular outdoor recreation activities [b]
(Current population recreation activities 161 million)

	Participants (Millions)	Share of Population
Picnicking	82.1	49%
Swimming	77.3	46%
Playing outdoor sports	60.0	36%
Driving for pleasure	59.6	35%
Attending sports events	59.4	35%
Walking for pleasure	50.3	30%
Fishing	49.4	29%
Sightseeing	46.4	27%
Boating	41.1	24%
Bicycling	37.1	22%
Camping	35.2	21%
Nature walks	30.5	18%
Hunting	20.9	12%
Horseback riding	16.1	10%
Bird watching	7.5	4%
Wildlife photography	4.9	3%
No participation in outdoor recreation	40.2	25%

[b]From LEISURE BOOM - BIGGEST EVER, U.S. News & World Report, April 17, 1972.

It is also interesting to note that driving for pleasure as well as walking for pleasure has dropped from the number 1 and number 2 outdoor recreation activities to number 4 and number 6. Number 8, sightseeing, would give some indication of the number of people involved in traveling and tourism primarily for travel's sake. The Outdoor Recreation Resources Review Commission initial study revealed that approximately 90 percent of all Americans participated in some form of outdoor recreation in the summer of 1960. The original ORRRC study encompassed 27 separate, detailed reports on the various activities in their study. They found that the four greatest influences for the demand for outdoor recreation were:[4]

1. A growing population with an increasing percentage living in cities and suburban metropolitan areas.
2. More and more leisure time available to individuals and families.
3. More money available to spend for recreation and for other discretionary purposes.
4. Increased mobility or ease and convenience of travel, often in modern automobiles.

[4]ORRRC Report, op. cit. 1965.

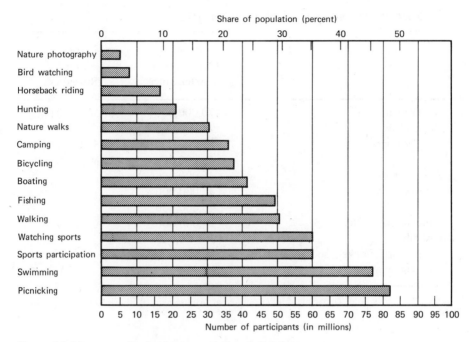

Figure 14 Most popular outdoor recreation activities.

According to the ORRRC reports, the population of the United States will virtually double by the year 2000, which will make our country a nation of over 350 million people. They predicted that the population will have 73 percent of the people living in metropolitan areas, compared to 63 percent in 1960. This figure, in some reports, has already been exceeded with urbanization approaching 80 percent or better according to some authorities.

Other reports by the Department of Commerce[5] attempted to study the number of trips people take by purpose of vacation. In 1972, the total number of person trips was 458.5 million with 26 percent taking trips for outdoor recreation, entertainment, and sightseeing. Another 38 or 175.9 million person trips were to friends or relatives and the remaining 36 percent were for business and other miscellaneous activities.

The study indicated that many of those visiting friends and relatives also participated in recreation activities, implying that 64 percent of the trips people took in 1972 were for recreation and tourism purposes, which accounted for 233 billion person miles traveled and 1.1 billion person nights spent away from home.

Some indication of the magnitude of recreation participation can be gotten from the statistics kept by federal, state, and local agencies providing parks and recreation.

[5] Bureau of Census, *National Travel Study,* The Department of Commerce, Census of Transportation and Travel, Superintendent of Documents, Washington, D.C. 1972.

Table III Most popular private recreation activities [c]

	People Participation or Attendance	Total Gross Revenues
Amusement parks	470,000,000	$1,500,000,000
Horseracing	74,000,000	–
22 major parks	55,000,000	570,000,000
Boating	48,000,000	$4,600,000,000
Auto racing	45,000,000	–
Football	42,000,000	–
Bowling	40,000,000	–
Professional baseball	39,000,000	–
Basketball	38,000,000	–
Other sports, hockey, soccer, boxing, wrestling	30,000,000	–

[c]Funspot Directory and Department of Commerce, Amusement Business Division, Billboard Publications.

In 1970 the National Parks reported over 212 billion visitors as compared with 79 million in 1960. In 1972, the National Forests had 230 million visitors with 40 percent of these visitors participating in camping, fishing, and hunting. The Corp of Engineers claimed 323 million visitors, the Bureau of Land Management, 91 million visitors in 1972. Attendance in state parks amounted to 483 million in 1970 as compared to 259 million in 1960.

One indication of the growth of tourism and travel is the number of visitors to large amusement parks in comparison to other spectator activities. In the first year of operation since October 1, 1971, Walt Disney World in Florida attracted over 10.7 million guests. When added to Disneyland in California, the parks entertained over 20 million visitors and the second year Disney World increased its attendance 3/4 of a million, which has resulted simultaneously in the rapid growth of hotels, motels, eating places, and other service and accommodation facilities which are a necessary part of these recreation complexes. Today there are over 24,000 rooms in the area with 3000 more committed to be built.

In other selected statistics, the Bicycle Institution estimates over 35 million bike riders in 1960 and 75 million in 1971. Tennis is one of the fastest growing of the 13 categories studied under the BOR report, and has increased from 5.6 million in 1960 to 15 million in 1973. Boating has also shown a definite increase with over 47 million persons participating with over 9.4 million pleasure craft, accommodated by 4620

Marinas and Boat Yards. Water skiing had 11 million participants in 1970 and camping excursions and backpacking were participated in by 50 million persons in 1973. Fishing estimates include 32.5 billion participants, skin and scuba diving 3.5 billion participants, in 1970 mini-bikes claimed over 2 million users, and over 12 million golfers played on over 10,500 courses in 1971. Snowmobiles numbered 500,000 in sales in 1972, over 5 million skiers traveled to the slopes in 1973, which was double the number of lift tickets sold five years previously. The Recreation Vehicle Institute indicates in 1972, 740,200 units were in use. This is compared to 80,300 units in 1962.[6]

The Bureau of Outdoor Recreation study concluded that in 1970 approximately 530 billion persons 12 years of age and over participated in 13 major (plus other minor) outdoor recreation activities. However the study showed that one-third of those surveyed did not participate in any of the 13 or more activities for one or more of the reasons listed in the following table. This would tend to conflict with the original 1965 ORRRC report that reported 90 percent of the population participating in some form of recreation during the summer of 1960.

Reasons	Percent
Lack of Time	29
Thought facilities inadequate	22
Lack skill	19
Lacked money	12
Lacked equipment	10
Listed other reasons	8

The report also indicated that 76 percent of Americans have a favorite outdoor recreation activity, however 64 percent of these thought restricted in enjoying it because of the following reasons.

Lack of time	58
Thought facilities or area resources inadequate	18
Didn't have enough money	12
Lacked a companion or other essentials	7
Lacked ability or skill	5

---

[6] Bureau of Outdoor Recreation, *1970 Survey of Outdoor Recreation Activities Preliminary Report,* U.S. Department of Interior, February 1972, Superintendent of Documents, Washington, D.C.

Figure 15 Bowling is one of the indoor activities for which national practicipation statistics are not kept by the United States Government.
Courtesy: American Hotel and Motel Association, New York, New York.

INDOOR RECREATION DEMAND

Watching television continues to be the most popular indoor activity by any sort of measure, with over 97 percent of the population 12 years of age and over watching the tube for an average of approximately 19 hours per week. About $3/4$ of the population listens to the radio for recreation, an average of $3^1/2$ hours per day and about half listen to records and tapes with average weekly hours well below the TV figure.

About 90 percent of the U.S. residents read newspapers about once a day, two-thirds read magazines for pleasure and over half read books.

Movies are by far the most important away from home spectator activity; 64 percent of the population 12 and under goes to movies an average of over one time per month. Interest in sports activities is much more limited with only 30 percent of the population 12 years of age and over attending indoor sports events, and only about $1/2$ or $1/3$ of this figure are involved in such participant activities as indoor swimming, bowling, court games, pool, and billiards and the participants in these activities do

Table IV Most popular indoor recreation activities[d]

	Participants Millions	Share of Population
Watching TV 19 hours per week	156	97%
Reading	145	90%
Entertaining guests at home, social gatherings "going out to eat"	112	70%
Movies (1 per month)	103	64%
Exhibits, museums, musical events, plays, etc.	51	32%
Attend indoor sports events	48	30%
Indoor activities, swimming, bowling, courtgames, pool, billards	19	12%

Total Population used Recreation Activities–161 Million

[d]From LEISURE BOOM - BIGGEST EVER, U.S. News & World Report, April 17, 1972.

so quite intently with average activity participations between 18 and 36 times per year.

Apparently the U.S. is still a nation of freeloaders in view of the fact that about half of the weekend-trip visitors nights and almost 40 percent of the vacation visitors nights were accounted for by staying with friends or relatives. It may be crowded but the price is right.

The national inventory of second or vacation homes is approaching the three million mark. Industry sources estimate the annual increase in about 150,000 units. A recent national leisure survey indicated potential levels of demand for second homes that could result in a yearly increase of at least twice the reported figure provided that land developers and builders can offer sufficiently attractive products.

According to some experts, housewives now have much more time for fun and leisure than any other group, with an average of nearly six hours per day spent on leisure activities. This is approximately one hour a day more than was available to working men and 1.5 hours more than working women. The biggest block of the housewives leisure time (two hours per day) was used for an activity described in the study as visiting. That apparently included conversation and social life but apparently does not include yelling at the children which would fall into the category of personal and family care.

The next largest amount of daily leisure time went to the expected watching television for an average of one hour and 36 minutes. The results did find that housewives put in a work day more than ten-hours long while the study showed husbands worked for pay less than eight hours per day.

RECREATION DEMAND AS MEASURED BY EXPENDITURES _____

Another method of evaluating the increase in recreation participation is through money spent for leisure activities. In 1972 the U.S. News and World Report[7] estimated the spending for leisure time activities in the United States then amounted to 98 billion as compared to 77 billion in 1967. Or a 27 percent increase in five years. They indicated the following breakdown.

1972.

Recreation equipment, admissions for sporting events, movies, stage plays, concerts, and other cultural activities	50 billion
Vacations, recreation trips within the United States	40 billion
The purchase of recreation land and lodging, vacation homes	7.5 billion

The office of Economic Opportunity estimated expenditure for travel in the United States at $55 billion in 1971-72 but stated that this was about $1/2$ the expenditures for all leisure time activities.

The Midwest Research Institute[8] estimated that $58 million was spent in 1970 for goods and services for recreation and leisure purposes but indicated that the figure did not include expenses for food, clothing, automobiles, and other recreation oriented items that could push the total between 100 billion and 200 billion.

The Outdoor Recreation Resources Review Commission estimated that expenditures for tourism activities were 50 billion in 1970 as compared to 23 billion in 1960-61. Converted into 1970 dollars, expenditures for 1960-61 totaled 30 billion and in 1980 would amount to 127 billion. The 50 billion expenditures for tourism in 1970 in the study was broken down according to the following.

Food	7.5 billion
Lodging	8.6 billion
Public transportation	7.4 billion
Recreation	1.2 billion
Other incidentals	5.2 billion
Owned vacation homes	0.7 billion

Travel and recreation in the 1960s became a necessity not a luxury. While the cost of food and clothing has gone up, airline tickets are now 36 percent cheaper than they were ten years ago. Coleco, a company that deals in recreational products like portable swimming pools, sleds, and sports action games indicates sales have increased 30 percent since 1970 from 29.1 million to 36.2 million. The company expects its sales

[7] U.S. News and World Report, "Leisure Boom-Biggest Ever and Still Growing," April 17, 1972 p. 42.

[8] Midwest Research Institute, *U.S. Leisure Markets: Pleasure is Big Business,* MRI-1102, 1971-72, Kansas City, Missouri.

in 1971 to be above 50 million. Al Greensburg, Executive Vice-President of Coleco explains the rapid growth of the company by the growing trend of making the home a family recreation center. "If a family can't afford a house in the country, they try to fix up the home they already have with recreational products. And every time there is an oil spillage on the beaches, it is a great aid for our business. With one of our pools, the family has it's own little ocean in the back yard."[9]

Less than two-billion dollars expenditures for public recreation opportunities and services represent little more than two percent of the total expenditures for leisure priorities.

No two sources seem to agree on the exact size of the total recreation expenditures in the United States today. Part of the problem is in the complexity of gathering data on such an overwhelming variety of activities, purchases, and services. Again, the major problem lies in clearly defining just what constitutes a "recreational expenditure."

A number of very large, personal, consumption expenditure categories, including food, clothing, automobiles, and personal care products, contain a substantial share of leisure or recreation expenditure, even though they are nominally classified as necessities. A reasonable range of these expenditures to leisure purposes raises the total U.S. leisure spending by somewhere between $100 and $200 billion, depending on the rationale employed, according to the Midwest Research Institute's[10] "Growth in Leisure Activities: A Significant Opportunity for the Midwest." Those figures mean that leisure represents one-sixth to one-third of the total consumer economy. All sources agree that the leisure percentage is increasing.

Table 5, which follows, is an attempt to put an order to the expenditure data from many sources. The individual categories are *not* mutually exclusive—one cannot simply run a total of all expenditures listed to come up with a grand total.

These kinds of isolated statistics do not tell the whole story by any means or manner. They do not include data on the portion of the over ten billion dollars per year spent in travel which was recreation associated, nor the huge second home market. Social drinking certainly is a form of recreation but no figure has been placed on the 134 million barrels of beer, 201 million gallons of distilled spirits, or the 596 million gallons of wine produced in America in 1971, we can only estimate.

Total spending since 1967 is up 12 percent, while spending for leisure pursuits over the same period is up 27 percent. Expenses are increasing by six billion dollars per year. In a number of states, tourism ranked as the first or second largest industry in the state. Overall, it accounts for 20 percent of the total economy, and the average American spends $1200 to $1800 per year on tourism and travel recreation and leisure pursuits, or about one dollar out of every eight.

[9] Kazickas, Jurate: Associated Press Writer, Columbia Daily Tribune, Columbia, Missouri, February 27,1972.

[10] Midwest Research Institute, *Growth in Leisure Activities: A Significant Opportunity for the Midwest*, Kansas City, Missouri.

Table V Recreation Expenditures[e]

Category	Expenditure	Year(s)	Other Facts	Source of Data
Admissions sporting events, movies, concerts, cultural attractions	$50.0 Billion	1971	Total U.S.	US News and World Report April 17, 1972
		1972	Up 101% from 1960	Columbia, Mo. Tribune May 6, 1973
		1972	64% of the population, 12 & over go to the movies an average of once a month	Midwest Research Institute unpublished, undated report
		1972	30% of the population, 12 & over attend exhibits, museums, musical events, plays and lectures, but at lower frequency.	Midwest Research Institute unpublished, undated report
Alcohol	$14.5 Billion	1970	Total U.S.	"Economics of Leisure Today" Parks and Recreation Aug., 1971
Bicycling	$ 9.6 Million	1972	13% over 1971	Columbia, Mo. Tribune May 6, 1973
		1971	Dept. of Interior claims 37 million enthusiasts 8.5 Million units sold '71	US News and World Report April 17, 1972
Boating	$ 3.5 Billion	1970	44 Million operators bought 8 Million boats	Columbia, Mo. Tribune Feb. 27, '72 AP story by Jurate Kazickas

74

Category	Amount	Year	Notes	Source
Books and magazines	$ 8.0 Billion	1971		unpublished article by Eva Culen "Road Maps of Industry"
		1972	Sales up 185% from 1960	Columbia, Mo. Tribune May 6, 1973
		1972	90% of US residents read one newspaper per day	Midwest Research Institute unpublished report
		1972	2/3 read magazines for pleas.	
		1972	over 1/2 read books for pleas.	
Camping equipment (excluding vehicles)	$ 2.0 Billion	1971	(see also Recreation Vehicles)	Columbia, Mo. Tribune Feb. 27, 1972
Clubs and fraternal org.	$ 1.3 Billion	1972	(estimated)	Mid-Continent Memo June, 12, 1972
Federal government	$ 1.6 Billion	1965-1972	For acquisition of recreation lands. Part channeled through land and water cons. fund, earmarked for state and local govts. through matching grants.	US News and World Report April 17, 1972
Garden materials	$ 1.6 Billion	1971	(estimated)	US News and World Report April 17, 1972

[e] Allan T. Smith, *Recreation Expenditures*, University of Missouri, Columbia, Missouri 1974.

Table V (continued)

Golf	$ 3.0 Billion	1971	for green fees, club mbshp. cart rental and other exp.	US News and World Report April 17, 1972
			12.25 Million golfers 10,500 courses	US News and World Report April 17, 1972
Home electronics radio, TV, records, and mus. inst.	$10.3 Billion	1972	(est.) up 186% since 1960	Columbia, Mo. Tribune May 6, 1973
Leisure equipment	$18.0 Billion (est)	1972	products used in pursuit of leisure or relaxation	Mid-Continent Memo June 12, 1972
			up 52% in the past 5 years	US News and World Report April 17, 1972
Leisure expenditures total	$105.0 Billion	1972 (est)	exceeds Nat. Defense costs, more than for const. of homes, more than total corp. profits, more than farm income, more than total US exports	US News and World Report April 17, 1972
			will more than double in 1970s, Rec. 14% of pers. consump. $42 Bill. on recreation alone double 1960	"Road Maps of Industry" by Eva Culen
			Govt, Vol. Agencies & Ind.	"Economics of Leisure Today"

Item	Amount	Year	Notes	Source
			spend est. $6.25 Bill./yr.	by Richard Kraus Parks and Recreation August, 1971
Home recreation	$36.2 Billion	1972 (est)	One of fastest growing areas of expenditure	"U.S. News and World Report" April 17, 1972
Motion pictures	$ 1.9 Billion	1974	25% increase over 1973, 1,011,700,000 tickets 1970 increase, 124 new films	
Minibikes		1971	2 Million in operation 10 times no. in 1965 cost from $130-400.	US News and World Report April 17, 1972
Municipal recreation expenditures (including parks)	$ 1.3 Billion	FY 1970	up 15% from FY '69 capital outlay 1/3 per capita $9.90-munic. res. per capita highest in cities 300-499,000 population per capita lowest in cities under 50,000 population	American City Magazine October, 1971
Race track receipts	$ 1.1 Billion	1972 (est)	includes gate and on-track betting, horses and dogs	Mid-Continent Memo June 12, 1972
Recreation, sports eqpt. and activities	$50. Billion	1972 (est)	48% of total Leisure expendit.	Research, Education and Action Mid-Continent Memo June 12, 1972

Table V (continued)

Recreational vehicles	$ 1.8 Billion	1972 (est)	motor homes, 72,000 sold for $720 Mill., travel trailers, 200,000 sold for $680 Mill., tent trailers & Pickup campers valued at $415 Mill., by 1978, total no. of camping vehicles will nearly double, to 7.5 mill. units	US News and World Report April 17, 1972
Snowmobiles	$ 1. Billion	1972 (est)	Exp. includes accessories, suits, helmets, sleds, etc. 600,000 sales forecast in 1972 average cost $1000. now 1.3 Mill. in operation	US News and World Report April 17, 1972
Second homes	$ 2. Billion	1971	2 Mill. Americans own them 150-200,000 units built/yr Rep. 2% of total Leis. Exp., 55% higher than 5 years ago total will double in 8 years 2/3 cost $10,000. or more 1/4 cost $20,000 or more 57% near lake, river or ocean	US News and World Report April 17, 1972

Skiing	$ 1.3 Billion	1971	4.25 Mill. enthusiasts spend on equip., lodging, travel, lift tickets, & entertainment at resorts predict $2 Bill./yr by 1974	US News and World Report April 17, 1972
Skin diving	$30. Million	1971	spent for equip. alone	US News and World Report April 17, 1972
States and localities	$ 1.8 Billion	1965-1972	raised for rec. purposes mainly through bond issues	US News and World Report April 17, 1972
Surfboarding	$ 3.4 Million	1972	equipment, beach fees, and travel, average devotee 17 yrs old	US News and World Report April 17, 1972
Tennis	$50. Million	1971	in racquets, balls, access. 10.7 Mill. play	Am. Lawn Tennis Assn. US News and World Report April 17, 1972
Tobacco	$ 9.3 Billion	1970	on tobacco and smoking supplies	"Economics of Leisure Today" Parks and Recreation August, 1971
Travel for pleasure (in the US)	$40. Billion	1972 (est)	38% of total Leis. Exp. second largest component of leisure budget includes vacation trips, overnight journeys, trips over 100 miles	US News and World Report April 17, 1972 info. source-AAA

Table V (continued)

			to and from vacations **300 Bill.** miles alone Rec. driving is 33% of total est. driving for private cars. 90% by private car 85% less than 300 miles	Columbia, Mo. Tribune May 8, 1973 (AP)
Travel abroad	$ 5. Billion	1972	7.4 Mill. travelers dollar devaluation did not slow number or expense 1960-1971 foreign travel up 153%	
TV watching	$ 7.4 Billion	1970	on radio and TV receivers	"Economics of Leisure Today" Richard Kraus Parks and Recreation August, 1971
		1972	97% of US pop 12 and over watches TV an average of 19 hr/week	Growth in Leisure Activities Midwest Research Institute unpublished report
		1973	96% of all Am. homes have TV av. set on 6 hrs. 12 min/day	Columbia, Missouri Tribune February 24, 1975 (AP)
Water skiing	$45 Million	1971	for skis *alone* 11 Mill. people tried it at least once in year.	US News and World Report April 17, 1972 source Am. Water Ski Assn.

Although the economy and inflation is tightening the belts of the nations people, many types of recreation seem not to be affected. Fans are still packing 60,000- and 70,000-seat arenas, and paying for tickets ranging from $7.50 to $11.50. The situation baffles psychologists and economists. The 24 major league baseball clubs drew 30,027,063 in 1974 visitors which is only slightly less than 1973 figures. However there attendance is 4.8 percent higher at mid-point 1975 than at the same time in 1974.

Hobbies are booming, partly because of the recession. The hobby and craft industry as we know it—a billion-dollar a year business—began during the 1930s when the depression victims sought inexpensive past times.

Retail hobby craft sales jumped from 652 million to 1.3 billion in the past ten years. According to the Association Councils of the Arts, two out of every five Americans now practive a craft with millions more pursuing other hobbies.

America's favorite hobby is gardening, followed by stamp collecting. Bird watching has grown ten-fold in the last decade. Photography, coin collecting, antiques, jigsaw puzzles, and "do it yourselfing" also are big. There are other hobbies on the increase. Model railroading had a 50 percent increase in sales each year since 1970; acrylic crafting—transforming plastic sheets into furniture and decorations—has increased 120 percent annually; two billion tropical fish are in home aquariums; table games, such as Monopoly, Napoleon, or Omar Bradley are increasingly popular. Entering contests for jingles, names, captions, or slogans are on the rise, according to Frederick Fell, Inc. publisher of the *Official Guide to Prize Contests and How to Win Them*.

Others on the upswing include model airplanes, antique auto collecting, kiting, and magic. More information can be obtained from the Hobby Industry Association of America, 200 5th Avenue New York, New York 10010 or the American Craft Council, 44 West 53rd Street, New York, New York 10019.

The motion picture industry reported box office receipts increased 25 percent over 1973 to reach 1.9 billion dollars according to Donald Baker, Vice President for Advertising for Lowe's Theater chain. This includes sales of 1,011,700,000 tickets, an increase of 17 percent over 1973. This attendance was achieved on 124 new films per year less than the number of previous years.

Although the explanation is undefinable at this time, it appears that the country as a whole, is considering recreation and leisure activities and interests as a necessary part of living, and are continuing to spend proportionally.

Although the recreation patterns have changed, many Americans continue to devote a substantial portion of their incomes to the pursuit of a good time. While entertainment has been curtailed, and many people may be taking less expensive trips that are closer to home they are still going. The close-to-home types of recreation including bowling, movies, museums, and others including the public sponsored programs are experiencing increased attendance as never before.[11]

[11] Columbia Daily Tribune, Associated Press, April 24, 1975.

Figure 16 Attending concerts and other social gatherings close to home account for large percentage increase in attendance in recreation activities.
Courtesy: International Association of Amusement Parks and Attraction, Oak Park, Illinois.

By whatever measure the demand for leisure, recreation, and tourism services is *big,* and growing—faster than any other major segment of our economy. The patterns of this participation and spending has significant implications for the private recreation enterprise manager.

Summary

The demand for commercial and public outdoor recreation is increasing yearly at an astonishing rate. There is no doubt that facilities are needed to satisfy this demand. The reason the commercial and private sector of the outdoor recreation industry is becoming so popular and prominent is that the sector increasingly:

1. Offers the opportunity to experience combinations of popular outdoor recreation activities.
2. Satisfies the sociological and psychological needs of the American public by packaging these recreational desires under one roof.

The fundamental difference is, of course, that the individual or family generally pays for recreation experiences in the private sector. The growing outdoor commercial recreation industry is a reflection that customers feel they are receiving a valuable return on their recreation investment.

The "demand" for recreation is usually measured in terms of participation in various types of activities. The "supply," on the other hand, is a measure of the number of facilities, programs, or services available. The "need" is usually an expression of what individuals would like to do if facilities were available but not necessarily what they are doing. There continues to be a significant problem in the definition of various terms used in assessing demand, particularly between government agencies, state agencies, private enterprises, and regional travel and tourism associations.

Only recently have those providing public leisure delivery systems been willing to recognize the contribution of the private sector in meeting the needs of the general population for recreation and leisure service. The public recreation administrator has traditionally provided the kinds of services that he feels the public will desire, usually with little regard for the cost as it has been tax supported and evaluated success in terms of the number of participants. The private recreation enterprises manager sells a recreation service for a fee. He must combine all the skills and tools of business with a sound philosophy of leisure to make his business a success. He has an on-going automatic indicator—the net profit produced—to show whether he is doing a good job and whether the service provided is in demand by the public.

The first major effort to assess the demand for recreation of the American public was undertaken by the Outdoor Recreation Resources Review Commission. Unfortunately, this and subsequent studies by the U.S. Department of Interior and Bureau of Outdoor Recreation has concentrated on the demand for *outdoor recreation* and omitted entirely the demand for other indoor recreational activities. Estimates on the demand for indoor recreation are available from a multitude of other sources, which indicate that the American public probably participates in indoor recreation in equal amounts as outdoor recreation.

Another way to measure demand is in terms of the amount of time people participate in the activities, the number of times they participate per year, as well as the amount of money they spend for the various leisure pursuits.

It is probably unrealistic to expect all of the needs to be met, as new facilities are considered the demand usually rises to saturate the supply.

Additional References

Books, Bulletins, and Reports
Bureau of Outdoor Recreation, *The 1970 Survey of Outdoor Recreation Activities, Preliminary Report,* U.S. Department of the Interior, Superintendent of Documents, February 1972.
Bureau of Outdoor Recreation, *The 1965 National Inventory of Publicly Owned Recreation Areas and An Assessment of Private Recreation Enterprises,* Superintendent of Documents, Washington, D.C. 1965.
Bureau of Outdoor Recreation, *The Recreation Imperative,* Department of the Interior,

Superintendent of Documents, Washington, D.C. 1974.

Doubleday, Doran and Co., *Sodom By The Sea,* Garden City, New York, 1941.

Griffin, Al, *Step Right Up Folks,* Henry Regnery Company, 114 W. Illinois Street, Chicago, Illinois; 1974.

Hines, Thomas I., *Revenue Sources Management in Parks and Recreation,* National Recreation and Park Association, Arlington, Virginia 1974.

Little, Arthur D. Inc., *Tourism and Recreation,* Superintendent of Documents, Washington, D.C. 20402.

Mangels, William F., *The Outdoor Amusement Industry,* Vantage Press, Inc., New York City, 1952, Library of Congress Catalog Card No. 52-13299.

Munson, Karl, *Minnesota Resort Management and Short Course,* Brainerd Federal Extension Service, Washington D.C., March 28, 1973.

Norem, Susan K., Mary Beth McCurry, and Ruth E. Poliyak, *A Glossary of Terms Used By The Bureau of Outdoor Recreation,* U.S. Department of Interior, September 1975.

Smith, C. Ray, *The American Endless Weekend,* American Institute of Architects, 1735 New York Avenue, N.W., Washington, D.C., May 1973.

Smith, Clodus R., Lloyd E. Partain, and James R. Champlin, *Rural Recreation For Profit,* Interstate Printers and Publishers, Inc. Danville, Illinois 1968.

Wilder, Robert L., *Inventory of Potential Recreation Assets,* Extension Service Oregon State University, Corvallis, Special Report 302, June 1970.

Discussion Questions

1. What are the differences between demand and need for recreation services?
2. What are the publics attitudes regarding public versus private recreation?
3. In what ways do nonprofit agencies fit into the recreation environs with the public and commercial recreation agencies?
4. What implications does the 1962 report of the Outdoor Recreation Resources Review Commission report have for the commercial recreation vendor?
5. What are the problems with definition and measurement as they relate to understanding leisure interests and participation in leisure activities by the American public?
6. How can a supply of leisure services create its own demand?
7. Which activities seem to offer the most promising immediate growth potential in commercial recreation?
8. What generalizations can you make about the growth of leisure expenditures since 1967?
9. How can the hobby industry meet some of the economic and social demands of the leisure consumer today?

CHAPTER 4

THE
SUPPLY

The previous chapter has discussed the demand for recreation and leisure services and opportunities as measured by the participation in terms of time, activities, and money spent. This chapter will attempt to look at the suppliers of leisure and recreation services and opportunities, and to group these providers into various categories so that the student who is considering a career in private and commercial recreation can have somewhat of an understanding of the breadth and the scope of those agencies that provide recreation and leisure services for profit, who they are, where they are, how many there are, and what kind of services they provide. The demand then looks at the participant and his choices, while the supply looks at the provider, and the services he makes available, whether a public tax supported agency or a private agency for profit. It will soon be seen, that the categories of public for free, public for a fee, or private for a fee overlap, and that the lines between them are anything but distinct.

The first portion of the chapter will look at the providers in general, by total numbers of acres, numbers of enterprises, and so on, and will attempt to compare various aspects of the public, quasi-public and private supply. The last portion of this chapter will describe, in so far as possible, the individual types of enterprises comprising the supply-in groups with common characteristics.

PUBLIC AREAS AND FACILITIES _____

Although the Federal government controls the most land in terms of recreation resources and accounts for the greatest attendance, as seen in Table 6, they also account for the smallest number of sites available. Federal involvement in outdoor recreation is vast. At the end of 1972 over 80 agencies, committees, and councils were engaged in over 300 separate outdoor recreation related programs. The eight federal recreation land managing agencies can be classified into 3 general groups based on divergencies and resource interests and practices: 1. those with recreation as a primary purpose; 2. those that emphasize recreation but administer it as one of several other basic purposes; and 3. those that administer recreation as a relatively

Table VI Number, acreage, and attendance of public and private outdoor recreation areas[a]

	Number of Sites	Acres	Attendance (1 year)
Federal	2,127	446,615,942	537,065,000
State	18,614	39,701,456	420,468,000
County	4,048	2,976,911	194,317,000
Municipal	40,030	2,003,610	1,562,101,000
Total public	65,219	491,297,919	2,713,951,000
Private (profit)	131,626	30,025,200	1,251,876,000
Private (nonprofit)	1,000,000	467,000,000	800,000,000

[a]Bureau of Outdoor Recreation, *The 1975 Nationwide Inventory of Publically Owned Recreation Areas and Assessment of Private Recreation Enterprises,* U.S. Department of Interior, Superintendent of Documents, Washington, D.C. pp. 49, 90, 112.

minor land management function. Agencies providing recreation areas, facilities, and services include the Bureau of Land Management, the National Park Service, the Bureau of Sports Fisheries and Wildlife, and the Bureau of Reclamation in the Department of Interior; the Forest Service in the Department of Àgriculture; the Department of Defense at various Army, Navy, and Air Force installations and the Army Corp of Engineers; and the Tennessee Valley Authority. Together, the 8 land-managing agencies administer a total of 775 million acres, although only a portion of this is managed for recreation as reflected in Table 6. As might be expected, there is substantial variation in locations, types of resources, and facilities involved, and the type of management and facilities or programs that are emphasized. No attempt will be made to describe the kinds of areas they administer, nor the differences in policies concerning land acquisition and development or operation. The relationship between areas and facilities made available by government owned agencies in comparison with those offered through private enterprise will be discussed later.

State programs and services play no small part in providing opportunities for recreation and leisure activities. Most state lands are more highly developed, and provide for more visitors per acre than do federal lands. Although, in 1972, states managed almost 42 million acres of land, only 11 percent of this represents parks, recreation areas, playgrounds, and play fields, with the remainder representing des-

Figure 17 Most boating and sailing takes place on water areas owned or controlled by the United States Government.
Courtesy: Boating Industrial Association, glastron boats, Austin, Texas.

ignated public fish and games areas or public forest areas.

Local cities, counties, regions, and other political subdivisions of the state are in the best position to know the needs of their citizens, and can provide facilities for the community and neighborhood and close to home areas better than any other public agency. Agencies of local government control approximately 11 million acres, and although of considerably smaller amount and magnitude than those administered by the federal or state agencies, is of considerable importance because of the high use per acre, and the responsibility for providing much of the nations close-to-home outdoor recreation opportunities. They also must provide recreation opportunities for those who have insufficient funds to participate in private activities, or are without the means to travel to other public recreational areas outside their home community. The 21,000 local governments operate over 40,000 areas or facilities and thus account for many of the high intensity-use areas that are not provided in many of the large forest or reservation type areas of the other managing authorities.

The amount of land available in this country to the public for recreation activities is indeed staggering. Of the land surface totaling 2.3 billion acres of 3.6 million square miles, the eight federal government recreation agencies mentioned previously own approximately 32 percent, with one percent designated as being available for recreation. This added with 1.7 percent that are state owned, 1.3 percent that are county owned, and 0.03 percent municipal owned, gives a total of 491 million acres available for recreation, almost one-fourth of all U.S. land on which any or all Americans are free to engage in recreational activities. These public lands comprise approximately 65,000 individual areas both large and small and present a significantly large number and variety of opportunities for Americans to pursue recreation and leisure activities and interests.

Availability is not necessarily accessibility. Almost one-half of the population lives in the northeast quadrant of our nation. By contrast, recreation lands located in the west have over 75 percent of the available land for only 18 percent of the population. The 1972 nationwide recreation plan[1] indicates that where 75 percent of our population is concentrated, only 25 percent of the recreational facilities and only three percent of the public recreation lands are reasonably available for recreation.

As it is unlikely that significantly large amounts of land and facilities can be obtained within economic limitations near urban areas, the major portion of the population must travel to enjoy the types of leisure and recreation opportunities they desire, or purchase these opportunities from a private or quasi-public agency near their homes.

PRIVATE AREAS AND FACILITIES

As can be seen from the variety of descriptions of types of recreation facilities and programs discussed later in this chapter, the contributions through outdoor recreation from the private sector is indeed a complex array, ranging from dude ranches, to resorts, to the manufacturers of recreation equipment.

---

[1] Bureau of Outdoor Recreation, *Outdoor Recreation, A Legacy for America*, U.S. Department of the Interior, Superintendent of Documents, Washington, D.C. 1973, pp. 6, 12.

Today the private sector owns or operates as much acreage as the public sector and involves more people and a much wider variety of organizations and interests, as well as activities. Officials of public agencies, whether on the federal or local level have come to recognize that their agencies in no way can begin to supply the total recreation needs of the American public. They are now beginning to see the need to cooperate, to plan jointly, to develop jointly, and to assist each other, so as to aviod unnecessary duplication, and fair competition or an imbalance of supply and demand. It is estimated[2] that at least 50 percent of all recreation opportunities is directly attributable to the private sector.

In 1965, an estimated 85,000 commercial enterprises with approximately 23 million acres provided outdoor recreation opportunities for the American public. Together they received more than 1 billion visits per year. Of this number, about 37,000 were full-time providers of facilities and on-site services. These range from dude ranches and resorts to hunting guides and outfitting services, charter fishing boats, golf courses, shooting reserves, and commercial campgrounds. Another 2000 enterprises provide similar services on a part-time basis. An estimated 46,000 commercial enterprises provide outdoor recreation facilities and services relating to amusement and spectator sports activities.

An example of the cooperation between private and public sectors can be shown by the 24,000 concessionaires that have private investments on federal recreational lands and waters.

PRIVATE NONPROFIT RECREATION EFFORTS

More than 1 million individual enterprises provided outdoor recreation opportunities to the American people without a profit motive in 1965.[3] It is estimated that they control about 467 million acres of land and receive about 800 million visits a year.

Of this number, there are an estimated 47,000 private and quasi-private nonprofit organizations, and an estimated 32,000 membership clubs in this group; boat, swimming, hunting, and fishing clubs.

The other nonprofit opportunities are provided by land-holding industries, farmers, or industrial concerns, or are of the quasi-public group, including conservation and related societies, local garden clubs, and religious and civic groups. The total membership of these groups and agencies which indeed has a significant impact on outdoor recreation resources can only be estimated. However, youth groups alone will number more than 200 million, with well over 4000 facilities in all 50 states, whose members are among the most active recreation participants. About 50,000 companies offer

[2] Ibid p. 81.

[3] Ibid p. 86.

some type of spare-time activities to their employees. Many of the nation's farmers and land owners allow public hunting and fishing on their properties. About 1 million farms with a total of approximately 400 million acres of land are open to hunters and fishermen, an provide over half of the recreation resources for the nation's 28 million fishermen and 5 million hunters. The 1965 Bureau of Outdoor Recreation study of private enterprise,[4] found a number of significant facts. Among them are the following:

1. An estimated 132,000 or private recreation enterprises owning 30 million acres of land accounted for 1.2 billion a day patrons.
2. Nationwide, 62.4 percent of these enterprises were under utilized, 24.1 percent were used to capacity, and 13.5 percent were overused.
3. Less than three percent of the 491 million acres available for public recreation is within one hour's drive of people living in urban areas.
4. Private recreation areas, both profit and nonprofit account for almost 2/3 of the total number of recreation areas.
5. Private sector including both personal and nonprofit agencies is by far the country's largest supplier of outdoor recreation resources and facilities.
6. The total private recreation estate amounts to almost ½ billion acres, slightly more than the total public estate; however, most of the private recreation lands is mainly incidental and largely limited.
7. Only 1/3 of the total private enterprises were found to be in cities and towns.

Characteristics of the individual private enterprises:[5]

1. Averages 230 acres each.
2. Serves 7 times as many people per acre as public areas.
3. Forty percent of the enterprises are near public areas.
4. Ten percent of the enterprises consider nearby government facilities as competitive liabilities.
5. More than half of the total number of enterprises offer water activities, and over 2/3 offer municipal activities.
6. Most enterprises report under use of their facilities.
7. Only 14 percent said they had to turn potential customers away.
8. Half the enterprises that remained in operation from 1960 to 1965 reported an increase in patronage, and only 13 percent reported that they had lost customers

[4] Bureau of Outdoor Recreation, The Recreation Imperative, U.S. Department of Interior, Superintendent of Documents, Washington, D.C. 1974, p. 191, 196, 197 and Appendix VI.

[5] Ibid p. 196 and Appendix VI.

during that period.

9. It appears that, by and large, commercial outdoor recreation enterprises have concentrated on non-urban areas to attract urban clientele and perhaps neglected profit making opportunities in or close to urban areas.

BUREAU OF OUTDOOR RECREATION 1965 PRIVATE OUTDOOR RECREATION ENTERPRISES STUDY

The first assessment of private outdoor recreation enterprises was done by BOR as a part of the nationwide outdoor recreation inventory and plan, covering privately owned-and-operated enterprises in the continental United States, including volunteer organizations and agencies not operated for profit, which were in existence in the summer of 1965.

The inventory was assessed on the basis of a stratefied random sample by counties and geographic locations within counties. Outdoor recreation enterprises were identified in pre-selected portions of randomly selected counties, and a total sample size of 2102 was investigated.

Facilities offering the following activities were studied:

Bicycling	Field trails
Boating and boat rentals	Fishing, salt, cold and warm
Camping—for instance tent,	fresh water
trailer, group residence,	Golf
and day	Hiking and walking
Caves	Horseback riding
Drama and concerts	Hunting—big and small game
Drive-in movies	and waterfowl
Driving and sightseeing	Ice skating
Lodging	Spectator sports
Mountain climbing	Sports and play fields—such as
Nature study	archery, tennis, or softball
Picnicking	Swimming beaches and pools
Shooting ranges	Vacation farms
Skiing—water and snow	Winter sports

Because of the small sample size such an assessment can only be an estimate and can vary as much as 7000 enterprises (one standard deviation of sampling tolerance) in the total number projected. However, this was the first attempt by anyone to even project an estimated number of enterprises, and the study does not purport to be 100 percent accurate.

Table VII Private outdoor recreation enterprises[b]

Multiple water-oriented enterprises	7,856	6%
Swimming	22,195	17%
Boating	4,449	3%
Fishing	10,138	8%
total water-oriented	(44,638)	(34%)
Multiple land-oriented enterprises	8,128	6%
Lodgings	17,577	13%
Camping (overnight and day)	6,273	5%
Hunting	13,651	10%
Active participation games or activities	25,991	20%
Passive spectator and miscellaneous	15,591	12%
total land-oriented	(87,211)	(66%)
Total number of enterprises investigated	131,849	100%

[b]*The 1965 Nationwide Inventory of Publically Owned Recreation Areas and Assessment of Private Recreation Enterprises,* op. cit. 1965, pp. 107-109.

Table VIII Private outdoor recreation enterprise employees[c]

Number of Full-Time Employees During Average Week of Season	Number of Enterprises Reporting	
0	111,791	86%
1-2	11,277	9%
3-10	4,861	4%
Over 10	1,028	1%

[c]Bureau of Outdoor Recreation, *The Recreation Imperative,* United States Department of Interior, Superintendent of Documents, Washington, D.C., 1974, p. 128.

It can readily be seen that the 1965 assessment is far from complete, and many of the wide range of activities and facilities that were surveyed do not contain complete information. It was, however, the first attempt to begin to look at the magnitude and categories of private agencies providing recreation and leisure services for profit.

BUREAU OF OUTDOOR RECREATION 1973 PRIVATE ENTERPRISE STUDY_____

In 1973, the Bureau initiated a program to inventory all of the private recreation business in various states. Cooperation was obtained from the National Association of Conservation Districts and the Association requested the assistance of the Soil and Water Conservation Service through their county Conservationists, which cover over 96 percent of the nation's areas, through 29,000 soil conservation districts. To date, the survey is approximately 75 percent complete with 34 states having returned completed surveys of recreation enterprises in their states. The local district conservationists enlisted the help of State Department of Conservation agents, extension specialists and others to inventory and categorize each outdoor recreation enterprise. It is expected that this survey will produce the most complete and reliable information on the private sectors yet to be available. It will be an invaluable tool in getting a first-hand look at the kind and types of recreation businesses in the various states and hopefully information concerning their facilities, length of tenure, etc. The survey attempts to do two things: 1. to assess the number of enterprises, profit and non-profit; and 2. assess the types of activities and facilities offered at each enterprise. In this particular assessment, the facilities were categorized by the primary facility or activity. Multiple recreation facility enterprises will not be reflected. The types of primary facilities inventoried can be seen in Table 9. The total number of activities can also be seen in Table 10. Inventories from California, Tennessee, and Texas were not available and are not included in Tables 9 and 10.

This inventory effort is the result of part of the Bureau of Outdoor Recreation's charge in the 1960s to assist and cooperate with the private recreation sector of outdoor recreation suppliers. Although their assistance and cooperation programs have not yet been fully implemented, the inventory will indeed be a great asset.

One difficulty in assessing the outdoor recreation enterprises for profit, can be seen in the number of changes in the list from year to year. Rand McNally,[6] who provides one of the most comprehensive campground directories for the nation, estimates that each year over 10 percent of the listings have not been in the previous years lists, and approximately one-half of that number that were listed in the previous year are not listed in the current year.

Also the problem of increased facilities is ever present. Few private recreation enterprises will remain constant in the kinds of facilities or activities that they provide or offer. The survey may in that respect be obsolete the day it was taken for a particular location.

The Soil Conservation Service has previously been involved in efforts to assess the private recreation potential in the various counties in the nation. In 1962 the initial portion of a 3-phase plan was begun. Each county was to be inventoried concerning

---

[6] Rand McNally, *Campground and Trailer Park Guide,* Rand McNally & Co., New York, New York, Annual.

Table IX National Association of Conservation Districts private sector recreation inventory—number of enterprises

Enterprises	Profit	Nonprofit	Total
Campgrounds	11,619	6,087	17,706
Field sports	742	2,805	3,547
Fishing waters	6,931	2,892	9,823
Golfing facilities	5,395	3,765	9,160
Historical/Archaeological site	351	938	1,289
Hunting areas	2,231	3,861	6,092
Natural scenic	346	838	1,184
Picnic areas	528	1,277	1,805
Race tracks	998	243	1,241
Recreation	5,550	306	5,856
Rockhounding	85	17	102
Rodeo, zoo, amusements	2,469	894	3,363
Shooting preserves	793	1,192	1,985
Snow ski areas	510	105	615
Trails	2,103	672	2,775
Vacation farms	909	65	974
Water sports	7,697	2,729	10,426

Number of states included = 47

the private recreation enterprises in that county. Because of the interest of some states and the lack of interest in others the inventory was never completed or published. In 1970 additional efforts were made to complete the inventory and to do a county-by-county assessment of the potential for private outdoor recreation development to provide a tool for potential private recreation developers to assist them in evaluating potential areas or sites for recreation businesses. This study has not yet been completed to date. Few know of its existence, and it is unfortunate that such efforts, although well-intended and adequately conceived, have not received sufficient emphasis or priority from top administrators in the Soil and Water Conservation to produce their completion.

One consistent problem that has plagued the recreation industry as a whole including the private enterprises is the dichotomy with which the Bureau of Outdoor Recreation continues to look only at outdoor recreation participation, demand and supply. It continues to be a one-sided look at what Americans' desire and the enterprises that supply only outdoor opportunities. Perhaps some day the federal agencies will recognize that individuals need recreation indoors in the winter months as much as they do outdoors in the milder months, and the dichotomy can be eliminated and a true look at the leisure pursuits of the individuals can be implemented.

Table X National Association of Conservation Districts, private sector recreation inventory—types of activities offered by enterprises

Activity	Number of Enterprises		
	Profit	Nonprofit	Total
Camping—canoe	213	99	312
Camping—day	829	1,108	1,937
Camping—pack	288	259	547
Camping—resident	2,413	2,094	4,507
Camping—transient	3,228	403	3,631
Camping—vacation	6,792	843	7,635
Archery	888	1,536	2,424
Shooting range	1,082	2,052	3,134
Tennis	1,756	2,332	4,088
Fish—ponds/lakes	7,256	3,721	10,977
Fishing enterprises	5,924	934	6,858
Golf—driving	1,783	780	2,563
Golf executive	337	110	447
Golf—miniature	1,284	91	1,375
Golf—par 3	528	184	715
Golf regulations	3,538	2,903	6,441
Historical/archeological	543	976	1,519
Hunting total area	2,616	3,636	6,252
Hunting	4,123	5,600	9,723
Natural scenic	1,273	1,219	2,492
Picnicking	2,777	6,321	9,908
Racing—viewing	1,131	179	1,310
Recreation resort	3,047	164	3,211
Rockhounding	234	52	286
Rodeo, zoo, park	2,511	956	3,467
Shooting—preserve	506	934	1,440
Snow skiing	1,212	275	1,487
Trails total	3,317	1,812	5,129
Bicycle trails	549	182	731
Hiking trails	2,650	2,248	4,898
Horse trails	3,002	583	3,540
Off-road vehicles	472	161	633
Snowmobiling	821	460	1,281
Vacation farm	561	8	569
Vacation ranch	430	16	446
Boating—nonmotor	5,344	1,126	6,470
Boating—motor	4,665	339	5,004
Boating—launch, storage	10,479	2,163	12,642
Swimming	11,251	6,883	18,084

THE SUPPLY AS MEASURED BY THE GOVERNMENT'S STANDARD INDUSTRIAL CLASSIFICATION (SIC) SYSTEM _____

A much overlooked source of valuable information is contained in the U.S. government's Census of Business Reports produced by the U.S. Department of Commerce and the Bureau of Census. (see Tables 11, 12, and 13).

The first economic census of the United States was conducted as part of the 1810 decennial census when inquiries of manufacturing were included with the census of population. Business censuses were subsequently taken over on a differing number of years, and in 1935 began to be collected with the population census. Beginning in 1954, the business census has been conducted concurrently with the census of manufacturers and mineral industries. The primary advantage of this census is its consistency from census to census in providing benchmarks for indices of production, productivity, prices, number of employees, number in the employment force, sales, and number of enterprises.

Tables 11, 12, and 13 list information about the various kinds of private and commercial recreation business establishments listed in the Census of Business concerning their total number; total payroll; total receipts, and the number of paid employees for the week including March 12.

In most cases those agencies operated by quasi-public or public agencies were not included, such as municipal golf courses, swimming pools, and so on, because no business reports were received from those agencies or facilities.

It can quickly be seen that the Census of Business contains an enormous amount of information that reflects current trends in private recreation enterprises. Only time will allow sufficient study to interpret the meaning of these data for use in forecasting in the future.

The one problem with census of business information is the time required for publication, normally about three years. The 1972 data was available in late Fall 1975. The 1976 data will probably not be available until sometime in 1979 or 1980. Definitions of the various categories can be found in Appendix B.

PRIVATE AND COMMERCIAL ENTERPRISES _____

To this point the supply of private and commercial enterprises has been discussed in generalities in terms of the numbers of various types of enterprises, and other characteristics that are of interest from available sources from BOR, the government SIC codes, and so on. In this portion an attempt will be made to look at individual types of private and commercial recreation enterprises in order that the student can obtain an understanding of the variety of recreation businesses falling into each category, and some of the characteristics of each.

One serious problem has been the lack of consistent, available information about these enterprises. For the most part, information has come from the trade association office or from articles in periodicals and newspapers. Every type of enterprise has its own trade association with membership of similar types of facilities across the country. In so far as possible the name and address of the trade association headquarters office for each type of enterprise will be listed. It is hoped that this material can be added to in the future, as more information becomes available about these kinds of recreation businesses. All factual data presented was supplied by the respective trade association offices.

PROBLEMS OF CATEGORIZATION

You have noticed already the different ways and methods of categorizing recreation businesses. These methods have already been noted, those in the 1965 BOR study, those used in the 1973 inventory, and those used by the Department of Commerce in their SIC information.

Other sources use different listings. The state of Wisconsin[7] uses the following classifications:

Winter sports	Vacation farms
Shooting reserves	Hunting areas
Campgrounds	Riding stables
Fishing waters	Water sports
Field sports	Scenic and historic sites

Others, such as Donnelly,[8] suggest all recreation enterprises can be categorized. into four main categories. 1) outdoor attractions, 2) clubs, 3) resorts, and 4) entertainment centers.

Other authors have divided them into outdoor and indoor recreation enterprises, or into other differentiating categories such as spectator enterprises and participation activities, or activities offering exercise and relaxation such as vacation farms, camping areas, nature trails, and so on.

It is also most difficult to differentiate the enterprise from the activity. There are many hunting facilities for instance, but few hunting enterprises. There are a number of enterprises that have nature trails, but no enterprise would be exclusively trails. Many enterprises have picnicking and sports areas, but no enterprises would be listed under this category in any kind of a framework attempting to help organize the the different aspects of recreation businesses to some manageable framework. Most previous textbooks have attempted to categorize the supply in terms of activities rather than by facilities.

[7] R.P. Cooper, S.C. Stanifort, A.C. Johnson Jr., and R.A. Christensen, *Research Report-Some Organizational and Income Determining Features of the Wisconsin Outdoor Recreation Industry,* College of Agricultural and Life Sciences, University of Wisconsin, Madison, 1972.

[8] Arlin Epperson, Editor; *Private and Commercial Recreation Education Kit,* Speeches given at NRPA Congress Session, 1974 "Implications for Commercial Recreation Education."

Table XI Total number of SIC establishments[a]

SIC	Kind of Business	Total Number Establishments				
		1954	1958	1963	1967	1972
701, 703	Hotels, Motels, Tourist Courts and Camps					
	Total	66,962	85,890	84,706	87,006	79,685
7011	Hotels, motels, and tourist courts	54,210	70,535	64,276	65,579	58,688
	Hotels	24,778	29,203	22,722	23,625	13,989
	Year round hotels, 25 or more guest rooms	xx	xx	10,377	xx	xx
	Year round hotels, less than 25 guest rooms	xx	xx	8,570	xx	xx
	Seasonal hotels	xx	xx	3,775	xx	NA
	Motels, motor hotels and tourist courts	29,432	41,332	41,584	41,954	44,699
	Motels, tourist courts	29,432	41,332	38,858	xx	xx
	Motor hotels	NA	NA	2,726	xx	xx
7031	Trailer parks	4,360	8,110	9,769	12,437	13,789[2]
7032	Sporting & recreational camps	8,392	6,935	10,661	8,990	xx
78	Motion Pictures					
	Total	20,843	19,657	16,381	16,752	8,555
781, 782	Motion Picture production, distribution, services	2,352	3,191	3,729	4,565	xx
7813	Motion pic. production (other than for TV)	541	910	720	xx	xx
7814	Motion pic. production for TV	234	428	527	xx	xx
7815	Production of still films & slide films	NA	NA	102	xx	NA
7816	Motion pic. film exchanges	798	797	764	xx	xx
7817	Film or tape distribution for TV	84	129	167	xx	xx

SIC	Industry					
7818	Service allied to motion pic. distribution	421	354	328	xx	xx
782	Motion pic service industries	421	573	1,121	xx	NA
783	Motion picture theaters	18,491	16,354	12,652	12,187	12,699
7832	Motion pic. theaters, except drive-in	14,716	12,291	9,150	xx	xx
7833	Drive-in motion pic. theaters	3,775	4,063	3,502	xx	xx
79	Amusement & Recreation Services Except Motion Pic					
	Total	52,509	74,696	79,451	96,029	145,983[3]
792	Producers, orchestras, entertainers	9,276	17,867	14,380	27,698	47,727
	Bands, orchestras, actors, other entertainers	xx	14,655	11,047	xx	xx
	dance bands, orchestras, except symphony	xx	6,750	5,118	xx	xx
	symphony orchestras, other classical groups	xx	461	302	xx	xx
	entertainers (radio-tv) except classical	xx	7,444	5,627	xx	xx
	Theatrical producers and services	xx	3,212	3,233	xx	xx
	operators, producers of legitimate theater	xx	NA	311	xx	xx
	producers of live, taped shows for tv-radio	xx	557	300	xx	xx
	stock & repertory companies	xx	197	147	xx	xx
	entertainers, mgrs, agents, concert bureaus	xx	1,311	1,105	xx	xx
	other theatrical services	xx	755	1,025	xx	xx
7922	other not elsewhere listed	NA	392	345	NA	xx

[d] United States Department of Commerce, Census of Business Reports, Superintendent of Documents, Washington, D.C. 1958, 1963, 1967, 1972.

Table XI (continued)

SIC	Kind of Business	Total Number Establishments				
		1954	1958	1963	1967	1972
793	Bowling alleys, billiard, pool establishments	12,701	13,916	15,927	15,497	14,320
7932	Billiard and pool establishments	7,639	7,045	7,069	xx	5,847
7933	Bowling alleys	5,062	6,871	8,858	xx	8,454
79, Ex. 792,3	Other amusement & recreation services	30,532	42,913	49,244	52,834	xx
791	Dance halls, studios, schools	2,265	6,869	7,301	xx	xx
	Public dance halls or ballrooms	xx	875	869	xx	xx
	Dance schools, incl. childrens, pro.	xx	5,994	6,432	xx	xx
7941, 7948	Commercial sports	2,517	6,028	6,488	xx	xx
	Baseball, football clubs, etc., promoters	672	752	445	xx	xx
	baseball clubs	271	200	158	xx	xx
	football clubs	25	20	41	xx	xx
	other pro athletic clubs	376	448	246	xx	xx
	managers and promoters	376	448	246	xx	xx
7948	Racetrack operation, including racing stables	1,845	5,276	6,043	xx	xx
	Automobile racing	454	578	458	xx	xx
	dog race tracks	xx	xx	55	xx	xx

SIC	Category					
	thoroughbred horse race tracks	xx	xx	235	xx	xx
	standardbred horse race tracks	xx	xx	235	xx	xx
	dog & horse racing stables	xx	xx	5,295	xx	xx
7942	Public golf courses	xx	1,014	851	1,047	xx
7945	Skating rinks	1,799	2,254	1,274	xx	NA
7946	Amusement parks (incl. kiddie, theme parks)	2,488	3,682	997	xx	xx
7943	Coin operated amusement devices	6,045	5,264	5,038	xx	xx
7949	Concession operators of amusement devices	xx	xx	2,776	xx	xx
	carnivals, circuses	1,090	801	363	xx	xx
	fairs	1,090	320	1,257	xx	xx
	other commercial recreation and amusements	13,314	16,844	22,703	xx	xx

[1] Fairs operated by gov't boards or subdivisions not included, but they were included in 1963.
[2] Classified as "Trailer Parks and Campsites for Transients" under SIC of 7033.
[3] Includes Motion Pictures.
NA-4 Not available, new category created for 1972 SIC Codes.
NA - Not applicable.
xx - classified at the next broader kind-of-business level.
Figures taken from *Census of Selected Service Industries*, U.S. Department of Commerce, 1954, 1958, 1963, 1967, 1972, Superintendent of Documents, Washington, D.C.

Table XII Total payroll and number of employees SIC index[e]

SIC	Kind of Business	1954	Total # with Payroll				1972 Paid Employees for week including March 12
			1958	1963	1967	1972	
701, 703	Hotels, Motels, Tourist Courts and Camps						
	Total	38,558	48,528	53,071	53,560	46,509	726,577
7011	Hotels, motels, and tourist courts	34,438	42,025	44,770	44,903	40,837	711,051
	Hotels	19,368	20,715	18,969	18,690	10,750	346,955
	Year round hotels, 25 or more guest rooms	15,950	11,141	10,234	9,575	7,382	333,716
	Year round hotels, less than 25 guest rooms	3,418	5,600	5,138	4,372	3,368	13,239
	Seasonal hotels	NA	3,974	3,597	4,743	NA	
	Motels, motor hotels and tourist courts	15,070	21,310	25,801	26,213	30,087	346,096
	Motels, tourist courts	15,070	21,310	23,159	22,697	21,739	273,056
	Motor hotels	NA	NA	2,642	3,516	2,348	91,040
7031	Trailer parks	1,224	2,356	3,402	4,065	2,507	5,002
7032	Sporting & recreational camps	2,896	3,923	4,899	4,682	3,165	10,524
78	Motion Pictures						
	Total	19,227	17,601	14,869	14,853		653,047
781, 782	Motion picture production, distribution, services	1,906	2,421	2,829	3,375	4,704	64,660
7813	Motion pic. production (other than for TV)	417	668	720	909	1,392	16,941
7814	Motion pic. production for TV	206	312	527	686	1,138	15,106
7815	Production of still films & slide films	NA	NA	58	80	NA	xx

SIC							
7816	Motion pic. film exchanges	700	721	730	710	877	15,110
7817	Film or tape distribution for TV	80	111	131	147	151	2,075
7818	Service allied to motion pic. distribution	256	266	238	289	291	3,453
782	Motion pic. service industries	247	343	425	554	855	xx
783	Motion picture theaters	17,371	15,076	12,040	11,478	11,670	127,435
7832	Motion pic theaters, except drive-in	13,760	11,271	8,665	8,094	8,328	101,737
7833	Drive-in motion pic. theaters	3,611	3,805	3,375	3,384	3,342	25,698
79	Amusement & Recreation Services Except Motion Pic. Total	32,945	37,640	44,353	43,752	66,064	307,716
792	Producers, orchestras, entertainers	7,354	7,981	7,964	8,085	7,641	58,359
	Bands, orchestras, actors, other entertainers	xx	6,219	6,121	5,789	1,795	15,880
	Dance bands, orchestras, except symphony	xx	5,274	5,118	4,221	3,016	xx
	Symphony orchestras, other classical groups	xx	209	302	382	389	9,659
	Entertainers (radio-tv) except classical	xx	736	701	1,186	NA	9,327
	Theatrical producers and services	xx	1,762	1,843	2,296	1,249	10,472
7922	Operators, producers of legitimate theater	xx	NA	255	586	NA	10,622
	Producers of live, taped shows for tv-radio	xx	343	300	353	258	2,399
	Stock & repertory companies	xx	161	147	293	NA	xx
	Entertainers, mgrs., agents, concert bureaus	xx	521	587	746	NA	4,396
	Other theatrical services	xx	429	275	318	440	6,076
	Other not elsewhere listed	NA	308	279	NA	NA	xx

[e]United States Department of Commerce, Census of Business Reports, Superintendent of Documents, Washington D.C. 1958, 1963, 1967, 1972.

Table XII (continued)

SIC	Kind of Business	Total # with Payroll					1972 Paid Employees for week including March 12
		1954	1958	1963	1967	1972	
793	Bowling alleys, billiard, pool establishments	8,321	9,292	12,045	11,367	9,048	94,877
7932	Billiard and pool establishments	3,539	3,053	3,702	3,666	2,531	6,463
7933	Bowling alleys	4,692	6,239	8,343	7,701	6,517	88,414
79, Ex. 792, 3	Other amusement & recreation services	17,360	20,367	24,344	24,300	33,001	307,716
791	Dance halls, studios, schools	1,735	3,641	3,078	2,780	2,370	10,756
	Public dance halls or ballrooms	xx	547	601	437	339	2,739
	Dance schools, incl. childrens, pro.	xx	3,094	2,477	2,343	2,031	8,017
7941, 7948	Commercial sports	1,303	1,744	2,092	2,401	2,733	48,308
	Baseball, football clubs, etc., promoters	500	486	445	455	537	14,515
	Baseball clubs	267	190	158	136	152	3,944
	Football clubs	17	16	41	44	46	1,509
	Other pro athletic clubs	216	274	246	144	339	9,062
	Managers and promoters	216	274	246	131	339	9,062
7948	Racetrack operation, including racing stables	803	1,258	1,647	1,446	2,196	33,793

	Automobile racing	292	292	458	460	593	4,201
	Dog race tracks	xx	xx	55	43	42	3,791
	Thoroughbred horse race tracks	xx	xx	235	159	247	19,894
	Standardbred horse race tracks	xx	xx	235	91	247	19,894
	Dog & horse racing stables	xx	xx	899	1,193	1,313	19,894
7942	Public golf courses	826	647	1,047	1,479	2,315	12,785
7945	Skating rinks	1,017	1,148	1,274	1,033	NA	NA-4
7946	Amusement parks (incl. kiddie, theme parks)	1,510	1,936	997	786	682	20,339
7943	Coin operated amusement devices	3,301	2,964	3,074	2,400	2,061	10,165
7949	Concession operators of amusement devices	xx	xx	1,315	1,187	1,041	3,893
	Carnivals, circuses	726	333	363	548		5,893
	Fairs	726	270	1,257	578		5,893
	Other commercial recreation and amusements	6,942	7,684	9,847	11,108	11,380	78,971

[1] Fairs operated by gov't boards or subdivisions not included, but they were included in 1963.

[2] Classified as "Trailer Parks and Campsites for Transients" under SIC of 7033.

[3] Includes Motion Pictures.

NA-4 Not available, new category created for 1972 SIC Codes.

NA - Not applicable.

xx - Classified at the next broader kind-of-business level.

Figures taken from *Census of Selected Service Industries*, U.S. Department of Commerce, 1954, 1958, 1963, 1967, 1972, Superintendent of Documents, Washington, D.C.

Table XIII Total receipts for recreation establishments, SIC index[f]

SIC	Kind of Business	Total Receipts ($1000)				
		1954	1958	1963	1967	1972
701, 703	Hotels, Motels, Tourist Courts and Camps					
	Total	3,026,899	3,923,756	5,049,255	7,038,890	10,638,153
7011	Hotels, motels, and tourist courts	2,861,594	3,644,396	4,667,063	6,532,725	10,087,819
	Hotels	2,404,529	2,794,015	3,005,692	3,823,158	4,794,289
	Year round hotels, 25 or more guest rooms	xx	xx	2,574,904	xx	NA
	Year round hotels, less than 25 guest rooms	xx	xx	164,522	xx	NA
	Seasonal hotels	xx	xx	266,266	xx	NA
	Motels, motor hotels and tourist courts	457,065	850,381	1,661,371	2,709,567	5,293,530
	Motels, tourist courts	457,065	850,381	1,175,754	xx	xx
	Motor hotels	NA	NA	485,617	xx	xx
7031	Trailer parks	48,273	102,709	169,406	272,468	284,369
7032	Sporting & recreational camps	117,032	141,012	212,786	233,697	265,965
78	Motion Pictures					
	Total	2,351,789	2,430,729	2,724,965	3,476,121	2,920,415
781, 782	Motion picture production, distribution, services	994,638	1,249,017	1,662,233	2,183,086	xx
7813	Motion pic. production (other than for TV)	75,607	156,294	134,460	xx	xx
7814	Motion pic. production for TV	61,348	96,532	270,602	xx	xx
7815	Production of still films & slide films	NA	NA	11,215	xx	xx

106

SIC	Industry				
7816	Motion pic. film exchanges	625,982	711,064	825,120	xx
7817	Film of tape distribution for TV	24,052	91,176	229,140	xx
7818	Service allied to motion pic. distribution	23,870	30,303	26,458	xx
782	Motion pic. service industries	133,779	163,648	190,238	xx
783	Motion picture theaters	1,407,151	1,171,783	1,062,732	1,832,968
7832	Motion pic. theaters, except drive-in	1,179,371	938,164	807,596	1,293,035
7833	Drive-in motion pic. theaters	227,780	233,619	255,136	xx
79	Amusement & Recreation Services Except Motion Pic.				
	Total	2,020,708	2,660,952	3,940,286	12,660,113
792	Producers, orchestras, entertainers	293,974	472,019	590,162	1,436,093
	Bands, orchestras, actors, other entertainers	xx	181,187	222,483	xx
	Dance bands, orchestras, except symphony	xx	82,369	86,323	xx
	Symphony orchestras, other classical groups	xx	29,147	54,708	xx
	Entertainers (radio-tv) except classical	xx	69,671	81,452	xx
7922	Theatrical producers and services	xx	290,832	367,679	xx
	Operators, produces of legitimate theater	xx	NA	73,287	xx
	Producers of live, taped shows for tv-radio	xx	78,385	102,203	xx
	Stock & repertory companies	xx	14,168	21,440	xx
	Entertainers, mgrs., agents, concert bureaus	xx	48,727	73,847	xx
	Other theatrical services	xx	47,813	29,446	xx
	Other not elsewhere listed	NA	11,739	67,456	NA

^{f} United States Department of Commerce, Census of Business Reports, Superintendent of Documents, Washington, D.C. 1958, 1963, 1967, 1972.

Table XIII (continued)

Code		1	2	3	4	5
793	Bowling alleys, billiard, pool establishments	271,821	505,442	1,016,228	1,010,591	1,204,037
7932	Billiard and pool establishments	74,981	71,990	116,534	xx	115,149
7933	Bowling alleys	196,840	433,452	899,694	xx	1,088,888
79,Ex. 792,3	Other amusement & recreation services	1,454,913	1,683,491	2,333,896	2,942,662	6,051,539
791	Dance Halls, studios, schools	72,795	125,108	99,081	xx	xx
	Public dance halls or ballrooms	xx	27,050	28,773	xx	xx
	Dance schools, incl. childrens, pro.	xx	98,058	70,308	xx	xx
7941, 7948	Commercial sports	404,094	542,123	727,356	xx	xx
	Baseball, football clubs, etc. promoters	103,351	120,520	158,804	xx	xx
	Baseball clubs	53,410	55,165	68,005	xx	xx
	Football clubs	12,153	14,594	30,183	xx	xx
	Other pro athletic clubs	37,788	49,699	60,616	xx	xx
	Managers and promoters	37,788	49,699	60,616	xx	xx
7948	Racetrack operation, including racing stables	300,743	421,603	568,552	xx	xx
	Automobile racing	16,347	16,234	37,711	xx	xx
	Dog race tracks	xx	xx	44,615	xx	xx

SIC	Category	1954	1958	1963	1967	1972
	Thoroughbred horse race tracks	xx	xx	406,660	xx	xx
	Standardbred horse race tracks	xx	xx	406,660	xx	xx
	Dog & horse racing stables	xx	xx	79,566	xx	xx
7942	Public golf courses	31,979	38,773	75,864	xx	xx
7945	Skating rinks	31,642	40,581	47,782	xx	xx
7946	Amusement parks (incl. kiddie, theme parks)	82,283	126,605	105,939	xx	xx
7943	Coin operated amusement devices	238,956	229,445	282,894	xx	xx
7949	Concession operators of amusement devices	xx	xx	69,550	xx	xx
	Carnivals, circuses	52,811	36,956	46,536	xx	xx
	Fairs	52,811	14,215	57,758	xx	xx
	Other commercial recreation and amusements	540,353	529,685	821,136	xx	xx

[1] Fairs operated by gov't boards or subdivisions not included, but they were included in 1963.

[2] Classified as "Trailer Parks and Campsites for Transients" under SIC of 7033.

[3] Includes Motion Pictures.

NA-4 Not available, new category created for 1972 SIC Codes.

NA- not applicable.

xx- classified at the next broader kind-of-business level.

Figures taken from Census of Selected Service Industries, U.S. Department of Commerce, 1954, 1958, 1963, 1967, 1972, Superintendent of Documents, Washington, D.C.

Because of the overlapping of the facilities and services with other components of travel and tourism, such as resort enterprises, which offer lodging, meals, recreation, and relaxation, it is most difficult to fit these recreation enterprises into a meaningful system of classification for easier understanding.

For the purposes of the division of the specifics of the enterprises providing the supply, the following categories will be used for facilities or enterprises providing opportunities for the following:

1. *Spectator activities:* college and professional sports, racing, movies, exhibitions, concerts, cultural—historical—educational attractions, eating and entertainment.
2. *Outdoor attractions and amusements:* county and state fairs, amusement parks, and tourist attractions.
3. *Participative activities:* skating (roller and ice), golf, tennis, skiing, camping, bowling.
4. *Mechanized sports:* supported strongly by manufacturing industries, boating, bicycling, snow mobiling, motorcycling, off-road-vehicles, recreation vehicles.
5. *Clubs—Resorts—Second homes:* multi-activity enterprises with either geographical or membership requirements, or those that provide lodging or both.

It should be recognized that the above categories overlap considerably and none is mutually exclusive. Resorts in particular may offer activities from all five areas. Others may indeed find categories or classifications that are more meaningful to them.

Detailed descriptions of a number of the elements of the supply follow. Not every activity provided by the private sector is discussed for obvious reasons. Those which encompass the largest number of participants, largest number of enterprises, and for which information was available have been included.

It will be noticed that some discussion contains more information than others, as the availability of information effected the discussion considerably.

Specific facts and figures about a particular segment of the industry were for the most part obtained from the trade association reports, information sheets, and other public relations information. Few regular public sources were found. Thus footnoting was impossible.

The various segments of the supply have been grouped according to the previously mentioned categories according to common characteristics. Additional references, agencies, and publications of recreation activities not listed in this book may be found in Directory of National Organizations Related to Recreation, Parks and Leisure, NRPA #12005, Temple Jarrell, 1974, 1601 North Kent Street, Arlington, Virginia 22209.

SPECTATOR SPORT FACILITIES

CULTURAL—HISTORICAL—EDUCATIONAL ATTRACTIONS _____

Museums, zoos, aquariums, libraries, and historical sites are the major institutions that comprise cultural attractions. They provide information to the visitor on something of

Figure 18 A gothic castle in Lyndhurst, Tarrytown. Such cultural and historical buildings make excellent tourism attractions.
Courtesy: National Trust for Historical Preservation, Washington, D.C.

interest. This information is usually acquired by observation, by guided tour and presentation given to the visitor, and/or by provision of brochures and pamphlets.

Most institutions of this type are either publicly owned or supported by one or more private foundations. In addition they are supported in part by donations from individuals.

The history and growth of the United States has been preserved by the states and national government. Many of the historic buildings and landmarks have been restored so interested people can view and learn about the story of America. The National Register of Historic Places is a record of all nationally recognized historic properties that are worthy of preservation for their historic value.

The properties on the register are either owned by the city of its locality, the county, state, or federal governments. There are also some that are privately owned and operated. Most of the sites that are owned and operated by a form of government are open to the public with or without an admission price. Those privately owned are not open to the public with a few exceptions.

The historic sites are one part of tourism that is always in demand. The area that probably attracts the most tourists is that of the thirteen original states where our country began. Independence Hall, for instance, housing the Liberty Bell, is one of the most important parts of our heritage. Visitors are welcome there twelve months a year with no admission price. In Missouri a record taken in 1972 showed that 112,364 people visited 7 of the state's 117 nationally recognized sites.

The National Register lists the following:

Total entries in national register of historic places:	10,636
National register properties:	9,438
National historic landmark	1,198
Historical structures open as museums	
Historic houses:	3,500
Historic buildings:	1,440
Historic sites:	411
Preservation projects:	74
Historic ships:	19
National Trust for Historic Preservation membership	
1965:	8,965
1975:	82,000
Total member organizations:	
1965:	630
1975:	1,333

Opportunities in this area are probably limited for students with recreation and/or business educations. Although each site, facility, or institution had a director, these are usually people trained at the college level in art, library science, or history.

Museums, zoos, and aquariums, rely heavily on the use of volunteers to act as guides, to raise funds, and to help maintain the facilities. Often, there is alot of competition even for the job of volunteer. If someone does become a volunteer, they are usually given preference if a permanent job opening becomes available.

TRADE ASSOCIATIONS

National Trust for Historic Preservation
740 Jackson Street, N.W.
Washington, D.C. 20006

Archives of American Art
41 East 65th Street
New York, N.Y. 10021

American Society for Aesthetics
Cleveland Museum of Art
Cleveland, Ohio 44106

American Scenic and Historical
  Preservation Society
15 Pine St.
New York, N.Y. 10005

American Institute for Conservation
  of Historical and Artistic Works
c/o C T Corporation System
918 16th St. N.W.
Washington, D.C. 20006

SPORTS, CONVENTION, AND ENTERTAINMENT FACILITIES _____

It is difficult to pinpoint the origin of the arena buildings and sports stadiums in history. Surely, though, the Colosseum in Rome would deserve consideration as the inspiration for many of the design concepts used today in facility development. By all accounts, the Colosseum's versatility and multiplicity of uses to which it was reportedly put was and still is a "miracle" of design and construction. Since that era, however, the predominant vessels of mass amusement have been designed and constructed with more or less a single purpose in mind. Although many of the famed opera houses of Europe or sports stadiums of the United States have at times served alternate uses, their arrangement and disposition were much better suited for the original purpose for which they were designed. The true birth of the modern concept of the multipurpose building may have been in the United States. During the periods of both world wars, towns and cities near military camps and forts found it both partiotic and profitable to erect "memorial" buildings where soldiers could frequent for a variety of sports, entertainment, and relaxations. After the wars, these buildings with their courts, dance floors, arts and crafts rooms, and gyms were easily converted for general public use into what we now call a community center. Many larger and more elaborate community centers have been built since then in cities all across the States. The multipurpose complex may owe the birth of its concept to the Depression years. During the Depression, the Federal government financed hundreds of make-work projects to give needy urbanites a chance to work and earn a living. Many projects focused on the construction of mighty monuments which were really glorified community centers. Many of them contained large auditoriums, concert halls, galleries, sports, convention, conference, and display facilities all under one roof. Amusement business managers lists approximately 5000 of these facilities that book at least one show or event per year. These shows vary from local art shows, to wrestling matches to traveling theatrical productions.

A new breed of facilities is rapidly becoming familiar to the landscape of a growing number of universities and major cities across America. In contrast to the single-purpose sports stadiums or music/theater halls with which many of us may be more familiar, the modern arena/auditorium/sports complex is a manifestation of the ever-broadening leisure interests of the American public and their resulting demand for a wider range of recreation facilities. In addition, the proliferation of these complexes is a tribute to the recognition on the part of both public and private entrepeneurs of the need to meet this demand through the planning, design, and development of multiple-use facilities.

Perhaps the major impetus in multiple-use complex development in America has come from the nation's colleges and universities. The University of Illinois, in 1963, dedicated its multiple-use arena, and soon more and more elaborate and embellished structures were built at Notre Dame, Purdue, Colorado University, Arizona State, Missouri, and many other college campuses.

Private enterprise, too, has entered the recreation complex field in a big way with some impressive and sometimes ominous structures like the Houston Astrodome, New Orleans Superdome, Kansas City's HST Sports Complex, and a host of others. Though these may be spectator sport oriented and many are actually publicly financed, the multiplicity of uses to which they can be converted and their financial success merit their inclusion in considering the future of commercial development of this type. More recently, multi-sport participation centers, more akin to the university concept of multipurpose facilities, are enjoying some success in Europe and America. To a certain extent, modern hotel/convention center complexes, along with these other private and commerical ventures, will bear watching as barometers of the possible success or failure of the multiple-use concept.

A quick look at the economics of the convention center business will give an indication as to why cities are building recreation complexes with convention centers partially in mind. In St. Louis, research has shown that the average conventionaire attending a convention in hat city will spend per day in St. Louis about $42.50. For a convention of say 6500 people, per 4 day stay, this means that they will leave over a million dollars in St. Louis. This "new money" from outside the region which goes mostly to hotels, restaurants, and retail establishments provides a number of new jobs, and additional spending by the primary establishments receiving the convention dollars. Hotels employ about one person per room, and expensive restaurants may employ as many as one person for every two place settings. When St. Louis landed the 33,000 National Baptist Convention for September 1975, it was estimated that they would leave approximately $5,000,100 at the end of their 4-day stay. In 1976, for instance, St Louis booked 435 conventions with an anticipated attendance of 389,585. This will produce an estimated 73 million in direct revenue.

This is typical of the convention business in major cities across the nation, and thus the scramble to build new and bigger complexes where the conventionaire can be lodged, fed, conventioned, and entertained all under one roof if possible.

Most cities have a convention and visitors bureau, which may or may not be a part of the Chamber of Commerce. Many of these convention bureaus are financed by a sales tax on hotel rooms, which produces from $500,000 to 2 million dollars, to be used to attract new conventions visitors to the city. The number of cultural events available to the Amercian public has decreased considerably in recent years. Except for the major cities, and some unique markets such as college communities, theatrical productions or symphony concerts have not attracted sufficient attendance to generate a profit on such tours or concerts. The main exception has been in the area of "pop concerts," either rock and roll groups whose main audience seems to be youthful, or some of the other big named Las Vegas-type entertainers who seem to appeal to all ages. Country music entertainers seem to be attracting the most audiences across the country. This is in significant contrast to the late 1940s and early 1950s, where almost every memorial building, municipal auditorium, or civic center had a waiting list for bookings sometimes years in advance. Americans continue to be avid spectators, and the numbers watching auto racing, dog and horse racing, rodeos, and sports events increases every year. These activities, particularly of a sports and racing nature of course, had their beginning many years ago in the Greek and Roman times. The colleges and universities had no small part to play in the roll of spectator sports development, particularly in the area of football and soccer. These big three, football, baseball, and basketball continue to be the favorite spectator sport activity of the American public, although as the previous chapter indicated, attendance at these events does not approach those numbers which watch racing events of various kinds.

Today, sports are a grimly serious business everywhere. Major league professional teams are bought, sold, and moved almost weekly, and sports continue to be a big business on many college campuses. The complexes in stadiums in which these teams play are managed like any other business and in some cases requires specialized training in the particular aspects of those they attempt to attract.

These facilities are in no means inexpensive to operate. In one major multipurpose center, it costs approximately $5000 a day just to run the air conditioning. Doormen and ushers for an event can cost $1500 to $2000. These prices may be extremely small compared with those of the Astrodome and the Superdome in New Orleans.

In most arenas, the logistics of the operation for each event are handled by the center or arena staff, and the promotor of the event is billed for services rendered, plus, which may or may not be included in a rental fee. Sometimes the rent will include a percentage of the gate. Each sponsoring group, on the other hand is responsible for the promotion of its event. In a large multipurpose complex, the maintenance crew works overlapping 8-hour shifts, each with specific areas and routine chores to be completed on a weekly or daily basis, and special technicians and custodians are called in and according to the needs of each event. At times the staff requirements for large events may reach as high as 250 people as ice rink facilities are removed, and basketball floors installed for example.

Although most multipurpose facilities are designed with a single purpose as top priority, compromises in this purpose are made to serve other functions. Because of these design compromises, many technical problems can surface during the many uses of the building for which the civic provisions might not have been made in the original design. At various times the lighting in the auditorium, the size of the back stage, the width and height of quarters, the location of the equipment room, the collapsable bleachers, the parking facilities, the orientation of the building, and the problems of simple maintenance have all created inconveniences, barriers, or hazards for either the public, the entertainers, or the center staff. It is indeed remarkable that in many cases the multitude of purposes which the buildings are supposed to accommodate have survived, and done so well.

It is, however, increasingly difficult to forsee exactly what the public will pay to see. Many multipurpose complexes are in financial difficulties because of poor attendance. Only time will tell whether or not those booking attractions can out guess the spectating public sufficiently well to keep the facilities in the black.

As a relatively young phenomenon the multipurpose facility enterprise will undoubtedly encounter difficulties and complications in many facets of their development and operation, and naturally future complexes will benefit in development from the experiences of their predecessors. There are, however, certain problems such as financing, design, construction, circulation, large operation budgets, compatibility of uses, and the like that are inherent in the size, scale, and dimension of such enormous undertakings that must be dealt with realistically and solved to the ultimate satisfaction and benefit of the public if the multiple use concept is to ultimately succeed.

TRADE ASSOCIATIONS

National Academy of Sports
220 East 63rd Street
New York, N.Y. 10021

National Art Museum of Sport
Madison Square Garden Center
Gallery of Art, Pennsylvania Plaza
New York, N.Y. 10001

National Association of Theater Owners
1501 Broadway
New York, N.Y. 10023

Institute for Study of Sport and Society
Hales Gymnasium
Oberlin, Ohio 44074

Professional Convention Management
  Association
P.O. Box 572
Northbrook, Ill. 60062

National Entertainment Conference
P.O. Box 11489
Columbia, S. Carolina 29211

International Association of
Convention Bureaus
334 E. Broadway
Louisville, Ky. 40202

TRADE JOURNALS

Abel
Abel News Agencies
300 West 17th Street
New York, New York 10011

Action World
Rm 324, 507 Fifth Avenue
New York, New York 10017
Ed. Richard Branciforte

Amusement Business
Billboard Publications Inc.
1719 West End Avenue,
Nashville, Tennessee 37203
Ed. Irwin Kirby Publ. Walter Heeney

Amusements
208 N. Tennessee Avenue
Atlantic City, New Jersey 08401

Funspot Directory
Billboard Publications Inc.
Amusement Business Directories
2160 Patterson Street
Cincinnati, Ohio 45214
Ed. Irwin Kirby Publ. Walter Heeney

OUTDOOR AMUSEMENT PARKS & ATTRACTIONS _____

The fastest growing and most popular segment of the entire entertainment and recreation industries including both private and public operations is the outdoor amusement industry. Amusement park attendance for 1973 was about 470 million, over twice the attendance of 1970.

This industry is American in origin. It took the enterprising Yankee to put the walk through concept of the English "green park" and the Punch and Judy, balloon accessions, and other free forms of entertainment found in French cities together and to charge an entrance fee to see the shows, to enjoy its walks, and for the entire group to have a picnic.

The first such permanently located outdoor amusement facility in the United States was Jones Woods built in 1857 and located on about 150 acres between 70th and

Figure 19 Walbash Cannonball. A part of an outdoor amusement facility–Opry Land U.S.A. in Nashville, Tennessee.
Courtesy: International Association Amusement Parks and Attraction, Oak Park, Illinois.

75th streets in New York City and lasted for 60 years. Coney Island began in the 1880s as a resort for the wealthy. It consisted of 6 miles of New York Beach and is credited with bringing the flashing and jangling amusement park into the 20th century.

During the period until World Was II the parks in this era were or two major types. Those emphasizing *culture and education,* and those emphasizing *production* forms of entertainment that produced revenue. In the former, one could enjoy John Phillip Sousa or the Roger Proyer bands, take a stroll down through landscape greens and gardens, become knowledgeable through a trip on a goal mine-type ride. The production type park emphasized rides, picnic grounds, early physical type games of skill, and other types of participating units of entertainment patrons paid money to enjoy.

After a while, the cultural type park began to disappear for a variety of reasons, operating expenses, lack of interest, the changing entertainment mood of the American public, the increased use of the automobile, and so forth.

The production type park continued to grow in popularity. They began to expand the forms of entertainment offered patrons. When the concession concept started to be introduced in the industry during the mid-1930s, entire families, for example, would become concession operators in a facility to sell taffy made on the spot to operate a "guess your weight and age," to run a hi-striker, or to operate one of several types of pitch games. Entertainers began specializing in free acts and shows specifically created for the outdoor amusement industry. These free shows brought more and more patrons to the parks, more ride tickets were sold, more cotton candy consumed, and more taffy apples were eaten.

The parks continued to do well until the impact of World War II when government restrictions on manufacturing of rides over $5000 produced a number of "kiddie car parks." However in retrospect, the 10 year state of flux after the war can only be viewed as a temporary period in the history of the industry.

The impact of the *"themed park"* with Disneyland in 1955; the Philadelphia Tobaggon Co. gamble in building a now bigger and better "coaster" ride at an unheard of price of $129,000 in 1961, the increased use of pay-one-price, and the ever expanding group business type accounts has been the basic reason why the increase in gross receipts to the expected $500,000,000.00 figure for 1975.

Up until 1955 and the opening of Disneyland (for which Walt Disney invested an unheard of price of 17.5 million dollars), the facilities found in the industry consisted of varying sizes of the traditional type of amusement parks, each dominated by mechanical rides of all kinds for young and old.

Today, Disneyland is currently the nation's number one tourist attraction with an investment of nearly $130 million and has drawn over ten million visitors and $65 million gross business a year. Disney pioneered the themed facility in the industry, although borrowing very heavily upon the basic and original concepts of the traditional type park. The basic differences he introduced that resulted in the development of the themed attraction segment of the industry are as follows:

Although the ride may be the same as those found in a traditional type park, the environment approaching or surrounding the ride is dominant.

There is a major archetectural theme that is continuous and carried throughout all aspects of the attractions.

A themed attraction will cost more money because money is spent for different and additional reasons than in a traditional type park. The new west coast park being built by Marriott will cost $60 million. In addition to spending more on their ride environment, most themed attractions sponsor more varied form and professionalism in their entertainment and shows, their dining facilities are more elaborate, there are specialty retail shops and area, and because patrons stay longer, the parking lots are larger and cost more to build, maintain, and operate, including the operation of a transportation system to move the patrons in a comfortable and easy manner to the front gate.

Themed attractions will hire more specialists (directors of entertainment, landscape architects, trained food managers) thereby increasing their payroll expenses as compared to a traditional type park.

The last major difference between the two types of facilities is concerned with their patron emphasis, who they are, where they come from, and how they are told about the respective facility.

A traditional type park concentrates on the patron within a two-hour drive. A themed attraction concentrated on customer potentials within both the two hour drive, plus those located further away with a heavy emphasis on their potential tourist market.

As a result, the methods of advertising, the amount spent, and other related aspects of how to let people know about the facility will differ. Traditional type parks are bigger users of newspapers and local TV. Attractions use more highway signs, do more business with the motels and restaurants patronized used by their customers, and their TV budget is spread over a larger geographical market area. "Theme parks, though they represent less than 10% of all amusement parks, attracted 25% of the total attendance, and generated approximately 40% of the total revenue which came to around $700 million in 1971."

The traditional amusement park is still enjoyed throughout the country. The merry-go-round, ferris wheel, and roller coaster with the midway fringed by concession stands, has received an un-altering loyality from one generation to the next. Almost all amusement parks, whether traditional or theme oriented, will contain these rides within its boundaries.

The operation of most amusement parks is confined to the warm summer months and an average season of about 120 days. The season generally is referred to as extending from Memorial Day through Labor Day, although many parks open after Easter and a few, where climate permits, stay open year around.

The new theme parks, designed to entice families into spending more of their leisure time while also more of their disposable income within its borders, appears to have launched the industry on a path of continual growth. The new theme parks are thriving because of mainly physical and social changes that have occurred. Suburban sprawl, rising affluence, and the extension of the international highways have made it feasible to locate a park well outside the big city, but conveniently closer to major traffic arteries.

The current economic situation has not drastically hurt the amusement park business. People are having to cut back spending, but few are doing away with vacations. Most are slightly decreasing the amount spent while vacationing.

These parks are accessible to many, but near to few so that most visitors drive for at least an hour and are inclined to stay longer. While staying longer, they spend more. Several parks are catering to the longer staying visitor by having two-day tickets and hotels convenient for overnight stays.

In many of the theme parks, visitors receive alot of commercials through the "co-sponsorship" program. For an annual fee, a corporation sponsors a ride, a service, or an attraction in return for the chance to sell the corporation name or products. Some of the corporations participating in this program are Ford, Coca-Cola, North American Van Lines, Marathon Oil, Super X Drugstores, Sherwin-Williams Paints, and Bank Americard. Through the short history of this program, it has been profitable for both the advertising corporation and the park.

Currently, there are approximately 900 amusement parks in the United States. The number is decreasing as small operations give way to the larger, but the sums invested keep growing. There are amusement parks located in all fifty states besides nineteen foreign countries. Canada, England, Germany, and Japan are experiencing rapid growth in this industry.

Professionals in the park business say there are only a few large potential markets left. Chicago, Milwaukee, San Francisco, Toronto-Buffalo, Seattle, Vancouver-Tacoma, and New England. However, there are numerous possibilities for "mini-parks" of 8 to 10 million dollars investment. One corporation is looking for ways to tap the all-children market with investments of less than 3 million dollars.

Building an amusement park is very expensive. The average theme park has invested at least 25 to 30 million dollars, with Disney World as of its opening day, spending "a staggering $282 million." While some parks are making it big, other parks are going downhill. Two essential ingredients are tight business management and sparkling salesmanship. Whether some parks show financial gains is up to the weather. Rainy springs give parks a slow start and take away drastically from the short fixed operating season.

Over twenty publicly held companies and firms are in the amusement park business. Some are major corporations that derive the largest part of their revenues from other activities, but dabble in parks as a means of diversification. Among these are the American Broadcasting Company, Holiday Inns, Anheuser-Busch, National Service Industries, Bristol-Myers, NLT Corporation, Taft Broadcasting, the Great Southwest Corporation, and Marriott.

Business is better than average where the number of tourists is up. This is the case in Florida in the first few months of 1975. As it has been shown in the past, when the economy and the people are depressed, the amusement park business shows an increase in attendance and profits. When times are good, more people have extra money and amusement parks also show a profit. Either way the economy goes, a well managed amusement park has a prosperous future.

Regardless of typing, through the years successful outdoor amusement facilities have been built and operated on three premises. First, that the restless American will be forced into physical inertia by big city conditions, apartment living, the use of the automobile, and less and less satisfaction being obtained by his easier and easier job to perform. Second, that if the American public is offered the chance to enjoy a clean, wholesome, harmonious outdoor environment that his family can also visit, even the most sedentary person will come back for more. Third, if the facility is designed and equipped to give the public what it needs, and the whole thing is topped off with some showmanship, the facility will be profitable.

Today, themed attractions and traditional amusement parks that utilize these three premises, mixed with showmanship, are doing well, and their future looks excellent. Traditional parks are constantly updating themselves, buying more and bigger rides, modernizing buildings, booking contemporary entertainment, adding more pieces in their arcades, expanding their picnic areas, building petting zoos and introducing the latest in food items. And, whereas the themed attractions do more tourist business, the traditional parks with their established picnic area and generally lower admisison charges, are doing more and more gross business. More and more people are realizing there is nothing like a ride on a roller coaster to get away from it all. More and more people are finding out that a visit to an amusement park is one of the most enjoyable ways of spending money to have fun. For the pure and young at heart, the make believe of amusement parks invites participation, invites all to suspend reality without really abandoning it.

Today, 20 years after Disneyland opened, the themed attraction segment exists as an equal partner with the older traditional type facility in the growing outdoor amusement industry. Today, there are 36 major themed attractions in 22 larger market areas of the United States, each facility drawing more than one million customers a year. During the 1975 season, it is estimated these attractions will draw a total of 70 million people. By comparison, this estimated 70 million figure is 40 percent more than the total attendance for all of professional baseball, football, and basketball games. Total attendance for the entire industry comprising all traditional type parks and all themed attractions regardless of size for 1975 is estimated to be between 475 to 500 million.

The industry has survived two world wars, other lesser conflicts, the great depression, competition from movies and television, changing social patterns, and opposition from spectator and participating sports. The dymanics of the industry will remain constant. The three premises the old-timers based everything on are still valid. Any changes effecting the industry will come from advancing technology and alterations in social patterns. There will not be any difference in the fundamental psychological impact surrounding the industry. The biggest problem effecting the industry will be the energy crisis. But, based on past experience, the industry's appeal will remain as strong as ever, and the people will compensate in order to continue to enjoy what the industry has to offer.

The outdoor amusement industry is serviced by its own trade association, the International Association of Amusement Parks and Attractions. Now in its 55th year, and headquartered in Oak Park, Illinois it is the only organization representing the permanently located outdoor amusement facilities industry.

It's membership is comprized of 350 leading amusement parks, themed and tourist attractions of the 900 or so now in operation and approximately 400 manufacturers and suppliers with a vested interest in the industry. These members are located in the United States and throughout the world.

The amusement park industry is an entrenched family-fun spot that has been

Figure 20 Mickey Mouse and all his famous friends from Disneyland, the beginning of the modern day theme amusement park.
Courtesy: International Association of Amusement Parks and Attractions, Oak Park, Illinois.

rapidly improving in the quality and variety of entertainment offered. In a period where rising costs are becoming a greater consumer concern, inflation seems to add to the favorable cost spread between established amusement parks and other leisure activities. Thus, a variety of entertainment, broad consumer appeal, and at competitive prices suggests a continued growth for the amusement park industry. It is a safe bet that the second billion in industry revenues will come sooner than the first.

Amusement parks in the nation employ approximately 125,000 people during the summer operating season. Up to 90 percent of them high school and college students. With few exceptions, these jobs are not year-round. However, students are frequently exposed to a variety of jobs within the amusement park, particularly for those students who return to work summer after summer.

About 85 percent of the parks are located in suburban areas. The remaining 15 percent includes the urban park and the themed attractions.

Employment opportunities vary according to the size of the facility and to the scope of the entire operation. The size of the park will determine the total number employees in addition to the degree of specialization within each broad category of the overall operation: food and beverage; rides and games; souvenirs and novelties; entertainment; management (accounting, administration, personnel, public relations/ advertising); and maintenance.

In a smaller attraction, naturally, several of these functions may be performed by one person. However, to paint a true picture of the entire employment spectrum within the industry, it is perhaps best to list the clusters of employment opportunities that are available at a major amusement attraction. This way, the student can gain a true perspective of the breadth of the industry, in addition to being able to size up employment opportunities at a park or attraction of particular interest.

TRADE ASSOCIATIONS

International Association of Amusement Parks and Attractions
1125 Lake Street Building
Suite 204-206
Oak Park, Ill. 60301

TRADE JOURNALS

Tourist Attractions and Parks Magazine
Souvenirs & Novelties Publishers Inc.
20-21 Wayaran Road, Building 30
Fairlawn, New Jersey 07410

Concession Handbook
National Association of Concessionaires
201 North Wells Street
Suite 614
Chicago, Illinois 60606

Fairs and Expositions
International Association of Fairs and Expositions
500 Ashland Avenue
Chicago Heights, Illinois 60411

INDIVIDUAL SPORTS AND SMALL GROUP ACTIVITIES
BICYCLING

Bicycling, or cycling as it if often referred to, is one of the true mass sports of modern America. With an estimated one hundred million cyclists now enjoying the sport of bike riding, nearly half of all Americans could be referred to as cyclists. To most people cycling is a very personal sport and the freedom and convenience of two-wheel travel does not readily lend itself to organization or commercialization. On the other hand, last year alone the number of bicycles manufactured and sold in the United States exceeded automobile manufacture and sales by a significant margin and so the opportunities to capitalize on the bike boom and commercialize the various aspects of cycling seem endless. This has not been the case, however, as the vast majority of bikers are primarily interested in simple and unorganized, casual recreational cycling.

Aside from the industrial and retail aspects of cycling, the only other cycling component to undergo extensive commercialization has been cycle touring or tripping. Cycle tours are organized trips conducted on a prearranged eating and sleeping accommodations and a host of other possible supportive services. Even these organized tours vary widely in their degree of commercialization, extent of services offered, and margins of profit to tour organizers. Again, most trippers prefer to make their own arrangements rather than go through a tour organizer, and so commercial bicycle touring operations are a relatively small though diversified aspect of cycling.

A diverse range of tour organizers constitute the organized tour market. Very few are profit-making ventures and many tours are organized as service amenities of the larger commerical and private travel and tourism sectors of the national economy.

American Youth Hostels Inc. (AYH) and the International Youth Hostel Foundation (IYHF) lead the tour organization sector of bicycling. AYH has 110 hostel clubs, 33 councils, and 130 hostels registered domestically. The IYHF has 48 national member councils and 4400 registered hostels in locations all over the world. Each club and council may organize and conduct its own bicycle tours, and the number actually held each year varies with public interest. The AYH Travel Department has from 50 to 75 special itineraries each summer for small groups of from 7 to 9 trippers and a trained leader.

Hundreds of trip clubs who exclusively cater to cicyclists exist all across the country. They range in size from small local clubs to the International Bycicle Touring Society with 700 members. These clubs exist to encourage touring activities and promote touring in their community and seldom are run for profit. The League of American Wheelman, with over 1000 members, helps plan tours and gives touring information among its many other supportive activities for its local chapters. The Sierra Club, American Automobile Association, and several state and municipal recreation related organizations provide information to prospective tourers and may organize annual tours and trip activities. Several domestic and international airlines offer tour packages that include bicycle itineraries. American Airlines sponsors the "New England Two

Figure 21 Happy riders enjoy bicycling the year-round on the Palm Springs' Ten Mile Bike Trail.
Courtesy: Bicycle Manufacturers Association of America, Washington, D.C.

Wheeler" tour utilizing hostel and/or hotel accomodations. Western Airlines has package vacations to Hawaii and San Francisco that offer bikes and suggested tours at these destinations. Lufthansa, KIM, SAS, and Swissair work in cooperation with local groups in providing tours of their home country.

The majority of bicycle tours are either undertaken by individuals independent of any organization or are conducted in conjunction with the AYH or local bike clubs. Little information is available on the commercial aspects of touring, since commercial tour operators are a minority of the total tour profile and because tours vary so widely in length, cost, and number of cyclists. However, two general types of extended tours seem in evidence. Classic bicycle tours include the convenience of light travel and itineraries geared around nightly accomodations at established hotels and restaurants. These are generally more expensive and appeal to the more pampered biker. These tours are more likely to be conducted by commercial tour operators or the larger bike clubs and organizations. Hostel tours and bike camping tours are more involved with equipment but are more flexible in their iteneraries and time schedules because of the lack of necessity to reach suitable accomodations each night. These tours appeal to the more sophisticated biker and are more likely to be self-initiated and/or organized by the small bike club.

Local bike clubs that sponsor tours typically are composed of between 30 and 60 members. Accomodations are arranged by the club members and paid for on a pay-as-you-go basis. Age-group tours of mixed-age tours may be conducted and are usually held in good weather months on Saturdays of Sundays for either day outings or weekend trips with overnight accommodations at camps or motels. Usually trips are rated by the mileage covered in one day and short (18 miles), middle (32 miles), and long (40-50 miles) distance trips are offered on the same or different outings. More involved tours are usually conducted by the larger organizations and may range in expenses from the very luxurious tours to the more economical hostel type trips. Potential trippers should not be discouraged by a lack of organized tour opportunities in their locality as numerous sources of free technical information and advice, trip itineraires, maps, and accommodations are available for organizing your own tour.

The newest innovation to the bicycling industry is moto-cross bicycling. These races, like their motorcycle counterparts, are on tracks of dirt through woods, open spaces, through shallow water, and other hazards and obstacles. The winners must have good judgment, above average ability in handling a bicycle, and some luck, as well as the speed found in most other races. Speed is less of a factor, than the others in determining a winner. There are now national events and local moto-cross tracks in many areas.

Cycling is here to stay as a recreational activity, a sport, and sensible low cost transportation. Apparently the bike boom has peaked and the market is generally depressed due to the fact that bicycle models do not become obsolete each year. Repairs and service are the mainstay of the business. The bicycle may have already grown from a youth oriented fad to a serious component of the modern alternative life styles as millions of Americans make the bicycle a part of their everyday lives.

*Figure 22 Bicycle touring involves a pleasant lunch in a beautiful park area.
Courtesy: Bicycle Manufacturers Association of America, Washington, D.C.*

National and local interest in providing bikeways and encouraging bicycle commuting has helped to establish cycling as a serious adult undertaking. As more and more bike paths and trails are developed, the likelihood of continued interest in cycling is greater. Touring, already an established activity for the young, should expand in the future as long distance trails and itineraries are developed. The National Park Service has already instituted a policy of allowing hostel operations within national parks. The Cape Cod National Seashore, Delaware Water Gap National Recreation Area, the Indiana Dunes National Lakeshore, and Point Reyes National Park in California have hostels, and the outlook for additional hostels in other parks is promising. These and other developments should provide bikers with the needed facilities and incentives to develop their interests and skills in cycling and establish this nation as a leader in promoting the many attributes biking has to offer.

TRADE JOURNALS

Amateur Bicycle League of America
P.O. Box 669, Wall Street-Station
New York, N.Y. 10005

American Youth Hostels, Inc.
20 West 17th Street
New York, N.Y. 10011

Bicycle Institute of America
122 East 42nd Street
New York, N.Y. 10017

Bicycle Manufacturers Association of America, Inc.
1101 Fifteenth Street N.W.
Washington, D.C. 20005

TRADE JOURNALS

Bicycling
55 Mitchell Blvd.
San Rafael, Calif. 94903

Bike World
Box 366
Mountain View, Calif. 94040

Bicycle Spokesman
119 East Palatine Road
Palatine, Ill. 60067

Bicycling
256 Sutter Street
San Francisco, Calif. 94108

Hostel Guide & Handbook
Ziff-Davis Publishing Company
3850 Hollywood Blvd.,
Hollywood, Calif. 90028

Bikers of America
2806 Fountain Boulevard
Tampa, Fla. 33609

BOWLING CENTERS

Bowling, as a sport and recreation activity, has seen its good times and bad. In its early years it was often viewed as a low status, cheap game with centers often times complying with this image. They were often times not well maintained, equipment was of a poor quality and insurance rates were high due to frequent accidents on the lanes. During the late 1950s bowling reached a peak nationally as facilities, equipment, and over all management improved vastly over the 1930s and 1940s. In this prosperous

Figure 23 A recently constructed, family bowling center.
Courtesy: Brunswick Corporation, Skokie, Illinois.

period many center owners had the mistaken idea that they could sit back and let the customers roll in without any special promotions or inducements. When the popularity of the sport declined in the mid-1960s houses that did not actively promote themselves often went out of business.

A manager of a typical 32-lane "house" must fill all 32 lanes during the early part of the evening mostly through league play. During the rest of the evening, as a new type and set of customers come in, he tries to keep about half of the lanes full. Typically it has taken him 5 to 6 years to build up his present successful level of customers.

League bowling is an important method of filling any center during the first part of the evening. Leagues promote consistency, new interest, growth, and development along with the all-important profit margin. Leagues have a propencity to utilize other components of the centers more so than individuals with this in turn increasing the multiplier effect, even if only slightly. They eat and drink more and also purchase much more from the pro shop than other occasional participants. Leagues containing six to sixteen teams each continue to be the mainstay of the bowling houses. Industrial mens leagues are still most common and very popular today. They are seen as status symbols by the bowlers and moral boosters by the employers. Other leagues include childrens, women, mixed, senior citizens, and most recently special handicapped leagues. As one can see, most centers truly attempt to serve the needs of all segments of the population. All, in some part, add to the profit, image, and service goals of the bowling center. A rough estimate of total bowlers in the United States would be fifteen to twenty million. This is in fact the most popular sport, participation-wise in the country, as it has just recently surpassed golf in this respect.

Most participants fall into the lower-middle to upper-middle class families. The increase in upper-middle class families is caused by a great change in attitudes of them towards alleys and also the more positive, wholesome image now portrayed and promoted by the modern, progressive bowling center. There was a time when it was not socially acceptable for a "lady" to be found in a bowling alley. Today at least half of all league bowlers are women.

Bowling centers, or alleys as they are more commonly referred to, are viewed by most of their proprietors as an opportunity for the entire family to entertain themselves, at a reasonable price the year round. There are provisions, of varied natures, for the young, middle-aged, and senior citizens alike. The very young can usually take advantage of the common place day-care center often provided by the house. This keeps junior busy with something to do while alleviating mother of much of the responsibility of having him around. For seven-years old and up there are opportunities for open-play bowling, special tournaments, and competitive league bowling. Each of these vary in fees, skill-level, and awards according to the age group involved and the general nature of the events.

The primary concern of any commercial bowling center is to offer a quality bowling experience, build up a consistent, interested clientele, and above all else realize a profit. The key words are service, image, and profit. All components of a center, whether pinball machines, the restaurant and lounge, or just the snack bar or pro shop accessory counter, enter into the profit-oriented picture, yet still the main product to be sold is bowling. If the bowling clientele is not pleased and sold on the image of the house the operation will not last long.

Bowling centers are found everywhere throughout the United States with their location normally being based on a one lane per 1000 population standard. Usually the smallest house would consist of eight lanes (unless in a resort of special facility) and the largest might be a maximum of seventy-two lanes. Surprisingly enough bowling is extremely popular in California, Florida, and other similar areas even though these are prime locations for outdoor recreation pursuits. The abundance of senior citizen and interested women bowlers seem to play a large role in the growing enthusiasm in these areas. All together there are approximately 6500 bowling centers, of various sizes, throughout the country.

An average bowling center ranges from twenty-four to thirty-two lanes. Anywhere from twelve to fifteen full-time personnel are employed and about ten part-time people are kept busy usually during peak business hours. For the most part these positions are uncategorized and the worker must be very versatile and flexible.

An initial investment of approximately $30,000 per lane bed (not including the building) is required to develop a modern facility. This includes all components, equipment, and miscellaneous items. If one would include the building the price goes up to around $48,000 per lane bed. In most cases though buildings are rented or leased on a long term (10 year) basis. Total development costs may approach $1,000,000 in initial investment. Gross sales figures are guarded closely and are not readily available.

Full-time personnel include a general manager, who oversees the entire operation and tends to administrative duties, a manager, who coordinates and supervises lower level personnel, a bar manager, two full-time, semi-skilled mechanics, one on days and one on nights, two full-time counter-cashier persons, and as many league coordinators as deemed necessary by the individual center. A janitor, who works mainly nights and early mornings, is also employed full-time to take care of routine maintenance tasks. Part-time personnel, as mentioned previously, supplements full-time help for the most part.

Qualifications for all employees are generally the same, excluding the managers. All employees must be reasonably personable, willing to work when needed and also remain flexible to the jobs they perform. The general manager must have skills in administrative tasks while other managers must be knowledgeable in their own special areas. No job descriptions or classifications are utilized, as employees may be required to perform a variety of tasks.

There are several recent developments in the area of bowling facilities that should be mentioned. One is the operation of bowling centers by large manufacturing corporations. Brunswick, for instance, operates over 250 bowling centers throughout the country, and has a management-training program which includes on the job training, as well as highly concentrated in-depth, "classroom" education sessions at their home office in Chicago. Because of this diversification, new ideas and procedures that work can be shared easily and quickly across the country, for the profitable benefit of all centers. The training program also allows consistent selection of bowling house managers to be, as well as an opportunity to view their work habits and potential in an on the job training situation under the auspices of the house manager. Their training program normally requires approximately 2 years, where the trainee may be required to work as many as 12 to 14 hours a day, 5 or 6 days a week. However, he can look forward to moving up to a manager's spot, with more managerial responsibility and more consistent hours.

The other recent innovation in bowling is incompassed in the family entertainment center concept. These take a variety of forms, but may include such facilities as a bowling alley, an ice rink, a billiards parlor, a games room, or other recreation activity facilities, which will indeed promote the recreation facility for all the family concept. This is in addition to the traditional restaurant, lounge, pro shop, and other auxillary enterprises normally associated with the center. In some areas these are built in conjunction with shopping centers and other centralized facilities, which already have parking facilities and are a drawing attraction which provides considerable increase market potential for the recreation facilities. Mom or Dad can come and even if they do not bowl or skate they can leave junior in the facility while they do their shopping.

The implications for trained experienced management personnel in these types of facilities (in the future) seems to be unlimited. His responsibilities would require him to be knowledgeable in 5 to 8 recreation activity enterprise areas, and although the same management financial and maintenance responsibilities might be similar, the markets for each might be slightly different.

As the automatic pin setting equipment seemed to represent a turning point in the bowling establishment from the smoke filled, dimly lit recreational areas of previous years into the wholesome family entertainment centers that now exist, so the future of bowling with scoring done with computers may represent another turning point, as new innovations and equipment make it easier for the individual to bowl and increase his interest to "see what its all about." There will probably continue to be peaks and valleys in bowling participation and development. There may be a problem with oversaturation, too many alleys and not enough bowlers. In light of this situation the bowling centers that will survive should be the ones that promote and provide for a quality experience at a competitive price.

This activity appears to be one of the best lifetime sports, and those houses that are successful in developing joint instructional programs with schools, churches, and other groups will probably be the ones in the years to come to enjoy the best margin of profit situation.

TRADE ASSOCIATIONS

Bowling Proprietors Association of America
615 Six Flags Drive
Arlington, Texas

American Bowling Association
Milwaukee, Wisconsin

National Bowling Council
1666 K Street, N.W.
Washington, D.C. 20006

TRADE JOURNALS

Bowling Proprietors Magazine, published by the Bowing Proprietors Assoc.
615 Six Flags Drive
Arlington, Texas

Bowlers Journal
National Bowlers Journal, Inc.
Suite 214, 1825 N. Lincoln Plaza
Chicago, Ill. 60614

COMMERCIAL WILDERNESS OUTFITTERS _____

Wilderness tripping has become big business. The Colorado River Grand Canyon rafting outfitters gross 4.5 million dollars per season. For a price Mountain Travel, Inc. will take you backpacking in Pantagonia, Nepal, the Andes, or any of a dozen other exotic places. With literally hundreds of businesses involved with the proposition of exchanging a wilderness experience for a bundle of dollars the variety of experiences offered are almost impossible to describe.

Exotic, exciting, educational, and expensive are the adjectives that best describe most of the trips offered by these outfitters. Some are very small operations, others are large corporations, and others that are included in this discussion are "not for profit" corporations. The not for profit corporations offer similar experiences and compete to some degree with the strictly commercial operations for clientele. Other operations offer educational experiences in the outdoors, education in wilderness travel skills, biological sciences, or leadership seminars.

Outfitters are reaching for a market that has grown fast, is affluent, and likely to continue its increase in numbers. A survey of the readership of "Wilderness Camping" magazine revealed that their average reader was; male, 35.5 years old, married, with 1.8 children, and earned an average annual income of $18,500.

The success of these businesses, at least some of them, is phenomenal. To get reservations for some of the raft trips one must apply 6 months to a year in advance. Schools like Outward Bound and National Outdoor Leadership School (NOLS) are expanding their programs continually. Yet for every successful business of this type another fails or is at best a marginal operation. If these enterprises are doing as well as the average recreation enterprise, three out of five will fail financially or go out of business for some other reason within 5 years after they start. The difference between success and failure as in most recreation enterprises relates to the business and manage-

Figure 24 One of the most unique experiences offered in any of our national parks is a day-long float trip down the twisting Snake River in Grand Teeton National Park. Courtesy: American Hotel and Motel Association, New York, New York.

ment ability of the manager/owner. Too often their entrepreneurial goals are other than maximizing profits. Many are in the business because they derive other rewards from their business and are not as concerned with financial objectives.

There are five main types of these wilderness outfitting businesses are: 1) hiking or backpacking trips; 2) river running, 3) mountain climbing, 4) instructional, and 5) Ski touring.

Some businesses are involved in two or more areas and there is some overlap generally between the types. A wilderness outfitting business can be a commercial operation that outfits persons with equipment and also provides a guide, leader, or instructor that escorts the person or group into a wilderness or semi-wilderness environment. The attainment of a wilderness experience is often in itself the goal of the trip. Often, however, there are other auxillary goals that are part of the experience. These may be excitement as provided in climbing a mountain or running whitewater; education in wilderness skills, ecological principles, group dymanics or personal introspection; or as in the Outward Bound program character building by meeting a challenge of all these things. The hunting and fishing outfitters will not be included because they are large enough and different enough to be treated separately.

Hiking and Backpacking. Outfitters offer backpacking trips just about anywhere in the world and they usually have equipment available if the customer wants to rent; provide food (freeze-dried), guide, and transportation to site if outside the continental United States, and will cater to almost any age group. Some of these businesses have been in operation for years and have year-round programs.

Mountain Climbing. Many of the same outfits that run backpacking or hiking tours also have mountain climbing trips. Here also all equipment can be provided, food is included (freeze-dried), and often some type of transportation to the base camp area. Because of the risk involved in climbing some level of expertise may be required of the participants for the more dangerous climbs.

River running. In rafts, canoes, kayaks, or inflatable kayaks, outfitters are offering the opportunity to run whitewater with all the thrills and little of the risk. Trips range from a one-day trip to an 18-day trip through the Grand Canyon, or even a longer more exotic trip is available on the Omo River of the Blue Nile in Ethiopia. More seasonal than some of the other types they are nevertheless the fastest growing segment of the commercial wilderness business. They have grown so fast in fact that the Federal agencies that control the streams that are used have found it necessary to impose quotas and restrictions so that the usage would not destroy the resource.

Because rafting outfitters are probably the more complicated form of wilderness outfitting and have as wide a range of services available. These operations will be covered in some detail, bearing in mind that many of the same general situations exist in the other types of outfitters.

Practically all of the raft trips include at least one boatman (or boatwomen) per raft or at a minimum with the self paddling raft trips a guide to escort them down the river. A boatman may start at $25 per day and a good one may get up to $50 or more per day if they return for subsequent seasons. Among the restrictions put on commercial river-running operations is that the boatmen must meet a series of requirements before they can qualify as a boatmen. First aid and life saving certification must be attained. Training in human waste disposal, cooking, and river running must be proven. Boatmen on the larger rafts can be responsible for up to 20 people.

There are about 100 commercial raft outfitters, many of which operate on more than one stream. When the government put quotas on the rivers some felt that the outfitters would be put out of business, but instead they have expanded their operations over a wider spectrum of streams and can therefore offer a wide range of experiences for their customers.

The logistics of raft outfitting can be staggering in getting 10 to 50 people to the "put in" point, and making sure that someone will have vehicles to meet them at the "take out." Rafts must be maintained and gotten back to the starting place for the next trip. Chemical toilets with adequate storage for effluent, a screen, and enough toilet paper are all taken along on the raft. Food for a week or more, with fuel and a fire pan for cooking must accompany longer trips. All this and more must be provided with clockwork precision in order to satisfy the customer.

Although most people are familiar with rafting in the western states there are also flourishing businesses in the east. The Cheat, Youghiogheny, New, and Chattoga Rivers are the main streams run in the east.

Because the business is seasonal some of the outfitters have been attempting to extend their season by finding trips in Mexico, South America, and even Africa. That they have found some customers for these trips suggests that these may eventually become permanent offerings and there will be raft trips, like hiking trips, almost anywhere in the world.

Liability insurance is mandatory for the raft operations if they operate in federally controlled waters and this restriction is being extended by states and other agencies that control the rivers or businesses in other areas.

One interesting sidelight is that the rafters, who in the eyes of the private river runners are destroying the wilderness experience on the rivers, have become a powerful and to some degree effective lobby for the preservation of our wilderness streams. They are also active in policing their own activities so that they will not ruin the resource and experience that they are selling. While they are concerned and take steps to limit their impact on the rivers it is hard to imagine how, with hoardes of people running the rivers, the wilderness experience can be preserved at all.

Instruction. Mountain climbing schools, Outward Bound, NOLS, Educational Experiences International, professional rafting schools, whitewater canoe, and kayaking schools are only some of the instruction and education types available. These operations differ essentially in that besides the wilderness experience a very major part of their program is geared toward attainment of specific skills and/or knowledge.

Ski-touring. Not to be confused with downhill skiing—Separate operations deal only with cross-country skiing but many of the older program find that cross country skiing is a good addition to an existing program thereby expanding their season.

Many of these businesses are very small and are operated almost solely by the owner. However, quite a few of these businesses are huge in comparison, have a sizable payroll, and have many permanent employees. How much upward mobility exists within the field is unknown at this writing but with some of the larger organizations there is good reason to believe that a person could start as an instructor or guide and work himself up to a permanent position. Most beginning jobs would be seasonal with pay ranging from minimum wage or less to $1000 per month or even more in some cases. The higher paid seasonal positions often require considerable experience and some prior work experience with that particular employer.

TRADE ASSOCIATIONS AND JOURNALS
American Guides Association, Inc.
Box B
Woodland, California 95695

CANOE LIVERIES

With canoeing enjoying a popularity it has not seen since the 1920s, there has been an increasing growth in canoe liveries. There are some 500,000 canoes owned in the continental United States but this does not begin to be enough to satisfy the needs of all that want to "trip their hand" at a paddle for a weekend or a vacation. Thousands and perhaps even millions of people who do not own their own canoes are taking to the streams and lakes for a weekend jaunt or a vacation experience.

Canoe liveries as a form of commercial recreation industry may be attractive to some as a business or a source of employment since, one reasons, it would offer a chance to be close to the outdoors and be an enjoyable job besides.

Existing canoe liveries vary considerably in the size and structure of the business. Some are "Mom and Pop operations" with as few as 6 canoes, and others are huge with organization structure, many employees, and hundreds of canoes. Some operations rent canoes only, others provide transportation, lodging, guide service, food, retail sales, and a variety of other services all revolving around the canoe livery theme.

The Mom and Pop operations traditionally start because the owner's home proximates a "good" location for a canoe livery. Living there and having seen an influx of canoeists using their nearby resource and other liveries sprouting up along the water and/or road, they have decided to get on the bandwagon. Seeking information from their neighboring liveries they decide to get into business and buy some canoes and maybe a trailer or truck to shuttle the canoes for the customers. And always there is the indispensible sign near the road, their first and sometimes only advertising.

Although mostly a weekend and usually a seasonal business, at least one of the family is around most of the time to take reservations and answer questions from potential customers. During the weekend the whole family will be involved with the successful operation of the business. From Friday evening, if they are successful, people will be calling and coming wanting the canoes, drivers for their cars, or just information. In the peak of the season they will insure that someone is there to handle the vacation parties using the canoes during the week.

In the typical Mom and Pop operation all of this is done in addition to one or more of the family having full-time jobs elsewhere with the children in school or college during the week. Or perhaps their main income is farming, which also takes much of their time and efforts. Whatever the situation the operators of the small livery will usually not be in a financial position to hire help to alleviate the demands put on them by the business.

In constrast the larger, successful canoe livery operation earns enough for the owner/operator so that he may be able to hire help and even make a decent living without moonlighting at other jobs. Some, in fact, depend solely on their operation as their only source of income.

There are more than 60 manufacturers that produce canoes. Price breaks, canoe construction, material durability, and customer satisfaction are probably what will weigh most heavily on the decision of what canoes to purchase. Price breaks are between the livery owner and the manufacturer. Traditionally, many but by no means all liveries are using aluminum canoes. As mentioned before the type of waters the canoe will encounter may be important in not only canoe design but the type of material from which it is made.

Liveries must be located where the floatable streams are, preferably in a favorable spot on a stream, although a number of operators are located in large cities, where the people are, and provide cartop carrier racks for the renter.

Canoes with equipment will cost 350 to 400 dollars, and expected life of the equipment is 2 to 3 years. Liability is a problem and the U.S. Coast Guard says canoeing is the most dangerous form of boating with an accident rate of more than 3 times the average for the rest of the industry.

There are canoe liveries nationwide, wherever it seems that there are clean flowing streams or unique outdoor opportunities accessable only by canoe. From San Antonio, Texas to Ely, California to the Everglades and up to Maine; almost anywhere in the country there are successful thriving canoe liveries. Whether they are all making their owners rich is questionable, perhaps doubtful, yet enough people are finding it rewarding enough to carry on and there are some to be sure that find it financially rewarding.

Obviously, due to the seasonal nature of most of these businesses, canoe liveries do not offer much in the way of employment and the real opportunity is as the owner/operator.

Canoe liveries are only one of many similar commercial recreation opportunities for those aspiring to go into business for themselves. But it is one that is currently enjoying success and is a business that along with its hassel would have its rewards. With a modest investment it might be possible to develop a business that would prosper for years to come.

TRADE ASSOCIATIONS AND JOURNALS

American Canoe Association
4260 E. Evans Ave.
Denver, Colo. 80222

American Whitewater Affiliation
Box 1584
San Burno, Calif. 94066

ICE SKATING RINKS _____

While interest in roller skating developed through the depression and war years to peak in the 1960s, interest in ice skating has developed in the 1960s and may not have reached its peak yet. The popularity of professional ice hockey, as well as high school varsity hockey teams, has no doubt added to this interest. Many communities have built their own ice facilities, through governmental bond issues or organized programs in conjunction with private facilities. Ice hockey leagues are as much a part of the program in northern states and cities during the winter as is the traditional basketball league or the softball league in the summer. The contrast between ice skating and roller skating facilities are considerable. While roller skating has been traditionally a recreational activity for children and families, little attempt has been made to develop the competitive aspects of the sport. The facilities are considerably less expensive to develop, and they cater to a middle to lower income family clientele.

Ice skating, on the other hand, has developed primarily from a competitive base, and most are not family operations, as are roller rinks, but are corporations because of the 700,000 to 1 million dollar investment required for facilities, cooling equipment, and other affiliated services. Most private ice rinks and many public rinks include restaurants, bars, snack bars, and other auxiliary services to increase the profit margin.

Figure 25 Sheraton Park (Washington) winter ice rink. In the summer the rink is a splashing fountain and pool.
Courtesy: American Hotel and Motel Association, New York, New York.

Traditionally, the cost to skate in an ice rink is somewhat higher than the roller skating prices.

Because of the high cost of capital investment, ice rink managers have needed to promote use of their rinks, and in many areas where rinks are at a premium, the rink may be used as much as 20 hours a day.

Although some ice sport centers can generate in excess of $500,000 gross revenue, a survey of ice skating rinks last year showed that 52 percent of the rinks in the United States have gross receipts of $50,000 or less. Thus "facility leasing" has been the name of the game. While the first step in developing a facility is no doubt a consideration of the ice sheet size (most prefer a 100 by 200 foot size area), the feasibility study must include an hour by hour, day by day program plan that will provide for a minimum of 50 weeks of operation in order to determine projections for income. Some cities, such as St. Louis where ice skating rinks far outnumber the number of roller rinks, may be reaching the saturation point. In other areas the potential remains relatively untapped.

The potential of participation in ice skating is yet to be reached, and as a result many rinks may be built on less than complete feasibility and financial analysis in an attempt to gain a share of the expanding market. Those that will remain after the sifting out period, will do so as a result of good management operation, promoting, and programming as with any other "successful" private or commercial recreation enterprise.

TRADE ASSOCIATIONS

Mr. Trumble, Executive Director
Amateur Hockey Association of U.S.
10 Lake Circle
Colorado Springs, Colo. 80906

ROLLER SKATING RINKS

Roller skating is a familiar sport to many who as children started on the streets and sidewalks in the neighborhood.

The first recorded successful skate was demonstrated in England in 1760 by a visiting Fench inventor named Joseph Merlin. However, it wasn't until 1863 that an American, James Plympton of Massachusettes, invented a skate that would permit sideway rotation, thus allowing a person on skates to turn and weave. With this innovation the popularity of the new sport quickly caught on in America. By 1880 roller skating was a favorite pastime of New York society.

The indoor skating rink business received its biggest boost in 1934 when Victor J. Brown, the manager of a Newark, New Jersey dance arena, beset like many other businesses with economic difficulties, dressed up a promotional stunt that he hoped would stimulate business. Brown built a banked-wooden track above his dance floor in Dreamland Park and began to organize, promote, and advertise a nonstop 21-day roller skating marathon. Since this event, the roller skating rink operation has emerged as a fixture in American cities of all sizes. The public's interest in roller skating has expanded along with the general rise of interest in recreation and physical fitness. The popularity of skating seemed to have peaked in the 1960s when thousands of rinks were built in hopes of cashing in on the general recreation boom. Oversupply of rinks, poor management techniques on the part of novice operators, and other factors contributed to the closing of many of the rinks in the late sixties, until a more realistic number of rinks based on a steady supply of confirmed skaters is in existence today.

The roller skating rink business is still considered in the commercial recreation field as a potentially profitable enterprise, and a more serious operation based on sound management, analysis, marketing, and financial skills has characterized the successful operations of the past few years.

In 1969 the United States Roller Skating Rink Operators Association estimated the number of participating skaters at a high of twenty-four million. Today there are between eighteen and twenty million rink participants depending on the reporting source. Projections of the Roller Skating Foundation of America estimate a future increase of participation of 25 million in 1980, and as many as 35 or 40 million by 1990. These estimates are based on expectations of more diverse participation of skating age groups, and the general national trend toward healthful exercise and physical fitness.

Traditionally, the greatest number of skaters have been youngsters and this trend is expected to continue. However, a general increase in adult skaters has been reported over the years, and this trend is expected to continue resulting in a substantial participation rate among these age groups. The philosophy of most successful rinks has been to encourage and promote skating among the young children.

It is essential to most operators to develop a returning clientele base so that a steady, predictable portion of the community will always avail themselves of recreational skating opportunities and insure the continued success of the rink enterprise. Without the regulars, the rink operator must rely on the casual skaters who turn out in usually substantial if somewhat unpredictable numbers.

In 1969 the U.S. Roller Skating Rink Operators Association (RSROA) reported a high of 5500 operating rinks in the United States. Today there are fewer than 5000 rinks, a majority of which are unaffiliated. Rink operators associations such as the RSROA account for only 1000 of the total number of rinks. In general, rinks are not restricted by climate, topography, population, or social factors. Skating rinks are located today in towns of 5000 and cities of millions and their success seems to be predicated more on the manager's abilities to promote and operate his facility rather than on any inherent social or economic characteristics of the community in which the rink is located. Although a location in communities or suburbs with a large proportion of young families will no doubt help once a market is established, a roller skating rink can be a significant contributor to a community's financial, civic, and recreational stability.

The greatest majority of skating rinks are family operations. Typically, the owner and manager of the rink are one in the same person and family members often help out in the operation of the rink at some point in their lives. More often than not, owners and operators are avid skaters themselves. When this is not the case, it takes an unusually talented and motivated individual to successfully manage and promote the rink without losing interest or succumbing to the pitfalls of not understanding and communicating with the skating public. There are, however, a number of roller skating rink "chain" operations and rinks owned by absentee owners. These are usually managed by professional managers with a sound management, personnel, and marketing background.

The size and complexity of rinks vary from location to location.. Skating area is the primary determining factor in classifying rinks, and a range of 5000 to 20,000 square feet of skating area separates the small rinks from the larger ones. The average-sized rink has approximately 8400 square feet of skate area. The costs of building and equipping a roller rink vary, of course, according to the size of operation, but they are generally less expensive developments than bowling alleys, amusement parks, ice rinks, outdoor theaters, and similar commercial recreation enterprises. Smaller rinks may be constructed for as little as $75,000.00 while the larger developments may require $200,000. investments and up. The average medium-sized rink could be constructed for between $100,000.00 and $150,000.00 depending on the quality of interior appointments, equipment, and supplies.

Roller rinks are considered an excellent investment because of the quick return on the original outlay of money. Based on a steady stream of return and new customers, low turn-over rate of equipment, relatively low maintenance costs, quality concessions, and relatively few employees, rinks can average annual gross profits of between 15 and 30 percent. At these rates most owners can quickly pay off deferred construction costs and realize a substantial income over the years.

A minimum number of employees are required in the operation of the rink and these positions seldom require any special expertise or professional training. One ticket seller, one skate and checkroom attendant, a concessions operator, one or more floor supervisors and a janitor are usually the required staff in rinks. A professional instructor who can also run an equipment sales and pro shop is usually an added income factor for most rinks rather than a personnel expense. The income components of rinks include ticket sales (1) concessions, (2) skate rentals, (3) equipment sales, and, (4) if instruction is offered the rink realizes a percentage of the instructor's fees.

The future of the roller skating business is bright. Simple and inexpensive forms of recreation have always been in great demand and the current economic situation bodes well for those recreation enterprises that are easily accessible, close to home, family serving, and relatively inexpensive. In addition, past successes in the roller skating business, like few other recreation enterprises, have generated from their ability to establish rapport with the surrounding community and provide a service that is socially rather than sport oriented. In addition, unlike some chain operations, the roller rink as a family-operated enterprise contributes to the community both economically and recreationally and is accepted as such. The outlook is good for existing rinks with established clientele and moderately hopeful for well-considered new operations. The possibility of high profits will be attractive to new developers but the success rate of rinks will continue to depend on the management practice of the owners and operators. Like any business a quality rink operation takes dedication to principles and determination to succeed.

TRADE ASSOCIATIONS

Roller Skating Rink Operators Association of America
7700 "A" Street
Lincoln, Nebraska 65810

Roller Skating Foundation of America
515 Madison Avenue
New York, New York 10022

TRADE JOURNALS

Skating Magazine
United States Figure Skating Association
178 Tremont Street
Boston, Massachusetts 02111

SNOW SKIING

Snow skiing is a sport that is very popular in todays society and is increasing in popularity every year, with a 15 percent increase projected each year to ten million by 1980. It is also a rather expensive sport, requiring funds for transportation, lodging, meals, lift tickets, clothes, equipment, and lessons if one is not able to ski. The one disadvantage is that for the major population of the country, snow skiing is not immediately accessible. The average skier spends an outlay of $300 for equipment and skiing is now the number one sport in money spent, surpassing golf with 1.5 billion spent each year in clothes, atmosphere, equipment, and travel. According to the National Ski Areas Association, income for ski operations amounted to 2.5 billion in 1973. It is estimated that 300 million dollars will be needed to build new areas for skiers to keep up with the demand within the next ten years.

Over the past Christmas or New Years holidays, many of the nations estimated six million skiers went to one of the 1100 ski areas in the United States. Although there are ski areas in at least 40 of our 50 states, and some of these are near metropolitan areas for which they serve, most ski resorts are much more removed, and must contain a ski lodge, one or more restaurants, a ski rental and repair shop, instruction programs, and lifts. Sometimes the living quarters are away from the ski lodge, in the form of apartments, condominiums, or cabins.

Ski areas each have their own character and are influenced largely by geography. As a rule the best ski areas are found in the higher altitudes and the northerly locations especially where the slopes face northward so they are protected from the sun's melt-

Figure 26 Ski instruction school at a skiing resort.
Courtesy: Photo by Peter Miller, courtesy Ski Industries America.

ing rays. In states or areas without mountainous areas, the ski slopes are generally much shorter.

Southern and Mid-Zone states such as Arizona, Alabama, Arkansas, and Georgia do not have sufficient snow to provide skiing areas, but they do have high enough elevations and cold enough temperatures to provide the necessary conditions. Many times in these areas as in other well known facilities, the operation has invested in a snow making machine that provides the snow for skiing. This also allows normal skiing resorts to extend their seasons and insure adequate conditions throughout the season, being less dependent on the mercy of the weather. The machines cost approximately 50,000 dollars, however, and the temperature must remain at least below 20 to 30 degrees.

Skiing is primarily a middle to upper class sport because of the cost. The average skiier is about 40 years old, and holds a professional, managerial, or supervisory position. College students however are increasing in numbers each year, they can indeed afford to take longer vacations.

The prospective ski resort developer has a number of problems to be concerned with. While most developers are not as imaginative as John Bintz, of the Michigan

Apple Mountain Ski Area Noteriety, who developed a 60-foot mound in relatively flat central Michigan from dirt scooped out of a pond and turned it into a ski resort. Later he added additional dirt to raise it to 200 feet and now has eight lifts, eight snow machines, a ski school and lodge, and can handle over 2400 people per day on the "Bintz Bump." The developer of such a facility elsewhere however usually must consider the local terrain and other considerations such as:

1. Site analysis.
2. Slope angles.
3. Exposure to sun.
4. Environmental impact on area.
5. Sanitation disposal.
6. Roads in.
7. Parking.
8. Visual impact studies.
9. Density of dwellings per acre.
10. Where melting, sliding snow will end up.
11. Design of ice dams and snow loads.

All of this can cost as much as $50,000 per ski development, without lodging facilities.

Twenty percent of the ski areas are on U.S. Forest Service Land, where companies can only lease 80 acres on long-term lease and must apply each year for special use permits. This makes investors very cautious in developing ski areas. These installations must install their own treatment plants for 6000 to 8000 people for high use weekends. Problems of handling 7000 to 10,000 people for weekends such as in Vail, Colorado presents no small problems. While the number of skiers on the slopes can be limited by capacity of the lifts, the other facilities are certainly taxed to capacity.

While there is much demand in short periods of time, a ski resort operator has about 70 days to make one million pre-tax dollars. Although some ski areas make more money, others must rely on four percent of their gross sales before taxes for their profit margin. Diversification is a must, to hedge against problems such as the Eastern Seaboard areas faced in 1973 and 1974 with a mild winter and short snow fall, in addition to the gasoline shortage. As a result, many of the Eastern ski resorts are now owned by banks because of financial difficulties. Housing in remote areas such as Vail must also provide for 2000 maids, instructors, and souvenir personnel. The construction of lodges and condominiums (2600 in the last five years) has increased the value of some development areas such as Vail from $100 per acre in 1957 to $300,000 per acre today. Such facilities can no longer be run by the seat of one's pants, and require long term investments as well as organization and administration as a refined and structured business.

While costs can run from $6 per day for dorm style housing to $50 or $60 per night, skiing lends itself excellently to ski packages. Fly and ski packages have been developed by the airlines from almost every metropolitan area.

Activities offered such as hotdogging, downhill and slalom competition, winter carnivals, fashion shows, wine and cheese parties, instruction, and mid-week specials such as five-days and nights lodging and airport transfers for less than $200 has contributed to the increase in skiing. Increased numbers have also come from skiers who have substituted a trip in the United States for previously more expensive trips to Europe because of inflation dollar devaluation.

In addition to skiing, a number of other activities can be found in some ski resorts, including: sleigh rides, snowmobiling, athletic club facilities, ice skating, curling, snow showing, inner tubing, riding, winter mountaineering, swimming, handball, night skiing, paddle tennis, dog sledding, sledding, ice fishing, hand gliding, or a hot springs pool.

Problems that the owner-operator must contend with include:

1. Bad weather.
2. The economy and inflation that makes development and improvements very difficult.
3. The problems with investors, as most banks are not familiar with recreation investments and require up to 60 percent down.
4. The short season, 150 days in Northern Michigan or Canada to 50 to 70 in some southern states, requiring one-third of the business to be done over the Christmas vacation.

The success of the ski operation is determined on a number of factors. The three most important ones that directly affect the probability are:

1. Number of days open or number of days weather provide good skiing.
2. Number of skiers providing a reasonable capacity utilization of the ski slope.
3. The age of the ski area in which the original investments have been paid off.

While the ski resort business may look very inviting and attractive, or work opportunities at them look appealing, the problems are probably as great as for any other type of recreation enterprise, and decisions should be weighed in that light.

TRADE ASSOCIATIONS

National Ski Areas Association
61 So. Main Street
P.O. Box 83
West Hartford, Conn. 06107

Association of Ski Area Consultants
700 Toedtli Drive South
Boulder, Colo. 80303

Ski Industries America
P.O. Box 2270
Peabody, Mass. 01960

United States Ski Association
1726 Champh Street
Suite 300
Devner, Colo. 80202

The United States Eastern Amateur Ski Association
20 Main Street
Littleton, New Hampshire 03561

National Ski Patrol System
2901 Sheridan Boulevard
Denver, Colo. 80214

Mr. R.F. Mattesich, President
Ski Touring Council
Troy, Vermont 05868

TRADE JOURNALS

Canadian Skier
McManus, Robertson Publ. Ltd.
1434 St. Catherine Street
W. Montreal, Quebec, Canada
Ed. J.W. McManus

Skier's Gazette
1801 York Street,
Denver Colo. 80206

Skiing Area News
Ziff-Davis Publ. Co.
1 Park Avenue
New York, N.Y. 10016
Ed. John Henry Auran

Skiing Illustrated
Skiing Illustrated Publ.
Box 8307, Station "F"
Calgary 13, Alberta, Canada
Ed. John Harder

Ski (published 7 times a year) September through March by Time
Mirror Magazines, Inc.
380 Madison Avenue
New York N.Y. 10017

The Student Skier
The Student Skier Association
Box 398
West Dover, Utah 05356

United States Ski News
United States Ski News
The Broadmoor
Colorado Springs, Colo. 80906

Western Ski Time Newsletter
Western Ski Time Magazine
3106 Clayton Road
Concord, Calif. 94520
Ed. James Jorden

RESIDENT CAMPS

Resident camping, as opposed to travel camping, provides specialized opportunities for individuals, groups, or families to obtain the camping experience, with little or no equipment other than clothes, footwear, and bedding. In these situations, housing is either provided in tents, cabins, or dormitories, which are of a permanent nature. The camper is charged a flat fee for the duration of the camp, whether it be for only a few days or several weeks or more. Many voluntary and social agencies have camps of this nature for their membership.

Because of the possibilities of concentrated education and the remoteness and beauty of the natural evnironment, many of these camps have been used primarily for places of specialized instruction or education. Although many of the previous camps have been primarily summer camps of a recreational nature for youth, the most recent trend is for these to be conference retreat facilities, or camps of a specialized nature. These specialized camps are similar to traditional summer residence camps in most aspects; their problems are even the same. Budgets, maintenance problems, food costs, and staff are problems experienced by both. A specialized camp is a camp that caters to a particular clientele and only people interested in that specialty participate in the camp. A summer residence camp normally has a variety of different activities of a recreational and leisure nature including archery, crafts and nature, swimming, hiking, boating, riding, and others and tries to provide a meaningful recreational experience to those who attend.

The camping movement in the United States cannot be traced to an exact starting point. One of the first organized camps was Camp Chocorna, founded by Ernest Balch in 1881. The camp had an average enrollment of 25 boys and five men on the "facility." Program emphasis was on swimming, rowing, fishing, and the practical work of camp life. Throughout the 1880s and 1890s, the movement began to accelerate.

After the turn of the century, the camping movement grew even more rapidly. In 1910, the Camp Directors Association of America was founded. 1916 was the founding of the National Association of Directors of Girls Camps. And in 1921 the Mid-West Camp Directors Association was formed. The amalgamation of these three associations in 1924 into the Camp Directors Association marked the first national organization, which changed names to the American Camping Association in 1935. The camping movement in the United States grew rapidly in the 1920s, but specialized camps did not become evident until the 1950s.

Camps always follow the patterns of the people. The current trend is toward the more specialized camps. Most handicap camps are well established with more than enough clientele than they need. Handicapped people patronize camps more heavily than the average camper, because these camps meet their exact needs. The staff and the program operate to help with the camper's problems. Also, it is easier to make friends and relax when everyone is having the same difficulties and problems. In addition to the traditional summer residence camps which have been so popular in past years but are decreasing in popularity in the past few years, three other groups of specialized camps have emerged. 1) Those for special groups of individuals, whether they are handicapped or of a particular social, organizational, or interest group. This type of camp is operated similarly to a summer residence camp except that the staff, facilities, and programming meet the prescribed needs of the specialized group. 2) Developed primarily for those interested in in-depth instruction of knowledge in certain areas. These camps are usually conducted in a school type atmosphere with scheduled meetings and concertrated educational programs and are referred to as educational camps. 3) Termed by many as the branch program, and usually is centered around outdoor skills like rock climbing, backpacking, or trip camping. This may be thought of as taking one aspect of the regualr summer resident camping program and pursuing it to the fullest. The "branch program" is operated as a branch of the summer camp using the camp's administration but does not necessarily operate on the camp's property or at the same time as a regular summer camp.

Some educational camps were founded early in the camping movement, but the majority were founded in the 1950s and 1960s. These camps are similar to summer schools that would concentrate on academics, sports, or other interests. People who feel the public educational system does not go into enough detail, or none at all, use these camps to gain additional knowledge in these areas. Their demand is not quite as constant as the handicapped camps. Economic hard times as we have experienced in the last few years, hurt these types of camps. The clientele use these camps not as a necessity, but more as an optional extra.

The specialized branch program camps are the newest type of specialized camp. The demand for these programs stem from the trend of "doing things in nature." The summer camps' older campers, who have been doing the same swimming, archery, and horseback riding summer after summer, wanted a new experience. The summer camps, in an effort to keep their clientele, devised branch programs of interest to the older campers and other interested people. These specialized branch program camps have the potential for much future growth. Some predict that eventually summer camps will have about 50 percent of their campers participating in off-camp specialized programs, with the younger campers staying on the camp property. Economic hard times have hurt these camps, too, because they are also considered optional extras.

The number of camps in the United States seems endless. The ACA, which has the largest number of members of a camp organization, publishes a directory that contains only member camps. This is only approximately one third of the existing camps. It would be difficult to determine the exact number of a certain type of specialized camp.

There are many sources that list camps. These directories list many of the same camps, but each directory has some different camps listed, also. As mentioned above, is the ACA directory, which lists all its member camps including resident summer camps and specialized camps. Porter Sargent annually publishes a book called "The Guide to Summer Camps and Summer Schools," which objectively describes the camps he lists across the country. Charlotte Shapiro and Lore Jarmul have "The Parent's Guide to Summer Camps" which has information for camps in the area of New England and the Middle Atlantic States. The ACA also combines with the American Academy of Pediatrics and the National Society for Crippled Children and Adults, to jointly publish the "Directory of Camps for the Handicapped." This is not all the directories of camps, but by comparing these lists, a fairly accurate list of specialized camps can be made.

Handicapped camps are usually listed by the certain handicap they serve. Some camps serve two or three types of handicaps that are closely related.

The supply of "educational camps" is quite varied. Some camps were established in the late 1880s, but these are more like schools that use the term "camp." There is a camp for almost any area in which a need might be present. An example of camps falling within this category would include:

Adventure	Basketball
Art	Creative writing
Astronomy	Dance
Baseball	

Being the newest type of camp, specialized branch programs, organized mainly by summer resident camps, have the least range of activities. But as interest in this area keeps increasing, more and more varieties should appear. Camps that currently exist in this area would include:

Repelling	Survival training
Riding	Wilderness camping
Rock mountain climbing	Wilderness canoe trips

Specialized camps are located wherever there is a demand. Sometimes climate and elevation dictate certain geographic locations, depending on the type of need being served. All three types of specialized camps can handle from the inexperienced to the advanced, and length of stay can be from one or two weeks to the whole summer.

The number of campers that can be handled differs from camp to camp according to the size of the camp's facilities, size of staff, and type of camp it is. Most handicapped camps have a ratio of campers to staff members of close to one to one, because of the problems involved in teaching handicapped people. An example of a handicapped camp's camper to staff ratio is the American Institute of Mental Studies located in Vineland, New Jersey. This camp has a maximum capacity of 325 children and a staff of about 270, which is supplemented with 30 summer counselors.

Educational and branch program camps usually do not have as low a ratio of campers to staff members as handicapped camps. Their ratio will range from two to one to six to one. The ratio here depends on how hard the material covered is to learn and how experienced the instructor is. Lake Side Farm Camp, located outside of Lawrence, Michigan, has a maximum of 50 campers and a staff of between 20 and 24. Outward Bound, Inc. has groups of 10 to 12 people with two leaders per group.

The cost of specialized camps depends on the curriculum, the ratio of staff to campers, the camp's facilities, and length of stay. Most handicapped camps have agreements with national handicapped organizations to make allowances for people who cannot afford the whole cost. This is because they feel that the camping experience is very beneficial to each handicapped person. Handicapped camps' tuitions range from 100 to over 200 dollars a week. Educational and branch program camps range around $100 to $150 per week. The difference is not as much specialized equipment but that professionally trained staff is needed with educational and branch program camps.

The investment required for a resident camp facility is significant in terms of the land required, upwards of an acre per person, plus the housing, dining hall, and recreation facilities. These would approach the cost of a small resort. In addition, OSHA requirements of the federal government are now being highly restrictive in terms of camp facilities. The youth camp safety bill presently in congress would put additional restrictions on resident camps. In essence, this would cause all camps to raise their fees in order to be able to finance upgrading and improvements as required. It will probably make the mediocre to good camps more in demand and would force the marginal ones out of business because the cost of updating and improvement would be insumountable.

Job opportunities in resident camping are numerous, however, they are widely scattered. The camp director usually spends 6 to 7 days a week during the summer months directing the camp, and the rest of the year promoting his camp, and in maintaining and developing the camp facilities. Many of the camps are owner operated, however, there are other positions open for individuals with specialized skills in outdoor education, waterfront, other recreational activities, and camp counselors. Traditionally many of these are part-time jobs, but in some of the larger camps one or two programming supervisors are retained on a year-round basis to plan programs, assist in promotional efforts and in the employment of the summer help.

Staff positions are varied among the different specialized camps. The handicapped camps need professionally trained people in their handicapped area. This is usually around half the camp's staff. The remainder of the staff do not need to be as trained, but do need to work well in a camp setting. They act as assistants to the trained staff members. Educational camps need almost all their staff to be knowledgeable in their concentrated area, and they must also be able to instruct others. This is also true for the branch program camps. People applying for a job in any type of camp should be able to enjoy a camp setting, work well with all types of people, and keep the welfare of others before his own.

The economy has affected camps in the last few years. The economy has made everyone stretch their budget and camp's clientele have been no exception. Generally, camps' attendance have been staying the same or down just a little. This hurts when all camps have been planning for increased enrollment each year. However, people are getting adjusted to the new state of the economy and camp attendance is expected to pick up again. It is believed that people do feel that a camping experience is beneficial and that camps in the United States are worth the expense.

TRADE ASSOCIATIONS

American Camping Association
Bradford Woods
Martinsville, Indiana 46151

National Campers & Hikers Association, Inc.
7172 Transit Road
Buffalo, N.Y. 14221

TRADE JOURNALS

Camping Magazine
American Camping Association
Bradford Woods
Martinsville, Indiana 46151

TRAVEL CAMPS

One of the most important aspects of camping is that it is one form of recreation in which all members of the family can experience and enjoy together, and there is no barrier for age or interests.

There is, however, and exteremely high turnover in campground operation. Apparently many farmers with land and other rural residents attempt to follow recommendations in years past provided by the U.S. Department of Agriculture to develop campgrounds to supplement their income. Not having the business expertise or the investment capital, and having a conflict in time with the height of the farming season and the campground season being identical, many of these have ended in financial disaster.

Camping in the United States is a major outdoor recreation activity. Campground ownership has changed from a near monopoly in public ownership in the late 1950s to private supremacy today.

In the private campground market nearly all campgrounds are variations of the "overnight" or "destination" type. The overnight is designed for the campers who want to stop for a night on their way to a particular spot. The destination campground, while it can be used as an overnighter, is designed for campers who are either visiting

Figure 27 Travel camping provides a number of recreation opportunities and can be a family affair.
Courtesy: Recreation Vehicle Industry Association, Chantilly, Virginia.

the area to see man-made or natural sights nearby, or who plan to "resort" primarily in the campground itself for a few weeks.

While most campgrounds fit into either the destination or overnight categories there are many interesting variations emerging. One of these is the urban campground system being set up by Jellystone Campgrounds. These campgrounds feature standard facilities such as a swimming pool, miniature golf course, ranger station, grocery store, and souvenir shop. Instead of being "away from it all," the camper is near all the action. These campgrounds are almost always located within the city limits of larger metropolises.

Another type of campground is what is termed by many as the "weekender." This type of campground is between an overnighter, which is usually located near a major highway, and a destination campground which is usually off the major highway near some attraction such as a lake. Campers may in some cases "own" this camp site at such facilities.

The winter campground is also growing in popularity. In a recent 3M National Vacation Camping study, one out of two respondents said they had camped during winter. It is likely many of these travel in the southern states, but with the boom in winter recreation activities such as snowmobiling and skiing, campers are heading north more frequently.

In 1973 it was estimated that one out of every two Americans was an active camper, an excamper, or a potential camper. The following statistics reflect the trends in camping.

1. *KOA (Kampgrounds of America, Inc.) 1972 Camper Survey*
   38% used travel trailers while camping.
   22% used tent trailers while camping.
   14% used truck campers.
   6% used motor homes.
   5% used van conversions.
   12% used a tent.

   35% prefer to camp in state or national parks.
   16% prefer to camp in state or national forests.
   45% prefer to camp in private campgrounds.

   46% go to a specific location and stay there for their camping vacation.
   54% prefer to move frequently throughout their vacation.

   ---

2. *The 1971 Study of Vacation Camping,* National Advertising Co.
   80% preferred campgrounds located near water.
   34 days were spent camping each year by the average camping family.
   $17.18 was spent per day by the average camping family.

3. *Camping Explosion: 1971 Recreation and Camping Study*
   Waite, Thomas L. 1971.
   Average camping family went on four to five campings trips in 1971.
   41% of the camping families planned trip less than 2 weeks in advance.
   One out of five campers owns a boat.
   Six out of ten campers used campground directories in selecting a site to stay.
   30% were members of a camping club.

The campground market is obviously still growing. With the increasing burdens place on state and national parks, private campgrounds are in need to handle the overflow.

Many people involved in the campground industry believe that destination campgrounds are more in demand than overnight.

One indication of this trend is the interest KOA is now taking in destination parks. Initially an overnight system, KOA is not only trying to serve the people going to and from national parks but is also building campgrounds to take those extra campers.

One tip given by the production manager of the Woodalls Directory, Linda Profaizer, is that in 1976 campers will be heading for the original 13 states for Bicentennial celebrations in Connecticut, Massachusetts, Maryland, Delaware, New Hampshire, New Jersey, New York, North Carolina, South Carolina, Pennsylvania, Rhode Island, Virginia, and Georgia. Some campgrounds in those states are already advertising in directories to get early reservations.

In 1973, it was estimated that 60 percent of the nation's 15,000 campgrounds were run by private enterprise.

Parks and campgrounds
in United States 1974

	Parks	Sites
Private parks	8,685	643,153
Public parks	5,439	32,673
Total	14,124	964,826

The type of campground developed is often dictated by the land and location. Many campground owners have found that destination campers do not want to stay for a couple of weeks in a campground of little natural beauty. The overnighter, however, who might stop for an evening in an unattractive campground, probably would not go 100 miles out of their way to stay in a more scenic spot for one evening.

State and local zoning regulations can also be a determinent because laws concerning RV campgrounds are often stricter than for housing because residents of many towns haven't accepted the presence of the campground.

Once the land is obtained to build the campground there are certain facilities that campers will expect when they arrive at the campground.

According to Don Ryan, President of KOA, it cost approximately $200,000 to develop what he considers a minimal facility, whether it is destination or overnight. Again, costs vary according to location and costs of labor and materials, but this $200,000 buys a recreation building, roads through the campground, sewage disposal, electricity and water to each site, a small general store, and laundry facilities. However, Ryan says that for a destination campground owner to hold his own against competition, it will cost 25 percent more for the campground than it will for an overnight park and that 25 percent will have to be pumped into recreational facilities to keep the campers happily occupied. Many campground owners easily spend more than one million dollars on their campground facilities.

Those who consider entering the campground business must make a decision to pay for a franchise or to develop the area on his own. The purchase of a franchise is quite expensive but brings it guidelines to the entire developmental process. Normally these guidelines have been developed by experts and tested in full by previous franchise purchasers. This reduces the probability that the developer will make a mistake, but still requires that experts be retained in such areas as real estate, law, architecture, engineering, and market analysis.

It is absolutely necessary to obtain an attorney to handle the maze of legal requirements, an architect to design the campground, an engineer to prepare the appropriate land and utility details, and an experienced market analysis expert to provide an unbiased third party opinion about the projects profitability.

The Small Business Administration releases data each year showing that more than ½ of the new businesses each year fail within two years. This is true over almost all types of business, including campgrounds! The primary reason most businesses fail is due to lack of either objectivity about the proposed firm or a lack of management expertise.

There are thirteen major steps involved in developing a campground from the first idea through the first year of operations. The following illustration shows these steps and the order in which they are normally taken.

1. Market selection
2. Site selection
3. Land procurement
4. Conceptual design
5. Zoning
6. Preliminary engineering
7. Market analysis
8. Economic feasibility study
9. Financing
10. Final engineering
11. Construction bidding
12. Construction
13. Operations

A more detailed discussion of these procedures will be made in the chapter on planning and development.

James E. Webb, Jellystone Campgrounds, says the proprietary approach to park merchandising is coming, that is, the time is approaching when one way to make money is to sell park sites. He also said that the camping scene is changing. Campers are staying longer in each park and closer to home, plus they want planned recreation. He said the combination will be good for condominium park sales.

TRADE ASSOCIATIONS

Family Camping Federation
Bradford Woods
Martinsville, Indiana 46151

National Campers & Hikers Association, Inc.
7172 Transit Road
Buffalo, N.Y. 14221

TRADE JOURNALS

Campground & RV Park Management
P.O. Box 1014
Grass Valley, Calif. 95945

TENNIS

The increase of specific facilities for the racket sports are among the fastest increasing of this group. These differ somewhat from the sports clubs in that they are specific to one activity, and may or may not include membership provisions but offer their facilities on a per hour or per season basis.

The sport of tennis is experiencing an upward surge in popularity and shows no signs of slowing down. The game now appears to surpass golf in overall popularity. New tennis courts (both indoor and outdoor) are being built at a rate of 5000 per year, public and private, 14 new courts everyday. Tennis courts are being developed everywhere. Housing developers are finding that tenants would rather have tennis courts than golf courses at a ratio of three to one. They have been promoted by big time tournaments, physical fitness buffs, recreation departments, and bottling companies. As a result, 34 million tennis players in 1975 spent 10.5 million dollars in 1970. Last year 100,000 adults spent at least one week at tennis camp. In 1973 there were 700 tennis clubs providing 2500 courts. There are over 500 summer tennis camps for kids. It has been largely a surburban and urban sport. The all-weather court has resulted in some popularity, allowing it to dry in 30 minutes to an hour. In 1972,

Figure 28 Tennis has become "the in sport" in many areas of the country particularly in resorts.
Courtesy: American Hotel and Motel Association, New York, New York.

there were an estimated 100,000 courts in operation. The A.C. Neilson survey suggests that there will be 400 million dollars spent per year on tennis. The avid tennis buff will spend 50 dollars per racket and 20 dollars for stringing. Other reasons for the increase includes the youth boom, health and physical fitness, the fact that it is an easy sport to learn and requires little or no travel, it is not a large investment, and it is beginning to be a status sport. It is estimated that three percent of the nation's courts are now covered. Books are even published, such as "Tennis for Travelers," showing where public and private tennis courts are in all the major cities.

While in years past clubs offered only tennis playing facilities, they now offer saunas, baby-sitting, cocktails, air condition, locker rooms, coffee, towels, pro-shop, and instruction. In 1965 there probably were no more than 30 indoor tennis clubs in the U.S. In 1973 there were over 1500 in operation with several more on the drawing board. The urban areas in cold weather cities tend to be the best supporters of the special facilities with over 100 near New York and 75 near Chicago. The success of the facility depends on the facility being located within a 25 minute drive of the middle to upper income housing, as the average indoor tennis player is between 30 and 55 and has a mean income of approximately 15,000 dollars a year.

Tennis resorts have also begun to be very popular, such as John Gardner's five-day tennis resort in Scottsdale, Arizona or the LaCosta Club in San Diego, California. Here physical fitness buffs as well as sports buffs can learn new skills, lose weight, become physically fit, and have all the amenities of the downtown convention hotel.

With pre-engineered steel frame buildings, a number of private investors in indoor tennis facilities have returned profits of 20 to 25 percent, and some have paid for themselves in four to six years. The United States Lawn and Tennis Association suggests that promoters budget approximately $90,000 per court for an indoor facility excluding land costs and frills. This includes the court building, clubhouse area, pro shop, plumbing, heating and ventilation, parking area, and so on. A minimum of four courts is suggested with six courts recommended to realize the highest rate or return.

Some experts believe that there is an over saturation of indoor racket club facilities. With the advent of the air structure, a number of developers have found that they can provide tennis facilities for around $500,000, about one-third to one-half what they normally would have to spend for the modern day facility with lounges, saunas, restaurants, and baby sitting. Unfortunately the frills are what is killing investors today, spending three times what a simple facility used to be built for. While air structures have been a boost to the development of these facilities, heating costs more than twice as much and lights also cost more. It appears that some tennis facilities, particularly in the New York area where there may be as many as 200 indoor courts within 30 miles, are going bankrupt similar to the bowling alley shakedown of two decades ago. There is also competition from municipal departments of parks and recreation who lease existing outdoor courts to private enterprise, who put air structures over them in the winter, and pay the city ten percent of the profit. There are some disadvantages to the private enterprise in that respect however, because the city normally requires lower rates and will not allow long term contracts.

To get a picture of what it costs to finance the facility, a $500,000 facility must be run at 75 percent of capacity around the clock to break even. This amounts to 600 hours of tennis play per week at about $12.00 per hour, or season passes for $300 to $600 per year. This has to be done in a 30-week season if not air conditioned. This means that 200 to 300 players must be on the courts every week to stay out the red.

The United States Lawn Tennis Association approximates an annual income from a four court "no frills" facility at about $128,000 plus membership fees. Facility expenses should total about $60,000 to break even a four court facility operating on a 13-hour day requires 100 members per court.

Some experts feel that the number of tennis players will to pay these kinds of prices for tennis has been reached, and that the only new markets are those who reach tennis playing age and are able to afford it.

TRADE ASSOCIATIONS

U.S. Lawn Tennis Association
71 University Place
Princeton, New Jersey 08540

Mr. Harry Humphries, Chairman
U.S. Tennis Court & Track Builders Association
1201 Waukegan Road
Glenview, Ill. 60025

National Tennis Educational Foundation
51 East 42nd Street
New York, N.Y. 10017

James E. Hillman, President
National Public Parks Tennis Association
155 West Washington Boulevard-8th Floor
Los Angeles, Calif. 90015

TRADE JOURNALS

Tennis Trade Magazine
370 Seventh Avenue
New York, N.Y. 10001

Gilbert Richards' Tennis for Travelers
Richards Industries Inc.
407 Blade Street
Cincinnati, Ohio 45216

Tennis U.S.A.
Popular Publications, Inc.
205 E. 42nd Street
New York, N.Y. 10017
Ed. F.E. Storer

Figure 29 Adequate facilities provide more satisfying boating.
Courtesy: Boating Industrial Association glastron boats, Austin, Texas.

MECHANIZED SPORTS

MARINAS/BOAT YARDS

It is difficult to know whether to classify such activities as boating in terms of recreation equipment manufacturers, or in terms of recreation enterprise suppliers. There are indeed over 16,500 boating dealers serving the industry and the public including some 1200 marine distributors and jobbers. According to the boating industry of these 200 are wholesale only.

These would be classified as recreation equipment manufacturers, distributors or sales outlets. On the other hand, there are close to 5050 marines, boatyards, yacht clubs, and fishing stations attempting to supply the needs of fishermen, boatmen, water skiers, and divers. Of this number, 1320 are yacht clubs.

Approximately 4.6 billion dollars was spent at the retail level for new and used equipment, services, insurance, fuel, morings and launching fees, repairs, and boat memberships. Other significant factors concerning the boating industry: 1) Even though there were probably less actual miles logged by boats and waterways during 1974, actual costs of operation was up. 2) Unit sales were down and most production categories with the exception of sailboats, canoes, and some accessories. The amount of service was up however. 3) Used equipment sales were brisk. 4) Diversification among boating retailers continued to increase as it has done for the past several years. 5) The boating industry hit a peak in dollar sales in 1973. It is interesting to note that the skilled worker was the top market for outboard motors and boats in 1974 surpassing that of the professional or manager category.

Water skiing continues to be a highly popular sport, with about 12 million people going water skiing last year. The boating industry estimated that 34 million fishermen wetted their lines last year, and 4 million people went skin and scuba diving.

As the marina and boatyard will be of primary interest because of its nature as a supplier of recreation activity, it is interesting to note that marina openings have been less frequent during the last few years. There has been considerable interest and growth in the "dry land marina" concept. This has come about because of the economies possible with this type of facility. The costs of storage and property, are all less.

The most important problem plaguing today's marina operator is that of investment versus return. To attract business and flourish, a marina must be located in a heavily populated area where real estate values are high. It must also make substantial investments in facilities and equipment. In many instances the costs of doing business are far too high for the income involved. An acute shortage of suitable land exists at any cost.

The entire marina industry needs to re-evaluate its standards of charges in order to produce a solvent business picture. More and better marina facilities are vital to the continued growth of pleasure boating. Municipal marinas, built with tax dollars, are only part of the answer to the need for facilities. They are, however, important. The average marine dealer or boat builder can yield considerable influence in his area relative to the building of such facilities.

Marinas offer a variety of services to their customers. In addition to service, fuel, dockage, storage, and repairs;

60% sell fishing supplies
40% have boats for hire
82% sell soft drinks
92% have rest room facilities
45% operate snack bars
23% operate restaurants (usually leased out)
11% sell groceries
Average gross sales
   volume $600,000
Average net profit (after
   owner's salary) $ 25,000
60% of the marina/boatyards have been in business 15 years or less.
95% of the marina/boatyards are located on the water.
80% of the marina/boatyard managers own their own facilities.

The facilities at the average marina/boatyard are utilized as follows:

28% for storage & warehouse
24% for service & repair

15% for sales & showroom
4% for office operations
29% for other functions

The average marina/boatyard employs:

7 full-time people
6 part-time people

The average marina/boatyard spends 2.5 percent of its annual gross on advertising, mostly in newspapers. Classified advertising is preferred by 95 percent of the operators and managers.

Those interested in the marina and boating business, should have some expertise in water sports, and be familiar with boats and boating. Two elements appear to be crucial in the success of marina or boatyard. One is the dock, or storage areas, which provide the "summer homes" for many yacht and boat owners, as they come to the lake and live on their boats, many times not even taking the boat out of its berth. The other element is that of a good mechanic. People will store their boat, buy their equipment, and buy their food supply where they can get good mechanical service for their boats.

Marina or beach recreation operators might also want to consider a profitable concession in the rental of boats. Sailboats are very popular and typically runs from $3.00 an hour for a $500 boat to $8.00 an hour for a $1300 boat. Introduction of sailing instruction programs can add even more to an operator's income with little additional expense. Particularly municipal operations should give this consideration. Of the several keel boats available, the Caprice is specifically designed for rental purposes. It is 14-feet long, is non-capsizable and sinkable, and costs about $1500. A qualified experienced employee can be assigned full-time to this sailboat operation if there are ten or fifteen boats. Needless to say he should be a skilled sailor.

Boating and skiing has enjoyed a steady growth over the past few years, and is among the fastest growing segments of the recreation spectrum.

TRADE ASSOCIATIONS

National Association of Engine &
    Boat Manufactures
Box 583
Greenwich, Conn. 06830

American Power Boat Assoc.
915 Burns Drive
Detroit, Mich. 48214

Outboard Boating Club of America
401 North Michigan Ave
Chicago, Ill. 60611

American Yachtsmen's Assoc.
3418 14th St. N.W.
Washington, D.C. 20010

International Swimming Hall of Fame
1 Hall of Fame Drive
Fort Lauderdale, Fla. 33316

National Water Ski Association
2806 Fountain Boulevard
Tampa, Fla. 33609

TRADE JOURNALS

Family Houseboating
Trailer Life Publishing Co.,
P.O. Box 2081
Toluca Lake Calif. 91602
Ed.- Publ. Art Rouse

Go Boating
Go Guide on the Waterways, Inc.
775 N.E. 79st St.
Miami Beach, Fla. 33138

Recreational Industry
Boating Industry Magazine,
Conover-Mast Publ.
205 E. 42nd Street,
New York, N.Y. 10017
Ed.-Publ. Charles Jones

MOTORCYCLES AND OFF-THE-ROAD VEHICLES

Recreational trail bikes, mini-bikes, and off-the-road motocycles as well as vehicles began to overwhelm the existing recreation park facilities of the United States in the late 1960s. Although off-road recreational and sporting riders have existed in this country since the 19th century their numbers probably didn't exceed 250,000 and they were scattered thinly throughout the United States. The impact first received official attention in the January 18, 1969 issue of the Federal Register, wherein the Department of the Interior recognized off-road vehicle recreation as a legitimate use of public lands and described brief guidelines for the establishment and management of facilities for this popular recreation.

There are approximately 35 different motorcycle manufacturers, with the top 6 or 8 having more than 75 percent of the business. A relationship of manufacturer-supplier-provider is similar to that of the recreation vehicle institute for camping, and the boating manufacturers for marinas. Much of the promotion and public relations, as well as education for off-road vehicles as an enjoyable and respectable sport, has come from the manufacturers themselves.

The American Motorcycle Association, a group of over 200,000 members has also done much to promote the family aspects of cycling, as well as to pursue objectives of the membership, education, safety, legislation, and so on. This group is similar to the AAA for automobiles, and offers medical insurance and benefits as well as death coverage for its members.

There are always those who enjoy the pleasure and satisfaction of man and machine. This can be seen in the beginning from the driving for pleasure activity, which ranks top among all recreation activities in BOR studies. The social implications of off-road vehicle clubs, groups, and others also stimulates interest. It is interesting to not that a late 1974 survey by Kawasaki Motors, Inc. showed that 8 percent of all households in the United States owned one or more motorcycles.

The American Motorcycle Association estimates over 5½ million motorcycles in use in 1973 with approximately 1.5 to 2 million new cycles being purchased each year.

The average buyer is male, in his 20's, and earns between $10,000 and $18,000 per year.

There appears to be three areas of opportunity as it relates to private recreation. The first is, of course, to work directly with the manufactureres. Several plants employ more than 400 people. However, the work probably is similar in nature to many other industrial manufacturing concerns. A few talented and specialized individuals pursue a job in the field of motorcycling for the company, such as joining a racing team for research and development. These positions, of course, are highly specialized and difficult to obtain.

The second opportunity of a similar nature is in dealership-sales and repair. This requires mechanical ability, interest and ability in riding and racing, and would tend to be open more to those who are highly specialized and interested in this area rather than the casual rider. This would also take a rather large investment of capital.

The third opportunity involves the operation of a motorcycle park. The majority of sites now are limited to small machines located adjacent to urban areas. These are places where owners of motorcycles or other off-road vehicles can ride on private land requiring no driver's licenses. Land to be set aside for recreational riding should contain as varied terrain as possible including meandering trails, gentle natural hills and grades, some flat areas, and one or two extremely difficult non-trails. Ideally, the proper combination of terrains range from difficult to easy.

Depending on the type of operation intended and the age of the users, park management can range from intermittent supervision to full-time staffs. Unless a user fee is charged at the gate, no paid personnel need be employed. Families may be expected to supervise the young at the free reserves, and everyone using the site agrees to do so at his own risk. Where greater control or supervision is desirable one or more park supervisors should be trained in rendering first aid. Training programs for management and control of personnel are being offered by some cycle dealers in California. If the park is intended as a profit-making operation, capital investment and management requirements will be proportionately greater. Several firms are currently in the business of providing consulting and management services for operations of this type.

Generally, to be successful, private motorcycle riding parks have found it necessary to provide facilities for family group riding. Additionally, spectator attractions have been found to be a requisite for profitable operations. If the park is limited to small machines, it will rule out the older family members who generally ride the larger machines. While private profit-directed parks can scarcely exist without spectator attractions, the publicly administered reserves should not rule out the possibility of letting its facilities be used for the same purpose for community organizations. Not only do spectator events serve a useful community purpose, but they are also effective advertising for the reserves' day to day operation.

The temptation should be avoided to offer motorcycle and accessory sales, fuel, gasoline, and services. This is in competition with those who recommend the facilities to their businesses. The future of motorcycle industries will depend on the price of possible rationing of gasoline, customer purchasing power, and the cost of automobiles. As far as motorcycle parks go, the proposed outlook is that they will be like private country clubs in the cities and in the rural areas may become exclusive resort-type facilities centered around the motorcycle enthusiasts.

Little has been said about the off-road vehicles (ORV's) of the four wheel variety, because little is known. Most off-road vehicles which are built by Jeep and other manufacturers, cost in the neighborhood of $4000 to $5000, and are relatively few in number compared to motorcycles. There are a number of "dune buggies" and other four wheel, off-road vehicles that have been constructed individually from Volkswagen chasis, motors, and so on or other small automobiles. These are not four-wheel drive vehicles normally, and as a result are not as adaptable to hilly terrain and other land elements. They are driven more for recreation while their four-wheel cousins are used more for transportation in other sports such as hunting and fishing. Many of the four-wheel drive models are now being engineered to use four-wheel drive on the road as well as off to eliminate having to make time consuming mechanical changes for four-wheel operation.

TRADE ASSOCIATIONS

The American Motorcycle Association
P.O. Box 141
Westerville, Ohio 43081

Motorcycle Industry Council
1001 Connecticut Ave. N.W.
Washington, D.C. 20036

TRADE JOURNALS

Road Rider
2201 Laguna Canyon Road
Box 678
Laguna Beach, Calif. 92677
Ed. Roger Hull

RECREATION VEHICLES _____

A closely associated industry to camping is that of recreation vehicles. Although made up entirely of manufacturers, this group has been highly instrumental in surveying and developing markets for camping, and in planning, developing, and promoting campgrounds. Although other recreation activities have similar manufacturing groups associated with them, such as boating, bowling, or bicycling, none has been as active in promoting participation as has the recreation vehicle group.

Recreation vehicles in the United States can be traced back to the 1920s when boxlike delivery vans were used by their owners for weekend fishing and hunting trips. Production on a commercial basis in the 1930s and continued quite moderately. In 1954 there were 15,370 vehicles being produced annually, and this increased to

Figure 30 Recreation Vehicles come in all shapes and sizes.
Courtesy: Recreation Vehicle Industry Association, Chantilly, Illinois.

62,000 by 1961. By 1970 manufacturers were producing 500,000 annually. So the industry has grown by leaps and bounds. This great growth happened basically in the 1960s.

A recreational vehicle is a moving unit, either powered by itself or pulled by another vehicle, and designed as temporary living quarters for recreation, camping, or travel use. There are five basic recreational vehicle categories:

1. camping trailers   4. motorhomes
2. truck campers   5. five wheelers
3. travel trailers

Camping trailers are the lowest priced ranging from 300 to 1,200. These are basically fold out tents. Truck campers are designed to fit the chassis of ordinary pickup trucks and are removeable. These usually have kitchen, toilets, and shower facilities. Prices range from $1,500 to $3,000. Travel trailers are the most popular and come in a wide range of sizes and prices. This range goes from a 14-foot trailer priced at $3,000 to 30-foot trailers for $20,000. Many of these are quite comfortable and one can be relaxed whether eating, sleeping, or just lounging around. Motorhomes power themselves and are built on truck or bus chassis. These are quite expensive and usually begin at $15,000. Now after the energy crises many of these type vehicles are priced at the $6,000 to $10,000 range and are built much smaller. Fifth wheelers are a new category pulled by pickups with a special hitch connection. The fifth wheel allows for easier driving with less swaying.

Recreational vehicles provide packaged mobility, economy, and convenience. They provide many people the opportunity to travel who may not be able to afford hotel and restaurant bills. They give people the freedom to get off the beaten track and explore new areas without fear of having a place to stay. RV's make winter camping more practical and generally provide a more comfortable vacationing experience.

There are approximately four million recreational vehicle owners in America. Couples 45 and up are the principle owners. Buyer profile statistics are available from the Recrational Vehicle Institute.

Recreational Vehicles can be found anywhere in the United States. Of course they will more commonly be found at locations that people are attracted to. Most likely these locations will offer some form of recreation such as sightseeing, water sports, or hunting. These locations will usually be at parks, whether state, national, private, or commercial recreational areas. Of the four million recreational vehicles, a fourth can be found in California. Other states that are more popular in terms of owners and places to visit are Ohio, Michigan, Florida, Illinois, Texas, and Pennsylvania.

RV's can be purchased in all fifty states and are manufactured in all but three. Before the energy crisis hit in 1973, there were over 800 factories. One year later during the crisis this number diminished to 555. Many more have gone out of business since hen but an up-to-date number is not available.

Winnebago, whose headquarters are in Forest City, Iowa, accounts for 40 percent of the production of RV's. In 1958 John Hanson bought the company for $12,000.

By mid 1972 its assets were worth 773 million dollars. Winnebago states that ½ of its vehicles are sold to retired couples. The corporation is one of the few industries whose shares are traded publicly.

The following table shows the distribution of sales.

Recreation vehicles
Sales Distribution

	No. of Manufacturers	No. of RV's in Use	% of Total RV's
Travel trailers	275	1,860,000	36
Truck campers	246	890,000	17
Camping trailers	42	1,160,000	22
Motor homes	194	350,000	7
Pickup covers	218	900,000	18
Total	555	5,160,000	100

Problems are evident in RV's with regard to safety features. RV's popularity grew so rapidly that it caught state and federal officials by surprise, and safety standards are just now catching up. Many shoddy manufacturers with little design skill or engineering knowledge were putting vehicles on the road while cutting expenses on safety features. The most common safety fault of manufacturers is to buy chassis suspensions too small to support the weight of houses on them, making them top heavy and more prone to swaying.

Research conducted by the Wisconsin Division of Motor Vehicles showed that of 1500 RV's spot checked a third were carrying twice the load their tires were designed for. And a St. Louis dealer stated that 90 percent of pickup campers and 30 percent of trailers are overloaded.

Apparently state and federal officials should be creating more stringent laws for RV's to protect citizens from possible accidents and damage to their expensive investments.

Recreational vehicle clubs seem to be quite popular. The Family Motor Coaching Club prints a monthly magazine which describes their activities and associated services. This organization has regional clubs such as Crusin Cajuns, Arkansas Travelers, and Rollin Gators. Many of these regional groups form rallies with their regions, trying to get other RV owners to come and visit.

The biggest problem with RV's now, and increasingly so in the future, whether they are intruding on the rights of people who are seeking a camping experience free from all signs of civilization. Conservationists and environmental groups feel that many RV owners are trying to take it all with them, instead of trying to get away from it all, which is why people basically camp and go on vacations.

Since the advent of RV's many wilderness areas previously untouched are beginning to show the signs of wear and tear. Many people, through RV's, are getting to these unspoiled places and either intruding on those seeking a more natural camping experience, or else polluting and littering the areas. Naturally people in RV's may not be experienced campers and are not aware of the proper code of ethics with regard to our natural landscape.

Many of the national and state parks are being overrun with the vehicles. Many RV owners aren't aware of alternative spots for camping and head to where they know other people will be. Across the nation there are 10,000 parks for RV's, which range from $1.50 to $8.00 for an overnight stay. Many of these types of parks provide electricity, water, showers, and rest room facilities. But a complaint with these types of parks is that they don't provide enough natural beauty.

In the future, recreation planners should be fully aware of the impact of these vehicles and should plan areas accordingly. Separate areas should be established for RV owners that would allow other campers a more natural setting, free from these vehicles. And yet while planning areas for RV's you should remember to provide the utmost in solitude and natural beauty. This problem can only be resolved in the initial planning stages and is quite difficult to solve after areas are in use. RV's are here to stay and it is the duty of our recreational professionals to maximize cooperation between the different groups seeking a camping and vacationing experience.

Critical to the future of RV's is our energy supply. As our fuel supplies are dwindling, RV's may be nonexistent if rationing becomes effective. RV's will most certainly be forced to cut down on size to gain better gas mileage. Some of the RV's get as little as six miles per gallon, which is quite absurd in these fuel crisis times. If the prices on gas keep rising the wealthy citizens may be the only people able to afford the gas for recreational purposes. Manufacturers were cut in half when the United States was first hit by the fuel crisis and many more are going out of business, leaving only the very large corporations.

If new energy supplies are found another boom in the industry could be seen. BOR has predicted that the demand for public camping will be 80 percent higher in 1980 than it was in 1965. The U.S. Forest Service estimates that ½ of the visitors who come to public parks travel in RV's. If these statistics are true a great increase can be expected in recreational vehicle owners in the future.

TRADE ASSOCIATIONS

Recreation Vehicle Institute
P.O. Box 204
14650 Lee Road
Chantilly, Virginia 22021

Recreational Vehicle Dealers of America, Inc.
711 Orchard Street
Deerfield, Ill. 60015

The Family Motor Coach Association, Inc.
P.O. Box 44144
Cincinnati, Ohio 45244

TRADE JOURNALS

Campground and RV Park Management
P.O. Box 1014
Grass Valley, Calif. 95945

SNOWMOBILING

Since the development of the first "motorized tabaggon" by Carl Eliason of Sanler, Wisconsin in 1917, snowmobiling has risen, particularly in the last 7 to 10 years, to one of the fastest growing recreation activities in the country, and undisputed king in the northern snow belt states. There are approximately 2 million snowmobiles in the United States and Canada. Ten years ago there were an estimated 15,000 vehicles. In 1971, there was a 20 percent increase in demand and production, and an estimated 600,000 machines were produced by over 100 factories. Because of an overestimated market and some bad snow years, this has dwindled to about 30 companies manufacturing about 65 different brands. The top 10 manufacturers produce 80 percent of the market.

After the winter of 1973, there were approximately 350,000 snowmobiles on inventory, as a result of the over-production and over-estimation of the supply and demand. As a result there is now much more industry cooperation and dealer manufacturer cooperation to eliminate such financial blunders in the future.

Like boating, motorcycling, recreation vehicles, and other mechanized recreation activities, the manufacturers have, to a large extent, been responsible for promoting and publicizing the activity in order to produce a market for their machinery. Like other industries, the snowmobile industry is quite interested in the welfare of the purchaser and spends a great deal of money for research, testing, education, and public acceptance.

While motives behind the first snowmobiles were for life survival, hunting, trapping, and winter work, 95 percent of the owners of snowmobiles today are using them for recreation. They require many of the skills of skiing but much less skill and training. Northern snow belt states such as Michigan, Minnesota, Wisconsin, and New York who have had a very short summer recreation season are finding opportunities to use snowmobiling resort centers to attract vacationers year round, particularly on weekends during the winter months. A recent industry survey found that 85 percent of snowmobile purchases were by families with 2 or 3 children, and that 2/3 were blue-collar workers, and 3/4 never attended college. More than 1/2 earned less than $10,000. Snowmobiling is indeed a popular activity and may have moved to a category of a semi-necessity rather than a luxury in the snow belt areas.

Maintenance has continued to be a problem, with an average user spending about $80 a year during the 4-month season for plugs, belts, cleets, and other necessities. Like other mechanized recreation activities, the opportunities for employment in the industry are primarily in the manufacturing, in a dealership, or in an enterprise which offers programming opportunities. Many state and national parks, as well as local departments of parks and recreation, while resisting snowmobiling in the past are now putting out welcome mats for conscientious owners of snow vehicles and are planning programs including racing, drag racing, ski-joring, drill teams, and cross country trips to attract the snowmobile owner. There are presently 630 parks and national forests in the United States that permit snowmobiles. Snowmobile clubs have been organized in almost every community, with over 3000 clubs in the United States.

A number of the summer resorts in the northern states have added winter facilities such as saunas, heated swimming pools, indoor tennis, racket courts, and other activities of interest for the vacationing snowmobiler, in order to make the total facility a winter recreation complex with a place to park his snowmobile beside his automobile outside of his resort room.

The most popular activity of snowmobile clubs is snow cruising. A variety of activities occur on these cruises such as campouts, cookouts, and other activities. Usually the club will travel on a well-maintained trail in groups of 10 to 20 for an average of 15 to 20 miles per hour. Like other mechanized recreation activities, there are also problems with snowmobiling. The effect on wildlife, the damage to the ground over which they travel, the noise, and the high accident rate have been publicized by many who would desire to see them banned as they are in France and Norway. There is not a sufficient number of trails and at present the concentration of snowmobiles in some areas has produced significant rises in accident rates. Operators of snowmobile parks will need to be cognizant of respecting the rights of those who live nearby, while trying to cater to the varied needs and desires of the snowmobiling public. Materials are available from the snowmobile association on the rules and regulations which should be incorporated and suggestions on programming and operation of snowmobile parks.

Snowmobiling has indeed provided a refreshing and new recreation opportunity for people who formerly looked toward winter as a period of snowbound isolation. It has enlarged people's lives and brightened their leisure hours. Thousands are employed in manufacturing and distribution, and cash registers are ringing in resorts and rural areas during the months when they have traditionally been silent, from late October throught April. Properly regulated and supervised, this activity will no doubt take a well deserved place among others of the mechanized recreation activity group in the society in which we live.

There continues to be a number of problems surrounding the snowmobile affecting those who sell, rent, provide snowmobiles, or places for them to operate. The first of these is the high accident rate. Because of a lack of licensing in most states, anyone can drive one, and sometimes the trails become crowded with inexperienced drivers. In other places, drivers do not follow trails and because of the noise of the machines it is difficult to tell when intercepting someone else's path.

The noise has continued to be a problem with the manufacturers desiring to reduce noise down to about 75 decibels at 50 feet. While they have had some success, non-snowmobile residents continue to complain about noise.

A number of environmentalists still conclude that the snowmobile damages the land and that snowmobile operators are not cognizant nor making any conscious efforts to protect the environment. It appears only continuing education will help alleviate this problem.

TRADE ASSOCIATIONS

American Snowmobile Assoc.
13104 Crooked Lake Blvd.
Anoka, Minn. 55303

International Snowmobile
 Industry Association
5205 Leesburg Pike
Falls Church, Virginia 22041

TRADE JOURNALS

U.S.S.A. Snotrack
Market Communications, Inc.
534 N. Broadway
Milwaukee, Wisconsin 53202

CLUBS—RESORTS—SECOND HOMES

COUNTRY CLUBS _____

While there are probably more country clubs in existence than any other type of private recreation enterprise most are private clubs and operate on a nonprofit basis. Although there are opportunities for employment, the number of employees are minimal. These may include a club manager of a restaurant, bar, or lounge in a country club facility; a golf pro who may or may not be the club manager; and possibly a part-time life guard or swimming instructor in the summer. Some of the larger, more expensive clubs with tennis courts may have a part-time tennis instructor. Most of the social activities of the country club are planned and organized by volunteer club members and various club committees with assistance for the club manager. The swimming pool lifeguard may report to the swimming pool chairman. Most country clubs continue to struggle for financial existence as maintenance and upkeep take a large part of their revenue. Golf continues to be the main activity of the country club, with swimming, social activities, and tennis being secondary activities.

*Figure 31   Golfing is the main activity of country clubs, resorts, and hotels.
Courtesy: American Hotel and Motel Association, New York, New York.*

TRADE ASSOCIATIONS

Golf Course Builders of America
632 Shoreham Building
Washington, D.C. 20036

National Golf Foundation
Room 707 Merchandise Mart
Chicago, Ill. 60654

TRADE JOURNALS

Club Operations
Golf Digest, Inc.
88 Scribner Avenue
South Norwalk, Conn.
Ed. L.S. Sheehan

Golf Course Guide
Rand McNally and Co.
P.O. Box 7600
Chicago, Ill. 60680

RX Sports and Travel
Rx Golf and Travel, Inc.
447 S. Main Street
Hillsboro, Ill.
Ed. Harry Luecke

Senior Golfer
Senior Golf Publications Co.
P.O. Box 4716
Clearwater, Fla. 33518

Golf Shop Operations
Golf Digest
88 Scribner Avenue
Norwalf Conn. 06850
Ed. Cal Brown

Golf Digest
297 Westport Avenue
Norwalk, Conn. 06856

DESTINATION RESORTS AND HOTELS

There is no commonality of definition when a hotel or motel becomes a resort or a resort hotel. BOR definitions in the ORRRC Study Report #11, page 9 indicates the following: "A resort: Have rooms for at least 20 persons, and provision for at least two types of recreational activities excluding lawn games, children's playgrounds, and swimming pool." No definition is given for the resort hotel, however a list of members of the resort hotel committee and the hotel redbook of the American Hotel Association was used for their mailing list. It is rather superfluous to try to differentiate between resorts and resort hotels, and the former definition probably is workable for both.

The large resort is not unlike the health and sports clubs mentioned previously, or the community associations or second homes associations. In fact, it attempts to take the best of both, to provide a suitable environment for a variety of recreational activities to meet the needs of the entire family, and to provide a comfortable and exciting environment for housing those who come to participate in the activities of programs of the resort. This is indeed a recreation business that is divided into many smaller component businesses, and while the recreation and entertainment portions of their enterprise probably account for less than 15 percent of the gross sales, it is these activities that attract the consumer to the facility. Although recreation and entertainment may be the primary selling point, along with these, the businessman basically sells lodging and meals, much like motel, hotel, and restaurant managers; however, these are done in specific motifs, arrangements, and through the use of unique facilities and programs so as to turn even the sleeping and eating functions into a recreational activity. Each resort may promote primarily one or two specific activities such as tennis or golf while another may promote water sports such as skiing, fishing, canoeing, or swimming. In resort operation the goal of the business is to provide adequate recreational activities and facilities for vacationing guests so that they will not leave the resort for their entertainment. Facilities for water oriented recreation were reported by a majority of the resort owners. A breakdown of facilities provided at most resorts follows: swimming 94 percent, fishing 80 percent, boating 66 percent, picnicking 38 percent, hunting 32 percent, camping-tennis-golf 17 percent, riding and winter sports 15 percent, and hiking 10 percent. Other facilities provided included 32 additional types of facilities such as archery, lawn and court games, dancing, and square dancing, mountain climbing, skiing, target shooting, bowling, and even wildlife photography.

The major problems listed by the resorts included:

Fire	31%
Trash	24%
Vandalism	15%
Crowded conditions and staff problems	8%

The top ten resorts as listed occasionally in Esquire Magazine, (December 1975, pages 43-44) as well as Holiday (April 1975, page 44) indicate that among these resorts, swimming, golf, spa and health facilities, and trap and skeet are popular, probably in that order. Most resorts feel they have to offer a variety of activities for the whole family and that tastes are becoming much more sophisticated. They are also finding that the public is attracted to a resort because of its distinction or uniqueness of the facility.

Sea Pines in South Carolina is one of the few places that experts believe has made a good merger between resort operations and land development. Most places that try to do both at the same time usually end up doing a better than average job in one area and a poor job in the other.

Big name hotels and motels apparently do not build facilities any longer because of the cost. They simply manage the ones already built by real estate interests, who in recent years have demanded a percentage of the profit or another "piece of the action." Some have developed hotels or resorts as catalysts to land sales in an area to raise the value. The condominium hotel—where rooms or apartments are sold to individuals but rented by the hotel manager when the owner is not using it—are becoming popular. Hotel rates may double by the year 1980, and experts believe that the hotel manager must reinforce uniqueness of where they are located if they are to have their share of the business.

Time Magazine, March 29, 1976 lists hotel management as one of the few bright employment markets in an otherwise bleak picture. There are a number of books including Podd and Lesure, PLANNING AND OPERATING MOTELS AND MOTOR

HOTELS, Ahrens, New York, 1964 that provides complete information on hotel-motel-resort management. There are also a number of excellent college curriculums available in the area, a list of which can be obtained from the Trade Associations.

TRADE ASSOCIATIONS

American Hotel and Motel Association
888 Seventh Avenue
New York, N.Y. 10019

The Educational Institute of American Hotel & Motel Association
1407 South Harrison Road
East Lansing, Mich. 48823

American Motor Hotel Association
1025 Vermont Ave., N.W.
Washington, D.C. 20005

Council of Hotel, Restaurant, and Institutional Education
Statler Hall
Cornell University
Ithaca, N.Y. 14850

Hotel-Motel Greeters International
166 East Superior Street, Suite 501
Chicago, Ill. 60611

Hotel Sales Management Association
55 East 43rd Street
New York, N.Y. 10017

National Association of Hotel-Motel Accountants
Essex House, 100 Central Park South
New York, N.Y. 10019

National Executive Housekeepers Association
Business and Professional Building
Second Avenue
Callipolis, Ohio 45631

TRADE JOURNALS

Mr. Allen Fagans, Editor
Resort Management Magazine
1509 Madison Avenue
P.O. Box 4169
Memphis, Tennessee 38104

Resort Management
Box 4169
Memphis, Tennessee 38104
Ed. Martin Judge; Publ. Wallace Witmer

Resort and Motel Administration
6500 Kelvin Avenue
Canoga Park, Calif. 91306

Northwest Resorter
Detroit Lakes, Minn. 56501

Official Hotel & Resort Guide
Ziff-Davis Publ. Co.
One Park Avenue
New York, N.Y. 10016

Dude Rancher
Dude Ranchers' Association
P.O. Box 1363 D
Billings, Montana 59103
Ed. Conna G. May

Dude Ranchers
N.Y.S. Department of Commerce, Travel Bureau
112 State Street
Albany 7, N.Y.
Ed. Joseph Horan

Farm & Ranch Vacation Guide
Farm & Ranch Vacation Guide Inc.
36 E. 57th Street
New York, N.Y. 10022
Ed. Pat Dickerman

HEALTH AND SPORTS CLUBS

The growth of sports clubs, health spas, and work-out gymnasiums has increased dramatically in recent years. Probably a spin-off from the traditional YMCA facility program, many of the modern day facilities would not be recognized by some of the previous managers of "Y's" in the past. The present-day facilities take the form of miniature indoor country clubs, and may include one or more of the following: 1) work-out gymnasiums, 2) saunas, 3) locker rooms, 4) ice skating, 5) tennis, 6) racketball, 7) handball, 8) weight lifting, and in some cases, a 9) restaurant, 10) bar or lounge, or 11) an area for social activity. Many of the clubs specialize in several of the above. Indoor tennis clubs are growing very fast, as are racket clubs, health spas, and health club gymnasiums. Although the specific audiences and purposes of these various types of clubs are somewhat different, the objective is the same; to provide an enjoyable atmosphere for social interests and for full participation in the sports activities.

Most clubs have full-time professional instructors to coordinate learning and competitive programs for all ages and abilities. Club participation is usually by annual membership, but may be by initiation fee and annual membership. Some have full membership privileges at a certain rate and partial membership privileges for a reduced rate. Other facilities have both indoor recreation facilities and outdoor recreation facilities to be used in good weather. All encouraged physical fitness, and the enjoyment of the activity of the individual's choice.

The work-out gymnasium, although related to the health spa, differs primarily in intensity and seriousness of the training atmosphere of those involved. Those associated with these types of facilities normally are concerned about bodily health, and tend to be buyers of health food supplements to add to physical growth and fitness.

No matter what the type of major recreation activity offered as a focal point of the facility, they must be within easy reach of large numbers of people in metropolitan areas. Most facilities require between 500 and 1000 members to realize a profit after the initial investment.

The private recreation implications would be similar to others mentioned, with the owner having a sizable investment required of a minimum of 150,000 to 1,000,000 dollars or more, depending on the number and types of recreation activities he desires to provide. Personnel consists of a general manager, and instructors or coordinators for each of the major facilities offered, although in small clubs one coordinator may have responsibility for a number of recreation activities. One successful club owner listed the following practices as being important to the success of his facility:

1. Total Organization.
2. Quality personnel—young, good health, proper attitude, sales ability—little future involved for them.
3. Good public relations in all facets—notoriety, brochures, flyers, word of mouth.
4. Sound quality and well-maintained equipment.
5. High quality membership.
6. Cleanliness and consistent maintenance of entire complex.
7. Sound sales and membership plans with constant promotion.
8. Sound bookkeeping.
9. A general feeling and love for this kind of business.

Many public governmental agencies are also developing complexes which approach those of the private sector. Public facilities containing indoor and/or outdoor swimming pools, ice skating rinks, saunas, tennis courts, racketball or handball courts, and community rooms are not nearly as unusual as they once were.

TRADE ASSOCIATIONS

Club Managers Association of America
1030 Fifteenth Street, N.W.
Washington, D.C. 20005

Mr. Lance Field, Executive Director
International Backpackers Association
P.O. Box 85
Lincoln Center, Maine 04458

TRADE JOURNALS

Cue Magazine
Cue Publishing Company
20 West 43 Street
New York, N.Y. 10036
Ed. Stanley Newman Publ. Ed. Leob

HOME'S ASSOCIATIONS _____

A growing number of people in the United States are purchasing homes in subdivisions, condominiums, or lake housing developments because of the location of the recreation and leisure services associated with the development, or the facilities that are built in conjunction with them. Developers long ago have found that added recreation facilities such as a swimming pool, large park area, golf course, lake, or other added recreation or leisure attraction help sell homes. In some of the more highly developed areas, the individual who purchases a home within the subdivision has access to a country club, a golf course, a lake, tennis courts, and a swimming pool restricted to those who are members of the subdivision and their friends. In most cases, as an individual purchases a home in these communities they automatically must become a member of the "Home's Association," and pay dues to help maintain and program the facilities. Many condominiums also have their own private swimming pool and tennis courts. These, as well as the home's associations, may have a part-time or full-time recreation-social director who is responsible for organizing, promoting, and implementing recreation programs and activities of various kinds for the adults and children belonging to the association. Some more highly organized and unified groups have incorporated themselves as a legal municipality within the state and the association then also becomes a form of government. Because of the diversity of the types of development corporations and contractors that are building these kinds of facilities, there is no accurate number at the present time of these types of associations. In one county in Missouri there were found over 40 lake housing subdivisions. In areas around large cities, the number of condominiums and home associations may run into the hundreds.

Another equally new development in this area is the use of park and recreation trained personnel to help plan and develop recreation oriented subdivisions or retirement areas. Although recreation land sales is by no means new, the trend toward orienting buyers is a recreation development. A number of large development corporations have employed park and recreation trained personnel to work as a part of the planning team, in the sales end of the enterprise, or in planning and operating recreation program sevices as an amenity to the projects.

Experts in the parks and recreation field see this as one of the growing areas of opportunities for park and recreation graduates in the future.

TRADE ASSOCIATIONS

The Community Associations Institute
1200 18th Street, N.W.
Washington, D.C. 20036

SECOND HOME DEVELOPMENTS

The second home market is a substantial one reflecting current changes in expenditures and desires by the American public. A good deal of work in this area has been done by the Urban Land Institute, 1200 18th Street, N.W., Washington, D.C. 10036. These second homes, although at first glance appear to be independent and unrelated to each other or to recreation facilities, are increasingly being developed in clusters and groups, to take advantage of ski lodges, beaches, mountain retreats, golf courses, harbors, campgrounds, park shopping service establishments, and a multitude of other facilities. The desire for a private recreation experience continues to grow each year with the increased problems with travel, crowds, and overused facilities. There are approximately 1.55 million second homes in the United States, with 38 percent being in the northeast, 30 percent being in the north central, 17 percent in the south, 15 percent in the west. Golf, snow skiing, water sports, and a variety of other recreational activities form the basis upon which most second home communities are built. Although many second homes are built in areas of aesthetic and natural beauty, and this is the primary purpose for the primary objection of those who purchase these, many more buy second homes in communities to participate in sports activities which more often is forming the heart of the successful second home or resort community. Most larger developments, rather than relying on a single form of recreation, combine two or more within the project and more and more are attempting to provide four-season appeal and desirability, with snowmobiling activities, or winter health spa work-out facilities, compliment and in conjunction with regular summer facilities activities and programs. These second home developers are using the same philosophies that the community associations developers are using, except that they normally are located in areas removed from the centers of population and cater to a higher income clientele because of the nature of the second home.

Since 1974 however, resort condominiums and second home developments are no longer the thriving business they once were, and they now face a very cloudy future because of a number of factors including high prices, tight money, over saturation, and construction and gasoline shortages. Sales are down one-third from 1973 on purchases in resort areas. It is estimated that there are 15 to 20 million unsold vacant lots in the country containing 35 to 40 million acres.

One million resort lots have been subdivided in the last five years, but homes have been built on only about 13 percent of the lots sold. According to the American Land Development Association, individuals may still be interested in buying, however they estimate that 25 percent of the potential customers have already bought lots, and 57 percent will have bought by 1977. They suggest that individuals should consider purchase for recreation use only, but not for speculation. The Southeast appears to be the primary vacation property area. The after-tax profit of land development companies have declined 50 percent since 1968. There are a number of problems which land developers have been confronted with in second home developments.

Municipalities and counties are down zoning land, to inhibit or retard growth. They have no growth policies in terms of planning, extension of city services, and so on. The gasoline shortages have also caused problems. The land developers are facing considerable pressure from the ecology and conservation groups as well as consumer groups.

Some experts believe there is still a market for the smaller town houses or condominiums at single sport resorts close to urban areas. The future suggests that condominiums be sold on a multiple ownership basis with each owner paying a part and sharing the facility at different times, a plan similar to Sea Pines 40 to 60 acre sports garden in cities which has a full range of leisure activities evening entertainment and shopping facilities to which memberships can be sold.

TRADE ASSOCIATIONS

Urban Land Institute
1200 18th Street, N.W.
Washington, D.C. 20036

Summary

The providers of Recreation and Leisure Services can be divided generally into three major groups, 1. Public agencies providing areas and facilities, 2. Private enterprises providing areas and facilities and service, and 3. Private nonprofit organizations and agencies providing areas, facilities, or services.

The ORRRC outdoor recreation 1965 study of private outdoor recreation enterprises was the first effort to assess the private leisure service sector as a whole. Even though a sample was taken, it supplied a wealth of information not previously on hand.

The United States Bureau of Standards Industrial Classification (SIC) System probably is the best and most accurate barometer of the actual increase in numbers and sales of recreation enterprises for profit.

The National Association of Conservation Districts private sector recreation inventory of 1975 is the most recent attempt to assess the number and location of the various types of recreation enterprises.

There continues to be a problem of categorization of private and commercial enterprises for profit. However the following categories seem to provide the least amount of overlap between areas.

1. Spectators activities.
2. Outdoor attractions and amusements
3. Participating individual activities.
4. Mechanized sports and activities.
5. Clubs, resorts, and second homes.

The past two years have seen a rapid increase in the number of enterprises providing recreation and leisure services, and a consistent upgrading of the facilities in these enterprises. It has exceeded the inflation rate, and is the fastest growing aspect of the national economy.

Regardless of the rate of increase of the supply however, it appears that the demand for recreation will continue to increase at a much faster rate, and probably is unrealistic to expect the supply to ever keep pace with the demand. As soon as an additional facility is developed, the demand rises to saturate it. Several alternatives still exist for meeting the demand. These include cooperative joint efforts between public and private enterprises, leasing, easements, concessions, by private enterprise on public lands, and the use of more private land for public and private services.

Additional References

Books, Bulletins, and Reports

Dice, Eugene F., *Michigan's Commercial Horse Enterprises—A Directory and Study, Department of Park and Recreation Resources,* Cooperative Extension Service—March 24, 1971, Michigan State University, East Lansing.

Hines, Thomas I., *Revenue Sources Management in Parks and Recreation,* National Recreation and Park Association, Arlington, Virginia 1974.

Outdoor Recreation Resources Review Commission, *Private Outdoor Recreation Facilities,* ORRRC Study Report II, Superintendent of Documents, Washington D.C. 1962.

Schroder, David R., *Now They're Hot—Consider Tennis, Sailing, Bicycling,* Cooperative Extension Service, University of Minnesota, Duluth, **10** No. 3. December 1972.

Discussion Questions

1. In what ways does the Federal Government provide recreation opportunities that no other agency can logically provide?
2. Why is it important that public agencies cooperate with private recreation agen-

cies? How can this cooperation be promoted?

3. What are the career implications of the Bureau of Outdoor Recreation study of private recreation enterprise to the recreator contemplating entering the commercial recreation field?

4. In what ways do outdoor amusement parks serve the needs of the American public?

5. Should sports convention and entertainment facilities be operated as public or private facilities? Why?

6. Why would a bowling center be a good investment? What services do they provide and how can they be expanded in their services?

7. In what respects are commercial wilderness outfitter partners with the federal government?

8. What special training should the owner of a wilderness outfitter possess?

9. What factors contributed to the growth of commercial resident camping in the United States?

10. What types of camps comprise the commercial camping movement in America?

11. Considering commercial travel camps are in competition with public campground facilities, what stratagies and opportunities are available to the private owner to successfully compete with the public agency?

12. What factors contributed to the renewed interest in bicycling? Do you see this interest continuing during the next decade? Why?

13. Analyze the factors necessary to be a successful private motorcycle riding park owner.

14. Suppose an investor offered to back you in building and developing a small boat mariner at a nearby lake. First, the investor wants you to answer the following questions: What are the advantages and disadvantages of this type of business; and what services would you recommend your marina offer the public? Discuss your answers to the investors questions.

15. Considering the cost of fuel and inflation what is you prediction for the future of recreational vehicle sales?

16. In what ways can recreation amenities support real estate sales?

CHAPTER 5

MANAGEMENT OF THE RECREATION ENTERPRISE

ORGANIZATIONAL THEORY

While it is not the purpose of this chapter to discuss the many types of organizations and management methods, a word about organizational theory is appropriate.

Any organization must have some form and structure in order to accomplish the goals or objectives of the enterprise. Everyone must answer to someone. In light of the objectives, someone must decide how the tasks are to be assigned in order to accomplish the ultimate objective. Obviously one person can not do it all, therefore an organization of some kind is enviable. Even in the smallest enterprises, such as a campground of 100 units, the owner must either do all the work, or assign part of it to his wife, his children, or others who are hired part time or full time. While the organizational structure in small enterprises usually will be implied and unwritten, there still must be levels of management.

If the objectives of the organization are to be accomplished, the following functions must be provided for.

1. *Planning.* What are the objectives of the enterprise. What programs, activities, or services should be provided to meet the objectives.
2. *Organizing.* How should the plans be carried out. How will the work be allocated or divided. What organizational or departmental units should be established to carry out the basic tasks, duties, or functions. What relationships should exist between units of operation.
3. *Staffing and Resourcing.* Who is to perform the many and varied tasks. What human, material, and financial resources are available.
4. *Directing.* Who will oversee how the work is being carried out. How are the orders to be issued to get the enterprise operating and carrying out its function. Who will direct the general operations.
5. *Coordinating.* How will the various units or departments work together as a team toward the enterprise objectives.
6. *Controlling.* How will the assigned tasks be carried out. Are they conforming to

agreed upon plans. Are they meeting the time schedules and quality desired.
7. *Evaluating.* Were the objectives accomplished. Could the services be improved.

A number of different management experts list the above elements of administration differently. While they may vary from organization to organization, the general functions will be found in every enterprise, regardless of its size or services.

A necessary by product of these functions is departmentalization. Groups of responsibilities and tasks must be grouped together. How this will be done depends on the kinds of services rendered. While there are a number of ways to group these tasks, the most common method is according to function or purpose such as food, lodging, recreation, construction and maintenance, finance and accounting, and personnel.

Because the effective span of control, that is, the number of persons another person can effectively supervise, is normally between 4 to 10, most enterprises of any size must departmentalize into 4 to 10 departments, usually based on the above functions. You will note the organizational chart illustrating these in Figure 32 as being roughly pyramid shaped. This is fairly common in business. The flatter the pyramid, the more delegation of authority, more autonomy of departments and personnel, the more independent the results, however, it will provide less control, and more problems with delegation of responsibilities. On the other hand, the taller the pyramid, the tighter the control, the better the delegation of authority, the more controlled work and output, more supervision, but the longer the time to communicate with the workers.

Regardless of the ways of considering the functions of management or the type of organization which will allow the objectives to be accomplished the best, these considerations should be given attention in all enterprises, large or small.

Every owner, operator, or manager of a recreation enterprise has for his ultimate objective making a profit. Unfortunately, according to the Small Business Administration, approximately 50 percent of all businesses fail. This fact is particularly significant in the recreation business area, where the percentage may be even higher. Every individual responsible for an enterprise wants that business to succeed, that is, to produce sufficient income above expenses, to provide for their family, and to supply a satisfactory return on the investment involved.

Unfortunately, many times the management aspects of the recreation business are taken for granted. This may be a result of a lack of understanding concerning the importance, or a lack of information and education on how to manage. The lack of understanding of the financial aspects of management probably contribute to more business failures than any other aspect. The Small Business Administration reports that the major cause of business failures is not lack of capital, as might be expected, but a lack of managerial expertise.

Although the manager or operator must eventually base all of his decisions on the effect they will have on his public, or his market, the ultimate test of management is how well those in that market can be attracted, provided service, and returned home happy to share the "good news" of the enterprise with others. The methods, procedures, and techniques to accomplish these goals are all encompassed under the managerial aspects and responsibilities of the operator.

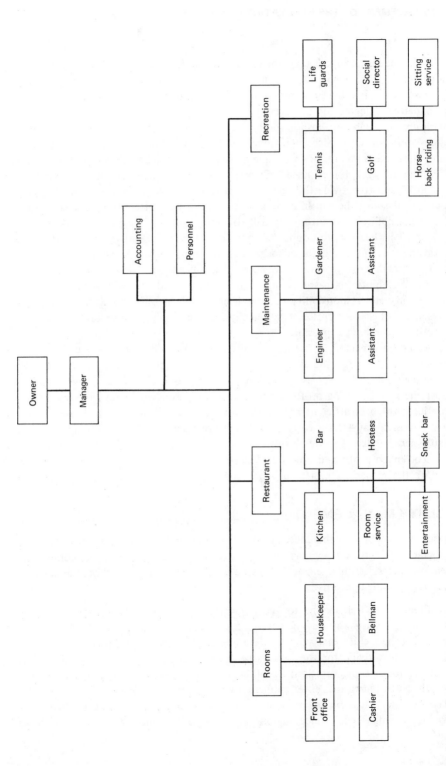

Figure 32 This organizational chart may be similar to those used in a number of recreation resorts. It reflects services in two components of travel, tourism, and recreation, that of food and lodging, recreation and entertainment.

Whether the farmer opens up a portion of his land for hunting, or a pond for fishing on a part-time basis, or whether a group of business executives invest in a large marina-motel resort complex, the principles of management are much the same, the difference being a matter of degree and complexity.

Basically the managers responsibility may be divided into five management areas; facilities, program or services, personnel, finances, and sales. As might be expected, each of these areas are inter-related, and a decision in one area will certainly affect the others. The manager, for instance, will desire to hire sufficient personnel to maintain the facilities and to provide the services or programs. However he is not limited in the amount of personnel he can hire, because this will indeed effect the financial portion of his responsibilities and ultimately will effect his "bottom line," that is, his profit or loss figure. Let there be no doubt, this bottom line profit or loss is the ultimate judge and yardstick of how well the manager has performed his responsibilities. Granted, outside factors that are beyond the managers control can effect this figure significantly, including availability of gasoline, location, weather, and others; however, it is the managers duty and responsibility to himself and to his investors to ultimately manage the resources of the enterprise, whether physical, personal, or financial—to cause the net profit to be as high as possible.

As would be expected, if the manager becomes too ambitious, and cuts personnel to below what is needed and slights attention to the program or services of the facilities, he may indeed be increasing his profit, at least for a short time. However, in the long run he may be losing profit, as the visitors or guests will detect an excessive profit motive with an insufficient program or service, and will not return. Therefore, the manager must always strive to strike the delicate balance between sufficient charges and sufficient service. Too much service and not enough profit results in the obvious result. Too much profit and not enough service, will in fact result in the same result. Therefore the manager's motto may be "the best service for the maximum profit."

FACILITY MANAGEMENT

It is not the function of this material to discuss in detail the management of facilities or programs, as these vary widely among the myriad types of private and commercial recreation enterprises that exist. The management of any facility should at least include the following concerns:

1. Facilities of sufficient size to accommodate the program or services. This may seem like an easy way out, however many individuals will in fact plan in reverse, providing the facility first and then determining the program and services.
2. Facilities to provide for the other aspects of the recreation experience, including lodging, food, transportation, or other services for which the guests are there, whether it be recreation, entertainment, or relaxation.
3. The facilities must be maintained in an attractive and acceptable manner. This would encompass daily cleaning and seasonal maintenance. The maintenance of

Figure 33 In some enterprises such as bowling, facility maintenance must be given a primary consideration in management.
Courtesy: AMF Bowling Products Group West Berry, New York.

the facility, must be accomplished through proper determination of priorities of the work to be done and either performed by the operator himself in a small enterprise, or assigned to other personnel.

It should be kept in mind that a significant portion of the recreation experience for the traveler involves aesthetics. The popularity of the theme attraction park would suggest that people want to go where the surroundings are beautifully designed as well as maintained, and will expect to find the facilities and grounds at least as well kept as the homes from which they come. Poor maintenance can contribute as much to a poor recreation experience for the visitor as can poor hospitality.

In an effort to provide the visitor with a beautiful and creative environment, most themed parks change decorations and decor every year and maintain them religiously during the tourist season. This also provides a much greater incentive for the return visit.

PROGRAM OR SERVICES MANAGEMENT

If the program or services are insufficient to attract visitors or gain their return business, all other aspects of management are mute issues. If the guests are not housed according to their desires, treated courteously in all transactions, fed to their liking, and entertained or recreated according to their desires, they probably will not return. As it will be seen later, up to 30 percent of the typical recreation businesses income may be from repeat visitors; therefore, this takes on a great deal of importance. Discussions in the chapter on marketing indicate that the manager must assess as closely as possible the expectations of the guests, and strive in every way to provide the guests with these amenities, in order that their experience may indeed match the managers expectations. If so they will return home happy and satisfied, and hopefully tell their friends. If not they will return disappointed, and probably also tell their friends.

Granted the small recreation enterprise manager perhaps will not have control over the lodging, food, or transportation aspects of the visit, however the manager does have control over the recreation, entertainment, or relaxation portions, which account for the primary purpose for which the guest is at the location at that time. The manager must strive in every way to provide a program and/or services that meet the needs of the guests—even to the extent of overcoming the inadequacies of some of the other aspects.

The manager must assess the programs or services offered by competition and strive to provide services of equal or better value. Visits to other similar enterprises would seem to be a necessity to gain additional ideas, and to evaluate the managers operation in light of the competition.

Program management can be accomplished through proper planning, and proper assignment of responsibilities.

PERSONNEL MANAGEMENT

Many managers will say that the management of personnel is the most difficult of the four management areas. The other aspects of management are in terms of tangibles, while management of people includes many intangibles, such as behavior, motivation, personality, or relationships. While goals can be set and obtained in the other three areas, personnel goals are difficult to establish and more difficult to measure. Successful management of personnel may be defined in terms of turnover rate, the comments of feedback of other employees, feedback for guests, and a very intangible and subjective judgement concerning employee or staff morale.

It is particularly important in the recreation business, because of the importance of hospitality to the guest, to achieve a friendly and cordial attitude on the part of the employees toward the guests. In many cases, the personality of the manager can influence the resulting attitudes and behaviors of the employees in the atmosphere of the enterprise as a whole. Therefore it is vitally important that the manager take stock of his own attitudes, behavior traits, and his relationships with his employees and the guests, for this will in many respects be the example and standard for the other employees, as well as the yardstick which the manager, whether he realizes it or not, will

Figure 34 In some recreation resorts such as dude ranches, obtaining qualified personnel is vital.
Courtesy: American Hotel and Motel Association, New York, New York.

use to measure how valuable the employees are to the organization. People tend to judge others according to themselves. Therefore the management of personnel, must be in with the manager.

The recreation enterprise will be judged by the guests to a greater extent on the basis of the impression of the staff and the courtesy's and hospitalities extended them, than by the facilities or program. The enterprise is judged by the friendliness of the staff, their alertness, their attitude, their outlook, and their desire to be of help and assistance.

The most important asset of any business is its human resources. The manager's job is then to organize these resources and to use their value in obtaining organizational objectives.

Those who have worked with people and employees find that the work is never simple, but the value of getting people to work not only for you but with you, can pay handsome dividends in the end. It is not only important to obtain good employees, train them to do their job well, but to retain them. Their feelings about their job, the employee morale, and motivation, all are important factors in the retention of employees.

RECRUITMENT

The first step in the personnel procedure is that of recruitment. In many recreation enterprises, because of their nature, location, or business, may be owner operated, with no additional full-time employees other than the members of the owners family. He may however require additional part-time help during the peak season, usually during the summer. If the manager anticipates employing even one person, the following procedures will be appropriate. However, the bigger the enterprise, the more sophisticated the procedures become.

The important prerequisites to recruiting employees, are (1) job descriptions and, (2) job specifications. Although the manager may have a clear idea in his mind of the responsibility he anticipates the employee to have, and the qualifications the potential employee needs to carry these out, many times it is difficult to convey these to perspective employees or employees after hiring. A good manager will set down in writing the job description as nearly as it can be described, which will include the duties and responsibilities of the potential employee. This of course should be done in light of responsibilities of other employees and a delineation of areas of responsibilities and authority to eliminate as much overlap as possible. This helps both prior to hiring and after hiring, as most personnel conflicts arise because of poor delineation of job responsibilities and authorities. It also helps in establishing lines of authority and accountability. The description should cover such things as what is to be done, the reason for doing it, how and when it is to be done, and who is to do it. It should also relate how the job may coordinate with other duties, responsibilities of others in the organization and the extent of authority assigned with it. A sample job description is shown in Figure 35.

The job specifications are also an intrical part of the job description. They outline the necessary physical and mental requirements, skills and training desired, hours and wage scales, qualifications, prerequisites required, and other benefits such as meals, insurance, vacations, bonuses, possibilities of advancement, etc.

In advertising the position, as much information as possible should be given so as to eliminate the necessity for communicating or interviewing numbers of applicants which are not really interested or qualified. Sources of possible applicants will vary according to the type of enterprise. Seasonal workers can many times be obtained from colleges and universities, and although they are not highly trained in the specific aspects of the recreation enterprise, they are usually amenable to education, and have extra amounts of enthusiasm and motivation. It is best to locate someone who has had some experience, if possible so that they understand the kind of work they will be employed to do, and will be able to learn how to relate to the guests much more quickly. The state unemployment service or colleges nearby may be possible sources of employment for applicants. Advertisements in newspapers, word-of-mouth by friends, are also important.

Figure 35 Sample Job Description[A]

DIRECTOR SPORTS AND ATHLETICS

Dependent on the needs of the recreation program, the sports and athletics director position may include specialization in programs for either sex or in one type of athletics.

Duties

1. Promotes and develops recreation programs for the enterprise through individual and team sports and athletics activities of all types.
2. Organizes and leads guest groups in athletics and sports activities with an emphasis on the activities' recreational and social value.
3. Incorporates sports and athletics into the total philosophy of recreation, and interprets this to guests and potential guests.
4. Helps participants to attain greater skills in and enjoyment from sports and athletics, and encourages individuals and groups to explore various related activities.
5. Plans and initiates a comprehensive program of games, athletics, and sports activities for all appropriate ages and for both sexes.
6. Assists in training and supervising assistants in athletics and sports.
7. Consults with the director of activities and entertainment (of there is one) and other superiors on the place of athletics and sports in the recreation program.
8. Searches out and adapts new experiences in games, sports and athletics for use in the recreation program.
9. Demonstrates above average playing skills in the activities for which he is responsible.
10. Arranges for and directs tournaments, exhibitions, public demonstrations, shows, or other special events in the specialty, as part of the enterprise program.
11. Recommends and assists in the optimum use of facilities and equipment available for games, sports, and athletics at the recreation center.
12. Insures that all desirable safety precautions are observed in each activity and gives first aid.
13. Keeps records and accounts; reports to supervisors on groups or individuals, plans and problems; recommends action, and carries out policies in leading the special activity.
14. Requisitions, issues, receives, and oversees the use of materials and equipment for athletic activities; recommends the repair or disposal of such equipment and materials for the athletics program.

SPECIAL QUALIFICATIONS

Personal skill in the leadership of sports and athletics and technical understanding of the rules, regulations and standards governing them. Professional ability to conduct recreation groups in athletics, games and sports at beginning and advanced skill levels. Ability to promote and organize team, dual and individual sports programs; and to develop an athletics program for all ages. Skill in establishing and maintaining effective working relationships with participants, associates and the public. Thorough knowledge of the theory and philosophy of recreation, and its application to individual and group behavior with particular emphasis on sports and athletics.

MINIMUM QUALIFICATIONS

Graduation from a college or university of recognized standing with either a Bachelor's degree based on a major in recreation leadership including supervised field work, and special emphasis in physical activities, sports and athletics; or a Bachelor's degree in physical education, and special emphasis equivalent to a minor concentration in recreation leadership, plus leadership experience in a variety of sports or in some other phase of recreation equivalent to a three-months period of full-time field work.

Figure 35 A job description is the first step in the recruiting and hiring process. Courtesy: Adapted from Personnel Standards in Community Recreation Leadership. National Recreation and Park Association, Arlington, Virginia 1957.

[A] Adapted from; *Personnel Standards in Community Recreation Leadership,* National Recreation and Park Association, Arlington V.A., 1957.

SELECTION

After the position has been publicized, the operator must screen the applicants, and will no doubt desire to interview those who he assumes will make the best employees. It is only courtesy to communicate either with a form letter or individual written letters to those who have applied indicating the status of their application particularly whether or not they have passed the initial screening process.

During the interview, the employer will attempt to discern such things as the following:

1. Analyze the background and experience.
2. Assess the enthusiasm and motivation.
3. Discern why the employee wants the job and what his/her goals and objectives are.
4. Will he/she return the following year.
5. Will he/she relate well to the rest of the staff.
6. Does he/she have some understanding of the nature of the duties and responsibilities at present.
7. Will he/she need sufficient orientation and inservice training or consultation.
8. Will he/she make a good impression upon the guests.
9. Is his/her appearance satisfactory.
10. What do others feel about his/her efforts.

Questions concerning the following may be contrary to civil rights and equal opportunity employment guidelines.[1]

1. Address.
2. Membership in organizations.
3. Photo.
4. Relatives.
5. Recommendations.
6. Military experience.
7. Academic background.
8. Educational level.
9. Arrests and convictions.
10. Social Security status.
11. Employment tests.
12. Height requirements.
13. Weight.
14. Marital status.
15. Ownership of a car or home.

Many personnel officers would advise that although they put a good deal of stock in the personal interview, they also run the risk of being mislead and making final

[1] From ADMINISTRATIVE MANAGEMENT MAGAZINE, Excerpted from Administrative Management, copyrighted © 1974 by Geyer-McAllister, Publications, Inc., New York.

judgements based primarily on personal impression and less on other information and facts available. One of the best resources for learning about the potential employee is the personal recommendation. References should be called if possible. Although many managers rush through the recruitment and selection process, extra time and care in this area may save many hours in future aspects of the personnel program including orientation, in-service training, and consultation. To some extent, the maximum potential of the position is established with the hiring of the employee. Individuals can improve, but only within limits. It is of significant importance to obtain the best individuals possible, so that the greatest potential for contribution goals and objectives of the enterprise are achieved.

ORIENTATION

No good manager would hire an employee and start him on the job without some kind of orientation procedure. Without this orientation, the employed would have to learn by trial and error, which consumes time and effort and many times creates a bad impression on the guests as well. On-the-job training is, of course, part of the learning process. The orientation should cover the following points:[2]

1. What is to be done? Do you state clearly what is to be done? Are materials, tools, and supplies ready or ordered? Do you indicate what equipment and tools are to be used? Do employees understand what to do?
2. How is it to be done? Do you explain clearly how the job is to be done? Do the employees understand the method to be used? Do you consider if there is a better way to do it? Do you provide for the employees to use their own judgment?
3. Why is it to be done? Do you explain why the job is important? Does the employee understand why you chose this method?
4. Who is going to do it? Do you state clearly who is to do it? Is the employee capable of doing it? How are they likely to react to your orders? Do they have enough authority to do it? Have they time to do it along with other work assignments? Is there a loophole to permit "buck passing"?
5. Where is it to be done? Do you indicate where the job is to be done? If materials or equipment are needed, do you indicate where to get them?
6. When is it to be done? Do you state clearly when the job is to start? Is it clear when the work is to be completed? If urgent, do you indicate urgency or priority over other work?
7. What are your own feelings and attitude toward the receiver? Are you friendly but firm? Do you confidently expect the order to be carried out?
8. Did you follow up to see if the order was carried out?

[2] Robert W. McIntosh, *Employee Motivation and Work Incentives,* Extension Bulletin 483, Cooperative Extention Service, Michigan State University, July 1966, p. 3.

IN-SERVICE TRAINING

Follow-up and continuous discussion of duties and responsibilities should be a part of the in-service training program. Weekly staff meetings, other follow-up orientation sessions more indepth than those at the beginning, and presentations by outside resource persons concerning specifics of the responsibility all contribute to a program of continued learning and education by the employee. It should not be assumed that the on-the-job training and day-to-day supervision is completely adequate for the best results. The in-service training program however is one of the most neglected aspects of personnel but offers the greatest potential to eliminate future problems and to act as a preventive measure for potential probelm causing situations in the future. It also helps instill confidence in the employee and interest in his job.

SUPERVISION OR CONSULTATION

The checklist mentioned previously is an excellent tool to use in evaluating effectiveness of supervision as well as orientation procedures. Unfortunately most personnel managers and supervisors only hold consultation sessions when they find actions or behaviors that are inappropriate. This creates a poor mental image for the employee. Regular individual consultation sessions should be scheduled to discuss both the favorable attributes of the employees work, as well as the unfavorable. It is in these sessions that the supervisor and the employee can become better acquainted, and can learn to relate better with each other, and discuss items of mutual concern with the least amount of anxiety and anticipation. The better the orientation and in-service training, the smaller amount of supervision and consultation sessions that eventually will be required. The supervisory process is not complete if the employee is only told what to do and inform the employee whether they are doing it correctly, and to show them how to do it correctly if they are not.

THE PROBATIONARY PERIOD

An all important aspect of the personnel procedure is the probationary period. Although many seasonal enterprises will not have the need or require such a period, its importance in the year-round position is highly underestimated. The employee should know that both the employee and the employer are on probation, and that either can terminate employment at any time during the probationary period. This allows the employer an opportunity to evaluate the work of the employee and to discern whether or not the employee is suitable for the task. It also allows the employee an opportunity to leave without the impression that she is quitting if she finds the work unsuitable. In essence this becomes separation by mutual consent. Such a period also gives additional emphasis to orientation and in-service training programs as well as evaluation, and will build in opportunities for the other valuable aspects of good personnel procedure.

EVALUATION

Many a personnel procedure ends with supervision. However, there is an additional step that is an integral part of the personnel policy, and must be given just consideration. The employee may be more effected by the evaluation, how it is done, on what basis it is done, and the rewards and punishments than on all the other aspects of the personnel procedure together. Every employee deserves to know on what basis they will be evaluated. This should be quantifiable as much as possible, and should relate directly to the job description. Explanations such as "do what I want done as quickly and as well as possible" are not effective. The staff members deserves to know exactly what is expected of them, in measurable terms with time limits prescribed, and what the rewards are for accomplishing those objectives. The whole philosophy of management by objectives or management by results hinges on this philosophy of determining with the employee the desired results in quantifiable and measurable terms, and the rewards or punishments or lack thereof for satisfactory attainment of those results. If possible the evaluation should be in written form, and should be periodic at specific intervals during the probationary period. These should be discussed in the supervisory consultation meetings. At the end of the probationary period, an evaluation should be rendered and a decision made whether the employee will be kept or terminated.

At regular intervals thereafter, evaluations should be prepared, incentives discussed, and discussion of morale made.

STAFF MORALE AND WORK INCENTIVES

The previous discussion of personnel related almost entirely to the objectives of the manager and of the organization or agency. In order for the employees to do the best job for the manager, some of their own objectives must be taken into consideration and ultimately met also, otherwise the employee will be or may be disgruntled, unmotivated, and less than a valuable resource for the agency.

The importance of the attitude and management method skills of the manager has previously been stated. A democratic type of delegating of responsibility, with the employees having the opportunity to share their ideas and agree with the manager on what the objectives of the work should be, creates much higher employee morale than does the autocratic type of organization where the manager makes all the decisions and the employees are more or less there to serve the manager. Many books on organizational structure in business have been written on this topic. Although the autocratic form is more immediately responsive and in the end perhaps more efficient, job satisfaction is less, labor turnover is higher, and employee morale is down. In an industry that counts heavily on the attitude of the employees as a selling point of the business, it would seem crucial that a democratic form of organization and supervision be established.

It must always be remembered that employees are people, not just a part of the organization or a cog in the machine that goes on hour after hour, day after day. They are individuals with likes, dislikes, feelings, and ideas, and can provide unlimited resources for the agency, or do the minimum required on their jobs. The question which must ultimately and continually be asked, is "what is the employee's goal, what is in it for him."

The processes, techniques, and procedures used in making the individual feel important to the total effort and the rewards given accordingly in an effort to help them meet their own personal objectives will help determine to a large extent the success of the agency in meeting its objectives through the use of human resources. Such items and fringe benefits as group life insurance, medical coverage bonuses, credit unions, and other events such as staff parties or meetings, which involve the employee as well as their families help to establish a good relationship between management and staff.

An effective mechanism must be established for the airing of complaints and grievances that the employees must have. If they are not encouraged to provide feedback or is made to feel out of place if they present a complaint, they will seek other ways to vent their pent-up dissatisfactions. This is how unions get their start. It is vitally important to seek and use the employees ideas, and to allow them flexibility to seek solutions to problems in their own areas.

Every successful agency must provide some mechanism for keeping employees informed. This tends to make employees feel important, and will minimize rumors that may start in various ways. Other ideas suggested by various authors for improving morale include expressing personal interest in employees, instilling pride in work well done, and providing effective supervision.

Many psychologists believe that people cannot motivate other people, they can only provide incentives for the individuals to motivate themselves. Others have written concerning the hierarchy of needs that each individual strives to achieve, beginning with the physiological needs of food, hunger, and bodily functions, safety and free from fear, social well being, sense of achievement and self esteem. It should be understood that while some work incentives are valuable for some of the employees, they are not valuable for others. Part of this reason hinges on which of the various needs in the hierarchy have been met. A met need is no longer a motivating incentive for the employee.

The primary reward of course is money, through raises, pay increases, bonuses, profit sharing, cost reduction for services or products, or deferred payment plans of various kinds. Psychologically the more frequently the bonuses paid the better. Rewards however may not be the same as motivating incentives. There are some psychologists however that have indicated that more money does not necessarily make a person work better. It may influence their behavior for a short time, but money can be used to reward those who have shown good work, and to provide the individual with the incentive to stay with the company so that they are not easily attracted elsewhere. It has been well established that after a person reaches a certain level of income, they are motivated by other types of incentives, and although money as an incentive is not eliminated, it is certainly not the first priority. "Job conditions" such as pay, work surroundings, vacations, and fringe benefits may tend to prevent an employee from being motivated if they are absent or substandard, but will not tend to be factors that can be used to motivate employees over a period of time. Factors that do tend to motivate include those listed by McIntosh;[3] recognition, praise, achievement, responsibility, promotion, better placement, and social prestige. It is difficult to determine which of these will be particularly effective with any one employee, but it is assured that superior employee performance will be obtained only when an employee's social and self-esteem needs are supplied on the job. A career ladder within the organization is an important tool. In the small enterprise, this of course is difficult, and may be the reason why they experience a good deal of turnover. With the owner-operator, several part-time employees and perhaps only one or more full-time employees, there is no upward mobility.

In the end however the employees must feel that their job helps them meet their individual needs, and improves their view of themselves. Their job must enhance this feeling for self confidence, strength, worth, and usefulness to the business organization. Denying these on the other hand will lead to discouragement, frustration, lower employee morale, and eventually perhaps sabotage.

It is therefore vital that each employee be invited and expected to assist and participate in management; thus each has a part to play in reaching the ultimate objectives of both the organization and those of the individual. The degree to which these are met on both sides will be the degree to which the manager is successful in an effort to build a better management team and strengthen the agency as well as himself as leader.

FINANCIAL MANAGEMENT

Every manager has as the ultimate objective to make a profit. It is only through the use of financial records that they can tell how close they are to achieving this goal, and gain the necessary information to change their course or plan to meet this objective.

It is not possible in this day and age to conduct even the simplest operation without some kind of records. Records are needed for a number of reasons.

1. To determine the current status of the business.
2. To assist in filing income taxes.
3. To determine the extent of income and expenses.
4. To evaluate the results of the responsibility that has been delegated to others.
5. To inform investors, lenders, and others concerning the status of the investment.
6. To inform potential buyers of the enterprise should that be the situation.
7. To comply with government regulations concerning Social Security, sales tax, and so on.

Whether the manager uses the simplest accounting form, which consists of a record of income, and the checkbook which is a record of expenses, or more complex departmentalized cash income and dispursement statements, elaborate balance sheets, or

[3] Ibid p. 4 and 5.

profit and loss statements, the type of records used must be determined by the kind of financial information desired.

Regardless of the type of management, or the financial objectives of the agency of the manager, his financial objectives are two.

1. *Liquidity.* The manager must provide for receiving the income or the receipts to the business and for paying the bills, and for making sure that there is enough cash so that the bills can be paid on time, so as not to effect the credit rating. The manager must therefore be concerned about the *cash inflow* and the *cash outflow* as he develops his cash budget. This can be predicted with some accuracy if good estimates can be made of income, and adequate records kept of dispursements. The forecast of the cash inflow and outflow is called a *cash budget*. The record of the actual amounts of transactions, will be kept on daily, monthly, and annual cash receipts and dispursements statements. In simple terms, the manager is concerned with keeping the income higher than the expenses. The seasonal aspect of the recreation business also complicates this process somewhat, as he will have significant expenses before the season opens, and therefore must allow for cash reserves or borrow money for short duration until such time as receipts are available. The income may indeed not exceed the expenses until late in the recreation season in some cases.

2. A second financial objective of the manager is to assure that the enterprise will provide sufficient income, and that the enterprise will generate enough additional profits to pay for the investment over a period of years. The manager is interested, of course, in maximizing his income, and maximizing the return on the investment, without endangering the liquidity or cash flow of the agency.

According to McIntosh[4] there are several things that can be done to maximize profit.

1. Improve the margin of profit on the sales. This can either be accomplished by increasing the sales volume or increasing the price.
2. Reducing expenses proportionately more than sales. A careful analysis will show areas where cuts can be saved or better buys can be made.
3. Improving turnover. Providing opportunities for more individuals to be served with the same number of facilities and employees.
4. Reducing the investment in certain assets such as making some buildings or facilities multiply use, leasing equipment or other arrangements.

Any of the above alternatives should be considered only after considerable thought and study of the "financial" status of enterprise, as determined from the financial records and reports of the enterprise.

---

[4] Robert W. McIntosh, *Management Through Figures*, Extension Bulletin 656, Cooperative Extension Service, Michigan State University, 1969, p. 5.

FUNCTIONS OF RECORDS

Financial records and reports service three basic functions: legal requirements, safeguarding assets, and plan and control operations.

To accomplish these functions, certain bookkeeping must be done. Bookkeeping is the clerical work of recording, posting, and filing the records of income and expenses. Accounting is the interpretation and analysis of the recorded transactions. The operator will need to decide early whether he intends to handle the bookkeeping and/or accounting functions himself, within his family, within his employees, or contract with someone outside the firm. Many small employers use small bookkeeping and accounting services that may handle a number of small accounts within a given area or community. Regardless of what procedure is used, there are a number of records and reports that are vital to the success of the operation. A number of these and other terms are defined in Appendix C.

1. Daily cash income.
2. Daily cash expenses.
3. Weekly, monthly, and annual income and expense record.
4. Profit and loss statements, weekly, monthly, or annually.
5. Tax records.
6. Mortgage and debt records.
7. Payroll records.
8. Balance sheet.
9. Inventory record.
10. Financial statements.

DAILY INCOME RECEIPTS

The income to the agency must be recorded daily. The daily income receipts are a record of the original transaction in whatever form that income comes to the agency or enterprise. The income may be grouped into various categories if there is more than one type of activity or enterprise for which money is received. It may be kept in the form of a cash register tape, handwritten receipts, admission tickets, or any number of other methods. The records should provide for some method of reconciling at the end of the day through numbered receipts, tickets, and so on.

DAILY EXPENSE RECORD

The expenses of the agency must also be recorded daily. The daily expense record normally will include all current expenses, whether by cash or check. These will include:

1. Personnel wages.
2. Utilities.
3. Supplies.

4. Equipment.
5. Advertising and promotion.
6. Repairs and maintenance.

A more elaborate breakdown can be developed if desired.

Other expenses that must be considered and charged on a monthly basis may include the following fixed charges.

1. Taxes.
2. Insurance.
3. Depreciation.
4. Interest.
5. Return on investment.

As many of the expenses as possible should be paid by check, which in essence acts as a receipt. If cash expenses must be met spontaneously, for delivery or purchases elsewhere, arrangements can be made for paid out slips and/or petty cash funds. Normally these are posted daily or weekly in a *general ledger journal.*

A double entry type of system of record keeping is the most desirable, where all the income is listed in one column near the left with various breakdowns in other columns to the right. This gives a double check on the totals and provides more financial information. The general ledger normally will include expenses for the fixed charges previously mentioned.

Unfortunately many managers have not followed sound accounting procedures in establishing separate reserve accounts for their various fixed charges. The government, for instance, requires a separate account for income tax withheld, and for Social Security withheld.

Special accounts should be established for depreciation and/or interest and return on investments. Many managers have failed to do so, and used these expenses as a part of their cash flow. When the time comes to pay insurance or to replace certain facilities, the funds are not there. This is certainly a short-sighted and hazardous type of financial management.

PROFIT AND LOSS STATEMENT OR SUMMARY

These statements can be prepared daily, weekly, or monthly to provide comparisons with past records and with the budget as prepared prior to the beginning of the period. An example of a profit and loss statement for a year can be found in Figure 37. It is a summary statement of revenues, expenses, and net income. It should also show the amount cash reserve.

TAX RECORDS

The state and federal governments require rather specific types of records to be kept for taxes and social security. Employee withholding records must be kept in two sep-

Figure 37 Profit and Loss Statement

CAMP GROUND

PROFIT AND LOSS STATEMENT
YEAR ENDING DECEMBER 31, 19

INCOME

Camp site rentals		$13,645	
Boat rentals		879	
Cost of goods sold			
Beginning inventory (store) January 1, 19	$1843		
Merchandise purchased	454		
Less ending inventory December 31, 19	1937		
Gross sales		360	
Total Income			$14,884

EXPENSES

Salaries and wages	$ 8,170	
Utilities	840	
Auto expenses	345	
Office supplies	251	
Pool supplies	240	
Advertising	259	
Repairs and maintenance	879	
Depreciation and amortization of land and facilities	1,670	
Total Expenses		$12,654
Profit from operation		$ 2,654
Income taxes		230
Net profit after taxes		$ 2,424

Figure 37 A simplified profit and loss statement for a campground.

arate places, which may be in the general ledger and in separate payroll records. Booklets are, of course, available from Internal Revenue Service to indicate the withholding rates. Social Security Records must also be kept very carefully. If the wrong amount of social security is withheld, the employer may not have any recourse but to make the additional contribution himself if the employee is no longer employed.

PAYROLL RECORDS

Payroll records should be kept in addition to the general ledger journal and should include rate of pay, gross pay for the pay period, amounts withheld for social security and local, state, and federal taxes. Space should be provided to add these amounts quarterly for social security and tax purposes.

MORTGAGE AND DEBT RECORDS

These records are rather individualized depending on the type of enterprise and the amount of the investment. These may include loans, bonds, or other types of mortgage or debt records.

BALANCE SHEET

In determining the amount of profit or loss, the rate of return usually increases as the risk goes up. For a marginal operation for which the investors are not sure whether a profit will be made, the return may be 15 to 20 percent. It probably always will be over ten percent, or the present value or time value of the earnings lost that could have been invested in treasury notes or other interest bearing accounts for an amount equal to the return on the investment on the enterprise.

The balance sheet, or the financial statement as it is sometimes called, will include the totals for the period, of revenue received, expenses, assets, liabilities, and is a summary of the organizations duties as of a particular date and is used in determining "actual" profit or loss, net worth, and return on investment. An example can be found in Figure 38.—

It will include a list of *current assets* which are those cash, marketables, securities, and other liquid assets such as receivables and inventories, which can be or will be consumed in a short time or converted into cash in an ordinary course of business.

Long-term assets are those of a more permanent nature concerning land, buildings, swimming pools, furniture, fixtures, and so on. Liabilities, items payable within one year, are likewise categorized.

The balance sheet may be departmentalized to show departmental profit, overhead, or fixed charges, if desired.

The balance sheet then is a statement of financial position. The assets indicate what is owned and the liabilities indicate what is owed, and the net worth indicates the value of the equity.

Figure 38 Balance Sheet

CAMP GROUND

BALANCE SHEET
DECEMBER 31, 19

Assets

Current Assets:			
Cash		$ 540	
Accounts receivables		56	
Inventory		1,904	
Total current assets			$ 2,500
Fixed Assets:			
Picnic tables, barbecue pits	$ 1,250		
less allowance for deprec.	750	$ 500	
Machinery and equipment	$ 3,500		
less allowance for deprec.	1,500	2,000	
Buildings—pool—campsites	$26,000		
less depreciation	4,000	22,000	
Land		13,000	
Total fixed assets			$37,500
Total Assets			$40,000

Liabilities

Current Liabilities:		
Accounts payable	$ 374	
Wages and salaries payable	188	
Allowance for taxes	438	
Total current liabilities		$ 1,000
Picnic tables, barbecue pits	750	
Machinery and equipment	2,500	
Buildings—pool—campsites	24,000	
Land	12,750	
Total Liabilities		$40,000

Figure 38 A simplified balance sheet for a campground.

BOOKKEEPING PROCEDURES

It goes without saying that all income should have receipts, and that all dispursements should have bills. A daily record should be kept of the revenue and expenses. An audit should also be taken annually that will pinpoint poor bookkeeping practices. If the manager has little accounting background himself, he may want to consider the services of a professional accountant to help him establish his record system for his particular operation.

There are a number of steps in the financial process.

1. Receiving the cash.
2. Post daily receipts.
3. Make deposits.
4. Record paid outs.
5. Verify invoices.
6. File invoices.
7. Write checks for bills.
8. Record purchases.
9. Post disbursements.
10. Prepare daily report.
11. Prepare payroll.
12. Prepare summary journals.
13. Prepare profit and loss statements.
14. Prepare other financial reports.
15. Reconcile bank statements.

WISCONSIN'S ONE-WRITE SYSTEM[5]

Because of the consistent poor booking practices found in many small recreation resort enterprises, Stephen Sellca of the Wisconsin Recreation Resources Center undertook a three-pronged program to help operators in his state with this problem. His program included the following:

1. Development of an accurate simple "one-write" in expensive bookkeeping control system that simplifies and organizes record systems and accounting information for operations control.
2. Development of a computerized management information system to provide managers with an analysis of his operation, marketing profiles, and comparisons between his operation and the industry as a whole.
3. Promotion of the above two programs and provide workshops and training sessions in their application and use.

---

[5] Stephen L. Selka, "One Write Bookkeeping and Management Information System for Wisconsin's Recreation Industry" Outlook, 3, Number 2, Summer, 1973, Cooperative Extension Programs, University of Wisconsin.

The *Bookkeeping Control System,* developed by McBee Brothers Forms, Inc., combines time-and-error-saving methods with records and forms designed for recreation businesses. More specifically, the system:

1. Collects income and cost data by profit center.
2. Complies information required for state and federal tax and labor forms.
3. Collects information needed for a daily business report, including the previous day's sales, cash balance, accounts payable, and accounts receivable position.

The "one-write" approach means that all necessary information concerning a transaction are written only once in the appropriate folding poster. The "appropriate" folding poster depends on the needs of the individual business.

The complete Bookkeeping Control System includes both a charges and receipts "sub-system," and some form of a disbursements sub-system. If the firm needs to compute FICA and withholding taxes on different amounts of employee earnings, separate cash disbursements and payroll sub-systems have been designed. In this case, the cash disbursements sub-system covers all expenses except payroll, and payroll expenses are handled by a separate sub-system. A combination disbursements and payroll sub-system is also available.

Since all of these sub-systems are complete in themselves, the "total package" doesn't need to be purchased, only the sub-systems applicable to industrial record-keeping. Each sub-system comes with a folding poster book, a journal binder for completed journal pages and the journal forms themselves. The separate payroll/disbursements sub-systems or the combination payroll/disbursements sub-system includes checks, envelopes and employee earnings record forms.

Pre-shingled checks or guest folios and duplicate journal pages are mechanically aligned in the folding poster. All forms are chemically coated paper (eliminating the need for carbon paper), so all forms may be filled out with only one writing. Thus, when a check is written or a guest folio prepared, the name of the person and the amount paid out or received are automatically recorded on two journal sheets. One is the journal page retained, and the Management Information System for analysis.

The second part of the program is the *Management Information System.* This system depends on the duplicate journal pages you provide but takes little of your effort since the actual analysis is done by computers at the University of Wisconsin.

If the Bookkeeping Control System is used, the completed journal pages can be sent to the Recreation Resources Center, where the information will be key punched and this data electronically manipulated to produce the desired management reports.

These management programs include internal data comparisons that show actual versus budgeted performance and current versus past performance. External comparisons show how the business stacks up against others of similar size and against the industry as a whole. Operating financial statements, marketing profiles, profit center analysis, pricing indicators, investments analysis, and some 13 important ration analyses (such as inventory turnover, debt-equity relationships, and profit margins) are all available as part of this system.

The entire system is flexible and readily adaptable to most small to medium sized businesses, including hotels, motels, restaurants, resorts, and campgrounds. It can be adapted to allow continued use of the business forms already on hand.

Send inquiries to Recreation Resources Center, University of Wisconsin-Extention, 1815 University Avenue, Madison, Wisconsin 53706. Telephone 608-263-2621.

At present, the forms are available to any who desire them for cost. The Management Control System may be available to specific states whose extension services cooperate.

This system should go a long way toward helping to solve the problem of poor record keeping and little time in the small recreation businesses.

PROCEDURES FOR REDUCING THEFT

In any organization there are opportunities for dishonest employees. Some means of control should be established. A list of suggestions to minimize embezzlement are:[6]

1. The payments received through the mail should be recorded by someone other than the one in charge of accounts receivable.
2. All receipts should be turned in daily and banked intact.
3. Invoices for merchandise delivered should be given to someone other than the person receiving the merchandise. This "blind tally" method used in connection with a receiving record is quite effective.
4. Someone other than the storekeeper should take the periodic inventories, preferably someone from the auditor's office.
5. The daily housekeeper's report should be checked against the report on rooms occupied.
6. The payroll checks should be given out by someone other than the person who calculates wages and prepares checks.
7. The bank statement should be reconciled by a person who does not keep the records of the motel pertaining to banking transactions.
8. Cash register readings should be taken by someone other than the clerk who acts as departmental cashier.
9. Each cashier should be provided with a fixed change fund (imprest fund) and a safe repository for it.
10. Quite often two signatures are required on any checks drawn on the motel's bank account.

ACCRUED ACCOUNTING

Many larger firms use an accrued basis for accounting and record the expenses when it is made, not when it is paid. This allows an immediate look at income and expenses, assets and liabilities which have been incurred but not necessarily paid.

[6] From PLANNING AND OPERATING MOTELS by George Podd and John Lesure, copyright © 1964.

BREAK EVEN CONCEPT

Another tool available to the manager is the break even concept or marginal analysis according to Kemper W. Merriam, Professor of Accounting, College of Business Administration, University of South Florida, Tampa, Florida. The break even concept assumes that the rates will be the same, and that the fixed costs will be the same over a given period of time. It determines the amount of expenses both current and fixed per day or per week that must be met, and then figures the number of rooms, the number of campsites, or the number of canoes that must be rented to meet the expenses. The manager then knows how many he must rent each day in order to be in the black. This can both provide incentive as well as a conscious knowledge of where the agency is from day to day in their activites.

SET PRICES

Determining the prices for the services that are to be sold is one of the most important aspects of financial management. If the prices are too low, the enterprise will not make a profit, if they are too high, the potential market (people) may go elsewhere, or decide to participate in other, less expensive, types of recreation. There are basically 4 ways to determine prices, and the good manager will determine what the prices should be under each method and probably set his prices somewhere in between as a compromise.

1. *Base it on the competition.* That is, the other campgrounds in the area are charging $3.50 per night, the manager may want to price his campsites between $3.25 and $3.75 depending on whether he feels he has a better product or an inferior product to his competition.
2. *Charge what the traffic will bear.* This method may only work if the enterprise is the only one in the area or if there is more demand (more people) desiring the service that he can accommodate.
3. *Use a formula developed by Hubbard[7] for the Hotel Motel industry in the late 1950's still in use today.* The steps in the use of that formula are as follows:
   a. Determine the cost of the land, construction and development, and the time it will take to repay them. Include the interest. Example. Cost of a campground for above is $100,000. To be repaid in 10 years with 10 percent interest. Thus cost per year will be approximately $15,000 to repay investment plus interest each year for the 10 year period.
   b. Determine the capital investment required for operation, that is, money needed for cash flow, inventories, and so on. This assumes that the income from operations will more than cover the costs of operation, and the next cost to the investor is what is needed for the formula. (example $5000 per year)
   c. Add 1 and 2 above. Total $15,000 plus $5000 is $20,000.

[7] From PLANNING AND OPERATING MOTELS by George Podd and John Lesure, copyright © 1964.

   d. Determine the fixed rate of investment return and multiply by the total of 1 and 2 above. (Example, 15 percent is desired, multiplied by $20,000 is $3000 per year.)

   e. Determine the average number of campsites that can be expected to be filled over the course of the season. Example 100 sites, filled 70 percent capacity on the average, multiplied by the number of days in the season. (Example, 100 × 70 percent equal 70 sites times 90 days is 630 sites days.)

   f. Divide the number of site days by the return desired, for the cost per site. (Example, 3000 divided by 630 is $4.75 per site per day.)

4. *Ask experts.* This is usually a good idea after all of the alternatives have been figured. It may cost something for the "consulting service" but an outside opinion may be a valuable asset, which may be given in addition to other recommendations on planning, development, construction, management, marketing or any of a number of other areas in which consultants specialize. This should be a part of the feasibility study discussed in the preceding chapter.

The manager should be ready to adjust prices upward or downward if he finds they are not satisfactory, (i.e., he is not making a profit, people are not coming, they are going elsewhere, or he may have more people than he can handle). He should do so only after sufficient time and considerable investigation to be assured that the prices are the problem and not poor marketing, location, or other factors.

TAX CONSIDERATIONS

Legitimate expenses of the business are deductable. Portions of use such as portional use of the house as an office, or the automobile are more complex, and must be prorated on a predetermined basis.

Charges should also be made in the form of expenses against capital, against equipment in the form of depreciation for equipment and furnishings, for interest, as well as for repair and maintenance. Anything that has a life of one year or less is included as an expense. If it improves the facility, or prolongs its life, it must be included as equipment, and depreciates over a prorated period.

Equipment is sometimes difficult to assess for tax purposes. Hand tools and other expendable equipment that has a normal life of a year or less, can be deducted completely within the year. Other items such as tractors, or canoes might depreciate yearly, and a prorata amount must be deducted each year for the life of the piece of equipment involved.

The collection of admission taxes and amusement taxes may be required under some circumstances. It is best to write for the tax guide from the Small Business Administration or from the Internal Revenue Service for information on these items.

A number of laws, both state and federal, will effect both the method of operation, and the fees collected. The manager or operator should obtain assistance from an appropriate income tax consultant and make specific efforts to locate laws or regulations from local, state, or federal regulatory agencies concerning the following.

1. Registration of guests, hotels, motels, or inns.
2. Retail sales tax.
3. Business activities tax or income tax.
4. Incorporation tax.
5. Franchise renewal.
6. Intangible tax.
7. Sanitation regulations.
8. Fire regulations.
9. Health and safety regulations.
10. Motor vehicle laws.
11. Zoning and building code.
12. Workman's compensation requirements.
13. Liability requirements.
14. Unemployment compensation requirements.
15. Federal income tax.
16. Social Security.
17. Fishing and game requirements.
18. Boating and watercraft regulations.
19. Insurance regulations.

CHARACTERISTICS OF GOOD BUSINESS MANAGEMENT

1. Current working cash to capital ratio of 1 to 1 or more. This shows adequate cash flow in most cases.
2. Large percentage of fixed assets in terms of land, building, and equipment 50 to 85 percent.
3. The current cash position; can obligations be met when due.
4. Equity investment, the ratio of long term debt to capital stock. Four point five is thin. One to one is excellent.
5. The ratio of long term debt to value of fixed cost. Can it be sold for a profit. Twenty five to one is a good ratio.
6. Ratio of accounts receivable to total sales.

HOW TO ANALYZE THE BUSINESS

Records are of little value unless they are analyzed in terms of the objective of the agency. The following suggestions may seem redundant but can serve as a reminder for those managers that find themselves "to busy" to give thought to the information adequate record keeping can furnish.

Figure 39 The aggressive manager will take advantage of every opportunity to supplement his gross sales, such as with boat rentals.
Courtesy: Bonair Boats, Lenexa, Kansas.

1. Keep adequate records.
2. Make a profit or loss statement.
3. Compare all accounts with budgets from last month, last year, or other yardsticks available from trade associations, trade presses, shows, or visits with other like enterprises.
4. Try to discover trends, and income up or down, expenses up or down, percent of income to operating expense.
5. Study the business conditions, the future outlook or travel trends to see what the future holds.
6. Know where you are going.

LIABILITY—INSURANCE—VANDALISM

Several other items that the operator must be concerned with in his business include liability, insurance, and vandalism.

With increasing magnitude of law suits being awarded, the manager cannot afford not to give due concerns to this area of management.

There are three classifications of visitors.

1. *Tresspasser.* The manager has no obligation for the tresspasser for injuries, other than to refrain from providing methods of entrapment, or to have any attractive nuisances. This is somewhat tempered if the manager has knowledge that the tresspasser tresspasses regularly and does not warn him of perils.
2. *Licensee.* The licensee is one who comes to the area designated for recreation for his own benefit, but does not pay a fee and is not invited. The owner must indeed warn him of perils, and take reasonable precautions to keep him from being injured.
3. *Invitee.* The invitee is one who comes to the area for the benefit of the owner, and usually pays a fee. The owner or manager owes to the invitee the highest degree of responsibility and care. He must not only warn him of perils, but must do everything possible to keep him from being injured. This may indeed require security people, in addition to signs, restraining barriers and of the precautions.

Normally in order for an injured party to collect damages, he must prove there has been negligence. Negligence usually must contain all of the following ingredients.

1. There must have been a duty that was the responsibility of some person, agency, or combination thereof.
2. This duty for safety must have been breached.
3. There must have been an accident of some sorts as a result of breaching of the duty or responsibility.
4. The accident caused injury and these injuries must then have a dollar value placed on them whether physical or psychological.

The operator should indeed secure liability insurance, which may be rated on the basis of the volume of receipts, and his rating will probably be determined by the degree of exposure as well as the age of the individuals.

The liability implications of negligence should be stressed very carefully in in-service training programs with staff, and a periodic inspection and observation must be taken to insure that standard operating procedures are designed to provide the patrons with the best possible protection from injury that can be done.

LIABILITY LIMITATIONS[8]

An owner or operator of a recreational enterprise can use several methods for limiting liability or transferring the risk of loss. These include: A) incorporation, B) carrying adequate liability insurance, and C) use of up-to-date safety inspection methods.

1. *Incorporation.* A corporation is a "legal person" created under the state corpora-

---

[8] John Pierce, *Liability and Insurance Protection Principles for Recreational Enterprises*, Extension Bulletin 505, Cooperative Extension Service, The Ohio State University, 1972.

tion laws and this legal procedure generally limits liability to the corporate assets. Theoretically an individual is not liable for any assets other than those he has assigned to the corporation. However, the corporate owners should be careful to satisfy all the legal requirements of establishing and maintaining such a form of business. This includes annual shareholders and directors meetings, the maintenance of records, minutes, and appropriate documentation. In addition, the corporation should have its books reviewed by an attorney periodically. This form of conducting business must be known as a corporation beyond a reasonable doubt, not to be confused with other noncorporate forms of business.

Incorporation may prove to be a desirable method of establishing an enterprise particularly if insurance costs are exceptionally high for the unincorporated business forms. There are many aspects to be considered before incorporation. These include high taxes, costs of incorporation, and such problems as zoning regulations. Attorneys and business advisors should be consulted before determining whether incorporation is desirable.

2. *Liability Insurance.* Insurance cannot eliminate risk, but it can transfer the risk of loss to a professional risk taker, that is, an insurance company. The possibility of a large, uncertain loss or cost of adverse settlement is replaced by a modest business expense—the insurance premium. In seeking insurance coverage, the operator should first see his local insurance agent. As premium rates and the basis for determining rates vary, it is wise to get a number of quotations before deciding on the final insurance policy. The demands for insurance coverage at private recreational enterprises is relatively new to many insurance companies. Some may refuse to insure; others may charge high fees in lieu of experience data on which to base more reasonable premiums.

Recent court awards for damages and injuries have been high. The function of juries in negligence cases is expanding and they play a major role in determining what is reasonable and what is negligence. Judicial statistics show that there is a tendency among juries to resolve doubts in accidental cases in favor of compensating the injured.

While liability insurance would seem to be a quick and easy way of reducing one liability it should be remembered that one or more claims may cause a rise or even cancellation of the insurance. Thus the conscious manager will do everything possible to "protect his insurability."

3. *Safety, Inspection, and Training.* Risks can be reduced by adopting all safety methods, equipment, and precautions presently being used at other recreation areas. Patrons should be informed of the need for safety through the spoken word as well as posted safety codes. Emergency phone numbers should be posted in case of injury. Full accident reports should be filed following any accident, no matter how slight. Insurance agents often provide their clients with these accident report forms free of charge. Filing of reports may lead to correction of unsafe conditions as well as provide accurate facts from which to determine causes of injury. Don't misjudge the safety angle, it's good business practice!

If the answer to all safety questions is not affirmative, then a re-examination of your business practices may be necessary. Not only will accident prevention reduce the chance of injury, but as already indicated, reasonable care is the basis for determining negligence. A safety program should begin with study of the recreation area by third persons. And followed by daily inspection by staff.

The recreation enterprise should have appropriate safety equipment such as fire extinguishers or life preservers, particularly at places of increased exposure to danger. An operator may have a difficult time defending a claim if there is a general lack of safety equipment. The omission of these precautions may cast doubts in the minds of jurors about your fulfillment of duty.

The best insurance against accidents is a trained and conscienscious staff. The implications of accidents and liability both to the individual and the enterprise should be made very clear to each employee early in his in-service training program.

Aggressive program of awareness on the part of employees will do much to prevent most accidents and resulting law suits.

FIRE

Other than normal investigative procedures, it is sometimes good to have the facility inspected by someone knowledgeable in this area so that little noticed or other potential fire causing hazards may be removed and eliminated. It goes without saying that fire insurance is a must.

VANDALISM

Vandalism is a problem in almost every public place. A number of methods have been used to try to reduce the vandalism, which of course can result in a significant expense to the owner-manager. Some of the better procedures have been as follows:

1. Provide an attractive, well-kept and well-maintained facility. Shoddy or ill-kept facilities attract individuals with this in mind.
2. Remove or replace vandalized equipment or repair vandalized areas, or repaint areas where graffitti is placed, as soon as possible. Vandalism begets vandalism.
3. Light the area well.
4. Provide as much security as possible, and encourage employees to be watchful of the actions of the visitors.

GOVERNMENTAL AGENCIES INVOLVED WITH COMMERCIAL RECREATION

A major deterrant to expansion of commercial recreation enterprises has been the lack of adequate capital, particularly for planning and development. Banks have traditionally been conservative, and with little consistent history of the financial success of recreation businesses, because of short seasons, uncertain weather conditions, lack of managerial expertise, and alternatives for capital improvements, have been extremely reluctant to make loans in this area. There is little doubt that recreation businesses, because of these reasons, is more of a risk than the average business.

The federal government has several programs which are of assistance although to a rather limited and specialized degree. The primary purposes of these governmental agencies is to promote local economies by creating additional jobs and income.

The Small Business Administration, the Economic Development Administration, the Department of Commerce, the Farmers Home Administration, and the Department of Agriculture are the primary federal government agencies whose purposes include either loans or technical assistance to those private enterprises that includes the recreation businesses.

Previously, the Farmers Home Administration limited its support to profit-making recreation operations that will supplement family farm income, or to associations of rural individuals, who desire to borrow funds to develop such recreation facilities as golf courses, swimming pools, and other opportunities not available in the area that hopefully will produce sufficient revenue to repay the investment.

The Economic Development Administration support is restricted to designated areas of economic distress. The Small Business Administration support is curtailed by (1) limited funds with disasters having first priority, and (2) the small size of loan guarantee which was previously $350,000.

Other agencies such as Soil Conservation Service has provided technical assistance in the use of land and water for fish and wildlife production and although assistance in developing recreation facilities has been primarily geared toward rural families or farmers wishing to provide their own services or provide additional supplementary services for profit. This has not been a primary concern or high priority objective of the Service.

The Federal Extension Service has been involved for a number of years, in cooperation with state land grant university Extension Services, in providing technical assistance in feasibility studies, planning, development, operations, and programming of private, or nonprofit recreation organizations and agencies. They have been an excellent resource in some states to the small recreation business executive in helping to provide information on which to base decisions.

Indeed, the managing of a successful private recreation enterprise takes a rare combination of abilities. The manager is no doubt the most important link in this system. If he does his job poorly, even the best enterprise with many visitors will fail. If he does his job well, a marginal operation may produce a moderate net profit. Figure 40 depicts many of the parts of the management puzzle.

Summary

Probably the most important ingredient in success or failure of a recreation enterprise is in the managerial skills and abilities of those who will manage the fiscal, financial, and personal resources of the enterprise.

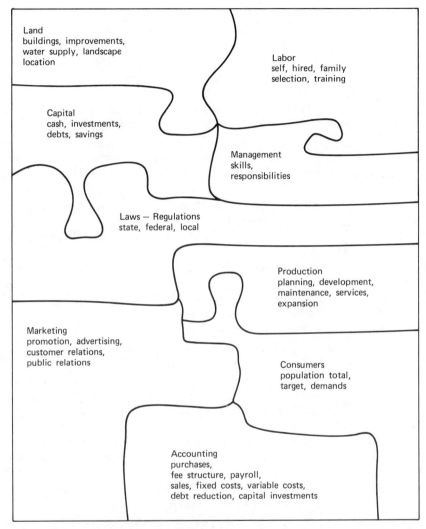

Figure 40 The manager must be skilled in many areas to be successful. If he is, the management puzzel will fit together.
Courtesy: Eugene Dices, Private Enterprise Recreation Managers Workshop Selected Paper, Department Park and Recreation Resources, Michigan State University, March 24, 1971.

It is impossible, of course, to present more than a superficial mentioning of the aspect of management and organizational theory; however, the four main aspects of management are: facility management, program service management, personnel management, and financial management. Other considerations for which the manager must be concerned are liability, insurance, and vandalism.

Additional References

Books, Bulletins, and Reports

De Vriend, A. J., H. M. Smith, and S. W. Weiss, *How To Evaluate Your Recreation Business,* C2437 Recreation Business Management Series - 6, Cooperative Extension Programs University of Wisconsin, Madison.

De Vriend, A. J., H. M. Smith, and S. W. Weiss, *How To Establish Rate Structures and Prices for your Services,* C2438 Recreation Business Management Series - 7, Cooperative Extension Programs, University of Wisconsin, Madison.

Dice, Eugene, editor, *The Private Campground Business: A Forward Focus,* Proceedings of the Michigan Campground Business Seminar, Michigan State University, March 24, 1972.

Farmers Home Administration, *Handbook of Outdoor Recreation Enterprises in Rural Areas,* Superintendent of Documents, Washington, D.C.

Greenaway, Donald, *Manual for Resort Operators,* State College of Washington, Pullman, Bulletin #13, 1950.

Gunn and McIntosh, *Motel Planning and Business Management,* Wm. C. Brown Co., 1964.

Hines, Thomas I. *Revenue Sources Management in Parks and Recreation,* #10021, National Recreation & Park Association, Arlington, Virginia, 1974.

Liability and Insurance Protection in Rural Recreation Enterprises, Extension Bulletin 580, Cooperative Extension Service, Michigan State University, 1967.

Liability Protection for Outdoor Recreation Enterprises, Circular 385, Cooperative Extension Service, New Mexico State University 1966.

Liability Risks in Operating a Farm Recreation Enterprise in Missouri, Bulletin 801, University of Missouri, Agricultural Experiment Station Resource Development Economics Division, 1963.

McIntosh, Robert W., *Business Methods for Cottage Resorts,* Tourist and Resort Series, Circular R-603, Michigan State University, Cooperative Extension Service, East Lansing, Michigan, June 1955.

Podd, George O. and John D. Lesure, *Planning and Operating Motels and Motor Hotels,* Ahrens Book Company, Inc., New York 1964.

School of Hotel, Restaurant, and Institutional Management, *Good Books for Good Managers,* College of Business, Michigan State University, East Lansing, Michigan.

Selka, Stephen L., *Bookkeeping Control and Management Information System,* Recreation Resources Center, University of Wisconsin, Extension, Madison, Wisconsin, 1974.

Shirley, Hardy L. and Paul F. Graves, *Forest Ownership for Pleasure and Profit,* Syracuse University Press, Syracuse, New York, 1967.

Small Business Enterprises in Outdoor Recreation and Tourism, Superintendent of Documents, Washington, D.C., 1974.

Small Business Opportunities in Outdoor Recreation and Tourism, Union Calendar #765, Superintendent of Documents, Washington, D.C.

Smith, Clodus R., Lloyd E. Partain, and James R. Champlin, *Rural Recreation for Profit,* Interstate Printers and Publishers, Inc., Danville, Illinois 1968.

United States Department of Agriculture, *Bibliography of Selected Publications on Rural Recreation as a Business,* Federal Extension Service, 1962.

USDA, *Rural Recreation–New Opportunities on Private Land,* U.S. Dept. of Agriculture, Miscellaneous Publication No. 930, June 1963.

USDA, *Forest Recreation For Profit,* U.S. Department of Agriculture, Forest Service, Agriculture Information Bulletin No. 265, 1963.

U.S. Department of Agriculture, *"Rural Recreation Enterprises for Profit",* Agriculture Information Bulletin No. 2/77, October 1963.

Van der Smissen, Betty, *Legal Liability of Cities and Schools for Injuries in Recreation and Parks,* W. H. Anderson Co., Cincinnati, Ohio, 1975.

Van Meter, Jerry R., *"Initial Counseling Guide for Recreation Enterprises",* Office of Recreation and Park Resources, Department of Recreation and Park Administration, University of Illinois at Urbana-Champaign, ORPR-17, January, 1970.

Vollmar, Glen J., *Budgeting Farm and Ranch Recreation Enterprises,* ESC. .559, Federal Extension Service. USDA, Washington, D.C., November 1964.

Unpublished Work

Murray, Roger Dee, *Commercial Campgrounds in Michigan: A Study of the Factors That Contribute to Their Financial Success,* Unpublished Thesis, Michigan State University, 1974.

Davis, Gary Joseph, *Management Characteristics of Private Profit-Oriented Golf Enterprises in Michigan,* Unpublished Thesis, Michigan State University, 1974.

Periodicals

Cornwell, George W., "The Private Outdoor Recreation Industry–Its Management", reproduced from the American Forests, October 1963 by E. J. Williamson, RDPA 118 (12/63).

"Is This Anytime to Start A Business?", Changing Times, the Kiplinger Magazine, October 1975.

Discussion Questions

1. Discuss the paramount issue as to why business fail.
2. Discuss how the five management areas of responsibility are inter-related.
3. In what ways do guests judge a resort operation?
4. Discuss how the questions employers are prohibited from asking may become a hardship on the employer in his/her hiring practices.
5. Do you feel maintenance and manual labor employees in a resort should receive formal on-the-job training? Why? What training would you recommend for these employees?
6. In what ways do sound financial management contribute to the success of a

recreation enterprise?

7. Why is record keeping important to the success of a business?

8. How does the "break-even" concept aid the recreation business manager in managing the day to day operation of the enterprise?

9. How does pricing of recreation services differ from pricing of legal or medical services? What are the similarities?

10. Which federal government agencies provide loans and/or technical assistance to recreation and other businesses?

CHAPTER 6

PLANNING AND DEVELOPMENT OF THE RECREATION ENTERPRISE

Whether the anticipated enterprise is to be a Walt Disney World, or a ten-unit campground, the ultimate objective of any private and commercial enterprise is to return a profit to the owner for the money invested. As can be expected, the more money that is invested, the more intensely the feasibility of the project is studied to determine if a profit is possible. However, the procedure for determining whether a Walt Disney World will make a profit as compared with a ten-campsite campground, is much the same, differing in the number of variables and the degree to which they are analyzed. Unfortunately over 50 percent of small recreation enterprises that are established annually, those with investments less than 50,000 dollars, fail. According to the Small Business Administration, only 12 percent of recreation enterprises make a profit. The percentage increases as the recreation enterprises grow in size. This may be for a number of factors: one, the care with which those with larger investments plan and assess their facilities; second, the professional manner in which they are managed. The Small Business Administration reports more businesses are losing money because of poor management than for any other single reason, including lack of capital.

In the late 1950s and early 1960s, several of the government agencies including the Federal Extension Service, Farmers Home Administration, and the Soil Conservation Service, developed extensive programs and publications encouraging the development of rural recreation enterprises, primarily as secondary incomes for farmers. Unfortunately, many of these enterprises were poorly planned, poorly managed, and based on assumptions rather than facts. It has now been learned that a substantial investment is required to make even the smallest percent return, and normally the management of a recreation enterprise is *at least* a full-time job. Those in rural areas found they lacked many of the human relations and hospitality skills, as well as the expertise, initiative, or interest to turn a part-time, secondary income producing enterprise into a full-fledged money making operation. Additional problems were encountered when it was realized the height of the tourist season paralleled the rural landowner's obligations to his primary duties of raising crops, taking care of cattle, and other responsibilities. Either one or the other was usually neglected.

Perhaps lessons can be learned from these experiences of the past, in more objectively and accurately evaluating the potential of a recreation facility, large or small.

THE FEASIBILITY ANALYSIS

Much has been said recently in the literature about the increased need for feasibility studies. There is little disagreement that they are indeed necessities. The differences of opinion, however, comes in determining exactly what should be included in the feasibility study. For the purposes of this material, the feasibility study (an outline of which can be seen in Figure 41) will be used in its broadest sense, and will encompass two broad, yet comprehensive areas:

1. *The Market Analysis.* This is an assessment of what is being sold, who it can be sold to, and how much it can be sold for. In short, it is an assessment of the *income* than can be generated, and the factors affecting income.
2. *A Management Analysis.* What will the enterprise cost to build and operate, and what will be the price to those who have been identified in the market analysis as the target buyers. In short, this is an analysis of the *expenses* of the enterprise and all of the factors affecting expenses.

In Chapter 7 we will see the operator exchanging services for fees. Therefore, the primary objective of the feasibility study is to determine if enough people can be attracted at a specific fee in exchange for services so the fees that are received will exceed the cost for providing the services. Whether this process is applied to a ten-unit campground or to a large hotel/resort complex requiring a complex computer programming, a number of common variables are inherent in each and the process of evaluating the factors affecting income and expenses remain the same. A lucid example of this can be found in the chapter on Feasibility Studies in the *Tourist Business*, by Donald E. Lundberg.[1]

DESCRIPTION, GOALS, AND OBJECTIVES

The first order of business that must be accomplished before a comprehensive analysis can be made of the marketing and management aspects of the study concerns the description of the services to be provided, and the goals and objectives of the enterprise. This will probably be the most difficult step in the planning process. It will, however, help to crystalize the specific objectives of the enterprise, in addition to providing a focal point in evaluating future steps in the planning process. This is a vital step to the owner, the designer, and the lenders of the capital. What are the fundamental reasons the owner wishes to build the enterprise? What are his objectives in building the facility? What purpose is to be served in constructing the facility?

---

[1] DonaldE. Lundberg, *Tourist Business,* Cahners Books, 89 Franklin Street, Boston, Massachusetts 02110.

Figure 41, Feasibility study outline

MARKET ANALYSIS

1. Goals and objectives of the enterprise.
2. Description of the services to be provided.
3. Description of the market, past, present, and future.
4. General characteristics of the market.
5. Location and accessability.
6. Evaluation of community attitudes.
7. Attractiveness of the locality.
8. Availability of utilities.
9. Consideration of the competition.
10. Projected attendance.
11. Projected revenues.

MANAGEMENT ANALYSIS

1. Initial or pre- opening expenses.
   a. Capital expenses.
   b. Equipment.
   c. Supplies.
2. Operating expenses.

FEASIBILITY ANALYSIS

1. Estimates of net income from market and management analysis data above.
2. Decision to develop or not develop.

Figure 41 A sound feasibility study should include all of the items mentioned in the outline.

1. Profit incentive alone?
2. To attract tourists and if so from where, when, and what type?
3. To attract the resident and nearby population?
4. To fill a commercial void or to help build an area or location?
5. To compliment or compete with already existing facilities or attractions in the area?
6. Will it be the primary concern of the owner or manager, or will it be a secondary one?
7. Is it more of a hobby that will be developed into a recreation business?
8. What is the minimum financial return that will be acceptable?
9. Must the family derive its entire living expenses from the enterprise?
10. Does the owner-manager have previous experience, expertise, or knowledge

of the type of activity or facility for which the enterprise will provide?

11. How much time will the owner-manager be willing to spend in the operation and management of the enterprise?
12. What funds will the owner have to contribute of his own to the enterprise?
13. Does he enjoy working with people, long hours of hard work, and will the family assist or will outside help be needed.

The owner-manager should outline in written form a description of the services to be provided, the types of facilities that will be required, the projected operating season to be provided, and as many other specific details as possible about the operation of the enterprise.

If the owner-manager finds the answers to the above incompatible with the long range plans, interests or capabilities, then pursuing the remaining portions of the feasibility study is an exercise in futility. Only after the above questions have been successfully answered, should the following steps in the feasibility study be attempted.

MARKET ANALYSIS

DESCRIPTION OF THE MARKET, PAST, PRESENT, AND FUTURE

It is of utmost importance that the service to be provided be analyzed in terms of the demand, as determined by such data as is available from, for example, the BOR participation studies, the U.S. Bureau of Travel Census Data, State Tourism Department studies, and/or Federal Extension Service, university, or other sources of information that will be able to tell the current demand for similar or identical enterprises. An effort should be made to determine whether the trend of the demand is up, down, or remaining constant. The implications of future factors limiting the participation should be: What effect will an energy shortage or gasoline shortage have on the participation rate of the public in the service or activity to be provided.

GENERAL CHARACTERISTICS OF THE MARKET

The questions to be asked in this portion of the feasibility study are discussed more in depth in the chapter on marketing. The sources of data to answer these questions are also discussed in that chapter. The following questions must be answered:

1. What are the general characteristics of those who will be participating in the activity offered, or desiring the service provided?
2. Who are they?
3. Where are they located?
4. What is the percent of the general population with this interest?
5. What is the percent of people with this interest who have incomes sufficient to participate?
6. What are the ages and sizes of their families?
7. What types of investments are required by those who desire to participate?

8. What is the length of time of their interests for participation?
9. How can these people be identified and reached?
10. Estimate the activity days per person if possible.

The Bureau of Outdoor Recreation conducts periodic surveys to determine the number of activity days per person individuals participate in a number of outdoor recreation activities. A copy of the latest data should be obtained. To illustrate how such data might be used, suppose a trade area with a total population of 10,000 is studied. By locating the general demographic information, it is determined that approximately 73 percent of the population is 12 years of age and over. This implies that there are 7300 individuals 12 and over of the 10,000 in the total trade area that would be available for the type of activity. From the report of the Bureau of Outdoor Recreation, it can be discerned, for instance, that the average number of activity days per person for camping for people 12 years of age and over is approximately 0.86. The 7300 population in the trade area is multiplied by 0.86, which results in 6278 activity days that might be anticipated to be the demand expected in that area for camping. This figure must, of course, be evaluated in terms of the supply and demand of other campgrounds in the area. More will be discussed in the supply and demand section. This can be done for each activity that is to be provided. Some individuals, however, may participate in more than one activity; therefore, they cannot be counted as different persons available for participation, but merely multiple participations by the same individuals.

LOCATION AND ACCESSABILITY

As this is a vital consideration, some of the standards to be considered in selecting and planning the site are as follows:

1. *Natural Attractions.* The area should contain, if possible and preferably on the site, some unique or unusual natural attractions of scenic beauty. Americans are primarily attracted to water as a natural resource, second to the mountains, and third to quiet areas of trees, shrubbery, and vegetation. Although man-made attractions do not necessarily completely depend on one of these to be successful, if it is possible to have these, it is a factor that will increase attendance and insure success. The availability of various types of geographical terrain, different types of vegetation, terrain, waterways, lakes and ponds for fishing, floating, boating, skiing, and other activities as well as an abundance of wildlife are great attractions to urban residents, particularly to children. Interesting geographic formations including various natural attractions, waterfalls, caves, and similar natural phenomena are all of interest to the recreationist.

    The presence of historical and educational attractions, structures, or sites is indeed a great advantage to the potential enterprise operator. These will diversify the market.

    Nearby tourist attractions may be more important to the recreation enterprise

Figure 42 Total overall planning as well as location and assessability are extremely important. This Valley Fair theme amusement park being built near Shakoppe, Minnesota is a 28-acre park with 28 additional acres for parking, located 3 miles east of the business district.
Courtesy: International Association of Amusement Parks and Attraction, Oak Park, Illinois.

than those actually located on the site. More and more it has been determined that tourists travel to a destination area in which they anticipate spending several days or more. Those areas that have a number of facilities and services available will be able to attract more tourists, and for longer periods of time. State and natural parks, recreation areas, forests, and wildlife refuges indeed provide tremendous drawing power. They appear on most maps, and large numbers of people may travel hundreds or even thousands of miles to visit them. It is not uncommon for privately owned recreation enterprises to develop on the fringes of such areas, and to provide such services and facilities not available to the government owned units, and to service the overflow of visitors.

2. *Man-Made Attractions.* Large, privately owned man-made attractions can also be

the major drawing power for an area. This happened at Disneyland and Disney World, with additional complimentary commercial attractions drawing upon the lure and success of the two Disney operations.

All public and privately owned recreation facilities should be inventoried and their annual visitations recorded in the feasibility study. Each visitor to such an area or attraction is a potential customer for the nearby privately owned enterprise.

Even though no major public or private attractions exist, the inventory should include all those available in the area, as a number of small attractions can be grouped to be a major destination attraction area.

3. *Historical Attractions.* Again, why is this important? All that has been said previously about state and federal recreation lands and geographical attractions can also be said of historical attractions. The areas surrounding Washington, D.C., Philadelphia, and Williamsburg will attest to the tremendous drawing power of historical attractions in the surrounding community.

4. *Sports Areas.* Large bodies of water suited for boating, or mountain areas suitable for skiing, and other natural sites suitable for sports activities tend to draw many enthusiasts. Many times they will visit other attractions or enterprises and need additional services in the process of participating in their sport, even though the services of the enterprise may not be directly related to the main interest of the visit.

5. *Other Complimentary Recreational Businesses.* There are many instances where the primary attraction at one enterprise supplements or compliments those of neighboring enterprises. In some cases those who come to visit historical or educational attractions find that special arrangements have been made for visitors to use nearby facilities such as golf, swimming, or horseback riding, that are component parts of neighboring enterprises.

In Miami Beach for example, a number of night clubs and supper clubs depend on the business brought to the area by the resort hotels on the "strip." Likewise, the hotels depend on the night spots for recreation and entertainment outlets for their guests who have laid in the sun or swam all day.

The recreation facilities of the community also must be considered. Few enterprises can provide their own golf courses. The city of Miami owns and operates a number of courses that are used, to a great extent, by out of state visitors staying in "beach" hotels.

Possibilities of this sort should be considered and included in the inventory along with the statement that initial contacts have been made to insure such use if desired.

6. *Industrial and Community Attractions.* The surrounding community may contain industries with scheduled tours that attract visitors. Travelers are interested in visiting Milwaukee breweries for an example, as well as theaters, dances, sporting events, parades, pageants, and a variety of community sponsored activities that may be an important contribution to the potential business of the enterprise manager. The existence of such attractions must also be included in the inventory.

Figure 43 Historical attractions are many times overlooked as potential assets to attract tourists. This Otlands' house with terrace and formal garden in Leesburg, Virginia is an outstanding tourist attraction.
Courtesy: National Trust for Historical Preservation, Washington, D.C.

EVALUATE THE ATTITUDE OF THE COMMUNITY

The number of tourists visiting the area currently is of primary importance to the investigator. The number of conventions held in the area, the number of delegates, the current retail sales for travel and tourist commodities, the attitude toward tourism by visitors and convention bureaus, local hotel and motel associations, chamber of commerce, state departments of tourism, and other tourism and visitor related agencies and individuals should be assessed in determining whether the location is the best possible for the tourist climate. The community can make important contributions to the recreation enterprise. Such services as health, sanitation, police and fire protection, road maintenance, churches, shopping centers, cultural activities, and entertainment are only a few community offerings. Communities that recognize the importance of tourism and recreation have a friendly and welcoming attitude toward the recreationist. If visitors are made to feel unwelcome or given the impression they are primarily a source of money, they will seek other communities where they feel more comfortable. Therefore, in the analysis it is important to describe potential community contributions and attitudes that they might influence the proposed enterprise.

EVALUATE THE ATTRACTIVENESS OF THE LOCALITY

Dr. Clare Gunn in his book, *Vacationscape*,[2] lists three important ingredients in the attractiveness of tourism attraction.

1. The element itself.
2. The setting in which it is located including the entrance and exit.
3. The surrounding countryside in which the enterprise is located.

If the attraction is located in a scenic and aesthetically appealing location, has many natural features, and is a drawing card in and of itself, this will be of considerable help.

However, if the road to the enterprise is ravaged by strip mines, abandoned houses, junk cars, or other characteristic reminders of the urban environment, these will indeed impair attractiveness of the enterprise. In Chapter 4, it was mentioned that there is a county by county assessment by the Soil Conservation Service of the potential use of the land for recreation enterprises, based on the attractiveness of the counties in which they might be located. This information is available from the Soil Conservation Service, and would be valuable in assessing the attractiveness of the county and locality in which the enterprise is proposed to be built.

CONSIDERATION OF SUPPLY AND DEMAND

A critical point in the feasibility study is an objective analysis of the number of similar or identical facilities surrounding or near the proposed enterprise. Although all public

[2] Clare Gunn, *Vacationscape, Designing Tourist Regions,* Bureau of Business Research, The University of Texas at Austin, 1972.

and private recreation enterprises operating in the area should be included in the inventory, particular note should be made of similar, privately owned enterprises. The feasibility study should include as much information as possible about the other outdoor recreation businesses, the potential areas of competition, and the ways in which they might compliment or compete with the proposed enterprise. It is difficult to obtain specific information directly from potential competitors. However, other information resources such as chambers of commerce, departments of tourism, or a regional planning commission may be able to provide some answers to the following questions:

1. What are they selling?
2. How well are they doing?
3. Are they well managed?
4. What rates do they charge?
5. Are they publicly or privately owned?
6. Any ideas on attendance or gross income?
7. How large is their staff?
8. What are their problems?
9. What can be learned from them?

It should be pointed out, that caution should be used in duplicating existing recreation enterprises. Too few potential users could result in dividing the customer between facilities to the point where all enterprises could become unprofitable. On the other hand, a certain amount of competition in the business world is considered both healthy and desirable. The feasibility study should state how the perspective operator proposed to compete. There are several possibilities:

1. *Plan to provide the highest quality of facility and services.*
2. *Offer a wide variety or distinctive form(s) of recreation opportunities.* In general the greater the number of opportunities the greater the competitive edge of the recreation business.
3. *Provide for original and creative management.* Recreationists are delighted by new ideas and management techniques that reflect a primary interest in the enjoyment of the recreationist rather than preoccupation with profit and ease of management.
4. *Provide for meeting special needs.* There are a great many organized groups and clubs with special needs and interests that may not currently be filled. Group-tour business is highly profitable, and usually is worked out in advance to the advantage of both parties.
5. *Provide a higher degree of hospitality.* The way the guest is treated will determine the rate of repeat business and the degree of favorable word of mouth advertising.

The feasibility plan should include plans and ideas for services or facilities that will compliment nearby recreation facilities. If a resort is to be built, for example, providing opportunities for fishing, riding, swimming, and other activities for other visitors to the area staying in campgrounds might provide additional income for the resort operator.

AVAILABILITY OF UTILITIES

Considerations concerning the availability of water, sanitation facilities, zoning, and energy requirements are of increasing importance. In many cases, the cost of supplying necessary utilities has been the factor that has caused many plans to be scrapped. It goes without saying that if the facility is to be located within a community, local zoning laws and regulations must be investigated and considered. The availability of public water supply, sanitation facilities, and energy for heating and cooling must also be considered. If the facility is located outside of a community, county, regional, and state regulations, if any, must be investigated. The State Department of Health will require certain regulations concerning sanitation disposal equipment. The regualtions concerning water supply may be administered by the Department of Health elsewhere.

The Department of Health will also be concerned about the food service. A number of inspections and regulatory information should be anticipated for following:

1. Food service.
2. Water supply.
3. Sanitation.
4. Federal safety requirements.
5. Building codes.
6. Youth camp safety.
7. Environmental impact study/analysis.
8. Swimming pools and bathing places.
9. Wildlife preservation.

The considerations necessary to meet each of these must be considered as a part of the feasibility study, so as not to incur additional problems or expenses later when regulations must be met that were overlooked previously.

The cost for heating and cooling has indeed been a major factor in the location of some facilities. In some areas the only available source is oil or propane. In others, electrical heat is the primary source of energy. Some areas, where they are still fortunate to have adequate supplies of natural gas, this question is not of significance. Estimated projections for future costs of energy should be investigated through the local utilities companies, as this has caused severe financial problems for some recreation enterprises built several years ago that now face this dilemma.

ACCESSIBILITY

The importance of accessibility, like location, cannot be underestimated in the feasibility study. From previous studies it has been determined that 53 percent of all families traveled less than 250 miles for recreation. The average driving time one way for one day trips was one hour. For an overnight stay, 75 to 100 miles was the average each way. The majority of families drove three to four hundred miles to a destination area for an extended vacation, and preferred to drive no more than 5 to 10 miles off the road from good highways. The question "is the facility close enough to potential users and are the highways adequate enough to insure accessibility," must be answered.

Zones of marketing opportunities should be considered, and can be broken down generally to three zones. Zone extends from the facility out to about 50 miles or one hours driving time. This is important particularly when considering the daily visitor potential.

Zone two extends from 50 to 100 miles and includes most overnight travel. If the ultimate proportion of the population is to be served in this zone, overnight accommodations must be available at the facility for participation on weekends and holidays.

The third zone includes 100-150 mile trips and more. Visitors from zone three are most likely to be overnight guests for weekends and longer vacation periods. Only enterprises of outstanding significance on a par with regional and state parks can expect to draw from distances beyond zone three. Examples are national and state parks and major commercial attractions such as Opryland in Tennessee and the Niagra Falls.

Research has shown that without a doubt the type of development influences the distance from which people are attracted. Likewise the recreation complex, that is, a destination area with a large number and variety of attractions providing a wide range of recreation opportunities, can be expected to draw from beyond this distance.

To carry out the "activity days computation" previously mentioned, it is necessary to define the marketing zones, and determine characteristics of the population for each zone. Therefore, a recreation enterprise can count the population in zone one as potential daily customers during the season and the population in zone two are potential customers for weekends and holidays. If the enterprise will attract customers from zone two or further, however, overnight accommodations such as campsites, cabins, or motor lodges will be required.

The influence of socioeconomic and related factors on outdoor recreation have been discussed elsewhere in this textbook. These data are available in the report entitled *Outdoor Recreation for America* available from the Superintendent of Documents, Washington, D.C. 20013 for $2.00.

HIGHWAY TRAVEL DATA

A useful component of the feasibility study is the volume of travel on the major highways leading to or passing by the recreation site. Most state highway departments conduct periodic visitor travel surveys that offer a great deal of useful information. Several studies done in the state of Missouri indicate that on any given day, from 20 to 30 percent of the traffic on any major highway is for recreation or vacation purposes. Information on out of state passenger cars visiting the state, number of persons per vehicle, origin or destination, travel purpose, length of stay, accommodations used, expenditures, and other similar information of great value in forecasting the business potential represented by the highway traveler is available from most state highway departments. State highway traffic counts along any roads are also available. This information is particularly important for those enterprises located on the main route of travel serving the potential recreation public for which the manager hopes to attract.

In summary then, the first steps in developing the feasibility study concerning location and accessibility should give consideration to the following:[3]

1. Area should contain the natural scenic beauty and necessary amenities such as a large body of water, trees, or shrubbery.
2. The area should not already be extensively developed as a recreational area, and should have a good selection of land available for development and future expansion, but should have some related tourist and recreation attractions.
3. The area should have a large population within one, two, and five hours driving time (i.e., the primary, secondary, and tertiary population markets) that will support the facility in varying degrees.
4. The area generally should be near a major traffic artery carrying large volumes of local and nonlocal traffic, and the facility should be both accessible to this major traffic artery and visible to the travelers if possible.

INFORMATION AND DIRECTIONS

The recent federal regulations restricting the use of directional signs on major highways, can be a significant factor in efforts to attract tourists and visitors from heavily traveled routes into the enterprise. The cost of signs large enough to be placed outside the affective distances of the federal regulations are extensive, perhaps averaging 3000 to 5000 dollars per year. In some cases state highway departments will advertise major tourist attraction areas by standard state highway signs. Restrictions and opportunities in this area should receive careful consideration. If sign boards and direction signs are restricted, alternatives must be considered, such as information or brochures in gas stations or restaurants all along the route, other advertisements on radio and local television, and even short range broadcasts by facilities or in tourist areas such as in Disney World, that can be actually picked up on the radio station in the automobile of the traveler.

Other elements and considerations in the market analysis are the factors influencing *attendance*.

ATTENDANCE

The basic factors influencing attendance at a commercial entertainment facility for example are:

1. Resident and local population, its movement and accessibility to the facility.
2. Tourist population.

[3] George W. Cornwell, *Conducting a Feasibility Study for a Proposed Outdoor Recreation Enterprise,* Cooperative Extension Service, Virginia Polytechnic Institute, Blacksburg, Virginia, April 1966.

3. Competitive and complimentary attractions.
4. Weather.
5. Flair, or showmanship.

These factors collectively determine any facility's attendance, capacity, admission price, staff, operating season and hours, and most efficient mode of operation. The key to a financially successful facility lies in tailoring the facility's content to adjust to the above five elements.

The first four factors can be felt and measured because they are tangible. The fifth and most important is intangible and ethereal, a "sixth" sense. It is the basic product of the facility. Without sufficient flair, repeat visits and favorable word of mouth advertising will be inadequate for success. Flair begins where design, planning, and construction ends. It is the combined result of many things, including live shows and attractions, event timing, background color and live music, wardrobe, good clean mechanical operations of rides and animation, sound effects, cleanliness, guest relations programs, crowd control, and host and hostess training.

In essence, the flair concept is what distinguishes the entire fabric, spirit, and intent of the private versus the public sector of the outdoor recreation industry.

The following planning element/consideration is fundamental to the determination of facility capacity requirements, minimum parking requirements, and most importantly, estimated first year gross revenue.

The element is *projected attendance* that can be adequately calculated by two common research methods:

1. Zone penetration by population.
2. Vehicular traffic flow patterns past the proposed facility.

The first method relies on comparative and mathematical analysis of the "primary," "secondary," and "tertiary" markets of the permanent or resident population surrounding the proposed facility. The second method accounts for the tourist segment of the population that would visit the facility while traveling by automotive transportation (i.e., car, bus, trailer, motorcycle, etc.).

An average attendance figure is produced for the facility under each method. The two averages are then added and divided by two. This produces a *projected attendance* under both methods. By adding and dividing the results of the two methods, the margin for attendance overlap is lessened and a fairer attendance projection is produced.

This is getting at the heart of the feasibility study. The potential income that can be expected will determine the maximum amount of money that can be spent for the development and construction of the project. A campground owner for example will need to know how many campsites he thinks will be filled per night if he develops a campground at a particular location. Thus he may determine, by methods to be discussed later in this chapter, that he can fill and average of 80 campsites per night for the camping season of 120 days. This would figure to be 9600 campsite days, and at a rate of say $3.00 per night per campsite, would produce gross income of $28,000 for the season. He may also estimate other income from auxiliary services such as boat rental, camp store, firewood, and so on, but the estimated number of persons camping on the campground for the season set the ceiling for the maximum gross income he can expect and ultimately use for construction and operation costs.

There is no cut and dry, black and white, solution-method-formula to precisely predict or project attendance for a facility that has yet to be built, let alone open. However, the above two methods, when they can be utilized, are excellent and adequate sources to make sophisticated, educated, and generally conservative guesstimates at an inherently illusive yet essential planning element. The methods are adequate because:

1. They reach out to the attendance experiences of other attractions/facilities.
2. They make allowances for the characteristics and scope of the proposed facility.
3. They are mathematically documentable.

Attendance projection must be attempted and documented to the greatest extent for two obvious reasons:

1. To give the planners a firm idea whether their facility will in the long term financially make money or break it, given the revenue envisioned from a projected attendance, and how that revenue matches against the project cost and expenses.
2. Because the financial community naturally must know the color and size of the bottom line before putting down some money.

The following is a description of each method. It is followed by some questions that deserve attention concerning the methods. Table 14 shows the figures arrived at under each method, and the average of the two.

The zone penetration method is achieved by applying to the proposed facility the attendance experiences of similar and different attractions within population "zones" of 50 (primary), 100 (secondary), and 150 (tertiary) miles from the attraction. The "experiences" are expressed as percentages, and attendance is expressed as a percentage of the total population within one and 150 miles of the attraction.

Let's say 1.5 million people live within 50 miles, 1.2 million people live within 50-100 miles, and 1.2 million people live within 100-150 miles of Attraction A. This

Table 14 Attraction A, projected attendance

Year	P-S-T Zones	Traffic Flow	Attraction A–Projected Attendance
1976	488,401	561,111	524,756
1977	540,165	617,222	578,693
1978	592,281	660,427	626,354
1979	665,128	693,448	679,288
1980	752,898	741,989	747,443

attraction historically draws about 24 percent of its total annual attendance from the primary market, 6.2 percent from the secondary market, and 3.7 percent from the tertiary market. (These are extremely realistic approximations, based on reports from several large themed attractions.)

The research shows many attractions have similar or constant attendance experiences within their respective population "zones." It is not unfair, then, to predict the proposed facility will realize attendance experience within its population "zones."

The second attendance projection method is through the analysis of vehicular traffic flow patterns adjacent to, or intersecting, the proposed facility. Traffic count figures for a specific location in most states can be obtained from the State or County Highway Departments.

Let's say we plan to build an amusement park the east side of Interstate Highway AB at the intersection of SR 55. (Thus, Highway AB runs N-S of the proposed facility.) In this case, north and south bound traffic from Highway AB has both exit and entrance access to SR 55, and thus the facility.

The state highway department reports in 1974 an average of 12,467 cars travel daily north and south on Interstate AB past the SR 55 entrance and exit ramps. Thus:

> 12,467 x 365 days = 4,550, 455 cars
> *2.74 persons per vehicle = 12,468, 246 persons
> **30% of above are recreation-oriented vehicles
> THUS: 12,468,246 x 30% = 3,740,474
> ***3,740,474 x 15% = 561,111
> 561,111 = first year attendance by this method

*National Average. Conservative for tourist-active states such as Florida, Texas and so on.

**In tourist-active states, the State Highway Department or the State Tourist Agency/Commission will utilize a percentage to represent the volume of recreation-oriented traffic as a part of the entire traffic volume on major highways. Naturally, it is almost impossible to predict the validity of such a percentage unless one were to physically stop each vehicle and ask the driver and passengers if they had immediate or eventual recreation plans in the state. Often, this percentage is a matter of professional judgment on the part of the state agency, or represents the total attendance of all state public and private attractions (if available) as a percentage of the estimated number of state highway visitors in one year. The researcher will usually be confronted with two obstacles when hunting for this recreational-oriented percentage:

1. If it is given, and available as a matter of record, it is usually optimistic or liberal. For instance, the Texas Highway Department in 1974 estimated 35 percent of its highway travelers were recreational-oriented. This probably was a liberal estimate when used to calculate tourist volume figures. A more conservative percentage was averaged with the Texas figure to project a more realistic reflection of the recreational-oriented estimate.

2. The second thing the researcher will find is that he or she will read a diversity of opinions on the subject before reaching a judgment on the percentage. Influencing

the final decision should be the consideration of the tourist popularity to other states in the country. Awareness of what another tourist-active state describes as a recreational-oriented percentage could be helpful in your own research.

***Again, this 15 percent is a matter of feel and judgment. In effect, it says one-half of the recreational-oriented travelers will visit my facility. This is actually a small number, when considering 70 percent of the travelers (in this case, at least) do not have recreation intentions, and would not have immediate plans or desires to stop at my facility. This 15 percent usually reflects the researcher's familiarity with the project, experiences at similar facilities, and consultation with experts and co-workers in the industry.

Several Questions deserve attention from this section:

1. What if zone penetration information is not available from attractions that are similar in scope, size, or location to the proposed facility?

The first thing to remember is that no two attractions/facilities are exactly alike. Unless they are part of a corporate chain, such as Sea World, Lion Country Safari, or Marriott's "Great America" parks, it is hard to measure physical similarities among commercial outdoor recreation centers/facilities. It's almost impossible to say Attraction A is like Attraction B. Second, the facilities/attractions upon which you are trying to match similar zone penetration data may be comparatively "small," and thus not have the marketing expertise, money, or staff to calculate what percentage of their visitors come from 50 or 100 miles. And they may not care to find out. Why should they, for instance, if they continue to "pack 'em in?" However, the owners or managers of these "smaller" attractions might be able to give you professional "guess-timates" based on their many years of experience in that area of in the industry.

Finally, the researcher will find many major and smaller attractions will have zone penetration data available, but not to you. It's simply a fact of life. It depends on the policy, the personality of the owner or manager, if you know the right person or have a connection, or it's entirely understood in writing what use will be made of the zone penetration data.

2. A second question is a natural follow-up to the first: What if vehicular traffic count figures are not available for your specific site, or the data is badly outdated?

This always presents problems. There's no easy solution. If figures aren't available near the proposed site, try to pinpoint a nearby site where traffic count readings are made. Then, try to obtain traffic count data for the nearest major traffic artery (arteries) that would feed travelers into your facility. An average of the counts might offer a clearer and truer reflection of actual vehicular flow upon which the proposed facility would draw. Finally, if data is outdated, ask the source for an opinion as to the increase or decrease along those routes since traffic count data were last reported.

As discussed, the development of attendance projection is a fulcrum to the establishment of three other elements which must be accounted for in the planning of an outdoor commercial recreation facility :

1. Facility capacity requirements.
2. Minimum parking space requirements.
3. Sources of income per yearly gross revenue projections.

Facility capacity requirements as shown in Table 15, represent the total number of guests that actually can be supported and manitained by Attraction A as a specific period of time (month, week, day), given the projected attendance. This can be understood by looking the the formula widely used in the chart below. Note that if Attraction A were to install amusement rides, hourly ride capacity can be calculated.

From the average high-day attendance, minimum parking requirements (not allowing for expansion) can be determined as follows :

8,887 ÷ 3 persons per car to account for bus/travelers, families = 2,962 cars

2,962 cars ÷ 114 cars per acre, and average which can be used both for amusement parks and shopping centers = 26 acres.

This figure is the minimum, for it does not allow for additional space that would be allotted to sustain park growth and thus larger average high-day attendance. As a general rule of thumb, in the private sector total parking acreage (which again is allotted

Table XV Attraction A, capacity requirements

	1976	1977	1978	1979	1980
Estimated attendance	524,756	578,693	626,354	679,288	747,443
Peak two months (60% of estimated)	314,853	347,215	375,812	407,573	448,466
Average weekly attendance peak two months ÷ 8857	35,548	39,202	42,431	46,017	50,634
Average high day attendance (25% of weekly)	8,887	9,800	10,607	11,504	12,658
Peak in-grounds attendance (60% of average high day)	5,332	5,880	6,364	6,920	7,595
Ratio of ride capacity to peak in-grounds attendance	1.5	1.5	1.5	1.5	1.5
Hourly ride capacity (peak x 1.5)	7,998	8,820	9,546	10,353	11,392
Annual capacity increase	N/A	822	726	807	1,039
Attendance increase	N/A	53,937	47,661	52,934	68,155

to support both peak crowd and park expansion) will be twice the acreage of the total recreation/amusement area.

Finally, after calculating projected attendance, first-year gross revenue can be estimated. This can be done once an admission price schedule has been determined for both adults and children. For example, an average admission calculated at three adults to every child (most amusement parks and attractions, for example, experience this ratio in "pay-one-price" operations):

$$3 \times \$5.00 + 1 \times \$3.00 = \$4.50$$

However, most commercial outdoor recreation facilities will have auxiliary sources of revenue: food and beverage, arcade, games, retail sales including crafts, special shows, and other sources. These sources of income will contribute to the overall per capita income. Thus, with a total per capita expenditure of $7.90 for example, Attraction A will realize a first year gross income of $4,140,324.

$$524,756 \times \$7.90 = \$4,140,324$$

Once the attendance projections and subsequent first-year gross revenue estimates are made, a similar procedure must be followed each year through the next five years, and generally estimated through the next ten to fifteen years, of the time required to amortize the capital investment.

In some market analysis and feasibility studies, several rates of return are estimated for comparison. For instance, in the case example illustrated above, projected attendance and income at a 40 percent level and a 50 percent level might be figured in addition to the 60 percent level, which is illustrated. This gives a clearer understanding of the breakeven point, estimating the incomes at various fees per "visitor day" that are plotted against total cost. A visitor day is defined as one visitor at the facility for any part of one day. The total visitor days is the total number of visitors multiplied by the total number of days of operation. The breakeven point is the number of users indicated by the point where the gross income line crosses the total cost line. In this way one can at least predict the number of visits required to breakeven at a given fee.

Table XVI shows the anticipated or projected income from gate receipts for our hypothetical amusement park: Table XVII lists projected income from sources other than gate receipts. Total anticipated revenues are shown in Table XVIII.

Let's look now at an example of estimating income for a much smaller campground operation. In terms of campground feasibility studies, a first consideration is whether the campground will be primarily a *transient* campground for single night and overnight stays for individuals traveling to and from other destination areas or whether the campground is in a *destination* area, close to other attractions where visitors will be expecting to stay several days, a week, or more.

The method of estimating the income for a transient campground will be similar to the previous procedure used in estimating attendance at the proposed amusement park example stated earlier. The highway traffic count past the location of the proposed facility should be obtained from the state highway department.

Table XVI Attraction A, gate receipts

	Attendance	Adults: Children	Adult-Child Admission	Per Capita	Gate Receipts
1976	524,756	3:1	$5.00-$3.00	$4.50	$2,361,402
1977	578,695	3:1	$5.25-$3.25	$4.75	$2,748,791
1978	626,354	3:1	$5.50-$3.50	$5.00	$3,131,770
1979	679,288	3:1	$6.00-$4.00	$5.50	$3,736,084
1980	752,898	3:1	$6.50-$4.50	$6.00	$4,517,388

Table XVII Attraction A, auxiliary revenues

	Attendance	Per Capita Food and Beverage	Per Capita Gift and Souvenir	Per Visitor Games and Arcade	Total Revenue	Estimated Gross Aux. Profit
1976	524,756	$1.38	$1.58	$.43	$1,778,922	$1,152,363
1977	578,693	$1.40	$1.60	$.45	$1,996,489	$1,296,270
1978	626,354	$1.42	$1.62	$.47	$2,198,501·	$1,430,691
1979	679,288	$1.44	$1.64	$.49	$2,425,057	$1,581,380
1980	752,898	$1.46	$1.66	$.51	$2,733,018	$1,785,870
Cost of Sales:		35%	45%			

Table XVIII Attraction A, total revenues

	Gate Receipts	Total Aux. Revenue	Total	Per Visitor Expense
1976	$2,361,402	$1,778,922	$4,140,324	$7.90
1977	$2,748,791	$1,996,489	$4,745,280	$8.20
1978	$3,131,770	$2,198,501	$5,330,271	$8.50
1979	$3,736,084	$2,425,057	$6,161,141	$9.00
1980	$4,517,388	$2,733,018	$7,250,406	$9.60

Using the previous example of 12,467 cars traveled daily through the intersection of Interstate AB and SR 55 the area where the campground is to be located, if an estimated 100 day season is calculated, then 12,467 times 100 = 1,246,700 cars will pass by the intersection.

If 30 percent of these cars are recreation oriented vehicles as determined by a number of previous research studies in tourism states, 374,010 cars are traveling for recreation purposes. According to the Bureau of Outdoor Recreation studies mentioned previously concerning the number of activity days per person individuals participate in specific activities, we can find that 46 percent of the population 12 years of age and over participate in camping at least one day during the summer. Thus, 46 percent of the recreation oriented vehicles passing this point is the maximum potential number of campsite days. This would allow a possibility of 172,045 camper site days to be anticipated for the season. This estimate must be reduced according to the number of campsite days other campgrounds can provide in the area along either Interstate AB or SR 55 for some 40 to 50 miles in either direction.

If ten other campgrounds are found with an average of 100 sites each, these would provide for 100 sites times 100 days times 10 campgrounds or 100,000 campsite days. This would allow 172,044 minus 100,000 or 72,044 campsite days as the potential for our new campground. This would suggest an excellent potential for the new campsite, as 100 sites times 100 days = 10,000 campsite days as the maximum potential of our proposed campground.

If the campground is in a destination area, the number of cars entering the area for recreation should be much higher than the previous 30 percent average for a state; let's assume it 60 percent. Thus 46 percent of the 60 percent recreation oriented travelers to the areas would be potential campers. The number must again be reduced by the number of other campsites in the area.

In estimating the income of a campground, usually the total number of potential campsite days are reduced by a certain percentage because of fluctuations in travel, that is, weekday, weekend, and holiday traffic. Thus a campground developed for 100 sites would assume that probably 45 to 50 percent of these would be filled during the weekend. Therefore an average capacity of 70 percent could be used as an overall season figure. Table XIX estimates the annual income from the campground for the next year.

Table XIX   Campground anticipated revenues

Fees collected from 100 sites (100 times 70% times $2.50/day)	$18,750
Profit from the camp store	1,000
Total	$19,750

Should the operator sell fireplace wood and collect fees for boats, motor rentals, or other auxuliary services, profits from these services would be added to the income listed above. These additional services would be more likely in conjunction with a distination camp rather than a transient campground.

It should be stated that the majority of persons who do their own feasibility studies tend to overestimate the anticipated income and underestimate the cost of construction and operation. Because of the self-confidence or ego of the individual, he will assume that he can be more efficient than others. Such planning obviously is disastrous in the long run. The reverse should be the rule. Be conservative in estimating income, and liberal in estimating expenses.

MANAGEMENT ANALYSIS

The management analysis is the second portion of the feasibility study and is primarily concerned with a detailed estimate of all expenses incurred in planning, acquiring, and developing the facility, and in operating it to provide the service for which it is designed in attracting the visitor. The management analysis can be divided into two major groups.

INITIAL OR PRE-OPENING EXPENSES

These include the following three categories:

1. *Capital expenses* including purchase of land, design, architectural and engineering fees, and the actual cost of construction for the site, entrance way, roads, utilities, buildings, and facilities themselves, along with supporting facilities, such as maintenance sheds and warehouses and any other permanent facilities.
2. *Equipment* includes any type of equipment for rides, food preparation, transportation, maintenance, or work that would have a life expectancy of from two to ten years or longer, but not of a permanent nature.
3. *Supplies* includes any items that would have a life expectancy of less than a year, such as handtools, office supplies, items that would be consumed in the process of sales such as foodstuffs, paper supplies, or other items used in maintaining or operating the facility.

To refer again to our outdoor amusement park example, Table XX gives an example of pre-opening expenses. An example of initial or pre-opening expenses for our 100 site campground can be seen in Table XXI.

The cost of developing and constructing a recreation enterprise varies widely and is difficult to assess in general terms. If the operator and his family are to provide all labor for development and construction, the actual cost will be less than if the work is contracted. Materials used in the construction of facilities will also affect cost. The type of facilities provided will affect cost. Flush type toilets cost more than pit type toilets. For each item the cost can vary and depends primarily on the decisions made

Table XX Attraction A, pre-opening expenses

Capital:	
Land	$400,000
Parking and entrance roads	$100,000
Grading and excavation	$ 60,000
Fencing and security	$ 40,000
Utilities and underground	$400,000
Landscape and drainage	$200,000
Design and engineering	$200,000
Amphitheatre	$300,000
Equipment:	
Kitchen equipment	$ 50,000
Rides	$1,700,000
Administrative equipment	$100,000
Supplies:	
Props and dressing (banners, poles, benches, etc.)	$100,000
Uniforms and costumes	$ 50,000
Scripts, sets, rehearsals, etc.	$300,000
Advertising	$100,000
Total	$5,000,000

by the individual for the enterprise.

Regardless of the type of recreation enterprise to be developed, a preliminary estimate of the development and construction costs must be made. List the items to be developed and constructed along with the best possible cost estimate available for each item. Break each item down into its lowest common denominator whenever possible. If the work is to be contracted, estimates can be obtained from the contractor. If the operator is to do his own constructing cost estimates on the materials, the information needed can be obtained from his supplier or some individuals who have constructed similar facilities.

Equipment cost must also be considered carefully. Various items of equipment are necessary for general maintenance, repair, and overall operation of the facility. These should not be overlooked in the original cost of constructing and developing the enterprise, and should have an annual depreciation rate similar to those indicated above.

OPERATING EXPENSES

The second category of expenses are those accompanying the operation of the facility. These are normally broken into two groups for bookkeeping and accounting purposes, and are called fixed costs and variable costs, as previously discussed in the chapter on management. However, for the purposes of our example in figuring projections for the

Table XXI Campground pre-opening expenses

Capital:	
Cost of Land 40 acres at $1000 per acre	$ 40,000
Road development and construction	$ 1,200
Clearing and constructing campsites (100 campsites at $200 each)	$ 20,000
Drilled well pipes, faucets utilities or etc.	$ 2,100
Construction of restrooms, toilets, etc.	$ 15,000
Office and campstore building	$ 7,000
Storage shed, maintenance shed	$ 5,000
Equipment:	
Tables (100 at $23 each)	$ 2,300
Garbage Cans (100 at $4.00 each)	$ 400
Fireplaces (100 at $12.00 each)	$ 1,200
Entrance sign	$ 100
Direction and miscellaneous signs	$ 50
Playground equipment	$ 500
Office equipment	$ 1,000
Pickup truck (used)	$ 1,200
Tractor and trailer (used)	$ 1,700
Tools and miscellaneous equipment	$ 1,200
Supplies:	
Office supplies	$ 500
Campstore supplies	$ 4,000
Total	$105,000

feasibility study these will be included together.

Fixed costs continue whether the enterprise is in operation or not. Included are expenses for taxes, insurance, and depreciation. These costs may be delayed but must be met in the long run if the enterprise is to succeed. It is a poor business practice to delay the setting aside of these expenses, as it no doubt will provide a day of reckoning sometime in the future.

Variable costs are direct cash expenses that exist when the enterprise is in operation. Included are expenses for utilities, hired labor, fuel, supplies, advertising, maintenance, and repairs. Variable costs must be met or the enterprise will actually be losing money.

Tables XXII and XXIII illustrate estimated operating expenses for our Attraction A and campground respectively.

Figure 44 Auxiliary services such as bicycling should be considered in the initial planning, both as a pre opening expense for equipment and the development of bike paths, and an operating expense to maintain the equipment after the facility is opened.
Courtesy: Bicycle Manufactureres Association of America, Washington, D.C.

Table XXII Attraction A, estimated operating expenses

Expense Salaries	1976	1977	1978	1979	1980
Begin with 40 full-time per 12 months (@ $10,000)	$400,000	$440,000	$500,000	$550,000	$610,000
Begin with 300 part-time per 13 weeks ($2.50/hr. 40 hrs)	$390,000	$450,000	$510,000	$570,000	$630,000
10% of payroll for taxes, insurance, benefits	$79,000	$89,000	$101,000	$112,000	$124,000
	$869,000	$978,000	$1111,000	$1232,000	$1364,000
Advertising and promotion (7% of gross revenue)	$289,822	$332,169	$373,119	$431,280	$507,528
Sales taxes (7% of gross revenue)	$289,822	$332,169	$373,119	$431,280	$507,528
Utilities (2.5% of gross revenue)	$103,508	$118,632	$133,256	$154,028	$181,260

Insurance (3.0% of gross revenue)	$124,209	$142,358	$159,908	$184,834	$217,512
Operating supplies (4% of gross revenue)	$165,612	$189,811	$213,211	$246,445	$290,016
Repairs and maintenance (4% of gross revenues)	$165,612	$189,811	$213,211	$246,445	$290,016
(1) Depreciation	$571,428	$571,428	$571,428	$571,428	$571,428
(2) Return on investment	$500,000	$500,000	$500,000	$500,000	$500,000
(3) Miscellaneous expenses (3% on gross revenues)	$124,209	$142,358	$159,908	$184,834	$217,512
Total	$3203,222	$3496,736	$3808,160	$4182,574	$4646,800

[1] Depreciation-refers to life expectancy of items of equipment and capital (except land) on Tables XX and XXI. An average of seven years was used as the average in depreciating those items.

[2] Return on investment-figured over 20 years at 10 percent interest.

[3] Includes legal fees, travel and entertainment, accounting fees, miscellaneous equipment rental, postage, dues, subscriptions, and general fees.

Note: the percentages above are based on percentages experienced by several attractions, a survey by Amusement Business, and an attractions audit by Funspot Magazine.

Table XXIII Campground estimated operating expenses

Hired labor: 1 man, 100 days at $10/day	$ 1,000
Taxes	250
Insurance	450
Advertising	200
Repairs and maintenance	500
Supplies	600
Utilities	500
Depreciation 1/7 of equipment from Table VII $8550	1,221
Return on investment-principal and interest for pre-opening costs-Table VII on 10 year payback	18,900
Total	$22,721

When computing depreciation for facilities, or items of equipment such as trucks, tractors, rowboats, and so on, the salvage value should be deducted from the original cost and the remainder divided by the number of years of life expectancy, to determine the annual depreciation rate. On buildings, a straight-line annual depreciation can be computed by dividing the years of life into the cost directly.

Since it is anticipated that the land will not depreciate, no annual depreciation rate will be specified for the cost of the land.

An annual depreciation rate for each facility and major equipment item must be included as an annual cost, and set aside each month as a part of the regular operating expenses so that when the time comes to repair or replace facilities or items of equipment, the money will be in hand.

ESTIMATING NET INCOME

By carefully estimating the gross income, and estimating as close as possible the gross expenses for both initial investments, fixed and variable separating costs, the estimated net income can be determined. The salary and wages of the manager or operator must be included in the annual operating expenses, as he will need to have some kind of income on which to live, regardless of the status of the enterprise.

Using our two previous examples, the net income and return on investment for the amusement park would look as follows:

Table XXIV Attraction A, estimated net income 1976

Total income from Table 18	$4,140,324
Total expense from Table 20	$3,203,222
Total Gross Profit (Before Taxes)	$ 937,102

Note: this includes payments of $571428 for depreciation, and $500,000 return on investment that will allow the $5,000,000 pre-opening costs (Table XX) to be repaid over a ten year period.

It would appear from Table XXIV that our attraction is planned for the right location and would be an excellent investment returning a profit of approximately 20 percent of investment.

The net income and return on the investments for the campground would look as follows:

Table XXV Campground estimated net income

Total income from Table XIX	$19,750
Total expenses from Table XXI	$22,721
	$ 2,971

From Table XXV it is obvious that the campground would not even make expenses the first year of operation, let alone returning enough for the camp director or manager to receive a salary. Allowing for increased attendance after the campground became known in subsequent years, it would be a number of years before it would return sufficient profit to support a manager and his family full-time for the year round. The results of this feasibility study would imply that the campground would not be feasible or profitable. This substantiates several studies on the profitability of small campgrounds, which found that over two-thirds of the campgrounds were not profitable, and those that were are larger, and have a number of auxiliary sources of income, or are in destination areas.

Table XXVI shows an actual analysis for a large campground with auxiliary services can be used to compare with the small operation discussed previously.

Table XXVI Safari systems campgrounds profit and loss statement

Safari Inn—Waco, Nebraska
Statement of Operating Income and Expense
For the Period July 15, 1971-December 31, 1971

Sales:	
Gasoline	$82,565.87
Resaurant	$47,960.22
Camp registration	$12,288.71
Gifts	$16,225.17
Groceries & convenience	$ 8,638.70
Mini-golf	$ 1,522.91
Total Sales	$168,773.52
Cost of goods sold:	
Gasoline	$62,214.13
Food-restaurant	$20,679.08
Gifts	$ 8,319.57
Groceries and convenience	$ 5,980.95
Total cost of good sold	$97,193.73
Gross Profit	$71,579.79
Expenses:	
Salaries	$39,650.27
Telephone & postage	$ 931.09
Utilities	$ 3,858.86
Repairs and maintenance	$ 579.73
Rental services	$ 1,035.45
Insurance	$ 1,626.88
Taxes-Payroll	$ 2,036.28
Supplies	$ 6,169.69
Advertising	$ 3,335.95
Miscellaneous	$ 2,399.98
Total expense	$61,624.18
Net operating profit	$ 9,955.61

The rate of return on the investment must eventually be computed to determine whether or not the investment will be profitable. Therefore, the gross income, gross expenses, and the net income must be carefully estimated each year for the first five years, and generally estimated for the remaining years over which the facility is amortized. It is anticipated that the income will increase as awareness of the facility increases, and repeat business is developed. Therefore, gross income for years following year one should increase. It is likely that operating expenses will exceed the gross income for the first three to five years, until sufficient attendance is obtained. The annual operating expenses will also increase somewhat with the rise in attendance; however, it takes a minimum amount of operating expense simply to open the door. It should be remembered that the fixed cost continues whether there are any visitors or not. These must be offset by larger profits over the long term of the investment. When these are averaged, the investor must obtain a minimum of 10 to 15 percent on the return of his investment. Otherwise, he would be better to invest the money in interest bearing notes and forget all the risk and work of development.

A projected return on investment should be prepared for each year for the length of time over which the capital investment must be amortized. If the investor determines that the cost of the land must be paid within 15 years, then one fifteenth of the cost of this land plus interest must be included as an expense each year and must be considered in figuring the return on the investment.

Likewise, if an investor has loaned money for all initial and operating costs, repayment of principal and interest must be included as a part of the operating cost.

If the owner or operator has the money for investment, he may require only the interest be paid on the amount of the investment as an operating cost.

Summary

Many small, private, recreation business enterprises attempt to save money by skimping on their preliminary planning and feasibility study. If perspective owners, operators, or managers of recreation enterprises would take the time and money to pursue the kind of feasibility study that they should, the percentage of successful operations would increase dramatically. Several studies may have to be made as different sites are considered, evaluated, and accepted or rejected. This, no doubt will increase the initial cost of the development of the final facility, as this cost must be recouped. However, a small number of dollars spent, initially to learn that a large number of dollars later should not be spent seems to be a step in the right direction. It is a wise person who follows the biblical instruction to "count the cost before he attempts to build the vineyard." Although the planning elements and principles previously discussed are probably applicable in the public sector as well, the fundamental difference in the private sector is that the facility must seek to satisfy the needs and desire of essentially two groups instead of one; the recreation and desire of the public, and the profit incentive of the entrepreneur/owner. The successful planner will seek to provide answers as to whether the public will be satisfied, and whether a profit will be made in a feasibility study encompassing a thorough investigation of the market, in terms of what is being sold and what the public will buy at what prices, at what location, including projected attendance and projected revenues. He will also make a thorough analysis of the management aspects, including estimated cost for capital expenses to to plan and develop the facility to make it ready for operation, as well as those funds necessary for the operation of the facility prior to the time when income will more than offset the expenses.

There is no question that in the final analysis a net profit must be projected that is satisfactory to the investor, otherwise alternative opportunities for investment of funds will be sought. It should be noted that human nature being what it is, people tend to overestimate their income and underestimate their expenses, and feel that they can do a better job of managing than their competitors, that they can construct facilities for less than their competitors, and can operate them more efficiently. Those attempting such developments should remember that only 12 percent of the recreation enterprise make substantial profits sufficient to support a man and his family, and that it takes two to five years to build x volumes over 50 percent of capacity.

Many owners may attempt to develop their facilities a piece at a time. Indeed an original plan should include plans for long-term projections; however, to build a piece at a time without an overall master plan for development is a shortcut for disaster. Many enterprises that have been developed piecemeal end up 10 to 15 years later looking just like that. Funds should be included in the initial cost, for an adequate master plan that should be re-evaluated periodically but followed unless there is significant reason for which to deviate.

A good sound feasibility study and analysis is the investors/owners best insurance against a poor investment. It should be remembered that if funds are not available for this type of investigation, and for the kind of capital analysis you suggest will be needed to open and operate the facility until it is making a profit, the wise investor will realize what the future holds.

Additional References

Books, Bulletins and Reports
Bureau of Commercial Recreation, *Wisconsin Recreation Development Opportunity,* Department of Natural Resources, P.O. Box 450, Madison, Wisconsin 53701.
Bureau of Commercial Recreation, *Wisconsin Recreation Development Opportunity— Campground,* Department of Natural Resources, P.O. Box 450, Madison, Wisconsin 53701.
Cornwell, George W *Guidelines to Planning, Developing and Managing Rural Recreation Enterprises* Bulletin # 301 Cooperative Extension Service, Virginia Polytechnic Institute, Blacksburg, Virginia, 1966.
DeVriend, A. J., H. M. Smith, and S. W. Weiss, *How to Analyze the Site and Location of Your Recreation Business,* C2436, Recreation Business Management Series 5, Cooperative Extension Programs, University of Wisconsin, December 1972.
Farmers Home Administration, *Handbook of Outdoor Recreation Enterprises in Rural Areas,* Superintendent of Documents, Washington, D.C.
Montville, Francis E., "How To Plan the Recreation Enterprise," Cooperative Extension Service, University of Maine, Orono, Maine, Circular 396, Revised February 1968.

Podd, George O. and John D. Lesure, *Planning and Operating Motels and Motor Hotels,* Ahrens Book Company, Inc., New York.

Safari Systems, Inc. and Subsidiaries, *Financing Proposal-Safari Inn,* at Abilene, Kansas, 1974.

Soil Conservation Service, United State Department of Agriculture, *Guide to Making Appraisals of Potentials for Outdoor Recreation Developments,* July 1966, U.S. Superintendent of Documents, Washington D.C.

Swart, William W., Charles E. Gearing, Tugart Var, *Planning For Tourism Development,* University of Miami, Coral Gables, Florida 1975.

Periodicals

Eyster, James J., "The Hotel-Motel Feasibility Study," The Cornell Hotel and Restaurant Administration Quarterly, School of Hotel Administration, Cornell University, Ithaca, New York, November 1973.

Lesure, John D., "A Cost Allocation System for Hotels," Reprinted form the Cornell Hotel and Restaurant Administration Quarterly, February 1973.

Discussion Questions

1. Discuss the elements of a feasibility analysis.
2. In selecting and planning a commercial recreation site, what are some of the standards to be considered?
3. What factors effect the supply and demand of recreation products and services?
4. What factors effect attendance at a commercial entertainment facility?
5. Assume you are considering the purchase of a recreation vehicle, overnight type campground. Discuss two ways of calculating the projected attendance at your facility.
6. In addition to an attendance projection what three other elements must be accounted for in planning of an outdoor commercial recreation facility. Explain each element as to its significance in managing the facility.
7. How would you estimate the gross income of a campground?
8. How can a campground owner minimize pre-opening expenses?
9. Why are fixed costs particularly significant to a recreation enterprise (for example, ski resort)?
10. How would you estimate the net income of a campgroud? Why is this important to the owner?

CHAPTER 7

MARKETING THE PRODUCT

Marketing means many different things to many different people. According to C. De-witt Coffman,[1] author of *Marketing for a Full House*, it is all of the planning and action that goes into:

1. Searching out all potential sources of business.
2. Finding just what it is that those potential customers want and need in the way of facilities and services.
3. Selling those potential customers.
4. Servicing them so that they spend the maximum amount of money.
5. Convincing them to return.

Another definition given by Professor Wentworth,[2] University of Indiana School of Business: "Marketing is the analysis, planning, implementation and control of carefully formulated programs to bring about voluntary exchange of values with target markets for the purpose of achieving organizational objectives."

Unfortunately, many enterprise operators in the past have mistakenly assumed that marketing meant selling. Selling is of course a part of marketing, but not necessarily the most important part. Marketing is:

1. Determining what people want.
2. Planning and providing products and services to meet those wants.
3. Selecting the most effective ways and means of reaching those who have these desires.

It has been said that more enterprises are operated on blind faith than on established capitol. A careful analysis of this statement may indeed be true. It is no doubt the

---

[1] From MARKETING THE FULL HOUSE, C. DeWitt Coffman, and Helen J. Recknagel, School of Hotel Administration, Cornell University, Ithaca, New York, 1975. Copyright © 1972, revised 1975.

[2] John Wentworth, Speech given at Executive Development Program, Indiana University, Bloomington, Indiana, March 1975.

most difficult but the most important part of the enterprise operators job. To be effective requires imagination, understanding, intuition, knowledge, creativity, and a great deal of good hard work. Marketing can best be thought of in terms of public relations. Favorable acceptance by the public is of paramount importance. Public relations may be defined as an attitude of management that places priority first on the public interest when making any management decisions. In other words, the enterprise operator trys first to determine what his guests desire, and second to provide those desires if possible for profit, third to entice them to return. Thus marketing is, in essence, people study.

The most important concept in understanding the modern-day philosophy of marketing is to reverse a previous idea about the owner being the boss, and realize the guests are the boss. Every aspect of the entire operation must be planned, managed, and operated with their wants and needs in mind. The enterprise is run to please the guests, rather than the employees. Many people, however, continue to think primarily in terms of sales when thinking of marketing rather than people.

The need for consumer orientation cannot be overstated. You should consider in your business operations and dealing with the public as well as your guests, the necessity of employing the golden rule, and/or operating your business according to Christian principles. "Do for others, what you would have them do for you if you were the guest." Good marketing and public relations procedures are merely giving of good will. The operator must give of his time, his talents, and his hospitality, in hopes of reaping some eventual financial reward. Good marketing and public relations programs can pay for themselves many times over, if planned and implemented correctly. Without them, they may have no hope of success.

The end objective of having the public and your guests recognize your business as one that provides the best services and products for the rates and prices charged cannot be attained over night. One dissatisfied customer may influence 25 to 50 of his friends, neighbors, and business acquaintenances adversely concerning your enterprise. One dissatisfied customer can indeed do more to take away business, than ten satisfied customers can do to increase it.

The business owner or operator, must think in terms of a plan and program to exchange services for reasonable fees. Figure 45 may help to illustrate. The arrows between the enterprise and the public indeed must be the same size. the operator cannot expect to remain in business long, if the fee arrow is larger than the service arrow, that is accepting a higher fee for the services he is providing than the public feels is warranted. He must indeed make every effort to provide the best service possible, and in return, the public will pay a fee. The idea of a voluntary equal exchange of values, is vital to the concept of marketing. If the enterprise charges higher fees than services warrant, his business will fall. If the enterprise operator provides more service than his fees will support, he will go bankrupt.

Values held by the public are of the utmost importance and these, in turn, are exchanged for the values of the enterprise operator (fees). The manager cannot forget that different people have different values and that each visitor is an individual. The old saying may describe it well, "Different strokes for different folks."

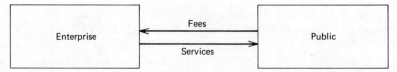

Figure 45 How fees must be exchanged for services between the public and the enterprise manager.

CURRENT CONDITIONS

There is indeed much uncertainty in the economy today. This increases the difficulty with which the values of the potential public determined. It is increasingly difficult to get a consensus on the ideas, concerns, and desires, of the market. The market however is growing in almost all segments of tourism travel and recreation, for reasons discussed previously.

Marketing then attempts to bring a goal of society closer to those of the enterprise or organization.

THREE MARKETING SINS

The primary three marketing sins according to Wentworth are as follows:[3]

1. Becoming industry, product, or activity oriented rather than people oriented.
2. Becoming market process oriented.
3. Becoming selling oriented. Selling is a one way street, marketing is a two way street.

Every decision must be made with the customer in mind. This is difficult for many energetic, enthusiastic, and self-confident managers to do, as the ego within us tends to tell us we are doing a good job, and rationalize our mistakes and inadequacies. Being objective is paramount to the business enterprise.

THE PROBLEM

Unfortunately, there is great diversity in the nature and kinds of private and commercial recreation enterprises. Many are sports and activity oriented such as golf courses, swimming pools, ski mobile agencies, canoe rental businesses, and so on. Others tend to be almost 100 percent in the lodging business, including campground operators or resorts. It is therefore difficult to prescribe a specific type of marketing plan that will fit each enterprise. There is little or no information available that would be directly applicable to all private and commercial recreation businesses. There are, however, several excellent publications that hold many valuable marketing ideas and suggestions that have been prepared for the lodging industry. Because of the inter-relatedness of

[3] Ibid

many of the private and commercial recreation enterprises with the hotel and lodging component, a good many of the ideas concerning marketing will apply equally well to those attempting to provide recreation opportunities or other leisure services for profit.

It has been previously stated, that recreation receives a somewhat smaller portion of the tourist dollar than do other components of the tourist and travel industry. A recent Florida study indicated that the tourism dollar was spent in the following manner:

Lodging	23¢
Food and drink	27¢
Recreation and amusement	13¢
Gasoline	8¢
Clothing and footwear	12¢
Jewelry, souvenirs, and gifts	7¢
Drugs, cosmetics, and tobacco	4¢
Services	2¢
Phones and other related utilities	1¢

WHY PEOPLE TRAVEL FOR RECREATION

It should be recalled from Chapter 2 that people travel for a variety of interests, motivations, and reasons, which relate to their values. It was also mentioned that these change considerably from group to group, and can be categorized to some extent in several classifications. The retired and elderly, as an example, tend to visit historic attractions much more than they will visit purely recreation facilities. The reverse is true of young married couples. The need to consider these individual values and motivations will be mentioned later in more detail.

Marketing can be divided into two primary considerations.

1. The analysis.
2. The plan and/or program.

MARKET ANALYSIS

To plan a marketing program without any information is to take a trip without a map. An analysis must be done which is primarily the information and fact gathering portion before a program can be planned. In keeping with previous discussions, it must be first determined what people want. They want a temporary home, with adequate sleep and rest, good food, and opportunities to take care of the other necessities of life. They also want to be entertained, amused, and recreated, but even though this may be the primary reason that they choose to visit the establishment, these are less likely to make them unsatisfied as poor food or lodging. Dissatisfaction in any one of the components, food, lodging, transportation, or amusement entertainment and recreation, can turn a potential asset into a definite liability. A number of questions must be asked and

Figure 46 Many students and young adults continue to prefer adventurous recreation activities away from well traveled areas.
Courtesy: Bonair Boats, Lenexa, Kansas.

answered insofar as possible. These would include:

1. Who are the present guests?
2. What do I know about them?
3. Who are the potential customers?
4. Where do they live?
5. What are their vacation and travel accommodation preferences?
6. What are their purchasing habits, shopping, and entertainment habits?
7. How did they hear about my particular enterprise?
8. Why did they decide to visit the enterprise?
9. Will they return?
10. What mode of transportation do they prefer to reach the establishment?
11. How long will they stay?
12. Are they transient or terminal visitors?
13. What is the potential?

Answers to many of the above questions must be obtained in order for the marketing plan and program to be effective. Every one should realize that a shotgun approach usually nets zero. Advertising and promotion expenditures cannot be productive unless sufficient answers are obtained. The need for answers or market research

Figure 47 A marketing plan begins with a thorough look at the product that is offered for sale, how it appeals to the market, particularly in comparison with other competing enterprises.
Courtesy: AMF Bowling Products Group, West Berry, New York.

is a necessity in determining the marketing plan and program. Additional questions to be asked of potential customers are the following:

1. The number of people I can expect.
2. Their effective buying income.
3. The cost of transportation.
4. Assessability.
5. Attractiveness.
6. Other factors.

A recent study reported in *Marketing for a Full House*[4] indicates that guests were attracted to a number of motels in the survey in the following priority.

[4] From MARKETING THE FULL HOUSE, C. DeWitt Coffman, and Helen J. Recknagel, School of Hotel Administration, Cornell University, Ithaca, New York, 1975. Copyright © 1972, revised 1975.

1. Location.
2. Housekeeping.
3. Courtesy.
4. Food.

It was interesting to note that of a long list of items, the last item on the list of how guests were attracted was the brochure.

Most enterprises probably are putting the minimum amount of time into their own marketing programs, and depending on what they read in trade journals or what they see others doing. They are probably relying on a few road signs, an entrance sign, and a few direct mail activities. Such limited programs cannot be expected to be adequate anymore than a motel operator can expect to house 100 guests in ten rooms. Word of mouth advertising concerning rate gouging, unclean rooms, poor food, or lack of courtesy travels much more quickly and broadly than does good advertisement.

MARKET SEGMENTATION

To answer some of the questions listed above, it is necessary to separate the total population into smaller units of people who have identical characteristics or values in terms of desiring the services the enterprise operator is trying to market. It is unrealistic to ever imagine that there is a single mass market. The management should expect that a large majority of the population will not be interested, and cannot be made to become interested, in his establishment under any circumstances. The objective of the operator is to isolate those individuals that have a desire or a potential desire, to make them aware of the services, and to motivate them to exchange their money for the services offered.

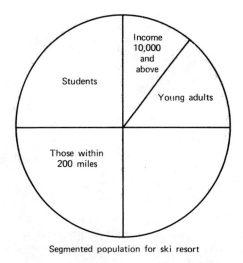

Segmented population for ski resort

Figure 48 The ski market may be segmented into at least four groups; students, those with incomes above $10,000 per year, young adults, and those living within 200 miles. In many cases manufacturers and manufacturers associations have data on characteristics on the primary market group, which can be obtained.

The concept of market segmentation is vital to the marketing program if a shotgun approach is to be avoided. As the market is more finely segmented, the proportion of individuals with interest and potential attendance increases. The ultimate in segmentation would be to isolate only those who had an interest and might be influenced to come. There are different market segmentations for every type of private and commercial recreation enterprise, and many of the segmented populations overlap considerably. Market segmentation is a group of people with similar characteristics that relate to a common product or service.

The potential customer has a number of "offers" to consider, and he looks at all aspects of each offer. Different offers appeal to different people in different ways, in relation to his values, his motivations, funds available, travel distance, and many other individualized considerations. Each operator must make every attempt to look at the segments rather than the total, and each operator will find he has a number of publics that make up a potential market for his services.

Walt Disney World for instance has segmented their markets into the following categories:

1. Distant residents (over 200 miles).
2. Regional residents (25 to 200 miles).
3. Local residents (within 25 miles).
4. Traveling tourists.
5. Arriving tourists.
6. On-site guests.
7. Leaving guests.

These are broken down further into retirees, couples with families, working couples without families, and teenagers.

Their marketing program includes advertising designed for each audience, through methods that have the best potential of reaching that particular audience.

The way to break down the population into segments then is the way that is most important to the operator.

Market segments in the camping equipment sales field are described later in this chapter and include zero potential, low potential, moderate potential, high potential, active campers, temporarily inactive, and permanently inactive.

Six Flags over Mid-America, a large amusement park near St. Louis, Missouri, lists among others the following markets: youth, families, senior citizens, and groups, in each of their primary, secondary, and tertiary zones.

Most markets can be divided into two basic segments. Demographic segmentation, which is a counting and classifying type of identification includes the following: age, sex, income, education, position in life cycle, social class, family size, race, religion, housing, nationality, and location geographically. The second type of segmentation is behavioralistic or psychographic. It has to do with motivations and values, and is very difficult to measure. Factors that effect this segment include values, motivations, interests, leadership ability, gregariousness, personality type, conservativeness, impulsiveness, desire for adventure, and independence.

Figure 49 Potential boaters comprise only a small part of the total population. Courtesy: Boating Industrial Association, glastron boats, Austin, Texas.

USER BEHAVIOR

The market segment therefore must be identified through one or more combinations of the above characteristics. The usage rate is based on a small, concise segment of the overall population. Users and potential users should be isolated from non-users. The potential users should be classified into one of five classifications.

1. Non-awareness, having no knowledge of either the recreation activity or the enterprise offering the activity.
2. Awareness, has skills and is aware of the recreation enterprise.
3. Readiness stage, can be influenced to visit the enterprise.
4. On-site visitor.
5. Past visitor.

The end purpose of the visit must be identified if possible whether it is indeed for recreation, for skill development, for social reasons to be with friends, or to relate the happenings of the visit to people back home.

SOURCES OF DATA FOR MARKET SEGMENTATION

Fortunately, much data is available on some aspects of demographic segmentation but only a few sources are available on other aspects, particularly those of the behavioralistic segmentation aspects. In attempting to locate sources of data on the particular segments of most interest to the enterprise operator the following sources should be investigated.

1. Primary Sources of Data.
   a. Own records. The best source of primary data is the records of the visitors to the site. If no records exist, this should be given high priority.
   b. Knowledge and experience of employees.
   c. Consumers, through the use of a sample survey. Unfortunately many enterprise operators begin with the sample survey first. This should be undertaken only after all of the previous sources mentioned above have been fully investigated. Also it is the most costly. The searching out of data increases as one moves down the list of sources. A sample survey many times can give misleading information because of a poor sample, poor interviewing, or poor questions.
   d. Experimental survey. In many cases small innovations or new ideas can be tried on an experimental basis with a small portion of the visitors and their reactions obtained. This is merely a matter of trying it and collecting data on it. Most changes can be piloted first, to reduce the initial expense for an untried venture.
2. Secondary sources.
   a. Government data, census information, or Discover America Travel Organization information.
   b. State information, in some cases state governments or state Departments of Tourism will have information services available.
   c. Local municipal sources concerning population projections, age, income, or education characteristics.
   d. University-Extension service, business schools, and other departments have valuable sources of data for demographic information.
   e. Trade Associations (a valuable source of information), usually available to members and others at a cost.
   f. Other sources such as banks, community development arms of utilities, Chamber of Commerce, and others.
   g. Consultants and/or experts.

Again, beware of ego involvement. Buying on the part of the visitor is the result of the total image of the enterprise, attitude of clerks, location, or price. Loss of only one can squelch the whole package. The total package is important. Several items of consideration in case a customer survey is desired might be the following:

1. List what information is desired and what is needed (what do you want to find out).
2. List a number of questions under each item, perhaps asking the same question in

several ways.

3. Go through the entire list of items of information needed in this manner.
4. Go back and pick out the best questions.
5. Look at order and sequence so that they naturally have some organized thread running through the total.
6. Get some input from experts. University Cooperative Extension Specialists can assist. Public opinion survey departments on University campuses can assist.
7. Keep it short. Most individuals will not spend more than 3 or 4 minutes filling out a questionnaire.
8. If possible, keep the questions to yes and no responses, or those of a forced choice nature where they can check.
9. Refrain from asking more than one or two open ended questions where the customer must write out his response.

When attempting to segment the population, ask the following questions.

1. What is the problem or the desired result intended by this segmentation and/or marketing program?
2. What kinds of steps or objectives will help me reach the end result or help me to solve a problem.
3. What kinds of information do I need to know to solve the problem or meet the objective.
4. How and where can I get the information I need.

One must always attempt to look at these final objectives or end results of an analysis to determine whether or not the actions he is taking to obtain data to segment the population will help him to reach that goal. Likewise the accumulation of much data does not always translate easily into marketing plans and programs. Many an individual has collected much data and then sat down and wondered what to do with it. One trained in marketing can be of great assistance on a one shot basis, or on a continuing basis, to help the enterprise operator determine exactly what it is he wants to know, what kinds of data will help him find the answers to these questions or obtain the objectives, and how to use the data that is collected to meet those ends. Then the analysis is much more efficient, and collecting only data that will provide answers or assist in the final planned program.

It is necessary to be as creative as possible in considering segmentation, as well as in locating sources of data. It must also be remembered that more of the same is not always best.

Every effort must be made to examine the behavior of the leisure customer, by asking the guests themselves, asking others, taking surveys, interviews, and by any other means available at hand to try to learn as much about the behavioral characteristics of the segmented population as possible.

As the enterprise operator has no doubt considered the *forecast*—that is the number of potential people that he can expect to attract—during his feasibility study either on developing or taking over the enterprise, that aspect will not be discussed further, other than to say that many of the items that would effect the potential attendance can be investigated and realistic estimates made.

PRODUCT ANALYSIS

A thorough investigation should be made of the services that are being sold and the type of activity involved in addition to the following:

1. The quality of the service.
2. The rates.
3. The appearance of the property, the condition of the facilities.
4. Transportation.
5. Location.
6. The business flow average.
7. The signs.
8. The advertising promotion and publicity.
9. The landscaping.
10. The lodging accommodations.
11. The food service.
12. The beverage service.
13. Quality and courtesy of the staff.
14. The attitude of the community concerning travel and tourism.
15. Other facilities near you with which you can cooperate.
16. Relationship with Chamber of Commerce, local or regional tourism or travel groups, and State Department of Tourism.
17. Length of season, comparison of facilities and services with averages of all enterprises of the same kind.
18. Routes used to get to the facility.
19. Types of transportation available and modes used.
20. Distance from densely populated centers.

In many of the items above the enterprise manager should not be the one to make the evaluation. Because of ego involvements mentioned previously, it is the rare operator that can be completely objective. A friend, acquaintance, expert, or competitor is in a much better position to make a frank and objective evaluation of the above, particularly concerning the physical condition of the facility and the services rendered.

It is an excellent suggestion to test your own property. Call on the phone and make a reservation, or have complications that will require the best response from your receptionist or will test their patience and other aspects of their public relations image with their public. Test the facility yourself, camp in the campsite, participate in the recreation activities, have your friends or friendly competitors do the same.

Analyze each employee's strengths and weaknesses, courteousness and patience, desire to serve, as well as the function of the position they hold or the department therein. Every effort should be made to solve in-house problems before attempting to solve outside facility problems.

Some of the information gathered will automatically imply action, and a plan should be prepared to aleviate those conditions found to be unsatisfactory. Consult with others who are knowledgeable in the field concerning corrective programs for other results found.

COMPETITOR ANALYSIS

This implies a frank and honest evaluation of similar facilities or enterprises within the area, or even in other areas. Although similar enterprises in the same area have traditionally looked upon their neighbors as competitors, the wise manager knows that in the minds of the visitor, the competition is between areas rather than enterprises. The Smokey Mountains is competing for the visitor against Yellowstone Park, and Lake of the Ozarks against Land Between the Lakes. Every effort should be made to investigate both the facilities and enterprises of a similar nature in the same area, as well as those in the other areas. One need not identify himself necessarily to find out the problems other operators may have.

The manager must evaluate whether or not his enterprise is at least as good as the average in every respect, if not better. It is not the mediocre enterprise that does the best business. It is the one that is unique and the one that does the best job of everything. Investigate the type of services offered, the cost, types of marketing programs used, types of visitors, and as much other specific information as is available.

MARKETING CYCLES

As one views the potential market for his services or product, another aspect of the marketing phenomena should be given careful consideration. Wilbur F. LaPage[5] of the U.S. Forest Service has spent many years developing, testing, and validating a market research model, which has significant implications for all managers and suppliers of leisure goods and services today. His model indicates that participation nationwide in any recreation activity will follow a growth curve similar to recreation activity of individuals according to age. Thus, as shown in Figure 50, the vertical axis can be in any specified terms, dollars invested, units of production, numbers of enterprises, capacity, or numbers of campers, skiers, or visitor days, while the horizontal axis is in terms of time. The model would indicate that the growth of any market over time follows the pattern of a generalized growth curve just as does the growth of a population. Thus, any recreation activity will experience growth in its infancy, rapid growth in its early years, continued rapid growth through its middle years, a slowdown of growth in its maturity, and a leveling off, almost horizontal growth, in a period of what LaPage terms as "senility." This model, of course, is independent of such unforseeable influences as shortages of energy and discretionary income.

[5] From RESEARCH FOR CHANGING TRAVEL PATTERNS by Wilbur LaPage, Travel Research Association Proceedings. Reprinted with permission of Mari Lou Wood, Executive Secretary.

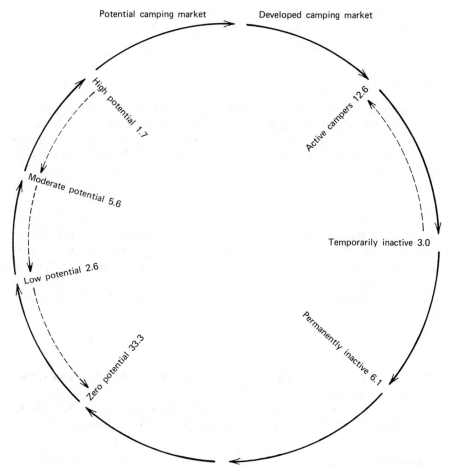

Potential camping market   Developed camping market

High potential 1.7

Active campers 12.6

Moderate potential 5.6

Low potential 2.6

Temporarily inactive 3.0

Zero potential 33.3

Permanently inactive 6.1

Figure 50 Most recreation activities have a marketing cycle and their growth follows a bell shaped curve.
Courtesy: From RESEARCH FOR CHANGING TRAVEL PATTERNS, by Wilbur LaPage, Travel Research Association Proceedings. Reprinted with permission of Mari Lou Wood, Executive Secretary.

1. INFANCY

In the infancy stage, there may be a number of entrepreneurs, all having a good idea at about the same time. There is little public awareness of the industry in terms of felt need, and no controls, licenses, registrations, or set standards.

2. ADOLESCENT

It must be understood that exact boundaries between growth stages are meaningless. As the industry begins to grow, the average investment per enterprise may be five to ten times that in Stage 1. Enterprise operators begin to be more business-minded.

Immediate returns are more important than retirement nest eggs. Established corporations looking for opportunities to diversify, conduct market studies on their own, and establish experimental developments.

3. YOUNG ADULTHOOD

This is primarily the "shake-down" period for the industry. Ma and Pa type enterprises can no longer compete in the market and begin to disappear from view. The larger, more efficient operations begin to succeed. Toward the middle of this stage there is a noticeable shift in trade organizations and associations away from communications and toward lobbying.

4. MATURITY

Growth in terms of new enterprises drops to the level of or below the rate of population expansion. Expansion of existing facilities may continue as a favored form of competition. Growth of individual enterprises now takes place at the expense of other enterprises. Broad, industry-wide promotions are now aimed at increasing the spending of people who are already in the market, as opposed to earlier efforts to expand the size of the market.

5. SENILITY

Senility has not been tested or validated as such, as most recreation activities are in one of the four previous stages.

Mr. LaPage has validated the model, specifically in the campground and recreation vehicle institute areas, and has substantial research to back up his findings.

EXPANDING THE MODEL

As research generates new information and is able to successfully integrate it with that information that has been lying on the shelf collecting dust, another important role of the market analysis emerges. Starting with a very simple but useful growth curve model, it is now possible to expand that model into a comprehensive guide for the entire recreation market.

The first step in graduating the growth model into a practical, useful tool comes with the realization that as the active recreation market of a particular activity expands, it's reservoir for future growth shrinks.

Using the camping market as an example once again, Figure 51 shows that those involved in camping as an activity more or less proceed through several levels of participation. Through results of a national camper market survey, figures in the millions have been obtained for each of the various steps in the cycle in terms of millions of households. Thus as the household has little awareness of camping they

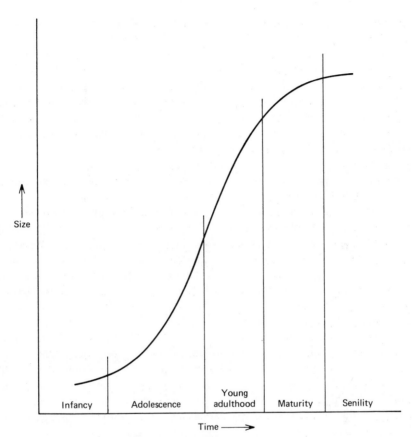

Figure 51 The marketing circle may be the result of increasing and decreasing levels of participation.
Courtesy: Wilbur LaPage proceedings of the Fourth Annual Conference Travel Research Association, Sun Valley, Idaho, August 19, 1972.

have a zero potential. As they become aware and are induced to go camping, they begin to move through the low potential to the moderate potential, up to the high potential, and then become active campers. It is interesting to note that the investment in equipment rises in relation to their potential. They may begin with an economical tent or tent-trailer, and very little equipment moving up to the cycle to the active camper status, to where they may have a hard-top travel trailer, or a recreation vehicle. After a time they become tired of this type of activity, and they move into the temporarily inactive role and begin to camp less. They then move on to the permanently inactive, perhaps sell their equipment, and look to other areas of recreation activity of their interest.

If the camping market, for example, expands much faster than facilities are developed, several results can be predicted. First with rising dissatisfaction, campers will begin to camp less, the average rate of camping participation will decline and that decline may offset whatever gains are achieved through market expansion and costly promotion. In addition to declining participation rates and increasing market dropouts rates, camper dissatisfaction may be expressed in other ways such as purchasing land for personal campsites, or otherwise changing camping styles. Campers may continue to camp just as much but in avoiding the crowds and waiting lines at public campsites they also eliminate much of their former economic impact.

The camping market is not unique among outdoor recreation markets. Each enterprise operator must assess at what point each segment of the population he is attempting to reach, may be in this cycle of potential active or inactive participants.

Although market studies indicate that camping participation, for instance, is declining, they do not indicate how much of the decline is due to: (a) the direct effort effective and inadequate supply of campsites, (b) indirect effect of camper dissatisfaction due to lack of quality, variety and appropriate geographic distribution of facilities, or (c) a normal social trend resulting from increased camper involvement and other activities competing for his free time. An artifacts of the data resulting in the fact that camping trips took more time in years past because of less mobile equipment, poorer highways, and poorer geographic distribution of developed campgrounds.

As the enterprise operator assesses his market he should also assess his growth and development in the various stages of the growth curve. There will come a time in each activity area where more and more must be spent to attract the same number of people into the market, inducing either active campers to remain active longer, or inducing low, moderate, or high potential participants to participate sooner, or to keep those who are temporarily inactive from being permanently inactive and to again participate in their chosen activity.

It will be interesting to watch this phenomena develop with each aspect of the recreation industrial complex.

As has been stated earlier, marketing is much related to *Why People Travel* for recreation. Additional materials concerning why destination areas rise and fall can be found in Chapter 2, and in other references following at the end of this chapter.

THE MARKETING PLAN AND PROGRAM _____

After you have identified the market segments or audiences that are most likely to visit your facility, investigated all of the aspects of your product and services, and have viewed what the competition has to offer, the next objective is to bring the prospects into your facility. It should be stated here, that the best laid plans, sales methods, promotions, or campaigns will be completely useless if the product is of inferior quality. The old addage "you can fool part of the people part of the time" is never more true than in the private and commercial recreation industry. The values of the word of mouth advertising has been mentioned previously. Unfortunately all too many enterprises embark upon marketing plans and programs without first carefully analyzing their own product to make it the best possible and better than most of those with similar services to offer.

What you have hopefully accomplished to this point:

1. Isolated the best prospective customers, and learned their principle needs and desires.
2. Determined how you can best fulfill these needs and desires.
3. Know what it takes in service and facilities to provide for the customers needs and make the best effort to provide them.

The next step is to set down in writing exactly what kind of a plan, through what vehicle, will attract the customer to your door, and supply him with what he wants and asks for. These are the steps in the *public relations* program. They can be broken down primarily into three areas.

1. *Promotion,* which includes all the ways and means that a tourist development group or recreation enterprise can instigate or contrive to attract attention or enhance visitors to come to his enterprise. They usually take the form of special events, special programs, or stunts or activities.
2. *Advertising* is generally thought of in terms of a service or product that is purchased to tell the story. This can take the form of ads in newspapers and trade journals, or in such things as placemats at restaurants or brochures.
3. *Publicity* is usually what advertising the agency can get for free by supplying materials to the various media with the hopes that they will use it in their publications.

The objective is to bring together the *product* that has been developed and the *people* (market) who have been discovered to be the most logical prospective customers. Utilizing the *package* that has been designed and *priced* for the product. The melting of these four components with the marketing mix is marketing.

Let us look at each one of these individually. The type of package that the enterprise has to offer will determine in what proportion and to what extent each of these three methods of public relations can be used most efficiently.

Many of the tools and activities possible under any of these three aspects, may overlap to some degree, and none is mutually exclusive.

PROMOTION _____

Many of the promotional ideas are encompassed in special events and festive activities, such as special days for particular ages, visitors from certain geographic locations, big name band entertainment, contests, and all of the opportunities for special day programs the calendar offers. Many ideas concerning festivities special events can be found in the booklet *Festival, U.S.A.* [6] Published each year, this lists all of the major festivities

---

[6] U.S. Department of Commerce, *Festival, U.S.A.,* Supt. of Documents, Washington, D.C.

and special events in all of the 50 states insofar as they have reported. Some of these will be regional in nature or may be a community wide event of significance, too large to be produced by a single enterprise.

PROMOTION THROUGH SALES

Sales promotion involves those activities in the day to day business of the enterprise that touch customers. It is not only the objective to persuade the visitor to visit your enterprise, but to also influence him through internal selling to patronize all the facilities of the business and either to stay longer if possible or to influence him to return again. Personal selling is a learned attribute used by staff personnel to invite guests to other facilities, such as a desk clerk, might say "Mr. Green the dining room will be open in 15 minutes, would you care for something to drink before dinner. Our lounge is open."

The response of the telephone operator is also vital to the promotional plan for the enterprise. Inquiries from guests about rooms from the outside can often be an opening for a polite and skillful sales effort. A lack of good public relations can also discourage sales. The local telephone company has several training programs to assist in this area. Promotion thru sales involves a fundamental process of training all employees to be sales minded.

PROMOTIONAL SALES THROUGH PRINTED MATTER AND OTHER MATERIALS

Internal selling can be done by means of various promotional pieces, printed or otherwise. In his book, *Marketing for a Full House,* C. DeWitt Coffman offers numerous suggestions for promoting internal and external selling through this means. Here are some of his examples: tent cards, post cards, lighted pictures in guest rooms, dining and beverage rooms, reminder cards, pencils, key chains, placemats, and dinner table placemats.

PRINTED LITERATURE

The average person is exposed to some 6000 advertising impressions per day from signs, post cards, newspapers, magazines, radio and TV, and other media. Because of the sheer magnitude of the many forces trying to make him an "offer" and persuade him to exchange his money for services, printed advertising and printed promotional materials must be exceptionally well done and efficiently distributed to be worth the cost. Here are some basic rules:

1. Get to the point, don't beat around the bush, be brief.
2. Provide the information that people want. If you are planning to vacation in an unfamiliar resort what do you wish to know about the place. Your answers to this

[7] Dewitt Coffman, *Marketing for a Full House,* Cornell University, Ithaca, New York, 1972, p. 166.

question will help outline the information needed in your folder. Quote prices, clothes to wear at the place, entertainment features, and similar information. A vital ingredient should be a map of sufficient description for people to find the location.

3. One of the keys to successful advertising is to be distinct, outstanding, or different to attract attention and induce the prospect to buy. This requires creative thinking and novel ideas, and many times will require the assistance of others, experts, and professionals in the field.

Printed materials include cards, pamphlets, descriptive folders, brochures, handbills, or place cards.

BROCHURES

The traditional four-color folder or brochure[8] constitutes one of the most effective forms of printed promotion. Nothing can completely tell the story of your place or enterprise as the brochure. Although most studies reflect the brochure is not the primary tool in bringing about an awareness to the prospect, it is in many cases the tool that helps him decide to visit, when he is in a state of readiness. Good four-color brochures are not expensive and should not be the place to cut corners. Many people evaluate the enterprise by the brochure that they read. Artwork should be professionally done, as should the full-color photographs. Good folders should include the following: location, attractions, special events, opening dates, how to get there, how and where to get additional information, telephone, services provided, eating facilities, transportation available, recreational attractions, as well as amusements and other attractions in the area. Smith, Partain, and Champlin[9] suggest that the brochure should cover the following eight points: Location, type of facility, climate, accommodations, facilities for children, recreational possibilities, special advantages, and price. An amateurish folder can be a detriment to your business. Better to have no folder at all than a poor one. By all means include printed descriptions of your nearby area. Prospective guests are more likely to come if you tell them about the many interesting and enjoyable attractions which they will find in your vicinity.

DIRECT MAIL[10]

Direct mail promotion has the advantage of preselection of prospects. The advertising message can go directly to that person privately and personally.

---

[8] Robert McIntosh, *Marketing Management,* Extension Bulletin E677 Cooperative Extension Service, Michigan State University, undated.

[9] Clodus R. Smith, Lloyd E. Partain, and James R. Champlin, *Rural Recreation for Profit,* Interstate Printers & Publishers, Inc. Danville, Illinois, 1966, pp. 273-4.

[10] Robert McIntosh, op. cit. Much of this material is adapted from this bulletin.

Its value depends on several important factors.

1. Quality and impact of the mailing piece.
2. The prospects interest and what you have to offer.
3. Frequency of mailing.
4. Newsworthyness.

The quality and the impact are of vital importance. A personal letter is, of course, best if you know the person. Be sure to send complete information to answer the prospect's questions. Ask yourself what you would be interested in if you were a prospective guest. Reprints from magazine or newspaper publicity can be advantageous. Orient toward children and mothers. Many times they determine where vacations are taken. Point out advantages for women and children.

Previous guests should be contacted periodically through greeting cards, invitations, information about new services, or new rates.

Purchased mailing lists are available from a number of sources but care should be taken to make sure they are indeed from the segmented group from which you seek.

Other sources might include those who have written but never made reservations, friends, and relatives of regular guests, or commercial establishments. One mailing seldom will produce satisfactory results. Several mailings made at least once a year may add to the success. Efforts should be made to answer all incoming mail the same day. Send folders, postcards, or personal letters and whatever else might encourage the individual to attend.

DISTRIBUTION

Prepare a list of possible outlets, which may include the following:

1. Direct Mail.
2. Chamber of Commerce.
3. Other vacation recreation travel groups, bureaus, or enterprises.
4. Sporting goods stores.
5. Restaurants, hotels, or motels.
6. Gas stations.
7. Retail outlets.
8. Distribute through agencies, or churches.

There are numerous devices to use to get out information and attract attention. In the beginning, try to determine which will be the most effective to use in reaching the market area. In addition, all local merchants and local industries should be urged to support the program in your own advertising such as in the use of billboards, radio, television, and direct mail. This especially applies to those who directly gain from the travel and recreation industry. For example, restaurants might use place mats to publicize the area, merchants might use sacks, shopping bags, wrapping paper with messages, and tobacco counters and cigarette machines might use matchbook covers to advertise the area or an event. Some of the firms might use flyers when sending out their statements and direct mail advertising. There are many opportunities if cooperation can be obtained.

Promotion is one of the most vital elements to success. Whatever you promote, be sure it is valid, a true representation of what you have to offer in the way of attractions, facilities, and accommodations. A dissatisfied customer can undo a lot of hard work. A good promotion program is actually a detailed plan, carefully thought out. It is a sustained system of communication of sending out messages, making sure they are received, and most important of all that they produce a response.

List the items to be worked on in terms of promotion. Make a promotion calendar. Certain things to do at prescribed times. Some things can be promoted continuously. Some will be seasonal, but this usually only means heavier emphasis three to four months in advance of the occasion or activity.

THE PROMOTION TARGET

The main promotional emphasis should be on attracting the independent visitor, those who visit public or private resorts, stay in motels or hotels, and eat in restaurants. This group of travelers consisting primarily of families of above average income in surrounding states, offers the greatest economic potential of any group, and should receive the most attention. Persons in this group are largely uninformed about the area and its attractions or if informed, tend to believe more and better tourist facilities are needed. Ultimately the message for all those who rely on the traveler for their income is that they, as individual business executives, must invest in their own tourist facilities and as a group, invest in tourist promotion.

This doesn't mean that the group travelers should be overlooked. Group business amounts to over 40 percent of the gross sales in some recreation businesses, companies, churches, schools, and clubs as well as professional tour operators, make excellent targets for promotional material, although most groups are the results of personal visits by a representative of the enterprise.

ADVERTISING

Advertising can be defined as paid, public messages designed to describe or praise your business. These can be provided through the use of posters, newspapers, radio, television, or other media. Effective advertising gains the attention of the prospective guest, holds it so that the message can be communicated, and makes a lasting positive impression on the prospects mind.

Every enterprise needs some form of advertising to keep revenues at a sufficient level to produce a profit. In addition to word of mouth referrals and endorsements, (the most valuable of all ways in increasing business), a well-organized advertising program is essential.

Before an intelligent and-well organized advertising program can be planned, the needs and desires of the prospective guest must be analyzed.

When applying market anaylsis to advertising, review the characteristics of each market group. Determine which of these groups can best be served. Always consider what additional groups could be served by remodeling or enlarging the facilities, or which entirely new markets that could be tapped.

After studying these possibilities, develop an advertising plan that will appeal to each prospective group. It is helpful if information is available concerning how many visitors came from a particular area in which you plan to advertise. To advertise "shotgun" is largely a waste of money. The market segmentation can best be used with advertising, because it can be more nearly directed to the particular segment of the population desired, as well as toward an awareness, readiness, or decision state.

A public relations director for Busch Gardens recently reported that during advertising spots on the Willy Wonka program watched by 15 million people they received 35,000 inquiries, but on spots during the Rose Bowl game watched by 70 million they received only 20,000 inquiries.[11] They determined that sports watchers were not their audiences.

WORD OF MOUTH ADVERTISING

Public relations is the process of having ones attitude place first priority on public interest in face to face operations as well as operations decisions and management. There is little question that word of mouth is by far the best advertising. In a recent survey in Missouri[12] of visitors to the Clearwater Lake area, 36 percent indicated they were attracted to the area by recommendations of others. One cannot take lightly the addage that repeat business makes the most profit. Few enterprises can expect to survive only on new customers.

This is the cheapest and most convincing form of personal advertising. A friendly, interested, and capable host encourages this type of personal advertising. Nearly every guest, if he feels welcome, will not only come back himself, but will recommend the place to his friends. All of your facilities and services, hospitality, and pricing policies will be directed to this one goal, a satisfied happy guest. Dick Pope, President of Cyprus Gardens, Florida, claims to have attributed his success to the fact that his "personnel smiled" when they accepted the admissions of the visitors.

---

[11] Speeches given at the First Annual Attractions Seminar in Lake Buena Vista, Florida, February 1975.

[12] Arlin F. Epperson, *Recreation and Tourism in the Clearwater lake Area,* University of Missouri, Columbia, Missouri 1974.

Figure 52 A full house depends on good advertising, publicity, and promotion as well as personal selling and word of mouth advertising.
Courtesy: Brunswick Corporation, Skokie, Illinois.

HOSPITALITY TRAINING

Public relations consists of every single contact that the operator and his staff has with the clientele, whether it is by telephone, correspondence, or personal conversation. Impressions that are made with the customer will mean success or failure to the enterprise because these customers pass the word along to potential future customers.

The primary responsibility of any employee, regardless of his position or duties, is to maximize the service to clients and customers. This does not happen by accident. A specific program must be designed to educate new employees in the need for good public relations, and to provide opportunities for training within the areas of their responsibility. The Marriott Hotel system, one of the leaders in this area, has extensive training sessions for each of their employees and ongoing in-service training sessions after they're employed.

Rules and regulations should be discussed, and the reasons for each. The importance of a cheerful and helpful attitude on the part of the manager will help reflect the same in the employees and hopefully to the customer. Patience and skill are required, particularly in cases of disgruntled or unsatisfied customers. During the training sessions, role playing can be used to depict these situations and discuss possible solutions.

Where local or regional tourism associations exist, hospitality training programs can be organized quite easily. Employees still must receive the support and enthusiasm of the manager to participate and put to use what they have learned. State Departments of Tourism, University Cooperative Extension Services, and State Departments of Distributive Education can be of vital assistance in developing these programs. Hospitality is the art of making people feel welcome and wanted. The operator and his staff must convince visitors that their coming is important, that it is desired, and that they are there to serve him. They want to be appreciated and to feel important; the staff should make every effort to make them feel wanted and satisfied. The rewards of practicing treating others the way you would desire to be treated are new friendships, happiness, satisfaction, and financial success. If one always gives more than is asked, in interest, sympathy, understanding, and patience, one will surely get something back in return.

USING AN ADVERTISING AGENCY

Some recreation businesses may desire to have an expert in advertising assist with the program. The purpose of an advertising agency is to increase business and do it profitably. They will assist in copy and layout, advise on choice of media vehicle, assist in conducting market analysis, and assist in planning and carrying out the advertising and public relations program.

Although there are a number of methods of advertising, recreation business executives will probably use less than half a dozen. The importance of timing cannot be overstated, particularly in working with newspapers, magazines, radio, or TV. Advertising should be timed for that period in the year when vacation plans are being made, usually early Spring. Such a time schedule is necessary for effective advertising.

OUTDOOR DISPLAY ADVERTISING

This medium is an important tool for those in the recreation industry. Between 85 and 90 percent of all travelers travel by automobile. The highway traveler is attracted to a large number of advertising and directional signs. Because of the many signs, outdoor advertising programs must be very skillfully planned and carried out to bring good results. Leave this to the outdoor advertising experts and companies.

With the changes in billboard sign regulations by state and federal governments, the future of outdoor display advertising, particularly long, heavily traveled tourist routes and interstate highway systems, is somewhat in question.

Feeder signs, which help give directions, are also important. Since 40 percent of the travel is done after dark, signs should be lighted.

NEWSPAPER ADVERTISING

Newspaper advertising may be of value, depending on the type of recreation business; however, the older segments of the population tend to be the most avid readers of newspapers. Perhaps it is best included with advertisement by regional tourism associations which would boost the area. It is sometimes advantageous to cooperate in a group advertisement sponsored by the Chamber of Commerce or Tourist Association. The newspaper will provide an attractive heading that features your resort area. Few recreation businesses are of sufficient size or provide sufficient diversity of interests and services to be able to afford the kind of advertising that will attract visitors to their particular facility alone.

MAGAZINE ADVERTISING

Although magazine advertising research indicates that heads of households that read magazines regularly do more pleasure traveling than heads of households who are regularly exposed to the major TV media, the practicality of a small recreation business advertising in a magazine is questionable particularly in light of the cost. The distribution of the magazine should be investigated closely, and particularly the circulation, to see whether there is sufficient readership in a given geographical area within driving distance of the facility to make it worthwhile. Ads in sports magazines should bring excellent results for recreation enterprises in good hunting and fishing areas.

RADIO

For transient business, radio is an important advertising medium. This may be of particular interest once the travelers are in the resort area. Again, it will depend on the type of recreation enterprise as to whether this will be truly effective or not.

Television is probably too costly to be practical for the average recreation enterprise. Although in combination with tourist associations of an area's Chamber of Commerce it may be feasible. This should help attract business to the area and each place could then get its share.

In any of the above types of advertising, newspaper, magazines, radio, television, or other paid ads, the agency usually will have professionals on their staff to assist in copy layout and development of advertising messages.

AWARENESS ADVERTISING

Awareness advertising dollars are relatively inefficient dollars because of the low potential dollar value. The hierarchy of advertising objectives are as follows:

1. Direct sales.
2. Reservations.
3. Inquiries.
4. Consumer awareness, customer awareness of product.

The majority of recreation business advertising, that is, brochures, flyers, and newspaper ads, is awareness advertising. Little added printing cost is incurred by adding dollar inducing offers to existing advertising. Emphasize direct sales and reservation objectives with appropriate offers or inducement. Tailor the approach around low occupancy periods that still offers customer enjoyment. Advertising efforts should include an offer and an irresistable inducement to create customer reactions. A legitimate offer should:

1. Be distinctive.
2. Promise a concrete customer benefit.
3. Force customer reaction.
4. Be irresistable.
5. Be easy and simple to obtain.

Put a dollar value, a time deadline, a customer benefit, and additional value into the offer package. The customer benefit should be as immediate as possible.

The offer should be a straightforward "no strings attached" promise.

Brochure advertising seems particularly awareness oriented. Many brochures are printed yearly. *Add an offer.* Include an offer on a separate less expensive change of year price sheet.

PACKAGE PLANS

Package plans deserve special attention, and usually consist of room, meals, and at least one other feature such as a tour, recreation participation, or show. They may or may not include transportation. Many of the transportation agencies have been leaders in developing special package offers. This is a rather sophisticated business, and can be done better by a travel agent, with help from a tourist association group, or others particularly knowledgeable or experienced in this area.

PUBLICITY

Publicity usually stems from timely announcements or information about newsworthy special events of interest. Although it might be assumed that few people are interested, this assumption should not be made prematurely. In writing news releases, the traditional questions of who, what, when, where, and why should be answered. The first paragraph should summarize the article, and each succeeding paragraph should discuss aspects of the main topic in descending order of importance. Most copy submitted to newspapers, television, and radio stations is typewritten, double spaced, with 6-inch lines. The deadlines for newspaper, television, and radio should be known to the manager so that the publicity will not give an advantage to the television station in the morning if the newspaper has only an afternoon edition.

It is well for the manager to visit the editor or the radio or TV station manager to discuss possible items of publicity, deadlines, and types of submission.

Although a recreation business manager should not assume that nothing he does is of newsworthy importance, neither should he assume that all things that he does are of newsworthy importance. Good judgment and wisdom will direct whether publicity is warranted, so that when releases are given to the media, they will in fact represent items of special interest. Good black and white glossy photographs should be sent with the release if available.

Some outdoor writers are available and can be invited as guests to the facility in the hope that they will refer to the business in their writings. The sports and travel editors for major metropolitan dailies and Sunday editions are additional outlets for publicity business to the area.

MARKETING BUDGET

The value of a well-developed market program has been reiterated many times. Such a program cannot be developed without incurring some cost. The recreation enterprise should expect to spend from three percent to six percent of its annual gross sales in promotion and advertising programs. Many professional advertising executives will attempt to evaluate the various advertising and promotional opportunities on the basis of the number of exposures per dollar. In other words, the number of cars passing a particular highway sign in a given period of time, times the percentage of those who will be expected to look, will give a unit advertising cost per exposure to the public. These can then be compared with readership in a newspaper ad or distribution of place mats. A good manager will utilize a variety of avenues to reach his varied segmented populations and markets.

There are three main ways that operators handle marketing programs.

1. By themselves.
2. Signing up with a public or private agency that handles promotion for them.
3. A third way is yet to be discussed, that of joining or forming an association with others to conduct marketing promotion and advertising jointly. Of course the successful manager uses a combination of all of these.

TOURISM ASSOCIATIONS

An individual operator can indeed advertise and promote by himself through a number of means, which have been previously discussed. There are, however, some types and methods that are either too costly as an individual or some that lend themselves more readily to attracting people to an area, rather than to an individual facility. These can accomplish a number of things that could not be done individually. Mr. Robert A. Elmore,[13] Executive Vice President of the Chatanooga Convention Visitors Bureau,

[13] Speeches given at the First Annual Attractions Seminar in Lake Buena Vista, Florida, February 1975.

lists the following advantages of a local or regional travel and tourism association. An association can:

1. Be the lowest paid employee, brings the highest degree of return and results.
2. Do more than any agency can do individually.
3. Provide an opportunity for multiplier effect.
4. Build support in the community for the total travel and tourism industry.
5. Provide protection against rate taxes by city for other purposes.
6. Save enterprises more money than it cost.
7. Keep people informed through a newsletter.
8. Provide public service announcements for private nonprofit organizations through the convention bureau.
9. Provide agencies for attracting and entertaining press, outdoor writers, and others.
10. Sponsor radio and TV spots, and coordinate promotion of enterprises and attractions in a total given area through this media.
11. Incorporate advertising and compliment what other attractions and enterprises are doing individually.
12. Provide joint advertising at reduced rates for quantity.
13. Provide cooperative advertising local and state avenues.
14. Help in publishing brochures.
15. Answer inquiries concerning attractions and enterprises cheaper.
16. Handle direct mail campaigns more efficiently and cheaper.
17. Assist with packaging programs for tours.
18. Take the lead in coordination and promotion of travel shows.
19. Provide speaker bureaus.
20. Handle photography for brochure production of members.
21. Handle convention bookings.
22. Develop opportunity lists.
23. Do studies or be involved in implementing recreation studies of needs and demands.
24. Solicit and serve tours.
25. Develop citizen involvement programs, special events, and special celebrations.
26. Take the lead in providing hospitality training for employees.
27. Assist in expanding the length of the tourism season.
28. Assist in obtaining federal and state funds and help to locate and obtain some.
29. Host welcome centers.
30. Provide support staff for conventions and special events.
31. Add a civic flavor to a private venture.
32. Save *you* money.

Indeed all local or regional tourism and travel associations are not large enough or as well funded to provide all of these services; however, they are a method by which things can be accomplished together that cannot be accomplished individually.

The old philosophy that all tourists are stolen from someone else because "there were only so many to go around" is just not true. A term *synergism* was coined at the DATO conference in San Diego in 1974 refers to individuals having to work together to accomplish common objectives. Enterprises, attractions, and amusements must all cooperate in any area and as an industry to gain the most benefit. In most cases the whole area must prosper for each to benefit. The enterprise owner should belong to the Chamber of Commerce, be interested in their activities as well as civic clubs, and definitely cooperate with their neighbors. Familiarization tours for all employees of every recreation business enterprise, or amusement in an area should be provided so that they will sell each other. Passes for all employees to all attractions in the area is helpful. Unfortunately it seems when the economy is good, people drop out of Chamber of Commerce and tourism groups, and when it is bad, they all join up hoping for better days or more assistance.

As the manager plans his marketing program he must consider both horizontal programs, with a variety of other attractions and facilities in a given area as well as vertical programs with others in the identical kind of business throughout the country. Many trade associations made up of like enterprises exist to help get favorable legislation passed and unfavorable legislation defeated, assist in educating members to run better and more profitable businesses, and assist in advertising and promoting an area so that enterprises within the area do a better business. Local or regional tourism associations may be both a referral type agency to help attractions promote one another, as well as to promote the area to outside residents through advertising and publicity. Some, however, only serve one of these functions, and this will vary from place to place.

CHAMBERS OF COMMERCE

Many community or area Chambers of Commerce do an outstanding job of tourist promotion and providing travel information services. Tourists frequently contact Chambers of Commerce in vacation areas. Many Chamber of Commerce have attractive and well located information offices that provide referrals to members. They can be important sources of business. Your memberships help get travelers into your community and your place of business.

TRAVEL AGENCIES

There are some 6000 authorized travel agents in the United States and Canada. The exact extent of business to recreation and enterprises obtained through travel agencies is not known. They do, however, provide considerable, diversified advertising to segmented portions of the market. In many cases, travel agencies can best be approached by preparing an area wide sales information booklet that has a brochure from every member whether lodging, food, attraction, or recreation establishment and an information sheet giving the following items about each:

1. Brief history.
2. Location.
3. Open season, days and times.
4. Admission prices.
5. Discounts if any.
6. Time required to visit or participate.
7. Food services.
8. Lodging.
9. Person to contact, address and phone number.
10. Accessibility to elderly and handicapped.
11. Information on advanced registrations.
12. Method of payment.
13. Location and parking.
14. Accessability by bus.
15. A two-paragraph description of the attraction.

This makes it relatively simple as well as encouraging to travel agents to book tours through particular areas. Some areas attribute 40 percent of their business from organized tours. There are several directories for travel agents and for the national Tour Brokers Association. It is wise to give special attention if possible to each guest that is sent by a travel agent. A favorable report back to the travel agent will encourage him to send others. If feasible, pay a personal visit to the travel agents in your area to become better acquainted and to give them your brochures.

STATE TOURISM DEPARTMENTS

State tourist departments also have assistance to offer to local enterprises and should be given as much support as possible. State tourism expenses increased 23 percent in 1973 in Texas, as a result of an increased state tourism department effort. Assistance from state departments will vary from state to state, but may include any of the following.

1. Marketing.
   a. Literature, writing, distributing.
   b. List of respondents to state advertising.
   c. Travel shows.
   d. Inclusion in state produced films, ads, publicities.
   e. Familiarization tours.
2. Development, package tours, field consulting, matching monies, and state travel conferences.

COMMUNITY AWARENESS _____

One of the serious problems in the travel and tourism industry today is the lack of awareness on the part of the community, on the part of other businesses and community leaders who do not understand the importance of tourism to the economy, the need for total community interest in tourism planning, and the attitude of the community toward the tourist as an invited visitor and guest. Unfortunately, many businesses who obtain a significant amount of their incomes from tourists or travelers make no effort to treat them as guests or to express the fact that they are welcome, and many times the opposite is true. It is often the lack of a friendly community attitude that makes the traveler look elsewhere for his recreation rather than the particular responsiveness of the specific facility. The attractiveness of the community, the streets and highways through the community as well as the location of various services, are all important aspects to the general impression the visitor receives of the areas to which he is traveling. These are of course under the primary control of the community elected officials. If no consideration is given in the community appearance, attitude, and location of facilities to tourism needs, the traveler will indeed sense this and react accordingly.

There is no easy answer as to how such a community attitude, responsive to the needs of the traveler, can be established. By becoming involved with the Chamber of Commerce, civic organizations, and other opportunities, the operator may effect some person to person awareness. Programs of education can be held in cooperation with the regional Tourism Association, State Tourism Department or the Cooperative Extension Service for those in the community. Unfortunately it is difficult to get attendance. This is a long and hard process, and community leaders may need to be sold on a one to one basis. Seldom do pressure tactics or antagonism produce satisfactory results. Hospitality training sessions and familiarization tours for local officials and individuals may help also. In some cases only time will help with this problem.

Summary

The old adage that nothing happens until something is sold is never more true than in the private and commercial recreation business. No matter how good the product or service, until it is exchanged for a fee, neither the participants nor the provider finds satisfaction. The marketing program must encompass all of the following; (1) search out potential persons interested in the product. (2) Find out what the potential customers want. (3) Sell the potential customers what they want. (4) Service them so that they spend a maximum amount of money. (5) Convince them to return. Marketing is persuading a potential customer to exchange a fee for a service.

It is vitally important to determine why people travel, so that the enterprise manager can discern the expectations of those who frequent his facility. If their expectations are met, they will leave satisfied with their recreation experience and will desire to return. If their expectations are not met, they will leave unsatisfied and will share their feelings with the others.

Market segmentation is a must in the private and commercial recreation business. Segmentation is pinpointing exactly what groups are most interested and most likely to be potential purchasers of the service and directing the marketing plan towards that specific group. The marketing plan must include provisions for promotion, advertising, and publicity, as well as programs of cooperation and membership and tourism associations, and to promote community awareness.

Additional References

Books, Bulletins, and Reports

DeVriend, A. J., H. M. Smith, and S. W. Weiss *Advertising, Promotion, Publicity,* Recreation Business Management Series - 8, December 1972, University of Wisconsin-Extension.

Kentucky Travel Council, *Community Travel Development Primer,* 670 South Third Street, Louisville 2, Kentucky.

McIntosh, Robert W., *Sales Promotion for Motels and Resorts,* Tourist and Resort Series, Circular R-605, Cooperative Extension Service, Michigan State University, East Lansing, November 1961.

Periodicals

Business Management Magazine, "A Marketing Manager's Guide to High-Risk Strategy in the 1970's", Special Report, 38, 5, August, 1970.

Plog, Stanly C., "Why Destination Areas Rise and Fall in Popularity", The Cornell Hotel and Restaurant Administration Quarterly, School of Hotel Administration, Cornell University, Ithaca, New York, August 1973.

Schink, Don, "Our Shifting Recreation/Tourism Market", Outlook, Cooperative Extension Programs, University of Wisconsin, Madison, IV, Number 1, Summer 1974.

Schink, Donald, "Photography for Brochures", Outlook, II, Number 2, Cooperative Extension Programs, University of Wisconsin, Madison.

Schroder, David R. "Advertising Summarized from 'How to Attract Attention' " The Wisconsin Restaurateur, March 1973, Recreation Resources Center, University of Wisconsin-Extension, 1815 University Avenue, Madison, Wisconsin 53706.

Schroder, David R. "Awareness Advertising VS. Action Advertising", Recreation Marketing Series, Recreation Resources Center, University of Wisconsin-Extension, 1815, University Avenue, Madison, Wisconsin 53706, February 1973.

Schroder, David R. "More Effective Promotion Planning-Understanding Customer Value", Outlook, Volume III, Number 1, Cooperative Extension Programs, University of Wisconsin, Madison, Spring, 1973.

Discussion Questions

1. In what ways does a sound marketing plan contribute to the successful operation of a commercial youth camp?
2. Describe and discuss the elements of a Market Analysis.

3. What value would the concept of market segmentation have to a travel agent? To an amusement park owner?

4. How does the understanding of the marketing cycle effect the prospective buyer of a recreation business? Define and describe the marketing cycles.

5. Do you agree with the statement: "as the active recreation market of a particular activity expands, its reservoir for future growth shrinks?" Why?

6. How does public relations differ from sales?

7. What are the essential elements and tools to a promotion program?

8. How is promotion related to sales?

9. What do you consider to be the five most important advantages to being a member of tourism association?

10. How can state tourism associations assist local recreation enterprises and general leisure industry?

CHAPTER 8

IMPLICATIONS
FOR
THE
FUTURE

It is an unusual individual, whether he be a provider or a participant, that is not interested in knowing what the future holds for leisure and recreation. For those whose livelihood is dependent upon wise judgment and future planning, the need to forecast as accurately as possible is compounded considerably.

Experts in the field of forecasting markets use a variety of methods to produce their predictions. In the days of consistent economic growth of five to seven percent annually, the future could accurately be predicted by plotting the history of the previous five to ten years on a graph, and projecting in the straight line for the next five to ten years. Other researchers have attempted to sample attitudes of individuals or households and base predictions on the resulting expressed needs and desires of those surveyed. Others have attempted to trace the cycles of civilization, human nature, and humanistic trends through history to predict in more general terms the trends of nations and communities in the future.

Any method of analysis and subsequent prediction is based on a consistent if not stable economy. Anyone remotely connected with the travel, tourism, or recreation industry knows that although the history has been fairly consistent up until 1973 or 1974, the subsequent years and those immediately ahead can by no means be classified as predictable or consistent. With the implications of an inflationary rate (in the past ten years) of ten to fifteen percent, and a reduction in the amount of energy available of ten to fifteen percent, with an increased energy demand of approximately six percent per year, these two factors are paramount in the consideration of what the future holds for the private and commercial recreation enterprise.

FORECASTING

There are three basic problems in forecasting the future of recreation participation in the nation as a whole. The first problem is the effect of outside influences on the phenomena, such as inflation, energy, mobility, and others that will be discussed in detail later.

A second problem is in terms of definition. As mentioned previously, the leisure industry encompasses such a wide variety of "bedfellows" and such a variety of definitions, that only those specific segments that can be defined specifically have any hope of being accurately projected. Influences that increase some aspects of the leisure and travel industry decrease others, and therefore the problem of definition is compounded when talking about the industry as a whole. For an example—gasoline allocation will help the airlines, as seen during the energy shortage of 1974. On the other hand, such an allocation tends to cripple the outdoor attractions industry.

The third problem concerns the inability of researchers to assess the psychological attitudes of individuals on their decision, and to adequately project how decisions are made, and in what priority order. The fact that two individuals, alike in every detail, education, occupation, income, location, and nearness to available facilities, may choose different recreation activities for totally different reasons gives example to the problem. It has been determined that an individual vacationer or potential recreator makes his decision based on a multitude of influences. Although this knowledge helps us understand why we cannot accurately predict, it does not help us with a possible solution.

EXTERNAL IMPLICATIONS

In spite of the problems mentioned previously, some trends can be identified. There are a number of implications external to the recreation enterprise that should be noted in attempting to project what the future will bring in the leisure industries for profit.

THE ATTITUDE OF THE PUBLIC

Almost any psychologist or sociologist will indicate that the mainstay of the work force is between 25 and 50, and these 31 million workers are expected to dominate the attitudes of the American public now and in the future. Indeed, todays worker is a different individual than his father or grandfather. If he had seen the great depression, it was as a youth. He has not grown up with Pearl Harbor, the bomb, cold war, or Korea, but has seen the confusion of the Viet Nam, Laos, city riots, and assassinations of our nations leaders. Most of these workers have aspired to suburbia, and spend much of their time and income attempting to keep up with the Joneses. They have faith in the ability of science to solve almost every problem but now see scientists and engineers in the unemployment lines. Military service is no longer of concern to them, and even for their children it seems something that is possible to be avoided. These workers indeed have a different philosophy about work and leisure than their predecessors. Their values concerning work differ considerably from their predecessors. Partially because of the changing trends in emphasis from the product orientation of old to the worker orientation of today, they feel they are entitled to challenging, rewarding, meaningful work, and opportunity to influence the decisions made in the work environment, and to be paid a higher than average wage, with significant fringe benefits including social benefits such as life insurance, medical insurance, educational benefits, and even unemployment insurance, which pays within ten to fifteen percent of full salary if the individual has a temporary layoff.

Todays worker, of course, like his father and grandfather was schooled in the work ethic and although he is much less satisfied with his job, he is not much better able to face mass leisure than his parents or grandparents, nor is he better equipped for mass unemployment.

"Experts" of years past have fallen fairly well into three groups. Some see the future as the Green Dream of the Ivy Professor, while others forecast the Sibernetic Society wherein there will be near total automation, while a third school holds that life styles in 1980s and 1990s will differ from those in the 1970s about as much as those of 1970 differ from those of 1956.

It is a fact and reality that everyone wants time off but few know what to do with it. Recent studies of the elderly conclude that more than 80 percent of the leisure skills possessed by the elderly were obtained before age 25. Often, because this group knows no other way, their leisure consists of conspicuous consumption, of the spectator sportsman, or more frequently the nonleisure of time filling and frustrating boredom. Many are leisure dilettantes in their leap from activity to activity, seldom acquiring any degree of expertise about anything pertaining to leisure. In short, for years and years our society has been oriented both in education and in employment

Figure 53 Increasing numbers of persons are considering the afternoon of golf or the vacation at the resort a necessity rather than a luxury.
Courtesy: American Hotel and Motel Association, New York, New York.

toward a world of work, and now most of our 31 million workers may be faced, at least in part if not in whole, with a world of leisure, forced or by choice.

Many of the "moonlighters" indicate that they took second jobs not primarily because they needed the extra money, but because they did not know what to do with their leisure.

Some however have seen the need to re-orient out present system of education and work environment to more realistically fit with the modern-day needs and practices. Norman Cousins[1] writing in Saturday Review has said, "Education can be just as relevant in preparing a person for creative and joyous living and for increased life expectancy as it is in preparing him to become an income producer and solid citizens."

Our John Doe, a typical product of the Protestant Calvinistic-Puritan work ethic, has had the desire to work inculcated in him since before he was born and in his father and grandfather before him. Leisure and recreation convey an almost sinful and definitely un-American connotation to him. Despite his drive to work, recent study after study has implied that American workers hate their jobs, and increasingly must turn elsewhere to find the rewards and challenge so much needed by individuals who have achieved the first several steps in Maslow's Hierarchy of physical and psychological needs, and are desperately searching to find other acivities and outlets that will give them these satisfactions. Work for many has lost its meaning, and they are there only to get the money, but try desperately eventually to escape the drudgery of the assembly line. Leisure to many still carries with it the concept of recreating for work. One who hates his work cannot enjoy recreating himself for that work.

Robin M. Williams, Jr.[2] lists 15 value clusters inherent in life in the United States. Work and activity top his list, while leisure has not yet made the list. A leisure-oriented work is finding acceptance with the youth and has been referred to as the new naturalism. The great majority of youth's parents however continue to live to work and hate their jobs.

What implications does this attitude have for the future? It implies a number of things, successive careers, multiple, part-time positions, short-contract employment, and constant retraining as well as periods of unemployment between jobs, more vacation time, and a need to readdress themselves to the meaning of leisure, education, and work as defined by his parents.[3] Part of the answer lies in the nature of the work to be done itself. This will be discussed further in the internal implications section of this chapter.

The external implications of attitude concerning work and leisure implies that everyone concerned with the leisure industry, whether for profit or through govern-

[1] Cousins, Norman, "Art, Adrenalin, and the Enjoyment of Living," Saturday Review, April 20, 1968, p. 20.

[2] Williams, Robin M., *Values and Beliefs in American Society, Character of Americans,* Michael McGiffert, E. D. Dorsey Press, New York 1964.

[3] Purcell, John J., "Getting Ready for 1984," The Adult Leadership Magazine, May 1974.

ment institutions, should be aware of the need to assist in changing the current attitude of the American public toward leisure through education, through opportunity while they are participating through skills training, through adult education courses, through many beginners "learn to" classes where individuals can begin to develop both an attitude toward leisure, and a skills repertoire to participate in leisure in many areas in which they may find enjoyment, without the risk of social embarrassment of learning these skills in front of his friends.

SPENDING IMPLICATIONS

Chapter 1 contains the current status of many of the reasons for increased travel, tourism, and recreation. A brief review of those factors which contributed to the increase to the present level would seem logical in attempting to predict future participation and consumption.

At present recreation, tourism, and travel are tied rather closely to the economy. This can be compared closely through the travel price index developed by the U.S. Travel Data Center, which is an index of the cost of goods and services purchased by travelers while away from home. Included are the prices away from home of food, hotel and motel rates, gasoline, public transportation fares, recreational services, and incidentals.[4]

During the 1950s and the first half of the 1960s the index was relatively high ranging in the upper 80s and 90s, reaching an all time high in 1965 of 103.4. During the last half of the 1960s it was good, but began to slip slightly in the 1970s through 1972. Beginning in 1973 the index began a downward trend unparalleled in the 20-year history of the index. In the first quarter of 1974 the index dropped to an all time low of 60.9. It turned upward in mid-1974 only to drop again and close with 58.4. Travel costs, of course, are not immune to changes in the economy. In fact there is evidence to suggest that they are increasing at a faster rate than other costs. Gasoline price increases led all other travel price increases. increasing 41 percent over the year. Railroad fares rose nearly 14 percent and food away from home rose 13 percent in the same period.

With the average annual raises being between five percent and six percent for the 31 million workers previously mentioned, the average inflation rate is somewhere between 8 and 12 percent for the last two years. Thus the buying power of the general public has been reduced at an average of three to six percent per year, while expenses for travel and recreation areas increased at a 12 percent rate per year. Spending for recreation and leisure services consisted of 16 percent of the gross national product in 1970, and is estimated to be at 30 percent of the gross national product by 1980. These forecasts however were made before the recession of 1974.[5]

[4] U.S. Travel Data Center. *1974 B, Travel Printout 3(8): 1-4,* Washington, D.C.

[5] Discover America Travel Organization *1973 Travel Data Study* Washington, D.C.

Figure 54 Expenditures for recreation have increased faster than the rate of inflation and probably will continue to do so because of the desire to travel and visit places of interest, such as Busch Gardens in Tampa Florida for a "Safari Trip."
Courtesy: International Association of Amusement Parks and Attractions, Oak Park, Illinois.

INCOME IMPLICATIONS

According to the U.S. Census Bureau[6] median family income rose seven percent to $12,840 last year. The number of people below the poverty line increased 5.6 percent, to 24.3 million, which is slightly over 11 percent of the population, or one American in every nine. This is income of $5000 for a nonfarm family of four.

Fifty six million families or 20 percent of the total had incomes of over $20,000 and five percent of the population have incomes over $32,000. One percent had incomes over $50,000.

The top fifth of all families have about $2/5$ of all family income, and the bottom fifth, only about $1/20$ of the total income. These percentages have stayed about the same for many years. It is easy to see that in this sense there has been no income redistribution in the American society for many years.

Among families whose bread winners managed to stay employed during the year of 1974, the median income was $16,072, up ten percent from the year 1973 and down only one percent in buying power. Real median family income has declined in all but one of the recessions since World War II. Even after these slight declines, real family income has increased, stands 90 percent higher than 1947, 37 percent higher than 1960, but only $147 higher than in 1969.

Although many people complain of reduced incomes, this is no doubt true among those who are partially of fully unemployed during some time in the past years. The other families however have probably received a reduction more in their mind than in reality. This has been accompanied by related reductions in expenditures in several areas.

There continues to be much discussion concerning what future incomes will be. One group indicated that after the median family income reaches 15,000 dollars a year, yearnings for money can fall off and income can be increasingly exchanged for time off. Another group believes that incomes will increase sharply and that this is the main interest and concern of the unions and of the American public. A third group implies that it will remain about the same, in terms of discretionary income. Persons will shift to higher levels of income, but material "needs" will rise along with leisure demands. This holds true if one is to analyze the distribution of income mentioned previously. The top and bottom percentiles of families has remained about the same.

There is no doubt a continued attitude that what used to be considered a need may now be considered a luxury, and is not determined by the income we have but by what our neighbors have. Few people would say that radios, televisions, air conditioners, or a second car are now luxuries. Likewise, many people are beginning to assume that vacations are no longer a luxury but a need and feel justified in taking vacations or shorter trips regardless of the circumstances, financial or otherwise.

---

[6] Milius, Peter; in the Washington Post, as printed in the Columbia Tribune, July 24, 1975.

Conclusions by the Conference Board Record[7] include the following.

1. There will be substantial rises in real income but consumers needs will also rise.
2. Leisure will have to share the discretionary portion of higher incomes with competing forms of nonessential and luxury spending.
3. Families with incomes over $15,000 will increase from 22 percent of the total population in 1970 to 42 percent in 1980.
4. Participation rates for married women in the work force will continue to rise, also reflecting pressures to reach adequate life syles.
5. Occupations that correlate best with high incomes, professional and managerial jobs also require the longest working hours, so that leisure time will not necessarily increase as income rises.

TIME IMPLICATIONS

There has been as much speculation by forecasters concerning the amount of leisure time that the average American will have in the future as there has been about the amount of income he will have. Table XXVII reflects some interesting forecasts concerning the percent of leisure time that will be available by the year 2000. Professor Holman takes the long historical approach in making her predictions. It is interesting to note however that time away from work increased only approximately 30 minutes during the last decade. Ten to fifteen years ago, in a period of growth and development, the working class saw leisure time as an alternative to increases in income. With present unemployment rates in the ten to fifteen percent bracket, the attitude is apparently changing to one of cherishing a job, and in some cases working either longer hours for the same weekly pay, or a shorter number of hours at the same rate per hour, in order to keep the company in business and to keep their job.

There is no question that free time in the future will be spent differently than it has been in the past. This is reflected both in the rising level of education and the occupational changes in the work force. It is difficult to find people who are satisfied with dirty or meaningless jobs, even though the pay is significant. More educated and satisfied workers may require more creative and challenging jobs.

There is no disagreement that the American public has more blocks of leisure time, with the institution of the three-day holiday weekend, more plant vacations, many four-day weeks, and other methods of blocking leisure time. The total amount of leisure, however, for this society as a whole has not increased that significantly. Reduced work time has been counter-balanced by increasing travel time as people move to the suburbs.

[7] From CONCEPT OF LEISURE, Conference Board Record, **10**, Number 6, p. 25 by Milton Leontiades. Reprinted with permission of Joseph L. Naar, Director of Public Information, the Conference Board.

Table XXVII National time budget and time division of leisure, 1900, 1950, and 2000

Use of Time	1900 Billion Hours	1900 Percent of Total Time	1900 Percent of Leisure Time	1950 Billion Hours	1950 Percent of Total Time	1950 Percent of Leisure Time	2000 Billion Hours	2000 Percent of Total Time	2000 Percent of Leisure Time
1. Total time for entire population	667	100		1329	100		2907	100	
2. Sleep	265	40		514	39		1131	39	
3. Work	86	15		132	10		206	7	
4. School	11	2		32	2		90	3	
5. Housekeeping	61	9		68	5		93	3	
6. Preschool population, nonsleeping hours	30	4		56	4		110	4	
7. Personal care	37	6		74	6		164	6	
8. Total (items 2-7)	490	73		876	66		1794	62	
9. Remaining hours, largely leisure	177	27	100	453	34	100	1113	38	100
10. Daily leisure hours	72		41	189		42	375		34
11. Weekend leisure hours	50		28	179		39	483		44
12. Vacation	17		10	35		8	182		16
13. Retired	6		3	24		5	56		5
14. Other, including unaccounted	32		18	26		6	16		1

Adapted from Mary A. Holman, "A National Time-Budget for the Year 2000," *Sociology and Social Research*, **46**, No. 1, October 1961. Reprinted with permission of Martin H. Neumeyer, Editor Emeritus.

Because of the desire for work, and its need to fill the traditional satisfactions desired by individuals in the past, it is felt that additional leisure time will not be sought after with as much diligence as previous decades have seen.

Again the Conference Board Record[8] makes several conclusions concerning the future in terms of leisure time.

1. There will only be a slight reduction in the work week, but there will be more paid time off, grouping of time off, a shift of services from agriculture and earlier retirement.
2. Paid vacations increased from 1.8 to 2.2 weeks per year in the 1960s. Personal time off increased slightly also. The increase in leisure time will be expected to increase proportionately in the 1970s and 1980s.
3. Time off will be taken in lumps rather than slivers, more three-day weekends and four-day weeks.
4. A shift from farming to service continues, meaning more part-time work and shorter work weeks.
5. Workers will retire early, 50 percent before age 65 versus 12 percent before 65 in 1960.
6. The work week declined only 30 minutes in the 1960s and the rate of decline slowed from previous decades. Thus, the 40-hour work week will continue for some time particularly in the service industries.
7. Many workers have chosen leisure. Young, old, and married women workers prefer shorter working hours. Married men, especially professional and managerial occupations age 25 to 44, work considerable overtime and 4 million workers hold second jobs.

MOBILITY IMPLICATIONS

One of the increases discussed in Chapter 1 implied that the access to available facilities, through new interstate highway systems and comfortable automobiles, has attributed greatly to the increased demand for recreation. With reduced speed limit, and a slow down in the expansion of the interstate highway system, the mobility factor would appear to remain about constant. There are several other indications however, that air travel will become less expensive, comparing favorably with the cost of bus transportation, and because of the time involved the increase in air travel will reduce the use of the private automobiles as a transporter to recreation participation sites. Group tours will increase because of the savings of moving groups of people in busses, trains, or airplanes. Use of package tours will also increase, which will include transportation to and from the site, perhaps land transportation while in the area at the destination, housing, meals, or recreation.

[8] From CONCEPT OF LEISURE, Conference Board Record, 10, Number 6, p. 25 by Milton Leontiades. Reprinted with permission of Joseph L. Naar, Director of Public Information, the Conference Board.

One of the biggest question marks in discussing mobility implications is the availability of fuel. The summer of 1973 saw a dramatic reduction in automobile travel because of the assumed inability to obtain fuel, reduced hours and Sunday closing of service stations. A similar reduction in the availability of energy could cause similar reductions in travel in the future. There is no doubt that our energy consumption is increasing at approximately six percent per year, and it is anticipated to be a number of years before our current efforts to develop our own supply will be able to meet the increased demand. Thus increased cost and limited availability will continue to reduce the desire and ability of people to travel by automobile to and from recreation desti- nations and sites. The "one-tank full" vacation is becoming very prevalent.

URBANIZATION IMPLICATIONS

The trend toward urbanization has apparently been halted, in fact the central cities are experiencing reduced population as more people move to suburbia and farther out to the countryside. Those who move in this direction will, of course, convert more of their leisure time to travel time if they continue to work in the cities, or if they attempt to make a living from the land, as many are doing now either part time or full time, this may require working from dawn till dark with corresponding reductions in leisure time.

EDUCATION IMPLICATIONS

It has been previously indicated that education effects the type of recreation and leisure pursuits of individuals. As the educational level increases, individuals tend to travel more, stay longer, and participate in activities that require more specialized recreation equipment and more specialized recreation skills. The increase in education may be tied somewhat closely to increases in income. Therefore some factors may be attributable to increased income as well as education.

There is little question that the level of education is increasing. Soon the average educational level will be high school graduate or more. At present, over one-half of those in college are from families whose parents did not graduate from high school. The increased level of education cannot help but contribute to an increased demand for recreation in the future.

IMPLICATIONS OF SOCIAL FACTORS

It is interesting to study the results of age on recreation demand. It is a fact that people are getting married later, and beginning their families later. It is a fact that people are retiring earlier, and traveling more in their retirement. It is a fact that college students are traveling more, expecting a summer vacation before returning to school, and treating this more as a necessity rather than a luxury. It is a fact that because of increased income and education, the blue collar worker is able now to

Figure 55 Those in the middle income group can now afford many of the types of recreation equipment previously available only to upper middle to higher income families.
Courtesy: Recreation Vehicle Industry Association, Chantilly, Virginia.

afford many of the recreation opportunities previously available only to the highly educated and highly salaried.

This has produced considerable increase in the demand for recreation, and will continue to produce a similar increased demand in the future.

CONFLICTING EXAMPLES

As the following examples will show, there are conflicting reports as to the present status and future trends of recreation demands. These may pertain to specific segments of the recreation and tourism market, and while there has been considerable fluctuation in some areas as a result of inflation and the energy shortages, other segments of the industry have increased consistently. The Associated Press reported in the fall of 1975[9] that overall resort business was up 12 percent from 1974, making this year the

[9] Columbia Tribune, Associated Press, Wednesday, September 10, 1975.

best year ever. "People are economy minded and are looking for less expensive places to eat or bring in their own food. Americans are spending their time closer to home, and spend time one place rather than traveling around. Most are not traveling more than 300 miles from their home. The Automobile Club of Michigan indicated that routing requests by state residents were up 11.5 for the upper peninsula and 46.6 for the lower peninsula."

AAA, the Automobile Club of America reported people were staying twice as long in private campgrounds as they did last year and added that revenues were up for state parks although no specifics were available. The Pocono Mountains Tourist Bureau in Pennsylvania said the area had 17 percent more visitors this year than it did in 1974. According to George C. Wilson[10] big resort areas, such as Miami Beach, is booming, recession or not. Even at the Miami Beach Dog Racing Track, R. J. Hart, General Manager predicted that people will bet on 35 million greyhounds by the end of the season running from January to May, an increase of 15 percent over last year. Miami apparently is experiencing full houses, in spite of the talk of poor economy and inflation prevalent at that time. Florida's tourism research director, Landon Haynes, reported that more cars with Michigan license plates came into Florida in January than from any other state, over 18,500. This came at a time with the major unemployment situation in the car and steel fabricating plants in Michigan. Haynes indicated that February and March traffic was running 30 percent higher than last year. Business in Miami Beach however is at the budget end of Miami, rather than at the luxury places at the north end. The very expensive luxury hotels appear to be doing as well as ever, which might imply that the rich people have not been hit hard as yet, and still have discretionary income. The Doral Beach Hotel, which rents from $60 to $200 a day, appears to have its best year ever. Others in the Miami Beach area reinforce the idea that apparently their patrons feel that they are entitled to a vacation, no matter what, and they are going to take it while they have the money before the prices go up.

It is interesting to note that in later articles concerning the Miami situation, written in the Fall of 1975, the Miami Beach area has been virtually deserted. The Miami Tourist Bureau had approached the Miami Beach city government for marketing capital to attempt to attract additional tourists to the south end of Florida.

A number of interesting statistics were shared at a recent nationwide meeting.[11] According to Dee Larson of Jefferson Motor Coach Tours in Minneapolis, the tour business is expanding significantly. Fifty percent of their business is first time riders, with over 5000 passengers in 1974. Jiffy jaunts of one- to two-day packages are of interest to many. Most travel tours are made up of elderly or retired people or young married couples. Delta Airlines sales indicates that their sales are up 200 percent in January of 1975 over 1974. Avis Rent-A-Car implies there is more fly/drive packages being taken advantage of but primarily by upper income brackets of people. Renters of Avis Cars seldom buy tours, and are more independent travelers. Their industry

---

[10] Wilson, George C., Washington Post, Sunday April 6, 1975.

[11] Presentations at the First Attractions Seminar, Orlando, Florida.

Figure 56 In spite of the gasoline shortage and tight money of a year or two ago the skiing business is booming.
Courtesy: Photo by Peter Miller courtesy Ski Industries America.

is experiencing growth paricularly during the energy crisis. The U.S. Travel Bureau estimates that foreign travel is down considerably and many of those normally taking trips abroad are taking trips within the continental United States. Hershey Park, Pennsylvania indicates a 25 percent increase in 1975 over 1974. Busch Gardens has indicated their attendance is 40 percent ahead of their best year, and 40 percent ahead of November, December, or January of 1974, and 34 percent ahead of 1973. Pat Callen of Cyprus Gardens indicates that 1975 attendance is in line with where 1974 should have been had the recession and energy shortage not influenced the travel situation. According to Dr. Douglas Freckling of the U.S. Travel Data Center, in the third quarter of 1974, automobile travel is up 13 percent, weekend travel is down five percent, and the vacation trips were up 30 percent. It appears that weekend travel is the first to be eliminated in a recession.

According to Robert Blundred, Executive Director of the International Association of Amusement Parks and Attractions, attendance at amusement parks has increased consistently in years past. He implies that one reason why the Outdoor Amusement industry appears to do so well during times of recession is the per hour-leisure expenditures rate. The pay-one-price admission at most parks encourage stays of eight to ten hours. Given the average length of stay and the per capita spending in the ten to twelve dollar range, spending during the day in the park is less than many other hourly leisure expenditures. Most of these attractions are also within the 100-mile to 300-mile radius to which most Americans are restricting their travel destinations. The influence of children in the family also has considerable impact on this industry, and even though Dad and Mom may not enjoy the visit as much as the youngsters, in many cases the summer is not complete until the youngsters have had an opportunity to go to Six Flags, Silver Dollar City, or Hershey Park.

CHANGING ACTIVITY INTERESTS

The Midwest Research Institute Nationwide Recreation Study[12] reveals that camping and bicycling are the two fastest growing leisure activities while outdoor games such as golf, tennis, and skiing rate third in growth. Also, the average American family now takes 2.8 vacations per year plus an average of 7.6 weekend trips away from home annually.

Electronic video games (ping-pong, hockey, etc.) are gaining in popularity (due to their silent operation compared with pin-ball machines no doubt!). About 50,000 coin operated games worth at least 40 million dollars were sold in 1973.

About two-thirds of the Corp of Engineers project lakes are located within a 50-mile radius of urban areas of populations of 50,000 or more. The Corp of Engineers

[12]Midwest Research Institute Nationwide Recreation Study, Midwest Research Institute, 425 Volker Boulevard, Kansas City, Missouri 64110, 1974.

Figure 57 Projections indicate that longer than average increases will be seen in bicycling.
Courtesy: Bicycling Institute of America, New York, New York.

speculate the growth will double over the next 15 years at these areas.[13]

The trend toward physical fitness and concern for the environment are also affecting the recreation behavior patterns. Larger than average increases in tennis, hiking, bicycling, canoeing, backpacking, nature study, cross country skiing, and primitive camping are examples of trends resulting from interest in physical fitness and environment. No doubt the relative low cost of these activities has also made them attractive.

Although they are not growing as rapidly, swimming, boating, and fishing are still the most popular.

One of the fastest growing aspects of recreational activities is that of recreation equipment facilities for private or home recreation space. Because of the problems found in travel, more and more people are buying swimming pools, building tennis

[13] U.S. Corp of Engineers, Water Spectrum, 3rd Quarter, 1974. Superintendent of Documents, Washington, D.C.

courts, and developing their own picnic areas and play spaces in their own backyards.

The adult education classes across the United States is growing at an unprecedented rate. Many people are taking the opportunity to attend classes either to update their vocational skills, or to participate and learn more about a leisure interest or activity.

Apparently the taste and desired facilities will change also. Eighty percent of the respondents of the people surveyed in a statewide Missouri Tourism Study[14] indicated that they desired more campsites with water and electricity provided, better restrooms with hot and cold showers, more picnic tables, and more water hydrants. Ninety five percent of the recreationists surveyed did not object to paying a user fee for different activities if they knew the fee would be spent for improvements for operation and maintenance.

Another changing aspect of recreation services for the future concerns the modern regional shopping mall, which is quickly establishing itself as a focal point in the life of American communities for retail purchasing, as well as community services. The center captured 44 percent of the total retail market industry in the country, and are fast becoming a nucleus of social, community, and cultural activity in the suburban United States.[15] Although one study shows that shopping trips account for only six percent of the total family trips, indications are that these trips to the shopping area are for more varied reasons and for longer duration than previously. Malls are now offering fashion shows, arts and crafts displays, travel exhibits, cooking demonstrations, decorating seminars, yoga programs, sports demonstrations, antique automobile shows, boat shows, camping and recreational vehicles displays. Teenagers often participate in baton twirling contests, public speaking competitions, square dances, and junior achievement affairs. Some malls are even offering accredited college courses. The shopping mall can be the public square of the future and encompass many recreation and leisure activities as well as be a focal point for public service activities and public education programs. The implications for private and commercial recreation here are obvious. In Pittsburgh, Pennsylvania for instance, increasing numbers of shopping malls are also including recreation facilities such as ice rinks, bowling alleys, arcade rooms, raquet clubs, cinema houses, and others.

SUMMARY—EXTERNAL IMPLICATIONS

To summarize the external implications it can be said that the forecast is partly cloudy, that is, because of the inconsistency of the energy availability, of the inflation rates, and because of the mood of the customer changes rapidly and is one of great uncertainty, the forecast for recreation in whatever form is somewhat in doubt. In other words, "they do not know" and tend to make sporatic decisions. There is little

[14] Epperson, Arlin F., *Recreation and Tourism in the Clearwater Lake Area*, Department of Recreation & Park Administration, University of Missouri, Columbia, Missouri 65201, Summer 1975.

[15] Sussman, Albert, Columbia Tribune, Missouri, Wednesday, June 12, 1974, New York Associated Press.

doubt that it will continue to grow, at a rate even or faster than other major expenditures in the economy. Whether or not it will continue to keep the pace it had begun through the early 1970s is doubtful.

Two sources have summarized in general the best guesses as to what the American public will do in terms of travel, tourism, and recreation. These are summarized below.

AMERICANS WILL STAY CLOSER TO HOME[16]

1. The current phenomenon will undoubtedly benefit some regions of the country. Those close to large population centers may witness significant increases in tourism and recreation while regions like the Southwest, Mountain West, Alaska, Hawaii, and others will experience decreases. Unfortunately, these areas are more tourism dependent than other regions of the United States.
2. Foreign and exotic vacations will be postponed and substituted by domestic vacations. This can only be beneficial as long as this group equals or exceeds those in lower income brackets who may postpone vacations altogether.
3. Some recreational activities will show less dramatic changes in use than others. Activities such as skiing, which attract higher-income households, may be less changed than automobile touring or camping.
4. Mass transit will grow in popularity as a mode of transportation to recreation areas. Many leaders are strongly suggesting that the American public must and will file for divorce in its marriage with the automobile. Given that two-thirds of all vacation travel spending is by households traveling by automobile, such a move will force major changes.
5. Sales of recreation vehicles and some recreation equipment will decrease. Although many envision camping as a cost saving device, the investment in new equipment may be less appealing than rentals or a shift to other activities.
6. Vacations and other recreation trips will be planned more carefully and over longer periods of time. Consequently, programs with continual and current information output will be the most likely to succeed. No longer can one expect to catch travelers along the highway or entice them to visit with glittering generalities. Vacationers will seek detailed information on areas, services, and accommodations thus reducing uncertainty and loss, and wants to maximize the benefit from their vacation dollar.
7. Successful marketing will be directed to highly specific target markets and special interest groups. Packages must be sold to clubs and other groups who will utilize mass transit and other group devices that cut individual cost.
8. Tourism will decline. Mass recreation and tourism as we know it in this country came with affluence and improved transportation. And although we may maintain a degree of affluence in this country, the energy problem will be with us for a long time.

[16] Hunt, John D., Tourism in the Second Half of the 70's, Tourism and Recreation Review, Utah; State University, 4, Number 1, January 1975.

WHAT TO LOOK FOR IN THE FUTURE[17]

1. More family oriented programs. A change in travel program patterns; less foreign travel, more *See America First* by bus, train and with family or group rates offered.
2. Domestic air travel complete package tours catering to the family group concept. Special charter arrangements will be offered.
3. Greatly reduced rates in motels/hotels and some resort facilities. In-tour rates to and from resort and attraction centers will be offered by motel/hotel chains.
4. Local attractions on the increase, a radius of 100 miles will be the target area for auto travelers.
5. A return to the special excursion promotions and rates. Combined travel and admission packages will be on the increase.
6. In-tour attractions, parks, restaurant, theaters, and sports centers will gear up and develop programs more for the neighborhood crowds. Look for a change in their promotional thinking.
7. Old established recreational institutions, agencies and services like the Y's civic recreation departments, and schools will begin to make changes in their programming, facilities and basic administrative patterns—concerning participants in the adult and family categories.
8. All programs will encourage strengthening the family ties. More parental involvement.
9. Retired employees will play a more active part in the recreation programs. Considerable help will be obtained, volunteer and paid, through these groups.
10. More intramural sports, more contests, greater participation, and large speculation audiences will be evident. Greater attention and recognition will be directed to intramural activities, less to the varsity semi-pro selective groups.
11. Increase in outdoor family activities. Bicycling will continue to gain participants. Family bicycle hikes will be popular.
12. Physical fitness programs will be more enjoyable, and desired. More adventure hiking groups, contests, games, and swim parties will be scheduled to involve the physical fitness concepts.
13. Entertaining at home will become more popular—cookouts, card parties, backyard sports and games, and a need for instruction in home entertainment will be welcome.
14. Look for vegetable gardens to spring up everywhere. Extensive use will be made of backyards, vacant lots, and even window boxes. Old victory garden programs should be dusted off and renewed.
15. Do it yourself-handyman aids will be most popular and from these instructional programs, groups will form to help each other in cutting costs for home maintenance.

[17] *Key Notes,* National Industrial Recreation Association Newsletter, **5,** Number 1, January/February 1975. Chicago, Ill.

16. Cultural activities will be on the increase. Learning programs, development of skills, exposure to higher education, art, music, theater, and dance appreciation will be welcomed.

INTERNAL IMPLICATIONS

Many of the problems of attitudes and working conditions affecting the total recreation market also affect the individual recreation enterprise. Because of the long hours and the nature of the work, the recreation enterprise operator should take a careful look at his own enterprise to see whether or not the factors that are causing changing attitudes in the work force as a whole are also affecting his own particular business.

In an attempt to get his own house in order, the enterprise operator should give first priority to analyzing each job he has to offer, to see if it can be made more rewarding and more challenging for those he employs. Because of the importance of hospitality and a satisfied customer, a satisfied employee is certainly a must. The working conditions that may result in others patronizing his recreation establishment more in the future, may also be the same conditions that confront the operator, that is, high turnover, excessive sick leave, or a high rate of error or omission, causing him reduced business in his own facility.

Every effort must be made in the personnel area to select qualified people, pay them competitively, train them well, and strive to make every job an enjoyable, creative, and challenging opportunity with as much associated responsibility as possible. Employee motivation is a key to successful business now and in the future. Employees must receive recognition and appreciation in their jobs, as well as find opportunities for creativeness and a challenge, if they are to be an asset in assisting the manager to meet the challenges of the future.

There is little question that recreation business people will continue to face increased cost of doing business, such as labor, advertising, equipment and repairs, interest, and cost of good sold. Recreation spending will still require effective advertising and promotion. Because of increased gasoline costs and energy consumption programs, people will likely travel shorter distances and stay in one place longer. They will also be more selective in facilities and services. The main thing the recreation industry must do to meet the challenge of the current economic energy situation is to respond positively.

The following suggestions should be given careful consideration:[18]

First, determine what you are selling: Identify the combination of services and/or facilities that attracts visitors to your business. Then, look objectively at your present customers. You need to know where they are from, and their incomes, occupations,

---

[18] Minnesota Tourist Travel Notes, "Tourism Spending Holding Up During Recession," University of Minnesota Cooperative Extension Service, **13,** Number 2, Summer 1975.

ages, family situations, and what they like to do when in your area.

Sell aggressively: People who want your specific services and facilities are your target for advertising and promotion programs. Stretch your promotion dollar by cooperating with others in your area to offer packages.

Offer Security: Offer a package—combine food, lodging, and activities in one advertised price. Offer low-cost entertainment.

Search for the best price: Estimate costs from the past year's costs and how much they will increase. Then estimate the occupancy and consequent gross income at each possible rate you could charge. Select the price that results in the highest net profit.

Figure 58 The enterprising manager may be able to turn his summer resort into a year round resort by providing winter activities
Courtesy: American Hotel and Motel Association, New York, New York.

Watch your Expenses: Explore new ways to cut costs, saving energy, and controlling your inventory. Keep accurate records to help you manage your business.

Try New Ideas: You have a unique business and it needs your personal touch. Be a business professional!

Study the Statistics Keep close tabs on research done by your state extension service, State Department of Tourism, or city or regional tourism or convention bureau, the U.S. Travel Data Center, economists, and sociologists who watch the travel and economic trends in various parts of the country. Keep an eye on the inflation rate, and watch for reports from organizations like the Conference Board Record who are experts in forecasting and projections for a number of large companies whose future depends upon correct "guesses" most of the time.

Finally, Even though the future is uncertain, develop a play—a probable course of action knowing full well that error is likely.

Summary

Every private and commercial recreation enterprise operator desires to know what the future holds for leisure services as a whole and to his enterprise in particular. He must do everything he can to accurately predict what the demand will be, the price people are willing to pay, and ultimately whether his enterprise will be able to show profit. He must consider a number of external implications in an effort to make his forecast. These include analysis of the public attitudes, spending and income implications, as well as energy, time, and transportation implications. He must also look at the historical perspective in terms of the long-term growth of his and other products or services.

While attempting to keep current on the external implications, the manager must also be concerned about internal implications, those problems, attitudes and working conditions that affect his individual employees as well as the total recreation enterprise as a whole. He must have his own house in order. This implies keeping abreast of fringe benefits programs, employee training programs, and in-service training and education programs that will keep good well-trained staff at this facility.

It is clearly evident that growing affluence and growing fractions of time will continue. These favorable factors should assure the share of personal incomes spent for leisure growing to at least remain in line with the growth in discretionary income. However, it must be remembered that long-term growth prospects can indeed be interrupted by short-term fluctuations.

The leisure market must have closer definition and study before one can make generalizations concerning the future.

The "leisure ethic" is in effect a term only useful with a specific product or consumer market in mind. The common observation that increases in time and income happily combined to guarantee growth in leisure time pursuits may be true for the economy as a whole but is not a real helpful guide for firms hoping to benefit from such growth. We must acknowledge that the concept of leisure for the future rests on an uneasy foundation of few facts and many assumptions and learn to separate the one from the other.

Discussion Questions

1. What problems must a recreation business forecaster consider in projecting recreation and leisure trends?
2. What social/psychological factors would you consider as having the most significant impact on todays work force and their attitudes toward leisure?
3. Considering the economic uncertainties of the 1970's, discuss and illustrate the paradoxical trends of the leisure industry.
4. Assuming you own a recreation and leisure consulting service that mails a newsletter to clients in the travel, resort, amusement park, and campground industries. What would be your predictions regarding recreation and leisure trends for the next ten years?

CHAPTER 9

IMPLICATIONS FOR COMMERCIAL RECREATION EDUCATION

Interest in private and commercial recreation has increased dramatically in recent years by those who have previously been concerned with providing leisure and recreation services in the public sector. This has been for a number of reasons, none the least of which has been the dramatic increase in tourism, travel, and expenditures for private and commercial recreation sercives, as well as the generalized attitude that it is indeed the participant that is most important, and since he does not distinguish between the services provided by private or public recreation agencies, perhaps those in these two sectors should indeed attempt to cooperate much more fully.

Another major reason for the increased interest and awareness of the private and commercial recreation field has to do with the job opportunities for graduates from recreation education curriculums that has heretofore been educated primarily in the three traditional areas of:

Municipal Recreation

Therapeutic Recreation

Outdoor Recreation

Several studies would imply now that there are two or three graduates of Recreation Education Curriculums for every one job that is available in the market place.[1]

There has been a dramatic increase in the number of curriculums over the past few years that are educating people for job opportunities in the public leisure services;[2] thus many of those in the public education curriculums are looking to new areas of job opportunities for students, as well as attempting to provide some assistance to

[1] Arlin F. Epperson; *A Profile of Selected Personal and Professional Characteristics of Recent Graduates from Recreation and Park Curriculums in The NRPA Great Lakes Region,* unpublished dissertation, Indiana University Bloomington, Indiana 1973.

[2] Don Henkel, "Personnel Referral Service", Park and Recreation Magazine NRPA, May 1974, 1601 North Kent Street, Arlington, Virginia 22209.

students who have a basic desire to work in leisure services that are tied much more closely to the economy and the market place than those in the public sector. It is for the above reasons that this chapter is included.

TYPES OF JOBS FOUND IN PRIVATE AND COMMERCIAL RECREATION _____

The first attempt to delineate those kinds of jobs that exist or would exist in the private and commercial recreation area are identified in a study by Drs. Peter Verhoven and Dennis Vinton of the University of Kentucky in 1972.[3] It was they who studied the leisure occupations under a grant from the Bureau of Education, Department of Health, Education, and Welfare.

The U.S. Office of Education has for many years attempted to provide career education materials for a variety of types of employment. The Department of Education has divided all kinds of employment into 15 career clusters, listed below.[4]

Agri-business and natural resources

Business and office

Communication and media

Construction

Consumer and homemaking

Public service

Fine arts and humanities

Environment

Health

Leisure (recreation, hospitality, and tourism)

Manufacturing

Marketing and distribution

Marine science

Transportation

Personnel services

The cluster concept of which the Hospitality and Recreation cluster is a part was developed by the U.S. Office of Education to facilitate the development and implementation of the concept of career education. U.S. Office of Education designed

---

[3] Peter J. Verhoven, and Dennis A. Vinton; *Career Education for Leisure Occupations Curriculum Guidelines for Recreation, Hospitality, and Tourism;* Superintendent of Documents, Washington, D.C. 1972.

[4] Ibid.

career clusters that group the many diverse occupations in the economy by common characteristics. As a result of this clustering however, many diverse types of occupations are grouped together, in sometimes what would appear to be with uncommon characteristics. "The Hospitality and Recreation occupations are those occupations which provide services to others away from their home, so that they can more fully enjoy their non-working time."*

Over the past years the U.S. Office of Education has been primarily concerned in developing career education materials in each one of these clusters primarily for those in junior and senior high school-age levels, to make students more aware of the types of opportunities that are available, and to help guide them as they attempt to make life-career decisions, or to pursue specialized education in high school or college toward a career end. The Verhoven and Vinton study prepared leisure-career curriculum and education guidelines to bring about an awareness on the part of students of the opportunities, requirements, and qualifications for jobs in the leisure, recreation, hospitality, and tourism cluster. The study primarily is oriented toward those who may not necessarily plan to complete four years of college as preparatory education.

The leisure career field as described in this study would be broadly descibed as follows:

> The Leisure Career field encompasses those occupations pursued by persons engaged in performing the functions required to meet the needs of persons engaged in leisure-time pursuits.

> An analysis of the primary functions of the leisure career field led to the identification of four major occupational groups:

> 1. *Recreation services*
> 2. *Recreation resources*
> 3. *Tourism*
> 4. *Amusement and entertainment*

RECREATION SERVICES

The main function of the recreation services group is to provide recreational activities. This group creates and supervises programs, plans, activities, and provides recreation leadership and instruction. These leisure-time experiences take place in a variety of settings—parks, playgrounds, camps, and community organizations to mention just a few. Careers in recreation services involve a great deal of personal interaction.

RECREATION RESOURCES

The recreation resources group includes jobs related to the planning, development, maintenance, and protection of resources, both natural and man-made, used for

---

*Contract Research Corporation: Career Development in Hospitality and Recreation Occupations, Belmont Massachusetts, in cooperation with the U.S. Office of Education, Superintendent of Documents, Washington, D.C. 1976 pT-3.

leisure-time experiences. These jobs deal primarily with recreational areas, facilities, products, goods, and with natural areas. In general, these jobs from a support system for the experiences provided by the recreation services group.

TOURISM

The tourism group includes jobs related to travel for pleasure (rather than for business or duty), to activities for tourists; and to money spent on a location other than the one where it was earned. Within this group are five major components:

1. Attracting a market for tourism experiences.
2. Providing transportation to places of interest.
3. Providing attractions for tourist participation.
4. Housing, feeding, entertaining, and serving tourists.
5. Informing people about attractions, services, facilities and transportation, and then making specific arrangements for them.

AMUSEMENT AND ENTERTAINMENT

Occupations in this group are primarily concerned with amusing, diverting, or informing people. Included here are jobs centered around:

1. Commercial amusements.
2. Live, filmed, or broadcast performance.
3. The presentation of those and athletic contests.
4. The training of persons or animals for entertainment.
5. The teaching of entertainment skills at a post-high school level.
6. Personal services in entertainment establishments.

In listing the sample job titles in each one of these general areas, the job titles are categorized into entry level groupings, including:

Level One. Those jobs that do not require a high school diploma.

Level Two. Includes those jobs that require a minimum of a high school diploma or its equivalent.

Level Three. Includes those jobs that require a minimum of two year post secondary degree from a Junior or Community College or Certification program.

Level Four. Includes those jobs that require a minimum of four-year post secondary degree.

We are, of course, primarily interested in those described in the tourism and amusement and entertainment occupational group, and those that are designated as entry level four, normally requiring a college degree. Those listed under the tourism occupational group were as follows:

1. Travel agency director.
2. Resort manager.
3. Director of food services.
4. Travel consultant.
5. Booking agent.
6. Tour time manager.

The material indicated the jobs at this level call for over-all planning, decision making, scheduling, budgeting, coordination of units, understanding of total organization function, supervision of unit supervisors, and responsibility for public relations—all leading to the efficient operation of the facility or program.

Those described under the amusement and entertainment occupational group include the following:

1. Stage director.
2. Arranger.
3. Producer.
4. Technical director.

Responsibilities for these are described as involving the over-all supervision of many different types of workers to accomplish a specific goal. All supervisory trades must be combined with special skills and talents in the specific area.

It can be readily seen that information in this material concerning jobs in level four are considerably limited.

The remaining portion of the study reflects the framework for refocusing present curriculums to include emphasis on career education for leisure occupations. It is interesting to note that the authors, in a 1967 man-power study, found a total of 303,000 jobs, and predicted that in 1980, there would be three jobs for every one person available, and there would be a total of 1.2 million jobs available in both public and private commercial recreation.

FOLLOW-UP STUDY BY CONTRACT RESEARCH

A follow-up study developed by Contract Research Corporation of Belmont, Massachusetts.[5]

The purpose of the second study was to develop curriculum guides designed for students in grades seven to nine, to provide them with the necessary tools and information to explore career opportunities in the fields of hospitality and recreation. The study indicates that the hospitality and recreation industry encompasses a large and diverse field including over 50 types of employers and over 200 types of occupations. These occupations vary in setting, complexity, responsibility, and training requirements.

[5] Contract Research Corporation; *Career Development in Hospitality and Recreation Occupations,* Belmont, Massachusetts; in cooperation with the U.S. Office of Education, Superintendent of Documents, Washington, D.C. 1976.

COMMON ENVIRONMENTS OF HOSPITALITY AND RECREATION

To organize this diverse field, the numerous occupations and employers have been grouped according to common environments or sub-clusters. They are:

1. *Lodging:* This environment includes all of those occupations involved in the management and operation of lodging facilities. People employed in this environment work for hotels, motels, resorts, convention centers, and steamship companies.
2. *Recreation:* This environment includes those occupations involved in the management, planning, and operation of recreational programs, facilities, and areas. Examples of employers are recreation centers, camps, hospitals, governmental agencies, and bowling alleys. Occupations range from grounds keepers to youth worker to director or owner of a recreational area.
3. *Entertainment services:* This includes those establishments and occupations involved in the management, promotion, and operation of entertainment. Movie theaters, amusement parks, and booking agencies are examples of employers. Occupations range from ushers to theater managers.
4. *Cultural services:* This includes those occupations involved in the management, services, and operation of cultural institutions such as libraries, museums, and zoos. Occupations range from ticket takers to curators.
5. *Sports:* This environment addresses the activities involved in professional sports. Occupations include professional athletes, referees, activities involved in the management and operation of sports centers such as stadium managers, and ticket sellers. Employers include professional sports teams and sports stadiums.
6. *Food and beverage services:* This environment ranges from food preparation, food service to food management. These occupations are found in a variety of industries including restaurants, school cafeterias, snack bars, or catering services. Occupations include waiters, chefs, and restaurant managers.
7. *Travel services:* This environment includes those occupations that are involved in the arrangement and support of travel. These occuapations include travel agents, flight attendants, and tour guides. Employers include airlines and travel agencies.

Those types of jobs that are identified by the study are illustrated on the following pages from that report.

HOSPITALITY AND RECREATION

1. *Lodging.* Steamship Companies, resorts, convention centers, hotels, motels, guest houses, or railroads.
2. *Recreation.* Skating rinks, dance studios, gun clubs, architectural and consulting firms, bowling alleys, municipal agencies, camps, health care facilities, golf courses, ski resorts, campgrounds, trailer parks, sporting and recreational camps, parks, or pool parlors.
3. *Entertainment bureaus.* Theatrical productions, ticket agencies, carnivals, race-

tracks, ballet companies, night clubs, rodeos, movie theaters, theaters, entertainment bureaus, circuses, or amusement parks.

4. *Cultural services.* Museums, zoos and aquaria, libraries, historical sites.

5. *Sports.* Sports centers, stadiums, or professional athletic teams.

6. *Food and beverage services.* Drinking places, flight kitchens, ships, catering services, food processing services, cafeterias, restaurants, hotels and motels, concession stands, coffee shops, and education and health institutions.

7. *Travel.* Airlines, railroads, tour bus lines, auto rental agencies, tour boat lines, governmental tourism agency, travel agencies, tour promoters/operators, or travel management private companies.

LODGING

1. *Steamship companies.* Cabin superintendent, steward, or maid.

2. *Resorts.* Manager, resident manager, convention manager, front office manager, service superintendent, executive housekeeper, reservations clerk, front desk clerk, bellman, doorman, or chambermaid.

3. *Convention centers.* Convention manager, sales manager, front office manager, service superintendent, executive housekeeper, reservations clerk, front desk clerk, bellman, doorman, or chambermaid.

4. *Hotels.* Hotel manager, resident manager, sales manager, convention manager, front office manager, salesman, superintendent, service, executive housekeeper, reservations clerk, bell captain, front desk clerk, bellman, doorman, or chambermaid.

5. *Motels.* Motel manager, front office manager, reservations clerk, desk clerk, service superintendent, bellman, or maid.

6. *Guest houses.* Guest house manager, lodging facilities attendant, or maid.

7. *Railroads.* Reservations manager, host/hostess, or maid.

RECREATION

1. *Skating Rinks.* Manager, skating ring, skating instuctor, attendant, or ticket seller.

2. *Dance studios.* Manager, Dance Studio, Salesman, dancing instructor, or dancing instuctor.

3. *Gun Clubs.* Manager of Gun Club, hunting and fishing guide, or equipment attendant.

4. *Architectural and consulting firms.* Landscape architect or draftsman.

5. *Bowling alleys.* Owner, manager, desk attendant, or service superintendent.

6. *Municipal Agencies.* Municipal Recreation Director, assistant director, recreation area planner, program director, recreational facility manager, playground director, activity director, playground leader, or attendant.

7. *Camps.* Owner of camp, camp director, program director, activities director, head counselor, head of waterfront, counselors, or junior counselors.

8. *Health-care facility.* Recreation therapist, activities director, or recreation aide.

9. *Golf courses.* Manager, golf pro, caddie master, golf course ranger, caddie, or golf range attendant.

10. *Ski Resorts.* Manager of ski resort, publicity director, head of ski school, ski instructor, head of ski patrol, ski patrolman, ticket seller, or lift attendant.

ENTERTAINMENT SERVICES

1. *Theatrical productions.* Producer, publicity director, stage director, road manager, wardrobe mistress, or wardrobe assistants.

2. *Ticket agencies.* Ticket broker or counter clerk.

3. *Carnivals.* Carnival manager, supervisor of rides, supervisor of games, ride operator, game operator, pony-ride operator, ticket seller, or ticket taker.

4. *Racetracks.* Owner, manager, publicity director, patrol judge, paddock judge, jockey/driver, animal attendant, or ticket seller.

5. *Ballet company.* Producer, publicity director, stage director, road manager, wardrobe mistress, or wardrobe assistants.

6. *Night clubs.* Owner, manager, booking agent, maitre d' hotel, host, hostess, or doorman.

7. *Rodeos.* Rodeo manager, rodeo performer, animal keeper, animal person-head, ticket seller, or ticket taker.

8. *Movie theaters.* Movie theater manager, booking agent, sales manager, motion picture projectionist, head usher, cashier, or usher.

9. *Theaters.* Theater manager, booking agent, sales manager, publicity director, head usher, cashier, or usher.

10. *Entertainment bureaus.* Concert promoter, booking agent, artist manager, or road manger.

11. *Circuses.* Circus superintendent, circus trainmaster, circus foreman, master of ceremonies, circus performer, costumer, circus laborer, or ticket seller.

12. *Amusement parks.* Amusement park manager, supervisor of rides, supervisor of games, ride operator, game operator, pony-ride operator, ticket seller, or ticket taker.

CULTURAL

1. *Museums.* Museum director, curator, archivist, public relations director, resorter, education director, tour guide, or attendant.

2. *Zoos and Aquaria.* Director, publicity director, head animal man, animal handler, tour guide, or attendant.

3. *Libraries.* Library director, librarian, library technical assistant, or desk clerk.

4. *Historical sites.* Historical site director, public relations director, tour guide, or attendant.

SPORTS

1. *Sports centers, stadiums.* Owner, manager, publicity director, ticket sales director, ticket seller, or usher.
2. *Professional athletic team.* Owner, publicity director, general manager, athlete manager, coach, athlete, umpire/referee, or bat person.

FOOD AND BEVERAGE SERVICES

1. *Drinking places.* Bar owner, bar manger, bartender, waiter/waitress, or barboy.
2. *Flight kitchens.* Manager, flight kitchen, production manager, cooks, or food assembler.
3. *Ships.* Director of food and beverage, chef, cook, kitchen supervisor, maitre d' hotel, steward of room and deck, bartender, wine steward, waiter/waitress, or busboy.
4. *Catering services.* Owner of catering service, manager of catering service, cook, kitchen supervisor, waiter/waitress, or busboy.
5. *Food processing services.* Owner of food processing, production supervisor, cook, food assembler, route representatives, or lunch truck driver.
6. *Cafeterias.* Cafeteria owner, cafeteria manager, kitchen supervisor, cooks, line supervisor, counter person, cashier, or counter supply person.
7. *Restaurants.* Restaurant owner, restaurant manager, executive chef, chef, baker, cook, kitchen supervisor, food controller, kitchen helper, baker helper, maitre d', hostess, bartender, wine steward, waiter/waitress, cashier, or busboy.
8. *Hotels and motels.* Director of food and beverages, function manager, restaurant manager, chef/cook, kitchen supervisor, food controller, maitre d', bartender, waiter/waitress, cashier, or busboy.
9. *Concession stands.* Owner/manager food concession, cook, or counter clerk.
10. *Coffee shop.* Coffee shop owner, coffee shop manager, cook/baker, counter clerk, cashier, or busboy.
11. *Education and health institutions.* Director of food service, kitchen supervisor, cook, line supervisor, counter person, cashier, or counter supply person.

TRAVEL SERVICES AND PROMOTION

1. *Airlines.* Group sales manager, chief flight attendant, reservation agent, or flight attendant.
2. *Railroads.* Manager railroad terminal, station/depot master, or railroad conductor.
3. *Tour bus lines.* Manager of tour bus lines, tour bus driver, or bus hostess.
4. *Auto rental agencies.* Owner of auto rental agency, manager of auto rental agency, dispatcher of car rentals, car rental clerk, or car rental parking attendant.
5. *Tour boat lines.* Owner of tour boat line, manager tour boat line, tour boat

captain, sightseeing guide, or steward.

6. *Governmental tourism agencies.* Director of tourism, publicity director, or sight-seeing guide.
7. *Travel agencies.* Owner of travel agency, sales manager, group sales manager, sales representative, travel counselor, reservation agent, or travel clerk.
8. *Tour promoters/operators.* Manager, sales manager, promotion manager, sales representative, travel counselor, reservation agent, tour guide, or travel clerk.
9. *Travel management for private company.* Tour arranger or reservations clerk.

It can be seen from the above job listings that there is no differentiation made in the study between those that require a high school education only, as compared with those that require a college education.

This study makes no claim that its job titles are adequate or conclusive. They are examples and should be accepted as such. The remaining portion of the materials is related to implementing the various kinds of information about the environments into the curriculum of the student through a variety of specialized games and activities.

INFORMATION SYSTEMS AND SERVICES INCORPORATED

Another attempt to organize the kinds of jobs available in recreation, parks, and youth services includes some discussion of those in private and commercial recreation is encompassed in a booklet produced by Information Systems and Services Incorporated, Sextant Systems Incorporated.[6]

This nonprofit organization has a number of similar booklets available in their Career Development Star Sextant Series, for the following age levels:

1. Beginning Series K through 4.
2. Junior Series 6 through 8.
3. Senior Series 9 through 14.

Included in the 9 through 14 series are the following cluster groups:

1. Manufacturing—salaried manufacturing—wage.
2. Banking.
3. Insurance.
4. Hospitals, professions, agriculture, grafic arts-publishing.
5. Construction.
6. Recreation and youth services.
7. Hotels and restaurants.
8. Public utilities.
9. Air transportation.
10. Motor transportation.

---

[6] *Information Systems and Services Incorporated;* Sextant Systems Incorporated, Milwaukee, Wisconsin 53201, 1972.

11. Protective agencies.
12. Merchandising.

The firm has excellent descriptive materials for teachers and counselors, to help include information about various careers in their teaching, as well as to be able to answer questions about certain jobs in each of the clusters. In addition to a number of jobs in the recreation, parks, and youth services cluster being described, they list requirements for entering, the promotional outlook, and suggested pay and skill levels. They also have a unique personal profiling system that allows the individual to test himself on some 70 questions under the following categories:

1. Scholastic ability.
2. Social abilities.
3. Mechanical.
4. Aesthetic and creative ability.
5. Physical ability.
6. Personal Traits.
7. Interests.
8. Needs.

The authors attempt to rate each job according to the level of need in each of the categories previously mentioned, and suggests that those students desiring a specific job should match their profile against the one suggested, and if their profile in terms of the grading system superior, good, fair, or poor, is less than those required, then the counselor can recommend they not pursue that career option.

It is interesting to note that although the job descriptions, pay information, requirements for entering, and so on in this cluster were apparently determined by a jury of competent recreation professionals from both public recreation and youth serving agencies, the jury was not asked to evaluate the personal qualifications required as determined by the self-evaluation. The following sub-categories in the recreation, parks, and youth service cluster were:

	Number of Job Titles Described
1. Parks	23
2. Recreation	11
3. Medical recreation	4
4. Independent professionals	8
5. Zoological gardens	10
6. Youth services—YMCA	16
7. Scouts of America	4
8. Boys club of America	5
9. Commercial recreation	12

    -Manager, bowling establishment
    -Program director, bowling establishment
    -Counterman, bowling establishment

-Instructor, bowling establishment
-Mechanic, bowling establishment
-Golf pro
-Athletics trainer
-Professional guide
-Auto mechanic, racing
-Masseur
-Lifeguard
-Lifeguard captain

No claim is made by these authors that their titles are anything more than examples, although they appear to be fairly conclusive in the public and semi-public areas, but appear to be terribly deficient in the commercial areas.

NRPA EMPLOY[7]

The National Recreation and Park Association, a long established agency of lay and professional people interested in public recreation, has become interested in the private and commercial area of recreation as well. One of their publications, *Employ,* attempted to describe job opportunities, employment settings, job opportunities, and related job information for prospective students and graduates interested in this area for possible employment. Badger divides the private and commercial sector into the following settings, with related agency contacts for prospective job seekers.

Attractions and Amusement Parks. These types of parks are viewed in two categories. (1) General Amusement parks such as Disneyland, Six Flags, Herald Winds, or Colonial Williamsburg, and, (2) specialized parks such as Lion Country, Sea World, or the Historical Town of Smithville.

Sports and Entertainment Centers. These include bowling alleys, ice rinks, golf ranges, roller skating rinks, swimming pools, or multipurpose facilities.

Tourist Attractions. These include springs, botanical gardens, fish and animal exhibits, caves, or museums.

Vacation Excursions. These include steamship-line tours, or historical tours.

Resorts and Camps. These enterprises are based initially on one or more of five appeals: Sun, water, mountains, serenity, or recreation. These resorts range from overnight camping grounds to total destination resorts where guests will stay up to two weeks. Examples of the latter are Hilton Head Island in South Carolina, Walt Disney World

[7] Chris Badger; *NRPA Employ,* **1,** Number 9, May 1975, National Recreation and Park Association, 1601 North Kent Street, Arlington, Virginia 22209.

in Florida, Mainline Corporations Adventure in Squaw Valley, California, Calloway Gardens in Georgia, and others. Other such resorts would be campgrounds, tennis resorts, dude ranches, sports camps, and private camps.

Clubs. There are two basic types of clubs (1) city clubs, which are usually private or closed membership facilities located in downtown city areas. There are a number of these clubs in each large city. The club is usually centered around food and entertainment as well as recreation, such as tennis, raquetball, handball, or a combination. (2) Country Clubs and Sports and Adventure Clubs, which are usually located in suburban areas and are private or semiprivate. In the past, these clubs have been heavily weighted toward golf, swimming, boating, and food. Now the emphasis is toward diversification into tennis, sailing, entertainment, cultural arts, and a multitude of programs and unprogrammed activities for all members of the family.

Additional samples of types of jobs available with duties and possible pay ranges are included. These categories were first described by Dr. Kevin Donnelly,[8] manager of Operations ABC Wildlife Preserve, Largo, Maryland.

A majority of the job opportunities in the private and commercial sector by virtue of the magnitude of participation by the public would indicate that the amusement park industry might offer the most potential for the prospective student. According to Blundred and Blundred,[9] the following are types of jobs that can be found in the amusement park industry.

1. General manager
2. Treasure-controller
3. Legal counsel
4. Office manager
5. Director of personnel
6. Cash control supervisor
7. Public relations director
8. Operations supervisor
9. Chief of security
10. Security lieutenant
11. Groundskeeping supervisor
12. Maintenance supervisor
13. Promotion manager
14. Head nurse and assistant
15. Park photographer
16. Purchasing agent
17. Chief mechanic
18. Warehouse supervisor
19. Landscape architect
20. Food and beverage director
21. Live show manager
22. Rides engineer
23. Animal curator
24. Employee relations director
25. Gifts and souvenir manager
26. Musical director
27. Wardrobe supervisor
28. Group sales director
29. Guest relations director

[8] Arlin Epperson, Editor; *Private & Commercial Recreation Education Kit,* Speeches given at NRPA Congress Session, 1974 "Implications for Community Recreation Education." Dept of Recreation and Park Administration University of Missouri, Columbia. Mo.

[9] Robert Blundred and Larry Blundred, Office of International Association of Amusement Parks and Attractions, Oak Park, Illinois, 1975.

Summary

No study has attempted to thoroughly investigate the types of jobs in private and commercial recreation that would be of interest to those with backgrounds primarily in recreation education. Those mentioned previously should not be construed to represent the totality of those available. Such a study would by necessity have to investigate each type of industry as indicated in the chapter on supply, and investigate specifically within that industry the kinds of jobs that are available, and those that could be entry level positions for recreation graduates.

It is hoped, however, that the preceeding will give some idea concerning the breadth and scope of recreation opportunities in the private sector, or both prospective job seekers, and educators attempting to prepare students for positions in this area.

COMPETENCIES NEEDED FOR POSITIONS IN PRIVATE AND COMMERCIAL RECREATION _____

Other than a few lines of description in the various studies mentioned previously, little has been done to determine the specific types of competencies needed for positions in private and commercial recreation. The only comprehensive effort to determine such competencies has been done by Langman,[10] who selected a jury of recreation educators and managers of recreation businesses, and asked them to rate various competencies in terms of those they felt were needed by people working in recreation enterprises. Competencies, as mentioned in Langman's material, refers to the ability to carry out duties, responsibilities, and obligations of a beginning level personnel for his employer. These were rated high priority, moderatly high priority, and minimal priority. Each competency was organized into three categories: technical (T), human-behavior (H), and conceptual (C). The study assumed that the following competencies would be obtained in a general due course of obtaining a degree from a university.

(T)-(1) Plan and organize his own work.

(T)-(2) Write effective letters, memos and other communiques.

(H)-(1) Follow through on detail in implementing decisions made by the policy makers.

(H)-(1) Accept responsibility.

(H)-(1) Have the quality of persistence in working towards goals.

(H)-(1) Demonstrate self-discipline.

(H)-(2) Have a competitive attitude.

(H)-(3) Practice a "positive" attitude.

(H)-(2) Empathize with and be sensitive to other's needs.

(H)-(2) Make constructive changes in himself.

[10] From DISSERTATION, COMMERCIAL RECREATION CURRICULUM by Robert R. Langman. Copyright © Robert Russell Langman, 1974. Reprinted with permission of Robert Russell Langman.

(H)-(3) Be willing to participate in civic organizations.

(H)-(3) Impress superiors and show others that he knows his job.

(C)-(1) Draw logical conclusions based upon facts available (ability to reason).

(C)-(1) Allocate time where it brings the greatest return.

(C)-(2) Have the knowledge that each decision affects later decisions.

(C)-(2) Understand that the greatest effort should be made where the most important results are needed at the moment.

The ratings are a composite of reactions by the jury in terms of their relative importance to forming duties in private and recreation enterprises.

Langman takes the competencies and relates them to specific courses as he describes course requirements for a major in commercial recreation. The ten top rated competencies that are specific to the commercial recreation field include the following:

1. Ability to understand tourist trends and patterns.
2. Ability to understand the mobility patterns as they affect commercial recreation.
3. Ability to know hotel, motel, and food service problems as they relate to commercial recreation.
4. Understand the values and limitations (philosophy) of commercial recreation agencies.
5. Recognize and analyze potential problems in commercial recreation agency areas and facilities.
6. Ability to understand the liability laws concerning commercial recreation.
7. Ability to know that one must handle problems in light of the total situation and move so as to improve the overall position of the company.
8. Ability to evaluate money producing potential of commercial recreation programs, areas, and facilities.
9. Understand economic aspects of business as they pertain to commercial recreation such as supply and demand, trade and growth, and income and profit.
10. Understand working functions of contracts, insurance, franchise, leasing, advertising, promotion, and publicity.

There was not total agreement between all the jury members. There seemed to be some significant differences that were associated with those of educational institutions and those in recreation enterprises as might be expected.

This study is summarized in a popular report published in the Parks and Recreation Magazine of NRPA.[11]

Other competencies suggested by other authors and speakers[12] are Arlin Epperson, University of Missouri; Roger Childers with the Calloway Gardens in Georgia; Stewart Aldridge, previously with Balboa Bay Club; and Dale Cruse, Chairman of the Depart-

---

[11] Robert R. Langman; "Be Prepared For A Career in Commercial Recreation" Parks and Recreation Magazine, July 1975, NRPA, Arlington, Virginia 22209.

[12] Epperson, *Private and Commercial Recreation Education Kit* op. cit.

ment of Recreation, University of Utah. They each have additional ideas concerning competencies that are needed by students preparing for positions in private and commercial recreation.

In visits with Paul Serff, General Manager of Hershey Park, Pennsylvania,[13] Mr. Serff indicated that he felt a person interested in working in private and commercial recreation should have as much education as possible in accounting, marketing, and management.

George Frantzis[14] indicates he would recommend people getting a law degree particularly to help handle some of the problems with the ten or twelve different kinds of inspections that are now required where only one or two were required five years ago. He indicated contracts are also a problem, which would lend support to a background in law or business and contractial agreements. He also recommends that maintenance is a bigger and bigger problem because people litter more and those who are hired are paid more and do less.

It is hoped that additional work will be done in terms of competencies for private and commercial recreation positions in the future. The Langman study is an excellent start, and it is hoped that others will follow.

CURRICULUM IMPLICATIONS

According to Cruse,[15] presently there is an unusual interest among college and university park and recreation personnel in development of a so-called commercial recreation curriculum. Many have embarked in a frantic and feverish effort to develop a new course or curriculum without knowing how to proceed.

The only study that attempts to evaluate the existence of courses in this area was prepared by the Southern Travel Directors Council in association with the state of North Carolina Department of Community Colleges in January of 1974.[16]

During the past five years the council became concerned over the apparent lack of educational opportunity oriented to tourism in their region, even though tourism had seen significant growth in the Southeast.

The study included three parts:

1. It attempted ways the council could increase educational opportunities in the tourism field.
2. To learn of educational programs already developed across the nation and those

[13] Paul Serff, General Manager of Hershey Park, Pennsylvania, Interview, August 19, 1975.

[14] George Frantzis, Personal Interview, August 21, 1975, Lake Quassapaug Amusement Park Inc. Route 64, Middlebury Connecticut 06762.

[15] Epperson, *Private and Commercial Recreation Education Kit* op. cit.

[16] Southern Travel Directors Council in Association with State of North Carolina Department of Community Colleges; *Tourism Education and National Impact Survey*, Atlanta, Georgia, 1974.

planned in the future.
3. To locate agencies with potential funding possibilities for tourism education in the future.

A sampling of 500 institutions from across the country was selected, including both public and private two- and four-year institutions. A total of 546 surveys were sent out in late September, 1963. The survey asked questions concerning tourism programs offered or planned, and student assistance and funding sources. The second portion of the survey for part three above was sent to 74 selected firms in the tourism area including oil companies, airlines, car rental agencies, motels, hotels, credit agencies, publications, federal agencies, as well as to professional trade groups to inquire of their support for such programs and the availability of finances in this regard. The study made the following recommendations.

1. There is substantial widespread interest in and support for the expansion and improvement of "Tourism Education" expressed at both the educational and the tourism industry levels.
2. There is a definite need for short and longer range tourism education program planning to insure the availability of qualified manpower to meet the future manpower demands of the tourism industry.
3. There is an implied need for an integrated data system that will periodically provide a comparison of tourism manpower demand and manpower supply in specific geographical areas for use in educational program and industrial development planning.
4. There is an indicated need for a system that will periodically provide up-to-date occupational information related to tourism oriented jobs, such as: entry wage rates, description of duties, working conditions, educational requirements, employment opportunities and outlook, and so on.
5. There is a definite need for a degree of standardization in tourism education in terms of: definitions, program titles, occupational titles, course content, and occupational skill requirements.
6. The development of new programs in tourism education, when viewed nationally, appears to be an uncoordinated and fragmented effort.
7. There is ample evidence that the council may become involved in more actively encouraging increased tourism educational opportunities through one or more avenues, dependent upon the desires of the council.
8. Funding prospects for tourism programs of the future will largely depend upon federal program sources unless more effort is directed to developing private support.

Several institutions in the Recreation and Park field including the University of Utah, Texas A & M, and Michigan State University have traditionally had courses that relate to private and commercial recreation. The study, of course, indicates a number of well-established curriculums in hotel management, and the food service industries, including Massachusetts, Cornell, and others.

There are a number of questions that are pertinent to the development of a commercial recreation program:

1. What is needed in the curriculum to give the student the necessary tools to compete in the leisure business world?
2. What classes are currently being offered in departments in universities to give students training for the development of needed competencies? If courses are not available to provide training toward the development of needed competencies new courses must be developed to fill in the deficiencies.
3. Where will these students be accepted to perform on-the-job training and where can they be exposed to the overall divisions of operation and management business?
4. Are the university-intern supervisors close enough to the agencies to personally supervise the commercial recreation student in his internship?
5. What kind of employment can the student expect to pursue upon graduating?
6. Will the commercial recreation agencies hire the competent commercial recreation graduate?
7. Has the department secured a written interdisciplinary approach agreement with on campus departments such as management, marketing, economics, or finances?[17]

Other questions that also must be answered before attempting to initiate a curriculum are:[18]

1. How do we get commercial, recreation agencies to accept our student interns and how do we get you to consider commercial recreation graduates for employment?
2. What kind of student product do you need?
3. What are you looking for in the student product?
4. What specific attributes are needed to be successful in the business world?
5. What suggestions do you have to aid us in developing a better graduate for commercial recreation?

The development of a private and commercial recreation curriculum must, by necessity, encompass much more than getting a course number approved by the department and, eventually, the university. It is one problem to desire to get a course established, and another to find qualified instructors to teach it. Ninety-nine percent of the present faculty in recreation curriculums are not qualified to teach private and commercial recreation courses. By its very nature, those in the industry themselves are the best qualified to teach. Every effort should be made to obtain them on a lectureship basis, to teach these courses until other qualified individuals can be included in recreation on recreation faculties with background and experience in the field. There are far too many courses now being taught by a faculty member with little or no experience in the areas in which they are attempting to teach. They end up being "textbook teachers."

---

[17] Epperson, *Private & Commercial Recreation Education Kit* op. cit.

[18] Ibid.

If we are to make the impact in the private and commercial recreation field that we hope to do, we have a selling job to do with these enterprise operators. If we furnish him a poor quality product, the word will spread and our endeavors will be severely handicapped. Instructors who wish to teach these types of courses must also make efforts to find field work opportunities for these students, and must visit almost on a one-to-one basis with managers of recreation enterprises in their area to sell them on recreation educated personnel, as most will not have even heard of such a curriculum.

We must make every effort to find individuals with background and experience in the type of industry in which they intend to do their field work and hopefully find employment, so as to give them every advantage. It is rather ridiculous to ask a ski resort manager to accept someone for a field work assignment or internship program in a ski resort, if they do not know how to ski.

PROBLEMS CONFRONTING FACULTY AND STUDENTS INTERESTED IN PURSUING PRIVATE AND COMMERCIAL RECREATION EDUCATION

Historically, few recreation graduates have been in top management in any of the private and commercial recreation establishments. The large majority of these executives have been business, finance, and marketing people. Among the reasons why these people are there instead of recreation graduates are:

1. The degree in recreation is new.
2. The option in commercial recreation is even newer.
3. The people on top grew up within the organization.

Donnelly[19] believes, however, the underlying reason is that we are not providing our students with the basic tools to become commercial recreation managers and executives. There is no question that in grass roots leadership and activity areas, a recreation graduate with his skills and training will quickly surpass other leaders in similar positions who have a business background. Usually the result is the recreation graduate will rise initially fast in the organizational structure to a management position. At this point the graduate will encounter stronger and stronger headwinds of administrative unknowns because he wasn't academically prepared for the new role he is now assuming. He now begins to "wing" some of his decisions and consequently his administrative decision making batting average begins to decrease. Of course, certain people are capable of bridging this by pulling themselves up by their own boot straps, so to speak, but this is still putting them at a disadvantage.[20]

Because of his decreased effectiveness as an administrator, the recreation graduate is placed in a holding pattern that, of course, retards his professional and financial growth.

[19] Ibid.

[20] Ibid.

On the other hand, the business graduate who has just now struggled out of the leadership level into management finds these administrative responsibilities familiar to him and his liking. This is what he has been trained for. This is what he knows. The doors and advancement start opening wider and wider as he moves up. Soon he becomes one one of those administrative executives we talked about earlier.

In the final analysis, commercial recreation is very much like any other business. The higher you go up the ladder, the more the company depends on your administrative abilities and less on your human relations or recreation activities skills. The question as to whether a recreation enterprise manager should hire a business major with some courses in recreation, or a recreator with some courses in business, is indeed an interesting question. We may not like the answer we receive from most business enterprise managers.

There is no question that business does not look primarily at credentials or past employment experience except in the application and hiring process. After that it is 100 percent on the ability of the individual, or his own "track record." It is very seldom that they will promote from outside, and most promotions, therefore, come from within after they have had an opportunity to look to see what the individual can do. Most students must begin their careers in private and commercial recreation at the introductory level. After they have shown their "stuff," they will be given additional opportunities.

Other problems that confront the students is the fact that a vast majority of the private and commercial recreation enterprises are small family owned and operated businesses. Campgrounds seldom will have more than one or two full-time people employed outside of the manager and they will primarily be maintenance people. Small amusement parks will hire part-time help, but the owner, his family, and maybe one or two others will provide the nucleus of the operation and be the full-time year-round staff. Thus, the career opportunities in 75 to 80 percent of the private and commercial recreation businesses is zero, either because of the smallness and the family owned and operated relationship, or because of the seasonality. Other problems that face the park and recreation graduate are as follows:[21]

1. Most employers in the private and commercial recreation field are not aware of (a) the park and recreation curricula, and (b) the talents and skills a park and recreation graduate possesses.
2. The recreation enterprise is basically providing recreation and leisure services for profit. It is a business similar to any other business only with recreation as the product. Therefore, in many cases, the enterprise will not be able to afford a recreation specialist on their payroll without that same individual possessing additional skills. In resorts, for example, there is often a heavy emphasis on a background in business administration, finances, marketing, and public relations. Even though many enterprises have private and commercial recreation opportunities,

[21] Badger, op cit.

they may be coupled with lodging and food establishments to help make the enterprise pay.

3. Most positions that are park and recreation oriented are at the lower entry level (not management), but there are usually opportunities for internal promotion and, as in many fields, being on the inside is the best way to meet the right people and sell them on the need for your professional skills.

4. As you move into the management level of the private and commercial sector the more you will be required to use business and administrative skills and the less you will have an opportunity to use your park and recreation skills. This also happens, to some extent, in other employment sectors for park and recreation but should be considered when looking at long range goals.

5. One of the major difficulties experienced by individuals seeking employment in the commercial and private sector is that there is no unifying organization for all of the many areas in this field; therefore, it is almost impossible to learn of job openings through a central source. This makes the job search process one that requires additional time and research effort on the part of the applicant.

6. Many enterprises (camps, clubs, resorts) hire recreation and park employees on a seasonal basis. This is changing with year-round programming (a concept that can be sold by a good recreation programmer) but it is often a problem faced by those interested in full-time employment.

It is most difficult to locate jobs in the private and commercial recreation business sector. There is no centralized organization to which each industry belongs. Each industry belongs to its own trade industry, that is, the campgrounds belong to the Campgrounds Owners Association, the amusement parks belong to the Amusement Parks Association, and so on.

The employment expectations continue to receive much speculation. The previous forecast by Verhoven and Vinton[22] would tend to be considerably optimistic.

In a special manpwer study report by Clapp and Cordell[23] indicates the following projections for future employment in private for profit recreation businesses. It can readily by seen that for the next five years the average number of new positions that can be expected in private and commercial recreation by 1980 in North Carolina is 52. If this is used as a nationwide average per state and multiplied by 50 this would allow a considerable opportunity for new employment in this area, however it is a far cry from the estimates of previous researchers.

Manpower projections are indeed a point of wide variance and discussion. It seems appropriate to quote from the Clapp and Cordell study,[24] which discusses this phenomena and gives an interesting example.

[22] Verhoven & Vinton, op, cit.

[23] Elvin B. Clapp and Harold K. Cordell; *1980 Projections of Recreation Employment Opportunities in North Carolina,* Special Manpower Report, North Carolina Recreation Review, July 1975.

[24] Ibid.

Projected 1980 employment levels for private, for profit recreation businesses.

Projected Level of Employment	Circumstances Under Which This Projected Level is Expected
320 (highest)	Combined population of cities with 5,000 or more residents increases to 1,930,324; percentage of county population which is Black decreases to 20% and percentage of labor force employed as professionals increases to 25%.
310	Combined city population increases to 1,930,324; percentage of county population which is Black decreases to 20% and percentage of labor force increases to only 23.90%.
307	Same as first projection except percentage of Blacks remains constant at the 1970 level of 23.75%.
298	Same as second projection except combined population of cities with 5000 or more residents increases to only 1,800,000.
297 (lowest)	Same as second projection except percentage of the population which is Black remains at the 1970 level of 23.75%.

The projections for numbers of recreation positions expected by 1980 cannot be guaranteed to be exact or without error. However, these projections are expected to be reliable from the standpoint that they are based on likely changes in the real-world factors that control levels of recreation emplyment in North Carolina. A range of the projected number of positions is offered to account for uncertainties in what the future may hold. But in all cases the interval represented by these ranges is relatively small.

Previous attempts to project employment opportunities for recreation professionals have been based on responses by agency heads to questions asking how many new positions they expect to have in the future. In all cases, the compiled results of these responses have reflected nothing more than wishful and inflated thinking! Reinforcement of this belief was accomplished by analyzing responses by top-level recreation administrators to a question asking how many new professional positions they expected to have by 1980. The results of this question are tabulated below:

Projected 1980 new recreation positions

Type of Position	Number
Administrative	466
Managerial	559
Supervisory	1023
Leadership	2767
Total	4815

The projections are approximately 10 times the number of new positions projected in this report. The median of the range of our projections for increase in total employment was 454. This vividly points toward a strong need to question the very optimistic numbers which sometimes appear in professional recreation journals and reports. Academic and manpower planning require a sound information base of some of the mistakes made in the past are to be avoided. It is our hope that the information in this report will lead to more realistic and efficient planning.

Needless to say, many present recreators have been a good deal more optimistic about opportunities in the private and commercial sector than they realistically should be. There will be opportunities for a limited number of well-qualified, well-trained graduates to enter into the private and commercial field. However, if the diversification of curriculums in the municipal outdoor education and therapeutic recreation areas is any example, private and commercial recreation curriculums will be soon to follow, thus resulting in an over supply in this area as now exists in the public recreation sector.

Curriculums and courses should be developed carefully, but with a view toward producing a quality product. Our future in this area depends on it.

Summary

Efforts are being made by a number of agencies to more specifically identify and classify the types of jobs found in private and commercial recreation and to estimate the number now in existence, and the potential for both individuals graduating from high school, and those graduating from the universities with bachelor degrees. While the job titles and areas have been identified, and some work has been accomplished concerning job duties and responsibilities, little has been done to determine exactly how many jobs of each type exist, and how many can be expected to be available in the future for high school or university graduates.

A number of studies have pinpointed competencies needed for various jobs in the private and commercial recreation industry and made suggestions for curriculums to provide such compensate.

There are a number of problems that confront faculty and students interested in pursuing private and commercial recreation education courses, curriculums, and degrees that will be slow in being resolved.

While early experts grossly overpredicted the number of jobs available in private and commercial recreation, those who have ventured guesses in small areas or regions have been much more realistic. While opportunities will exist, it appears they will be neither large in number, nor easy to obtain. However it appears that those students who desire to find employment in the private and commercial recreation service areas and human relations skills, and gain as much experience as possible in the area of private and commercial recreation in which they wish to be employed.

Discussion Questions

1. Discuss the "cluster concept" developed by the U.S. Office of Education and its usefulness in career planning for commercial recreation students.

2. Using the Verhoven and Vinton study and its four major occupational groups, how would you classify the following commercial recreation enterprises?
   A. Backpacking store.
   B. Mountaineering school.
   C. Leisure counseling.
   D. River rafting company.
   E. Sporting goods manufacturer.
   F. Hunting lodge.

3. "Level Four" jobs require a four-year post secondary degree and calls for certain key management skills. Discuss which skills are generally included in the traditional recreation curriculum and which skills must be obtained outside the recreation department.

4. What educational skills does the general recreation graduate possess that will enable him to compete with the general business graduate for jobs in commercial recreation?

5. In reviewing the various categories of job titles available in commercial recreation, what shortcomings do these grouping have for career planning.

6. Describe the various studies and booklets available for career planning for commercial recreation.

7. List and briefly discuss some of the more pertinent problems confronting students interested in pursuing careers in commercial recreation.

CHALLENGING PROFESSION AVAILABLE IN COMMERCIAL RECREATION

by Robert Langman*

How does one qualify for a career in commercial recreation? There is wide agreement among executives on what it takes to get a position with a commercial recreation company and those willing to adapt a program geared toward this field can more adequately prepare for a good position. It is believed by many that students who graduate from college will earn more money, become better people, and learn to be more responsible citizens than those who don't attend college. This case for college has been accepted without question for more than a generation.

But college has not been able to work its magic for everyone. College graduates are selling shoes, driving taxis, and working at other such semi-skilled and unskilled jobs while waiting for a chance to get into the field of their training or into management. Where has college failed?

The main criticism levied against the college education is its inability to prepare students for the available job market. It has been traditional for colleges to be a place (1) to fellowship educated men and women, (2) to develop the ability to think and express one's self, (3) to formulate values and goals of life, and (4) to learn to get along with others in developing social skills.

Much of the contemporary thinking maintains that all of these traits can be easily acquired while gaining experience on the job, especially, when the employee is climbing the ladder of success. Generally speaking, colleges have not tried to train students for specific skills for a job. It is a fact that many employers still have to train a man for a position after he is hired. This is especially true in commercial recreation.

However, employers feel that a four year college degree has some value. An employer expects the student to have initiative, a sense of responsibility, and a willingness to discipline himself if he has a degree. For these reasons, a diploma is a good thing to have when seeking a job.

*Dr. Langman was previously President, American Ranch and Recreation Inc. Salt Lake City, Utah; currently assistant professor Dept. of Recreation and Parks, California State College at Northridge, California.

When new employees are hired by a company they are, generally speaking, hired for a specific skill. However, the most important ability that can be demonstrated by an employee is his ability to manage. It is assumed in this article that those who take a position in commercial recreation will eventually accept management positions. With this in mind, the following recommendations are forwarded, based on concepts developed in doctoral research, commercial recreation at the University of Utah, and interviews and experiences with executives of large recreation management enterprises.

1. *A sought after employee is one who has a vision for the overall work program.* He can visulize how his job or task helps accomplish an overall goal. He is able to learn the philosophy and climate, folkways and folklore, customs and mores, friendships and jealousies, cordialities and frictions, ambitions of the company and hopes destroyed. Cliques and special interest groups abound. Individual ambitions and common loyalties are real. Cooperation and competition abide side by side. Since these things are true of any social system, employees must work with people on the basis of an accurate analysis of the company system. They must know how to fit into the overall social system, as well as accomplish these tasks.

2. *A sought after employee communicates well.* To get the work accomplished with a maximum of efficiency and a minimum of wasted time and energy, employees must establish free flowing and candid communication with superiors and peers and subordinates. He does his best to keep everyone filled in on what they need to know relative to the job performance. He does his best to keep them filled in on what they need to know, what they should know, and what they would like to know as being job relevant.

   Additionally, although he recognizes the essentiality of techniques, the employee "takes to heart the realization that communication is geared to three "C's." In communicating, he seeks to build a climate of *cooperation* and *coordination.* " He tries to increase the areas and concerns that they have in common, for the perimeters of commonality set the boundaries within which he must and can communicate competently. Once these skills are accomplished and he demonstrates top quality verbal skills, his ability to write effectively is equally essential.

3. *A sought after employee exercises good judgment.* "Good judgement ranks high." This applies not only to objective situations but to men. The employee appreciates the fact that no company is perfect, that inequities will exist that cannot be altered immediately. He knows that many good ideas cannot be implemented because of built in constraints. He realizes that a company must deal with reality. Accordingly, he learns to accept his situation while his superiors are working to increase the efficiency of the overall operation. He does not over-reach himself, nor promise what he cannot produce. More importantly, he is sensitive to the possibilities of "unanticipated consequences" that can be side effects of even the most logical and "on paper" plan or procedure.

4. *A sought after employee is persistent.* However, he is patiently persistant. He follows the advice of Pope Paul, "See everything, overlook alot, correct a little." To see everything is to deal with the company as it is, not what he would like it to be. He overlooks a lot because he is dealing with imperfect human beings. And, he corrects a little and zeros in on only those things that he has as his assignment and that results in better performance. He corrects a little by zeroing in on those things which spell the difference between mediocrity and excellence so far as results are concerned. Yet, if he is patient in helping people to change for the better, he is persistent in his efforts to insure that they do so.

5. *A sought after employee inspires confidence on the part of his fellow workers.* This is by no means populartity, but respect for him and the assignment given him. He deals with company assignment given him. He deals with company assignments with enthusiasm which is positive in nature. His estimate of timing for completion of a project is accurate. His evaluation of a task to do is sound equally is his ability to smooth over problems which results in success of all concerned. When he is promoted, no one is surprised.

Ineffective employees expect or demand respect and confidence. Their more realistic peers realize that such desirables must be earned and merited. Respect cannot be rigorously exacted; confidence cannot be commanded. Thus, the employee asks himself, now and then, two questions: 1) To what extent and for what reasons do I tend to gain the respect of superiors and peers? 2) To what extent and for what reasons do I tend to make it hard for each of these groups to respect me? He then evolves a practical program for capitalizing on the former and remedying the latter.

As for confidence, he realizes that a good prospective leader inspires confidence on the part of his subordinates in himself; a great leader inspires confidence on the part of his people in themselves.

6. *A sought after employee has the ability to attract competent people around him.* This includes customers and fellow workers. He exerts a certain expertise in assignments given him which helps to radiate confidence and sureness of action. His personnal magnetism seems to inspire performance.

It is absolutely essential to acquire the ability to achieve effective relationships with those who work around him, with him, and above him. The best way a person can pick up this ability is to immediately start watching successful and respected superiors and attempt to develop some of their more worthwhile working habits.

7. *A sought after employee is one who is anxious to work.* The employee knows that enthusiasm for his work is more caught than taught. Accordingly, despite the annoyances and irritations of the work and work environment, he gets a kick out of his job, for he understands that if he does not receive his fair share of satisfaction from what he does, he will never do it very well for any length of time. Lacklustre performance is organizationally impermissible; those who cannot or will not cut the mustard must be either transferred or replaced. Treating employees as though they were mere minions or machines, on the other hand, is equally unacceptable. They have a right to satisfy their needs as well as those of the company, with the help of a supervisor who is supportive and friendly without going over the edge of familiarity. The employee needs to accept this in the spirit it is given.

8. *A sought after employee is a professional, who is consistent in his dealings with people without being inflexible.* He is truly smooth. He stands up well under pressure and handles over time well. He is authentic in his dealings with others, he levels with them in his communication. This means he does not frequently change his mind. He can be depended upon to follow through on assignments. His loyalty and attitudes are consistent.

Everyone respects a man who adheres prudently and graciously to his values; no one feels secure with a moral chameleon. Yet the employee is consistent, not rigid. If he refuses to yield his basic principles to coercive pressures, he also refuses to impose them on others who are not similarly persuaded. He is neither a fawning "yes man" nor a negative resistor for the sake of being oppositional.

He does not so much learn to "agree to disagree," which is a spineless reaction at best, but rather he has mastered the art of "disagreeing agreeably." The latter attitude prompts him to recognize disagreements while striving to enlarge the areas of agreement.

9. *A sought after employee must "first learn to obey."* For an employee to experience greater responsibility with his company, it seems, he needs to have been a subordinate, vividly feeling all the disappointments and all the uncertainties that are associated with personal growth.

All of us grow up in stages and the same thing applies to our progress in a profession or occupation. Starting near the bottom and going up the ladder of success in a particular field may seem quite slow and unnecessary to many people nowadays and yet it is very worthwhile to establish a solid base for future progression and advancement. It is my firm belief that a person who follows this prodecure will have very few anxious moments even after he nears the top of his particular field of endeavor. This is because he not only understands the organizational structure but he has experienced the everyday operational problems that exist at many of the steps of the organization. Through this type of training experience he has not only been exposed to and hopefully mastered the technical aspects of his profession, but has also acquired an inside knowledge of how it affects human beings. Thus he is capable of realizing the frustrations and pressures as well as the rewards of certain jobs and how they might in turn affect his subordinates. This could help him analyze how certain jobs could be made not only more efficient, but more challenging and rewarding.

10. *A sought after employee needs the ability to seize an opportunity.* A clear recognition of essential needs and a careful evaluation of opportunity enable him to

develop a workable scheme. In order to have this ability, he must possess one of the rarest of qualities, namely—common sense. A talented opportunist seems to have a sort of sixth sense by which he knows a wildcat scheme from a sound one. An employee must learn quickly the cardinal sin of organizations is complacency, he strives not merely to keep abreast of his field and the competition, but ahead of them. He knows that drive is as contagious as apathy. Yet his desire to outstrip the competition is balanced by an appreciation of the efforts of his peers to make them and his firm look good. Because he is sensitive to the fact that any time they wish they can facilitate or hamper his success, he takes to heart the truth that the two most important works in the English language are "Thank you."

11. *A sought after employee is able to adjust to new situations.* This implies that he is well-adjusted, integrated person with the ability to move in good and bad times with poise and security. He has the ability to flexible, to roll with the punches. It means that he can deal with hostility, apathy, and aggressiveness. Change becomes second nature, he accepts it and makes the most of it.

Improvement and innovation are not pious platitudes; they are essentials for survival and growth. The attitude of the employee is that anything which man has devised, man can improve if he thinks hard enough about the matter. The incompetent seeks salvation without effort by chasing facile prescriptions which promise easy success. The professional is wary of too easy solutions, for he knows that progress comes through hard thinking and prudent implementation lest he throw away what is good in the firm in his quest for merely new.

It has been said that the worst enemy of organizational progress is not ignorance but rather the stubborn clinging to ways of doing things that have outlived their usefulness. Second to this is an inability to stop doing the unproductive. When the employee plans he follows the dictum, "Examine the past, scrutinize the present, seek out future opportunities." Thus, his forecasting takes unto account those events and changes that are likely to take place, but his planning is geared to those opportunities on which he is determined to capitalize.

12. *A sought after employee understands the values and limitations of commercial recreation.* The employee should have a "sense" about what will go and what will not. If he does, it will be easy to know why people are willing to spend their money for his services.

13. *A sought after employee needs to have and communicate his knowledge of the technical aspect of; government regulations, legal liability, economics, accounting principles, land, and facility development.* This technical knowledge tends to enhance the credibility of a suggestion made to superiors. The ability to portray this expertise is a needed asset to his personal career. An employee seeking management positions must acquire skills. Because of increasing complexity within each field an executive today has to understand and keep up on the latest development of various specialties within his area. This is necessary so that he may keep proper communication going, sensibly analyze and appraise projects for which they expect him to find financial and/or political support, and tie them in

with the overall goals of the department. With a working comprehension of skills he can make decisions effectively. He can serve only as a rubber stamp that is used by others to approve their decisions if he is without the necessary skills. Moreover, he will never gain the respect of the people of his agency when they believe that he doesn't really know what they are talking about.

In conclusion, a college graduate has developed general skills that are used, hopefully, to qualify him for a job. The sought after employee not only has the usual skills but has management skills which are displayed effectively to the employer so that advancement is forthcoming. With this type of employee the employer feels he has a potentially strong manager, who will be of great value to the business. He will advance naturally helping to make business decisions that get things done and follow through on details which accomplish objectives.

In the "making of a quality commercial recreation manager" it seems the college could provide better training. As it is now most of the training has to come "on the job."

As the business community verbalizes the need for specific job skills to the colleges, the colleges should review their programs and hopefully, by common dialogue develop a viable, practical training for students interested in advanced commercial recreation skills.

COMMERCIAL RECREATION SALARIED EMPLOYMENT VS ENTREPRENEURSHIP

by John J. Bullaro*

The recreation movement is in the midst of change more rapid, perhaps than in my other period of its history. Social, political and economic forces are pressuring the movement to update its programs, change personnel preparatory programs in higher education and to expand its professional concerns to include commercial recreation.

Commercial recreation offers new opportunities and challenges to the profession by way of an expanded job market for graduates of two and four years colleges. Economic growth in the United States has slowed considerably since 1970 with the effect of forcing many municipalities to curtail recreation services and to limit growth. This economic recession has not only reduced many career opportunities in public recreation it also has effected expansion plans of many non-profit agencies. United Way funds are more difficult to raise and monies for new programs and staff are not available to the extent they were in the 1960's.

Compounding this economic problem is the awarness on the part of employed professionals that the job market is limited thus restricting the usual career upgrading that takes places. A supervisor for a city park department might normally look for an assistant director job after some five years of service. Or he or she might consider a lateral move to a larger district for more salary. But this movement has all but stopped in many sector of the country with the effect of shutting off openings for new graduates.

Commercial recreation, by contrast, has continued to grow despite a sagging economy and double digit inflation. Depending on where you read the statistics, indicators show that the leisure market generated dollar revenue in 1972 of approximately $102

*John J. Bullaro is assistant professor and coordinator, Commercial Recreation, Department of Recreation and Leisure Studies, California State University, Northridge.

billion and in 1975 produced revenues of almost $150 billion (these figures include travel and tourism)[1].

These remarks should not be interpreted as suggesting that the commercial sector of recreation is exempt from uncertainities of economic shifts. Nothing could be further from the truth. While recreation and leisure spending did not decline appreciably in 1974 from 1973 new spending patterns did emerge as a result of gasoline shortages and massive lay-offs in industry. These were trying times for those persons charged with the task of charting the course of the enterprise. How these people handled their responsibility during these times often meant the difference between success or failure of the firm and thousands of dollars. A fact, little of the traditional education of recreators would have prepared them to solve these problems of marketing shifts, financing stratagies and material shortages.

Commercial recreation offers many promises and frustrations not found in traditional recreation. Many recreation graduates facing the task of landing their first professional employment will almost be required to consider commerical recreation because of the availability of positions. One question must be answered before securing that first commercial recreation job: do I want to work in an environment that places profit as its number one concern? People entering medicine and law must ask the same question. Assuming an affirmative answer, a question that might arise next is: do I want to work as an employee or do I want to start my own commercial recreaation agency. This paper is an attempt to help the student answer these, and the following questions:

1. Is commercial recreation an area that I could find career satisfaction?
2. What special skills and training do I need to succeed in commercial recreation?
3. What are my chances for success in running my own business and would I gain certain nonmonetary rewards not available to the employee?

The first question will be discussed as part of two and three however a discussion about commercial recreation in general will help set the stage for consideration of questions two and three.

CAREER POTENTIAL IN COMMERCIAL RECREATION[2]

The recreation profession is directing its focus on commercial recreation for such reasons as bright employment opportunities; government and nonprofit agencies not being able to meet all the needs of a leisure oriented society, and an awakening professional responsibility for providing properly trained personnel in commercial agencies.

---

[1] U.S. News and World Report, "Leisure Boom: Biggest Ever and Still Growing," April 1972. p. 42.

[2] Leisure Today. Career Potential In Commercial Recreation. JOPER, November-December 1975. P. 5.

This new professional focus will keep more professionaly trained people in the field, provide opportunities for higher incomes, and generate more and varied working opportunities. This new focus should ultimately provide an upgrading of the leisure products and services offered to the public.

There are many problems facing the recreation graduate seeking employment in commercial recreation. Employers are not aware of the training and potential of the graduate. The recreation graduate must compete with other graduates for the same jobs. Management level positions require more business and adminstrative skills than the typical recreation graduate may possess. Currently there is no organization within the profession that identifies and announces job openings. This makes the job search process one that requires additional time and research effort on the part of the applicant.

Almost every type of job offered in the traditional professional milieu has a counterpart in commercial recreation. The paramount difference in the commercial recreation positions is the profit pressure which is implied if not expressed in most program and adminstrative decisions.

Beside the similarity between positions in traditional and commercial recreation one finds in the commercial sector a whole range of opportunities not available to the traditional job seeker. This include positions in such areas as: tourism, hotel and resort management, sales, marketing and public relations, restaurant operations, amusement and theme parks owners and managers, and owner/operator of many retail outlets.

To further illustrate the varied career potential of commercial recreation the reader is direct to the categories of commercial recreation by Kraus.[3]

Categories of Commercial Recreation Programs

A. Facilities and Areas for Self-Directed Activity: Golf courses, swimming pools, ski center, ice rinks, bowling alleys, billiard parlors, riding stables, fish preserves, driving ranges, camp grounds and boat marinas. In each of these the individual is more or less active in providing his own recreation.

B. Facilities or Enterprises Providing Entertainment: Here the consumer is entertained in a generally passive way; this category includes theaters; indoor and outdoor movies; concert halls; commercial sports stadiums; fairs, and amusement parks.

C. Commercial Enterprises Providing Instructional Services: This include special schools, studies; or health center; that give instruction in music; dancing; the arts; physical fitness; gymnastics; self-defense classes; palaestras; riding schools; day camps; residential camps, travel camps; adventure programs; tour guides; mountain climbing schools; sailing schools; and swim schools.

D. Commercial Enterprises and Selling Manufacturing Recreation Equipment: Musical equipment; including tape recorders; record players; and instruments; toys; games;

[3] Kraus, Richard. "Recreation and Leisure In a Modern Society." Appleton-Century-Crafts, 1971.

gardening equipment; books; magazines; play clothing and a host of other products which represent commercial recreation involvement.[4]

E. Leisure Counseling and Consultation Service: This includes services for counseling groups and individuals about their leisure opportunities and specialized consultation regarding the construction adminstration and service of specialized recreation facilities, such as golf courses, swimming pools, and sports playing surfaces.

This rather extensive list of employment possibilities does require further explanation. For the new generalist-graduate or practicing recreation professional wishing to enter commercial recreation they should be advised that specific skills may be lacking in their professional preparation and specialized training may be required to insure their gaining entrance to the field and becoming successful. Langman's Ph.D. dissertation,[4] "Development of a commercial recreation curriculum," should be consulted for guidance in career planning by undergraduate recreation majors and practicing professionals desiring to enter the commercial recreation field.

Some of Langman's conclusions suggest that recreation graduates already possess many of the competencies required for success in commercial recreation. The following selected competencies were deemed essential for a beginning level commercial recreationist and should be part of the typical recreation graduates skills:

a. General skills and attitudes that all university graduates are assumed to have.
b. Dynamic personality ("good politician, mover, operator, stateman, and/or public relations expert").
c. Be able to perceive unethical practices-act in an ethical way.
d. Be able to obtain useful information from competitors without exposing one's position."

In addition to the above skills Langman's dissertation suggested that commercial recreation aspirants have training in accounting, business law, marketing, leadership training, politics and decision-making processes. Other attributes and skills judged desirable by this study include the ability to:[5]

A. Write effectively.
B. Be competitive.
C. Be positive in ones attitude.
D. Be self-disciplined.
E. Be persistant in working towards goals.
F. Be empathetic.
G. Be self-motivated.
H. Be able to impress superiors and show others that he knows his job.

---

[4] Langman, Robert Russell. "Development of a Commercial Recreation Curriculum." Unpublished dissertation. University of Utah. Ph. D. in Leisure Studies. June 1974

[5] Ibid, p. 151.

I. Reason well.

J. Use time wisely.

Langman's study further illustrates the diversity of background required to work in commercial recreation. Recreation personnel and students seem well adapted in work in commercial recreation agencies because the competencies they do possess (being people oriented for instance) are not skills that can be easily taught. The other, more technical competencies (accounting, law, politics) that recreators may be deficient in do lend themselves to formal instruction.

If the reader has determined that commercial recreation offer the best career track then the next question becomes important to consider: Shall I work for someone else or become an entrepreneur. For the moment we shall set the financial considerations aside and focus on the more personal considerations.

SALARIED EMPLOYMENT-ADVANTAGES

There are several advantages to being an employee of a commercial recreation enterprise. The most commonly preferred ones are:

A. No risk to Personal savings.

B. Security and fringe benefits.

C. Better working conditions.

D. Member of a "Family."

E. Opportunity for growth.

F. Pre-entrepreneurial training.

NO RISK TO PERSONAL SAVINGS

A salary of $10,000 is preferable to a profit of $10,000 if the lateral requires a substantial capital investment. This advantage is for some, off-set by foregoing the chance of realizing growth of the growth of the capital investment over the modest income produced by leaving a given sum invested in commercial banks or a savings and loans institution. In addition, one may invest this capital in some other investment over which he/she has no control with considerable risk.

SECURITY AND FRINGE BENEFITS

One strong incentive to being an employee is having a ready made organization to step into the job to be done is usually spelled out and the firm may have a long history of successful operation thus suggesting the job will be around for years to come.

Salaries in commercial agencies are often higher than public and non-profit agencies, however, this discrepancy is gradually disappearing.

Fringe benefits usually include paid group medical insurance, retirement plan, and paid holidays. For the employee reaching the upper echlons of management there are a host of other benefits that may be available.

BETTER WORKING CONDITIONS

Employees can leave work at the end of the day and leave their troubles at the office. Usually, entry level positions require an eight hour day and no more. Moving up the ladder changes all this as competition for the better paying, more prestigous jobs increases. Numerous studies show that executives typically work 60 to 80 hours weekly.

An employee with a grievance usually has access to someone higher up who, if nothing else, will listen. The entrepreneur generally feels alienated from others in the firm due to his ownership interest. When the entrepreneur has a grievance he or she solves the problem themselves or pays for advice from a professional business consultant.

"MEMBER OF A FAMILY"

Employees generally enjoy being associated with a company whose pretige and business position are both secure and well-known. The employee may find satisfaction in identifying with Disney Productions, Winnebago Industries, Brunswick Corporation or the Marriott Hotels, Inc. Others prefer to take pride in building their own "empire" rather than feel pride vicariously in the size and accomplishments of an employer company. It is possible to combine individuality with team membership and be a leader within a company employer and within an industry.

OPPORTUNITY FOR GROWTH

Many companies operating in the leisure industry are experiencing steady growth. Estimates are that this growth will continue and expenditures for leisure products and services will more than double during the '70's.[6] This growth should create more opportunities for promotion within the individual companies and increase the number of jobs available. These opportunities will require recreation professionals and new graduates to prepare themselves with certain business skills and be willing to accept less desirable beginning assignments and possibly at a salary less than expected in order to prove oneself to top management.

Private industry generally regards creative, dedicated and profit oriented individuals quicker and more tangibly than the public and non-profit sector of recreation. This is especially true if one is employeed in a line function, directly related to the product or service distribution of the country. In these positions results speak louder than politics and commercial recreation companies survive only if they get results. When a company hires an employee they look upon his or her salary as an investment. If they are realizing a profit on their investment then the employees future is secure . . . its that simple! When considering ones goals in a commerical recreation company keep in mind the desirability of being in a position of having your efforts measurable. If this is not possible at the entry level position then it should be viewed as a possibility later on.

---

[6] U.S. News and World Report, op. cit., p. 42.

PRE-ENTREPRENEURIAL TRAINING

A final advantage is that of procuring training and experience on the payroll of another firm. This has many advantages over striking out immediately on your own after graduation.

First, you gain a "feel" for the business. Working as a manager for a ski resort will often save you time and money when it comes to handling the wide spectrum of problems that besel a resort owner. Experience in a ski resort has carry-over value to other enterprises such as the hotel and restaurant business.

Working for someone else might take the luster off the entrepreneurial dream by mixing in some reality. After a short term behind the reservation counter at the ski resort, for example, you might decide that dealing with peoples' eating, drinking, and sleeping needs is just too demanding.

Finally, working for an established company in your field will enhance your chances of obtaining financing for your future enterprise. Lending institutions and private individuals (venture capitalists) want to know they are putting money into experienced hands.

SALARIED EMPLOYMENT-DISADVANTAGES

Perhaps every decision we make has some disadvantages attached to it. This is certainly true for being an employee. To name just a few of the most common:
A. Subordination.
B. Mobility.
C. Politics.
D. Fixed Income.

SUBORDINATION

In the tight job market that characterizes the '70s the employer has extraordinary power over the day to day operations of the employee. Extra work, cutting short a vacation, special projects or other such demands are more apt to be accommodate in silence than would have been the case, say, in the mid 1960's. During the '60's a disgrunted employee could in all likelihood find another, better job, if demands of the employer became unreasonable. Today the employer is more omnipotent. Despite the gains made by unions in providing arbitration rights for better working conditions, these benefits generally do not extend to management/administrative personnel. It's at the management/administrative level that most commercial recreation graduates will eventually work.

MOBILITY

Recently, a speaker representing one of the nations largest hotel chains told a group of commercial recreation students, "There are jobs waiting for all of you in the hotel industry but you must be prepared to start at the bottom and move your place of residence often."

Not all company representatives are this candid but if you go to work for a national company be prepared to move if you expect promotions.

POLITICS

Politics, according to sociologist Harold Laswell, is the process of who gets what, when, and how. Others define politics as the process which involves the allocation and distribution of valued things. In a company these processes, in time, bureaucraticed. Often who gets what is dependent on who is doing the allocating of job, promotions, windowed offices, company cars, and private secretaries. In most organizations personalities come into play in these allocations. There are corporate games that one must play and to the extent one is willing to play them often detemines success or failure of the individual in the long run.

As discussed earlier, the closer one is tied to the direct production of company revenue the less the political factors come into play, however the further one moves up the corporate ladder the more political becomes the position. A super salesperson for a backpacking manufacturer is valued primarily for his or her performance in selling. This individuals manager, while still being rated as a producer, nevertheless is exposed to the political pressures of middle management because of the prestige of the position and the money bonuses that may go with position. Much of the managers day is spent in close proximity to other executives thus the manager is a member of the "corporate family" and has an image to maintain that has little relationship to being a revenue producer.

FIXED INCOME

Broom and Longenecker state[7], "Earnings statistics show that lifetime earnings of employees are smaller in total than for entrepreneurs." However, there are many cases of employees outearning entrepreneurs. In any case the salary of an employee is usually fixed and rarely does the employee have an opportunity to dictate the amount of salary he or she will earn.

ENTREPRENEURSHIP

It is expected that most properly trained commerical recreation students will find jobs in the leisure industry. However, there is a growing number of recreation practitioners who are opting to become entrepreneurs.

The vision of owning ones own business is mutured in American folklore and history. The vision of the rugged individualist piloting his or her own business looms be-

---

[7] Broom, Longenecker. "Small Business Management." Fourth Edition, South-western Publishing Co., Palo Atto, California, p. 51.

hind the docil facade of many a disgrunted employee. Indeed the urge to "strike a blow" for personal freedom becomes so strong that over 500,000 individuals per year actually start a new company.

Who are these people? What makes them go it alone? What happens to them? What does it take to succeed? These are common questions one should asks before asking the more final questions if; how do I do it? and how much will it cost?

Albert Shapero[8] writes in Psychology Today: "When you go into business for yourself you trade off the familiar and the safe for the unknown and the risky." You generally invest every cent you have, borrow heavily, work fourteen hours a day, all to beat the odds which indicate that by the fifth year you and 75% of the others that started with you will probably have failed.

People that take on this kind of challenge have certain aptitudes, skills and motivations that set them apart. To better understand the entrepreneur we will examine the following categories:

A. Motivation.
B. General Aptitude.
C. Specific Skills.
D. Special Requirements.

MOTIVATION

Shapero's article suggests that the prime motivation for individuals to become entrepreneurs is their having been "dislodged from some nice, familiar niche." Shapero calls these people D.P.'s (Displaced Persons). An individual becomes a D.P. in several ways: (1) political refugees seeking a new life in America; (2) a person is fired or someone else is hired to fill a job the D.P. was hoping to get; (3) an opportunity arises that jars him from his original career goal; (4) threat of transfer.

The description of the D.P. indicates that some powerful event serves to motivate people to become entrepreneurs. In one study completed at the University of Texas 65 percent of the respondants stated they started their own companies in response to being a D.P. However, many individuals start their own business because it just seemed like the thing to do.

GENERAL APTITUDE

These are some qualities most successful commercial recreation entrepreneurs usually have. They are:

1. Hard workers who get satisfaction from accomplishment.
2. Willing to take the sole and final responsibility for decisions, with the capability to make sound decisions.

---

[8] Shapero, Albert. "The Displace Uncomfortable Entrepreneur." Psychology Today. November, 1975.

3. Unwilling to let worries and fears interfere with their decision-making, and they use their full productive potential.
4. Able to concentrate on the most important matters, and do not get side-tracked into immediate problems of minor importance.
5. Able to work at a high energy level.
6. Versatile and adaptable. (If lucky, they may have a few people they can depend on, but they are prepared to pinch-hit in every phase of administrative work.)
7. Willing to get into details (99% complete is not enough), yet are able to see the overall picture in spite of the details.
8. Imaginative, unorthodox, innovative, creative.
9. Optimists—able to inspire others in spite of problems and failures; they do not get discouraged, but see the bright side of situations. (Most people see what is wrong with an idea; the entrepreneur sees what is right and its potentital.)
10. Able to handle money wisely.
11. Good instructors—able to get satisfaction from helping others achieve their potential.
12. Patient—cheerfully and confidently maintaining faith in being able to overcome the delays and obstacles that inevitably get in the way.
13. Have a sincere interest in their product or service.
14. Belief that their leisure product or service is filling a genuine need.

SPECIFIC SKILLS

In a recent study completed at California State University, Northridge students from two commercial recreation classes took and opinion poll of 168 commercial recreation practitioners to determine attitudinal and skill differences and/or similarities between employees and entrepreneurs. The poll looked at the following:

A. Experience or special training.
B. Personal Intellectual skills. This included such self evaluations as good writing skills, organization, reading, and pursuit of continuing education.
C. Authoritarianism.
D. Attitudes towards the past, present, and future.
E. Hobbies.
F. Family history.

According to the study it seems that there was considerable agreement between both groups as to the necessity of having good verbal skills, planning, and organizing their work well, having above average writing skills, and belief in living a conservative life style. (I will leave it to the reader to interpret what a conservative life style is.) Both groups felt it was important to know the laws effecting their businesses.

Neither group indicated any interest in pursuing non-business related courses at night but both groups said they read business literature regularly; the entrepreneur more than the employee suggesting that his interest in business is more serious than the employee. On a question relating to whether their friends considered them intellectuals, entrepreneurs tended to respond negatively while employees responses were more positive. This suggest that individuals with strong intellectual interests tend to work for others possibly because there is more time to follow these outside intellectual interest.

Sixty percent of the entrepreneurs had prior management experience while only 30 percent of employees had this background. Entrepreneurs had more accounting and finance background than did the employees and this seems to confirm the suggestions in Lagman's dissertation that accounting and finance be part of the commercial recreation curriculum especially for the entrepreneur.

One final note of interest brought out in the California State University, Northridge study was in reference to Authoritarianism. There are inidcations that the entrepreneur is more critical of other people, less concerned with loyality, less flexible in decision making than is the employee.

SPECIAL REQUIREMENTS

Neither group had special requirements they felt were necessary for success other than that which has been stated.

CONCLUSION

Are there "types" that fit the notion of the entrepreneur and the employee? Certainly any attempt at classifying individuals is dangerous and at best misleading but certain patterns emerge from the literature suggesting tendencies that seem to fit one group more than the other.

It should be noted that entrepreneurs are also found in public: agencies, non-profit corporations, and large commercial companies working as employees. Entrepreneurs in these ambients display the same qualities as the successful founder of a new enterprise.

Some of the qualities entrepreneurs display include: drive, enthusiasm for the work, intelligence, independence-seeking, risk-assuming, resource-organizing, and leadership-taking. These are the types that lead charity drives, head national professional organizations, become president of social agency boards of directors, presidents of universities as well starting a business like disneyland.

On the other hand loyal devoted employees concerned with security and working on a team are essential for the continuing day to day operations of the recreation enterprise. In fact many entrepreneurs would not have been able to build their empire if it were not for the loyality, dedication, and security needs of the employee.

It is for each individual recreator to determine where he or she fits in best. The profession is expanding rapidly, opening up opportunities that past generations of professional were not required to consider.

Commercial recreation is changing the scope of the profession. The new recreation graduate and practicing professional wanting to become a part of this phase of recreation needs to consider their interests, philosophy, skills, and aptitude carefully. Then they can make intelligent decisions:Commercial Recreation?Employee or Entrepreneur?

APPENDIX A
KEY TERMS

1. **Recreation area**—A tract of land or water, ranging in size from a fraction of an acre to many thousands of acres—on which outdoor recreation is either the major use or one of several major uses. Recreational areas can be either public or private. Example: a National Park, National Forest, National Recreation Area, Seashore, or Lakeshore; a State, county, or municipal park, playground, or forest; a private resort, hunting preserve or campground.

   The equating of one national forest or national park containing numerous recreation sites and other recreation opportunities with a small, single-purpose city park has little meaning. The number of recreation areas is much less significant than the acres involved. For practical reasons, however, the enumeration of recreation areas is presented in the manner reported by the administering agencies.

2. **Recreation site**—A specific tract of public or private land or water within a recreation area that is used or developed primarily or exclusively for a particular recreation use or activity. Sites are usually very much smaller than the recreation areas in which they occur. Example: a campground site, boat marina, or designated ski run.

3. **Recreation facility**—The structures and/or developments on a recreation site placed for the purpose of enhancing recreation opportunuty. Example: a picnic table, a fireplace, a trail, or a boat ramp.

4. **Recreation unit**—The term for counting facilities. Example: a tent or trailer space within a campground site. To illustrate, a recreation campground may have 50 or 100 recreation camp units. Some units, such as swimming, or snowskiing sites, are recorded in acres, and others in capacity, numbers, miles, or feet.

5. **Enterprise**—A privately operated, profit or nonprofit business providing recreation services to the general public or a segment of the public. Enterprises include private camps, clubs, and recreation operations by nonprofit, quasi-public groups such as churches, Boy Scouts, or YMCA's The definition excludes private homes and the recreation facilities associated with them, such as home swimming pools.

6. **Recreation activity**—A leisure time activity which aids in promoting entertainment, pleasure, relaxation, instruction, and other physical, mental, and cultural benefits.

7. **Visit**—One entry of one person into a recreation area or site to carry on one or more recreation activities.

8. **Recreation occasion**—Participation in a recreation activity for all or part of one day. More than one recreation occasion may occur during one day. For example: fishing, picnicking, and hiking during one day count as three recreation occasions—one for each activity. On the other hand, if a person swims two or three times a day, it is counted as one swimming occasion.

9. **Metropolitan area**—As used in this report, is the same as a standard metropolitan statistical area as defined by the Bureau of the Budget. The entire territory of the United States has been classified by the Bureau of the Budget as either: (a) metropolitan, or "inside Standard Metropolitan Statistical Areas (SMSA's)," or (b) nonmetropolitan, or "outside SMSA's." An SMSA is a county or group of contiguous counties, except in New England,[1] which contains at least one city of 50,000 inhabitants or more, or "twin cities" with a combined population of at least 50,000. In addition, other contiguous counties are included in an SMSA if, according to certain criteria, they are essentially metropolitan in character and are socially and economically integrated with the central city.

10. **Urban population**—According to the 1960 Census definition, the urban population comprises all persons living in: (a) places of 2500 inhabitants or more incorporated as cities, boroughs, villages, and towns (except towns in New England, New York, and Wisconsin); (b) the densely settled urban fringe, whether incorporated or unincorporated, of urbanized areas; (c) towns in New England and townships in New Jersey and Pennsylvania which contain no incorporated municipalities as subdivisions and have either 25,000 inhabitants or more or a population of 2500 to 25,000 and a density of 1500 persons or more per square mile; (d) counties in States other than the New England States, New Jersey, and Pennsylvania that have no incorporated municipalities within their boundaries and have a density of 1500 persons or more per square mile; and (e) unincorporated places of 2500 inhabitants or more.

11. **Rural population**—Rural population comprises all persons not included in urban population.

12. **Urbanized areas**—An urbanized area comprise at least one city of 50,000 inhabitants (a central city) plus contiguous closely settled areas generally referred to as the urban fringe.

13. **Urban complex**—An urban complex consists of all countries half or more of which are located within 120 miles of the central city of SMSA's of 500,000 or more

inhabitants. In instances where such cities are within 120 miles of each other, the surrounding counties are combined to form one complex. Within each complex two use zones are established for recreation purposes. The first, the day-use zone, comprises a grouping of counties all or more than half of which are within 40 miles of the selected city(s). The second, the overnight-use zone, includes counties all or more than half of which are within 40 to 120 miles of the selected city(s).

Bureau of Outdoor Recreation, *The Recreation Imperative,* Dept. of the Interior, Superintendent of Documents, Washington D.C. 1974 page 78.

APPENDIX B

STANDARD INDUSTRIAL CLASSIFICATION INDEX DEFINITIONS

DEFINITIONS SIC CODES-1963

Hotels, motels (SIC 7011)—presented in separate categories—Year-round hotels with 25 or more guest rooms, (2) year-round hotels, with less than 25 guest rooms, (3) seasonal hotels (4) motels, tourist courts & (5) Motor hotels. The classification of individual establishments into hotels, motor hotels and motels and tourist courts was based on the respondent's self-designation.

Trailer parks (SIC 7031)—Establishments known as trailer parks primarily engaged in renting trailer space and providing utilities, such as water & electricity.

Sporting, recreational camps (SIC 7032)—Commercially operated sporting or recreational camps providing lodging or lodging and meals. These include boys' and girls' camps, fishing and hunting camps, and dude ranches. Day camps are also included. Camps primarily receiving their financial support from subsidies, donations, contributions, etc. are not included. Also excluded are establishments operated by membership organizations and not open to the general public.

Motion Pictures (SIC 78)—Establishments producing and distributing motion picture and still films and television tapes for theatrical, non-theatrical and television exhibitors, and establishments engaged in services allied to the production and distribution of the films. It also included theater engaged in the exhibition of motion picture films.

Motion picture production, distribution, services (SIC 781, 782)—Establishments primarily engaged in (1) production of theatrical, industrial, educational, and religious motion picture films, (2) production of films and tapes for television (3) production of still and slide films (4) the distribution of motion picture films, other than to television outlets (5) distribution of films and tapes to TV (6) services allied to motion picture distributors such as film delivery service, film buying and booking agencies, and film libraries and (7) services allied to motion picture production such as film processing, editing and titling, casting bureaus, wardrobe and studio property rental, and rental and repair of cameras, etc.

Motion picture theaters, except drive-in (SIC 783)—Commercially operated regular theaters engaged in the exhibition of motion pictures. These establishments are also known as conventional or four-wall theaters. Also those engaged on an itinerant basis with portable projection and sound equipment are included.

Drive-in motion picture (SIC 783)—Commercially operated "open air" or drive-in engaged in the outdoor exhibition of motion pictures.

Amusement and Recreation Services (SIC 79)—Establishments primarily engaged in providing amusement, recreation or entertainment. Symphony orchestras, ballet and opera companies, and similar services organized on a nonprofit basis are included. Those establishments are exempt from payment of Federal income tax under the provisions of Sec. 501 of the Internal Revenue Code which are operated to provide recreational facilities for their own members are excluded. Gambling businesses operated in the state of Nevada, where such businesses are legal, are included., excluded in all other states.

Dance Hall, studios, schools, including chidren's (SIC 791)—Dance halls or ballrooms catering to the general public, dance schools engaged in teaching dancing to adults and children, and dance schools for professionals. The renting of halls for private dances for occasional dances sponsored by fraternal or other organizations is classified as real estate and is excluded here.

Dance Bands, orchestras (except symphonies) (SIC 792)—Dance, bands, orchestras, combos quintets, and similar instrumental organizations presenting popular music on a contract or fee basis for private dances, restaurants, night clubs, radio and TV programs, etc. Symphony orchestras, opera companies, and classical music included elsewhere.

Entertainers (radio and TV) except classical (SIC 792)—Entertainment groups (other than dance bands, orchestras, or similar organizations) who operate on radio and TV. Also included those who entertain in restaurants or night clubs.

Classical music groups (SIC 792)—Symphony orchestras, opera companies, ballet companies, ice shows, concert organizations, and other classical music organizations, such as chamber music groups. Those organized on a non-profit basis also included.

Theatrical presentations, services (SIC 792)—Companies engaged in presenting "live" productions, such as road companies, stock companies, summer theater, burlesques houses, and producers of night club, live radio and TV shows. This included services allied such as theatrical, radio and TV casting agencies, booking agencies for plays, artists, and concerts, scenery lighting, and other equipment services, and ticket agencies for theater and sports events. Also includes the following groups (11 of them) rodeos and marionette puppet shows are included elsewhere.

U.S. Dept of Commerce, Census of Business Reports, U.S. Supt of Documents, Washington D.C. 1958, 1963, 1967, 1972.

Billiard, pool parlors (SIC 793)—engaged in the operating on billiard and pool parlors. Those which have merchandise or food sales equal to 75 percent of total receipts classified under retail trade.

Bowling establishments (SIC 793)75 percent rule as above.

Baseball, football clubs, promoters (SIC 7941)—Operators or promoter of professional or semi-professional baseball, football, hockey and basketball clubs, and promoters of boxing, wrestling and other athletic events. Receipts of such establishments do not include revenue from radio or TV broadcasts from sales of players, from concession operators, or from non-customer revenue. Establishments primarily engaged in renting of stadiums and athletic fields to sports promoters and clubs are classified as real estate.

Race track operations, including racing stables (SIC 7948)—Primarily engaged in the promotion of horse racing, dog racing and automobile and motor cycle racing. Also included those engaged in operation of racing stables, kennels operated by owners of greyhound racing for purses. In 1958 racing dog kennels were combined with "dog race tracks" and horse racing stables were combined with "horse race tracks."

Public golf course (SIC 7942)—Those privately owned and primarily engaged in the operation of courses open to the public on a fee basis. Municipally owned and operated golf courses not included. Membership golf and country clubs in a separate category. Miniature golf and golf driving ranges under "other commercial recreation."

Golf clubs, country clubs (SIC 7947)—Primarily engaged in the operation of golf or country clubs restricted to club members or their invited guests. Clubs exempt from payment of Federal income tax are excluded.

Skating rinks (SIC 7945)—Primarily engaged in operating rinks open to the general public for a fee for roller or ice skating.

Swimming pools (SIC 7949)—Primarily engaged in the operation of swimming pools open to the public for a fee. Municipally operated swimming pools are excluded. Membership operated swimming pools, exempt from Federal income tax are also excluded.

Boat, canoe rentals (SIC 7949)—Commercial establishments primarily engaged in renting small boats and canoes to the general public. Establishments which rent craft with operators or furnish power boat rides are in "other commercial amusements."

Other commercial recreation, not elsewhere classified (SIC 7949)—Other commercial participating sports facilities, such as commercially operated bathing beaches, riding academies, badminton, croquet, and handball courts, miniature golf, par-3golf courses, and golf driving ranges.

Amusement parks, kiddie parks, theme parks (SIC 7949)—Primarily engaged in the operation of amusement parks, kiddielands, and parks devoted to a particular theme. Municipally owned amusement parks are not included. Amusement devices located in amusement parks or operated in connection with fairs, circuses, etc. are included under "concession operators of amusement devices rides, etc." if they are operated on a concession basis.

Concession operators of amusement devices, rides (SIC 7949)–Operators on a concession basis, of amusement devices and rides in amusement parks, fairs, carnivals, and circuses. This was combined with the classification above in the 1958 census.

Carnival, circuses (SIC 7949)–Establishments operating a group of amusement service and/or retail units, and generally know as carnivals, which do not have any fixed exhibition sites, or companies engages in the operation of circuses having acrobatic and animal shows, and individual circus acts. Side shows are also included in this.

Fairs (SIC 7949)–Primarily engaged in arranging and operating the exibitions and related activities usually associated with county or state fairs. Carnivals and side shows which may be part of the fair, but which are independently owned and operated, are included in the classification "carnivals and circuses." Other amusement device concessions independently owned and operated are under "concession operators of amusement devices, rides."

Tourist attractions, natural wonders (SIC 7949)–Privately owned natural or man-made attractions primarily appealing to the tourist trade. Roadside animal farms and botanical exhibits are excluded.

Coin operated amusement devices (SIC 7949)–Primarily engaged in operating coin-operated amusement devices either in their own or in other places of business. Such amusement machines include juke boxes, pinball machines mechanical games, slot machines (where legally authorized) and any similar types of amusement equipment. Penny arcades and amusement parlors are also included.

Other commercial amusements, not elsewhere classified (SIC 7949)–Primarily engaged in the operation of commercial amusements or recreational services, not elsewhere classified such as golf professionals, swimming or ski instructors, ice skating schools, bicycle rentals, domino parlors, boat rent with operator, powerboat rides, pony tracks, wired music, etc.

In efforts to correct previous definitions and to more clearly align related services together, a number of changes in definitions have been made over the years. These are summarized as follows:

DIFFERENCES IN DEFINITIONS

1. As indicated on the chart in 1954 and 1958 the category "amusement parks" included the "consession operators of amusement devices" so the figures for "amusement parks" in 1958 and 1954 are not comparable to later years.
2. In 1954, 1954, and 1963, "swimming pools," "boat, canoe rentals," "bathing beaches," "riding academies, stables," "tourist attractions, natural wonders," and "golf clubs, country clubs" had each been counted separately. In 1967 they were all lumped in with "other commercial recreation and amusements."
3. Fairs operated by government boards or subdivisions were not included in 1967 but they were in earlier censuses.
4. In 1958 and 1954 stable and race tracks were counted together—divided only into

auto racing, dog racing, and horse racing, but the total should not be affected.

5. 1967 was the first year thoroughbred and standardbred horse race tracks were counted separately.

6. In 1967 "other pro athletic clubs" and "Managers and Promoters" were counted separately for the first time.

7. In 1954 symphony orchestras, opera companies and classical music organizations (i.e., string quartets) are included under "theatrical presentations, services" rather than "bands, orchestras, entertainers" so only the total 792 is comparable.

8. The "other not elsewhere listed" under "theatrical presentations" in 1963 and 1958 consists of items not listed separately in the other years— "operators of hall/tent-live theatrical shows" (1963 only); "producer only of New York or road shows" (both yrs.); "producers of summer shows" (1963 only); these included in "other theatrical services."

9. In 1954 "dance halls, studios and schools" did not include childrens or professional schools. This would change totals for 791 and for 79, Ex. 792,3 and for 79.

10. In 1954, 1958 there were no listings for "motor hotels." In later years these have been self-designated so probably will not throw off comparability of totals.

APPENDIX C

GLOSSARY OF ACCOUNTING LANGUAGE*

Accounting—Reporting, recording, analyzing and interpreting the financial transactions of a business enterprise.

Accounting Period—Any time unit decided upon by management. A fiscal year is a 12 month accounting period.

Accounts Receivable—Amounts due the business from guests, customers, credit card agencies and similar sources.

Acid Test or "Quick Ratio"—An approximate measure of the ability of a business to meet its current obligations. Thus, only immediately "liquid" assets of cash, accounts and notes receivable and marketable securities would be used.

Amortization of Intangibles—Annual charge for improvements made to leased assets.

Asset—The cost of goods or services which have been acquired. They may be utilized in either the present or in the future.

Average Rate per Rented Room—Total room revenues divided by number of rooms rented during accounting period.

Balance Sheet—Summary of the organization's assets, liabilities, and owner's equities as of a particular date.

Bonds—Written obligations to repay a given sum of money on a specific date with interest at a fixed rate.

Bookkeeping—The process of collecting, classifying, and recording money transactions. It is a part of the accounting function.

Break-Even—A point in the accounting period when total accumulated revenues are equal to total variable expenses to that particular date, plus fixed expenses for the year.

*Robert W. McIntosh, Management Through Figures, Extension Bulletin 656, Cooperative Extension Service, Michigan State University, 1969, pg 18, 19.

Capital Budgeting—Planning capital expenditures for the most favorable long-range returns.

Cash Flow—Profit (net profit) after federal, state, and local income taxes, plus added back depreciation; the amount of cash actually available to management during an accounting period—for debt reduction or other non-operating usage.

Additional cash flow could be obtained from borrowing or by issuing securities. These are external sources of cash and are not used in comparing investment alternatives. Similarly, sale of fixed assets increase cash flow but are usually not a part of cash flow projection.

Classification of Accounts—Grouping account titles under standard headings and definitions, to make possible meaningful comparisons among lodging establishments.

Control—Function of management concerned with arrangement of operations and the reporting system to be employed for the protection of owners. Involves enforcement of corrections needed to achieve goals and promote efficiency.

Current Ratio—Approximate measure of the ability of the business to meet current liabilities. Computed by dividing current assets by current liabilities.

Debt to Net Worth—Comparison of dollars invested in the business by creditors (shown as short and long-term debt), with dollars invested by owners. Computed by dividing *total debt* by *tangible net worth* (Net worth items such as goodwill, organizational or development expenses are deducted.)

Depreciation—Costs represented by fixed assets, the original cost of which is partly recaptured, currently. Can also be thought of as lost usefulness or expired utility.

Expenditure—Transaction involving present or future payment of cash or other property for goods or services.

Expense—Cost of goods or services which have already been used up or consumed during the current accounting period.

Fixed Expenses—Expenses which do not change as business volume changes, such as real estate taxes, interest on mortgage, depreciation, insurance, manager's salary and similar items.

Funds—Net working capital, figured by subtracting current liabilities from current assets; synonymous with "cash."

Goodwill—Above normal earning power of a business. An amount paid for a successful business that exceeds the fair value of the tangible assets purchased.

Income Statement—Summary of revenue and expense transactions occurring during the reporting period.

Leverage—Earning a higher return on investments as residual owners of common stock in a corporation than would be paid as a fixed return to holders of preferred stock.

Liquidity—Convertibility of assets to cash.

Long-lived Assets (fixed)—Real and personal property which provide needed facilities and services. These costs (except land) are gradually charged as operating expenses over their useful lives through depreciation or amortization.

Long-term Liabilities—Creditor equities which help make possible purchase of fixed assets. Such liabilities must be ultimately liquidated through cash funds created by operations.

Loss—A reverse of the conditions required for a net profit.

Net Cash Benefits—Present value of the total cash flow which obtained through operations during the useful life of the business investment.

Owner's Equity (net worth)—Total investments made in the business plus profits earned through operations which have remained in the business (retained earnings).

Present Value—Comparison of dollars to be received in the future with dollars at hand today using various discount percentages; Important when comparing today's costs of providing business assets with profits to be received in a future time stream.

Profit—Whenever revenues exceed expenses during a given accounting period, a profit has been made.

Profitability Indes—Fraction, ratio, or index number which compares the present value of cash outlay with the present value of total estimated future net cash benefits by present value of the cash outlay. In comparing various investment alternatives, the higher the profitability index, the better the investment.

Revenue—In-flow of assets from transactions involving the provision of services to guests, or the sale of goods to customers.

Semi-variable Expenses—Expenses which are partly fixed and partly variable (electricity). Part of the electricity expense, such as outside lighting, must be incurred regardless of the volume of business, while other uses (guest-room lamps and TV) will vary directly with room occupancy or activity; must be allocated—part to fixed expense, and the remainder to variable expenses.

Stocks—Shares of ownership in a corporation—common or preferred. Preferred owners receive dividends first and common owners last.

Variable Expenses—Expenses incurred in the production of revenues which are directly related to volume of sales. Laundry is a good example.

Stream of Benefits—Net profits estimated over the total future useful life of the investment.

Working Capital—Excess of current assets over current liabilities.

APPENDIX D

INSTRUCTORS
GUIDE
TO
COMMERCIAL
RECREATION:
ONE
APPROACH

One approach by John Bullaro,
a second approach by Arlin Epperson
can be found on page 376.

The value of any fact or theory as bearing on human activity is, in the long run, determined by practical application—that is, by using it for accomplishing some definite purpose.

John Dewey (Dewey: 195)

Commercial recreation education is a comparatively new area of focus for recreation educators. (Instructors: read Chapter 9) Therefore, even the most experienced educator might wince at the prospect of teaching a course in commercial recreation. This hesitation might arise from a feeling of inadequancy about the subject matter or just plain confusion as to the nature of such a course.

Professor Epperson has surveyed this vast area called commercial recreation and brought together a wealth of data. Within this one text is enough material and references to develop the frame work for several courses. It is this wealth of material that suggest the first course in commercial recreation be of a survey type.

SAMPLE COURSE DESCRIPTION AND OUTLINE
as used at

California State University, Northridge
Department of Recreation and Leisure Administration

NUMBER AND TITLE COURSE

Recreation 270—Commercial Recreation

PLACE IN THE COLLEGE CURRICULUM

A lower division course designed to acquaint the recreation major with the many career opportunities available in the commercial field of recreation. Since operating a recreation program for profit involves knowledge of basic business processes, the course is designed to present these processes in an easy to understand—nontechnical— format.

CATALOGUE DESCRIPTION

Study of the nature and function of recreation in commercial agencies and settings. Survey of the development and operation of commercial goods and services offered in the leisure market.

COURSE OBJECTIVES

To provide a broad search of the commercial recreation field to enable the student uncover a possible career choice.

To present business methods and terminology in such a way as to be readily understood by the nonbusiness orientated student.

To develop within each student the ability to synthesis business skills with sound professional recreation philosophy and practice.

To provide each student with an opportunity to blend these newly acquired skills into a potential recreation enterprise of his/her own choosing.

METHODS AND PROCEDURES

Field interviews, lectures, guest speakers, class visits, student presentations, workshops, group discussions.

COURSE OUTLINE

1. Over-view of commercial recreation:
   a. Growth—looking at the current boom.
   b. New emphasis—impact of current energy and economic problem on Recreation.
   c. Compatibility with traditional recreation agencies.
2. Research of the career potential—career notebook project begins 2nd week.
3. Student field interviews of commercial recreation practitioners. Class breaks into groups for discussion and oral reports.
4. What is the profile of a successful entrepreneur?
5. Survey of commercial ventures:
   a. Camping.

    b. Resorts.

    c. Marinas.

    d. Trailer parks.

    e. Retail outlets.

    f. Travel agencies.

    g. Corporations (Disneyland, Magic Mountain).

    h. Franchises.

6. Legal questions relating to commercial recreations; torts, partnership and corporation problems, tax liabilities, elements of contracts.

7. Employment in large commercial corporations:

    a. Is it for you?

    b. Corporate structure.

    c. Political game plan.

    d. Management opportunities and skills.

8. Class field visits:

    a. Commercial camp.

    b. Background manufacturer.

    c. Bicycle shop.

    d. Evaluations.

9. Developing a commercial recreation delivery system:

    a. Financing.

    b. Marketing.

    c. Facilities.

    d. Product.

    e. Sole proprietorship; partnerships; corporations.

    f. Feasibility studies.

10. Preparing proposals:

    a. What are lenders looking for?

    b. What are your chances for success?

    c. Dealing with lenders—what kind of people are they?

11. Leadership for Success: Planning, delegating, time control, personal grooming, writing skills, oral skills, interpersonal relationships.

12. Individual Consultation with instructor on class project.

PROJECTS:

A. Career opportunities = 20%.

B. Profiles of success = 20%.

C. Business proposal = 30%.

D. Book report = 10%.

E. Final examination = 20%.

Note: this is usually handed out the first day of class and reviewed carefully.

Substantively, commercial recreation is not new. We now know that is has been around at least since the early phoenicians traveled throughout the Middle East. But as a formalized discipline it has, within the past five years, only begun to gain acceptance by the profession as a legitimate field of inquiry. This shift of interest to include commercial recreation brings with it many new challenges for educators.

Recreation is an eclectic profession, having absorbed and synthesized data from such fields as sociology, antropology, physical education, psychology, and education into the discipline we refer to as recreation and leisure. Commercial recreation adds a new discipline, business education, into this amalgam of disciplines.

The following is a listing of some behaviorial objectives that the students in this course will hopefully achieve.

BEHAVIORAL OBJECTIVES FOR COMMERCIAL RECREATION _____

Upon completion of the course on commercial recreation the student should be able to perform as follows:

1. Identify the various catagories of commercial recreation.
2. To differentiate between public, nonprofit, and commercial delivery systems.
3. To develop a financial proposal suitable for presentation to a financial institution or investor.
4. To solve simple marketing problems related to recreation services and products.
5. To use common business and legal terms.
6. To understand the personality differences between the organizational practitioner and the entrepreneurial type.
7. To identify situations that are potential liability problems in recreation.
8. To write acceptable business letters and memos.
9. To evaluate business financial statements and to identify problem areas.
10. To locate potential career opportunities in commercial recreation.

A personal philisophical foundation helps to convey to students how their study of commercial recreation will serve many professional settings. It is helpful to realize that practitioners do not practice in a vacuum. Most every ambient where recreation needs are served requires, on the part of the practitioner, some understanding of business. Several years ago a graduate student submitted a thesis based on a descriptive study of a YMCA director. One recommendation by the thesis committee to the student was to include basic business courses in programs that prepare students to work in these type of agencies. The respondants reported spending as much as 60 percent of their time on business related activities. Also, the recent economic recession closed many agencies due to lack of funds. Stated another way—the recession may have required recreation agency directors to be competitive in the market place but they were not prepared for the battle.

This outline and the course it serves are not supposed to convince the student of the value of commercial recreation education. Rather, the outline illustrates the basic premise upon which this course is built: commercial recreation concepts and practice are applicable to most professional settings.

This reasoning suggests the first step: establishing the legitimacy of the course.

STEP 1-LEGITIMATING-TEXT: CHAPTERS 1-3

To legitimate some ideas, phenomena, or action often means establishing the basis upon which others can accept what it is you are try to accomplish.

In regards to commercial recreation, students will tend to accept the notion that "selling recreation" is not the antithesis to professional ethics when they understand how the use of certain business skills can upgrade the quality of recreation delivery systems in general.

To further legitimize the course it is helpful to review the economic, social, and political basis of free enterprise. This philisophical foundation will help the student place recreation services in the over-all scheme of the American business scene.

PROJECT

To further legitimate the course, the students should be made aware of the many opportunities that exist in commercial recreation.

To get the student attuned to unique career opportunities I use the CAREER OPPORTUNITIES PROJECT (COP). Since few, if any, positions in this field are listed under "Commercial Recreation" the COP project will point the student to potential sources of job leads.

The following outline has proven to yield excellent projects.

COMMERCIAL RECREATION 270	Dept. of Rec. & Les.
CAREER OPPORTUNITY PROJECT	Cal. State Univ.
	Northridge

PURPOSE

This project is intended to help you become opportunity oriented. One of the most critical challenges of your life will be marketing what you know. Obtaining meaningful and relevant employment does not just happen, it comes about by design. It has been said that, luck is where preparation and opportunity cross. This project should provide the opportunity while your general curriculum pursuit provides the preparation.

METHOD

It is obvious that many students will not seek careers in the commercial sector of recreation but will work in public, private, and institution settings. Considering most recreation delivery systems are commercial in nature it is possible that interim employment will be needed before a specific career choice opens up. Begin immediately to scan newspapers, journals, and other publications for announcements, articles, and discussions relating to careers in commercial recreation.

Start a folder marked *Career Opportunities*, and cut out all relevant material. Include resort ads that appeal to you as a nice place to work, articles about certain recreation industires, and so forth.

By mid-term you should have collected 70 to 100 different "opportunities." Your career portfolio is ready to assemble.

Portfolio outline:

A. Table of contents.

B. Your personal resume.

C. A statement about your career interests.

   1. What are your strengths.

   2. What are your hobbies.

   3. How does your view of the future effect your outlook on life.

   4. What is your vision about the future of recreation.

   5. What advice has been given you about your career.

D. Divide career opportunities into a classification system (such as Krauses).

E. Comment on each opportunity or classifications of opportunities as to how you see them relating to you. What job do you see for recreators that are either apparent or implied? What recreation services could you suggest that would make this particular agency more successful?

Sources:

A. Wall Street Journal.

B. Christian Science Monitor.

C. Regional newspaper.

D. Forbes-Newsweek-U.S. News and World Report.

E. Small Business Administration.

F. Business opportunities catalogue: Strout Reality, United Farm.

G. Travel section-Sunday newspaper.

H. Trade publications.

Instructors should emphasize to the students the importance of beginning the project at the beginning of the term. The project may sound redundent (to cut and paste); therefore, the tendency to procrastinate. The student is learning to research career opportunities and to develop sound research habits take time.

I generally hand out the COP project formate in the first week of class. This would also be a good time to assign, and later review, Chapters 1-3 of text. Use study questions in the back of each chapter.

Chapter 4, The Supply, should be dealt with separately. I would suggest completing this chapter before commencing Step 2.

STEP 2 UNDERSTANDING THE RECREATION BUSINESS ENTERPRISE: TEXT: CHAPTER 6 AND 7 _____

Developing an understanding of the business enterprise. Chapter 6, Planning and Development of the Recreation enterprise, could be assigned reading at this time. Instructors might find chapter 7, Marketing the Product, valuable material to have mastered while discussing Chapter 6.

I generally initiate this step with a two session lecture on "Who Succeeds in Commercial Recreation."

This section of the course is designed to explore success, isolate certain common denominators, and encourage students to discover answers for themselves. The following outline has been helpful in preparing the lectures.

Some qualities most successful entrepreneurs usually have:
1. Accomplishment.
2. Responsibility for decisions.
3. Concentration.
4. High energy.
5. Versatile.
6. Handle details.
7. Full potential.
8. Imaginative.
9. Optimistic.
10. Handle money wisely.
11. Help others.
12. Patient.
13. Ethical.

In attempting to convey the essence of the business environment the textbook uses the microcosm of the small retail operations. One can usually find all the elements of large corporation (save the element of manufacturing, which is beyond the parameters of this course) in the study of a backpacking store, tennis pro-shop, or a private children camp. To this end a guest speaker or, preferrable a field trip, will help to take the abstract notions of a successful entrepreneur and make them more personal to the student.

PROJECT

To further acquaint the student with the commercial recreation environment the field interview guide project takes the student into the field on his/her own to interview two business owners in an area of special interest.

This project hopes to accomplish the following:
A. Give the student experience in approaching business owners;
   1. The student writes an introductory letter to the proposed interviewee stating his mission and that he/she will be calling to arrange for an appointment.

2. The student follows up the letter with a telephone call attempting to make a firm appointment.

B. Give the student an opportunity to gain deeper insights into a particular segment of commercial recreation that is of special interest.

The student is urged to give a copy of the outline to the business owner at the time of interview. Students are urged to send follow-up thank-you notes. Copies of all correspondence sent to employer must accompany the final report. The project is shared with other members of the class.

Following is a draft of the field interview guide:

COMMERCIAL RECREATION 270
FIELD INTERVIEW GUIDE

  I. Background data
    A. A description of the business (what does it offer the consumer).
    B. What were the preliminary reasons for starting the business.
    C. What research was done prior to opening of the business?
    D. How did the owners background influence them in starting this business? (Did they have experience in this field, were employed in a similar business, etc.)
    E. Financing:
      1. Did the owner feel an adequate estimate of costs was made initially?
      2. Does the owner feel he had adequate financing in the beginning?
      3. What sources would the owner suggest you go to to raise necessary capital?
    F. What outside professional help was employed at the beginning?
    G. What problems did he/she face in the beginning? Why did they arise?
    H. At any point in the beginning did the owner feel discouraged? why?
    I. If they had an opportunity to start their business all over again what would they do differently? why?
  II. Operating the business
    A. What advertising was done initially?
    B. What advertising is done today?
    C. How is successful advertising judged?
      1. Does competition affect the business? How?
      2. What is the owner doing to meet competition?
      3. How many competitors in the area?
    D. Is there a customer profile?
    E. How many employees are there today? How many were there when the business first started?
 III. Summary and conclusions (student answers)
    A. What did you learn from this interview?
    B. What would you have done differently and why?
    C. How do you size up Mr./Ms.   and their business?

STEP 3 LEGAL AND FINANCIAL CONSIDERATIONS ⎯⎯⎯⎯⎯

To understand this section students are required to go to the library and write out definitions to the following legal terms.

COMMERCIAL RECREATION 270
LEGAL AND BUSINESS TERMS ⎯⎯⎯⎯⎯⎯⎯⎯⎯⎯⎯⎯⎯⎯

1. Abstract of title.	22. Bona fide.	43. Injunction.
2. Acknowledgment.	23. Capacity.	44. Insured.
3. Action.	24. Caveat emptor.	45. Joint tenancy.
4. Adjudication.	25. Certified check.	46. Invalid.
5. Administrator.	26. Charter.	47. Lease.
6. Affidavit.	27. Civil action.	48. Lien.
7. Alias.	28. Claimant.	49. Merchanics lein.
8. Amortise.	29. Copyright.	50. Mortgage.
9. Anser.	30. Close corporation.	51. Offeree.
10. Appeal.	31. Deed.	52. Offeror.
11. Arbitration.	32. Defendant.	53. Option.
12. Assignee.	33. Draft.	54. Referee.
13. Assignor.	34. Easement.	55. Rescind.
14. Attachment.	35. Endorse.	56. Sinking fund.
15. Bankrupt.	36. Encumbrance.	57. Tenant.
16. Beneficiary.	37. Estate.	58. Tort.
17. Bequeath.	38. Fee simple.	59. Trust deed.
18. Bill of exchange.	39. Fiduciary.	60. Usury.
19. Bill of lading.	40. Foreclosure.	61. Writ.
20. Bill of sale.	41. Goodwill.	62. Zoning.
21. Binder.	42. Incapacity.	

This section is composed of approximately six lectures and discussions sessions on the following:

A. General Business
  1. Sale proprietor:
    a. Advantages.
    b. Disadvantages.
    c. Examples.
    d. Guest speaker.
  2. Partnerships
    a. Advantages.
    b. Disadvantages.
    c. Examples.

        d. Guest speaker.
   3. Corporations
        a. Advantages.
        b. Disadvantages.
        c. Examples.
        d. Guest speaker (usually from a large hotel or amusement theme part who talks about career opportunities).
   4. Principals of leadership. (Usually a short review of some of the basic recreation leadership literature: One Lecture). Review study questions 5, Management of the Recreation Enterprise.
B. Legal concepts
   1. Negligence—tort law.
   2. Law of contracts.

STEP 4 "STARTING MY OWN RECREATION BUSINESS" TEXT: CHAPTER 8

Here is the place to begin tying together the material covered in Steps 1-3. The student will gain an elementary experience in preparing a feasibility study. The Small Business Administration (SBA) provides many pamphlets and brochures at no cost that can assist the instructor and students. The SBA also will provide guest speakers to address this subject in depth.

PROJECT

The following outline is taken from the SBA's, Small Marketers Aid No. 150. The student is asked to develop a fictitious business by answering the following questions:
1. What business am I in?
2. What goods or service do I provide?
3. Where is my market? Who will buy? Why will they buy? When?
4. Who is my competition? Why?
5. My sales strategy?
6. Construction Plans—a rough layout of facilities.
7. Financing Plans-Where will the money come from?
8. Organization and personnel.
9. Optional—Cashflow and breakeven charts.
10. Management controls—feed back. How will you know how you are doing?

   The above outline should be covered in detail by the instructor. This will take 2 class hours.

   This project can be expanded or simplified according to the course emphasis.

   In the past two years eight students have taken this final project and started their own recreation business. These business include:

Backpacking store
Pet shop
Book store
Speed and performance center
Private therapeutic recreation practice
Swim school
Ski rental business
Student ski travel agency

This step is concluded with students making a report on their projects.

CONCLUSION

Since there is a great deal of outside work given to the students, you may want to give class time off to compensate for the additional hours spent in field trips and interviewing. During these "off" hours the instructor should be available to counsel students on their projects. This might be the most important part of the course is the projects.

Recreation students are a very special group of people. They often express a deep disinterest in business and business related matters. They say they choose recreation as a profession because they want to work with people on a "deep and personal level." To a great extent, this is true. That is why it is imperative that the instructor present the business and legal data in an understandable and useful format. Step 1, legitimating the course, is important in that it ties the students needs and interests to the course content, so my most poignant observation is that the instructor do a thorough job in preparing step 1.

This chapter opened with a quote form the leading historical exponent of student-centered education, John Dewey. It will close with some thoughts from a contemporary exponent of student-centered education, Carl Rogers (Rogers: 157-163).

1. Human beings have a natural potentiality for learning.
2. "Significant learning takes place when the subject matter is perceived by the student as having relevance for his own purpose."
3. "Learning which involves a change in the perception of oneself is threatening and tends to be resisted."
4. "Much significant learning is acquired through doing."
5. "Learning is facilitated when the student participates responsibility in the learning process."

It has been attempted to convey these concepts in the writing of this chapter. Your personal commitment is to move your teaching methods in this direction—student centered.

It is hoped that this chapter may provide a skeleton by which others may proceed. As we have done with other disciplines, let us do with business—bring its concepts to bear on making the leisure experience more re-creating for more people.

Selected Bibliography

Appenzeller, Herb. *Athletics and the Law.* The Mechie Company, Charlottesville, Virginia. 1975.

Broom, H. N., and Longenecker. *Small Business Management.* South-Western Publishing Company, Fourth Edition. 1975.

Bursk, Edward and Chapman, John F. *Modern Marketing Strategy.* A mentor Book. New York. 1965.

Coughlin, George Cordon. *Your Introduction to Law.* Barnes and Noble Books. New York, 2nd edition. 1975.

Dewey, John. *John Dewey on Education* Selected Writings. Reginald D. Archambault, Ed. The University of Chicago Press. 1974.

Gatti, Richard D. and Gatti, Daniel J. *Encyclopedia Dictionary of School Law.* Parker Publishing Company, Inc. West Myach, New York. 1975.

Kotler, Philip. *Marketing For Nonprofit Organization.* Prentice-Hall, Inc., 1975.

Rogers, Carl R. *Freedom to Learn, Studies of the Person.* Edited by Carl Rogers and William R. Coulson. Charles E. Merrill Publishing Company, Columbus, Ohio. 1969.

Van Der Smissen, Betty. *Legal Liability of Cities and Schools for Injuries in Recreation and Parks.* The W. H. Anderson Company, Cincinnati, 1968.

RESERVE READING LIST
UNDERGRADUATE LIBRARY

1. "Is This Any Time To Start A Business?" *Changing Times,* October 1975 pp.24-28.
2. "Mood of the Consumer," Paul Novak, Supervising Consultant, Harris-Kerr-Foster.
3. "Why Consumer Attitudes Matter More Than Economics," *Nation's Business,* September 1975, pp 34-38.
4. "What Makes Advertising Effective?" *Harvard Business Review,* March-April 1975 pp 96-103.
5. "Advertising: The Battle Against Mediocrity," Tom Dillon, *Vital Speeches of the Day,* pp 491-495.
6. "America's Eating-Out Splurge," *Business Week,* October 27,1975, pp 43-61.
7. "Technical Writing: A Special Section," *Writers Digest,* October 1975, pp 14-20.
8. "The Leisure Industries: Investigations of Commercial Recreation and Tourism" Leisure Today, A special insert of the *Journal of Physical Education and Recreation,* November-December 1975

SAMPLE COURSE DESCRIPTION AND OUTLINE _____

RPA 391 PRIVATE AND COMMERCIAL RECREATION
Department of Recreation & Park Administration
University of Missouri-Columbia

2:30-4:30 Tuesdays   Arlin Epperson
(3 hours credit with lab and field trips)

I. COURSE OBJECTIVES:

1. *Awareness*—scope and nature of private and commercial recreation, travel, and tourism.
2. *Employment*—explore the area for potential employment in the private and commercial recreation field.
3. *Investigation*—by the student into a specific commercial and private recreation enterprise, and a specific career opportunity.
4. *Skills*—to assist the student in acquiring the knowledges, insights, and attitudes that should help him to work in or manage a successful commercial recreation enterprise.

II. COURSE REQUIREMENTS (see attached for descriptions):

1. 100 points for Assignment #1.
2. 100 points for Assignment #2.
3. 50 points for take-home final exam (to be discussed and explained in class).
4. 50 points for one quiz on reserve reading articles (see attached list).
5. 50 points for attendance at three scheduled field trips (approximately 16.6 points per field trip).

TAKE-HOME FINAL EXAM (50 points)

This take-home final exam will be assigned and discussed. It can be turned in before or during the final exam period. It will be based on all information presented in the course, and need not exceed five pages.

DESCRIPTION OF ASSIGNMENTS _____

ASSIGNMENT # 1 (100 Points)

JOB DESCRIPTION:

The purpose of this assignment is for the student to research and investigate a specific position in a commercial enterprise. The position's reponsibilities, its relation to other positions in the enterprise, its overall relation and importance to the operation of the enterprise, an idea of how many of these positions exist, and your own opinion as to the prospectus for these positions in the future.

GROUND RULES:

1. The student is encouraged to select a position that he or she is personally interested in, or that can be found at a commercial enterprise of specific interest.
2. The assignment will be discussed the first day of class.
3. The student will submit his or her position the second day of class.
4. While students may select identical positions, the papers are to be written and researched independently.
5. The instructor will have a list of positions for students to review only if they cannot select or decide a position themselves.
6. The instructor will be available to discuss this assignment and specific positions upon request.
7. The assignment is due 2/24. The length is not to exceed five type-written pages.

ASSIGNMENT # 2 (100 Points)

OPERATIONAL INVESTIGATION:

The purpose of this assignment is for two students—working together—to personally investigate/review/research the operation of a specific commercial recreation enterprise on the basis of all information presented in the class and field trips.

GROUND RULES:

1. The enterprise may be located in Columbia, adjacent towns, in the student's home town, or elsewhere.
2. The assignment will be due the last class period prior to stop day.
3. An example of the investigative process will be made in class to give students a clearer idea of the nature of the assignment (i.e., what to look for, ask for, and why).

DATE	TOPIC	SPEAKERS	ASSIGNMENTS
1/13	Travel & Tourism: Today's Commercial Leisure Market.	Arlin Epperson	Assignments discussed; Field trip schedules: Introduction read Chapters 1-2.
1/20	Travel & Tourism & the Missouri Economy	Jim Pasley, Director Mo. Division Tourism	Read Chapter 9 and selected reading following. Submit job titles per research in Assign. 1.
1/27	Demand and Supply	Arlin Epperson	Have read Chapters 3 & 4.
2/3	Financing & Budgeting for a Commercial Enterprise.	Arlin Epperson	Have read Chapter 5.
2/10	How to Operate a Commercial Facility & Why; What it takes for careers in Commercial Recreation and Why.	Robert Blundred, Exec. Director, International Assoc. of Amusement Parks and Attractions	First assignment due.
2/17	Feasibility & The Planning Process.	Arlin Epperson	Have read Chapter 6; Field trip to bowling alley and ice chalet scheduled this week.
2/24	Planning & Building an Amusement Attraction.	Mike Jenkins, Pres. Leisure & Rec. Concept Inc., Dallas, Texas	
3/2	Marketing	Arlin Epperson	Have read chapter 7. Submit enterprises to be researched for Assignment #2.
3/6-3/15	SPRING BREAK		

3/16	Marketing at a Major Themed Attraction	Dave Holt, Director of Marketing, Worlds of Fun	Discuss details of Kansas City field trip.
3/23	Working with your TV, Radio, and Newspaper Ad Sales Persons.	Mike Kelpe, Rick Wise & Mary Beth Winslow Sales Representatives from KFMZ-FM, *Col. Missourian* and KOMU-T.V. respectively	
3/30	Hospitality & Employee Relations	Arlin Epperson	Quiz over reserve reading articles.
4/6	Franchise Operations, Commercial Camp-grounds & Food Ser-vice.	Jim Estes & Fred Cooper Formerly Executives with Sa-fari Inn Campgrounds. Mr. Cooper is manager of Jona's in Columbia. Mr. Estes is with Cheese Villa, Inc.	
4/13	Open in-class discussion of first papers and material covered up to this point. Possible field trip to Woodrail Tennis Club & Country Club of Misssouri.	Arlin Epperson	
4/20	What the Future Holds.	Arlin Epperson	Have read Chapter 8. Field trip to Wood-rail Tennis Club and Country Club Tues. or Thurs. during class period. Take-home final exam papers as-signed and discussed.
4/27	Field Trip to Kansas City scheduled.		Monday 4/26/ As-signment #2 due.
5/3	Final Exam Period Scheduled.	Arlin Epperson	Exams due. Papers discussed.

INDEX

Accessibility, 88, 225, 231
Accrued accounting, 208
Activity days, 65
Advertising, 75
  awareness, 279
  magazine, 279
  newspaper, 279
  outdoor display, 278
  radio, 279
  television, 14
Age, 40
Allocentric/cosmopolitans, 32
American Express, 10
Amusement and entertainment, 315
Analyzing business, 211
Anticipated revenues, 241
Associations, 21, 22, 113, 116, 124, 129, 133,
      138, 139, 141, 144, 147, 153, 157,
      160, 163, 166, 170, 173, 174, 177,
      180, 181, 182
  American Society of Travel Agents, 11
  Discover America Travel, 3
  International Union of Official Travel
      Organizations, 16
  National Association of Conservation
      Districts, 93
  National Recreation and Parks Association,
      110
  Retail Travel Agents, 11
  Tourism and Travel, 5
Attendance, 86, 233
  peak, 238

  projected, 234, 238
Attitude of luxury, 16
Attitude of community, 229
Attractiveness of locality, 229
Automobile, 8, 36, 37
Automobile Club of America, 300
Auxiliary revenues, 240

Balance sheet, 204, 235
Benefits of travel, 26
Bookkeeping, control systems, 207
      procedures, 206
Bottom line, 188
Break even concept, 209
Brochures, 273
Bureau of Census, 19, 96
Bureau of Outdoor Recreation (BOR), 59, 60,
      225, 241
  1965 study, 91
  1973 study, 93

Capacity requirements, 238
Capital expenses, 242
Career cluster, 312
Cash budget, 200
Cash inflow, 200
Cash outflow, 200
Chamber of Commerce, 20, 283
Chambers of Commerce, 283
Characteristics, of market, 224
  of private enterprise, 90
Civil rights, 194

College enrollment, 13
Community awareness, 284
Competencies needed, 324
Competitor analysis, 266
Consumer orientation, 255
Controlling, 185
Coordinating, 185
Cost, 39
Cultural objectives, 14
Current assets, 204
Curriculum implications, 326, 328

Daily expense record, 201
Daily income receipt record, 201
Definitions:
  accounting language, 362
  camper day, 19
  demand, 54
  key terms, 353
  need, 54
  occasion day, 19
  outdoor recreation, 18
  outing, 19
  problems of, 16, 63, 289
  recreation, 18, 20
    expenditure, 73
  Standard Industrial Classification Index,
    357
  tourism, 20
  tourist, 17
  travel, 20
  trip, 19
  vacation, 19
  visitor day, 19
Degrees in commercial recreation, 329
Demand, 64, 83
  indoor recreation, 70
  manpower, 327
  measuring, 64
  outdoor recreation, 65
  recreation, 2, 54–84
Department of Agriculture, 216
  Department of Commerce, 96, 216
  Department of Health, 231
  tion of services, 224
  area, 239
  of hotels and motels, 10

Direct mail marketing, 273
Disney, 51, 68, 221, 227

Economic Development Administration, 216
Economics of travel and tourism, 6
Education, 13, 28, 40, 295
  implications for commercial recreation,
    311–334
Employment, levels, 332
  projections, 322
Enterprises, 157
  bicycling, 125
  bowling, 130
  canoe liveries, 138
  categories of, 110
  country clubs, 173
  cultural-historical-educational, 110
  health and sports clubs, 178
  homes associations, 180
  ice skating rinks, 140
  marinas/boat yards, 161
  motorcycles, off road vehicles, 164
  outdoor amusement parks & attractions, 117
  recreation vehicles, 167
  resident camps, 149
  resorts and hotels, 175
  roller skating rinks, 141
  second homes, 181
  snowmobiling, 171
  snow skiing, 144
  sports, convention and entertainment, 113
  tennis, 157
  travel camps, 153
  wilderness outfitters, 134
Entertainment, 6, 16, 45
Equal Opportunity Employment Guidelines,
  194
Estimating net income, 248
Evaluating, 186
Expenditures, for recreation, 72–82
  for tourism, 72

Family, activities, 48, 53
  business, 330
  income, 294
  spending, 13
Farmers Home Administration, 216, 221
Feasibility analysis, 222–242

Federal Extension Service, 216, 221
Federal lands, 86
Fees, 256
Financial management, 199
Financial records, 201
Financial resources, 199
Fire, 215
Fixed costs, 244
Flair, showmanship, 51, 234
Food and lodging, 6
Forecasting, 288
Functions of management, 185
Future forecasting, 298, 306
    education implications for, 298
    external implications for, 289, 304
    income implications for, 294
    internal implications for, 307
    mobility implications for, 297
    social implications for, 298
    spending implications for, 289
    time implications for, 295
    urbanization implications for, 298
Future implications, 288–310

Gate receipts, 240
Goals and objectives, 222

Health spas, 8
Highway travel data, 232
Historical attractions, 227
Home, 305
Hospitality, 230
    and recreation, 316
    resources, 5
    training, 276
Human resources, 191

Income, disposable, 11
    real family, 11
Industrial and community attractions, 227
Industrialization, 36
Information systems and services, 320
Initial expenses, 242
Inservice training, 196
Insurance, 212
Interest structures, 5
Interstate freeways, 9, 13
Invitee, 213

Job description, 192, 193
Jobs, in commercial recreation, 312
Job specifications, 192

Legacy for America, 62
Leisure, activities, 17
    career field, 313
    time, 2, 14, 18, 42, 71, 295
Leisure oriented work, 291
Liability, 212
    limitations, 213
Licensee, 213
Liquidity, 200
Local recreation areas, 87
Lodging, 317
Long-term assets, 204

Management, 185–220
    analysis, 222, 223, 242
    characteristics of good business, 211
    creative, 230
    financial, 199
    theory of, 217
Management analysis, 223, 242–253
Management Information System, 207
Management of, facilities, 188
    personnel, 190
    programs or services, 190
Manager, recreation enterprise, 54
Man made attractions, 226
Manpower, demand, 327
    study, 333
    supply, 327
Market, 6
    analysis, 222–242
    characteristics of, 224
    forecasting, 264
    setmentation, 260
    travel, 16
    travel and tourism, 6
Market analysis, 257
Marketing, 27, 254–287
    budget, 281
    cycles, 266
    plan, 270
    sins, 256
    zones, 232
Mobility, 13
Mortgage and debt records, 204

National Resources Review Commission, 16, 18
Natural attractions, 225
Natural resources, 5
Negligence, 213
Nonprofit organizations, 57
NRPA employ, 322

Occupational environments, 316
Occupations in, amusement and entertainment, 313
  attractions and amusement parks, 322
  clubs, 323
  cultural services, 316
  entertainment services, 316
  food and beverage services, 316
  hospitality and recreation, 313
  lodging, 316
  recreation, 316
  recreation resources, 313
  recreation services, 313
  resorts and camps, 322
  sports, 316
  sports and entertainment centers, 322
  tourism, 313
  tourist attractions, 322
  travel services, 316
  vacation excursions, 322
One-write system, 206
Operating expenses, 243
Organizational chart, 187
Organizational theory, 186
Organizing, 185
Outdoor amusement industry, 45–53
Outdoor recreation, areas, 86
  research, 59, 68
  resources review, 37, 58

Package plans, 280
Participation, 64, 66, 69
  reasons for no, 69
Payroll records, 204
Personality, 33, 44
Personnel, 196
  evaluation, 197
  inservice training, 196
  orientation, 195
  recruitment, 192

  selection, 192
  supervison, 196
Planning, 185
  accessibility in, 231
  attitude of community in, 229
  goals and objectives in, 222
  information and directions in, 233
  location and accessibility in, 225
  market for, description, 224
  services in, description, 224
  Zone penetration in, 235
Planning and development, 221–253
Pre-opening expenses, 242, 243, 244
Pricing, 209
Private areas and facilities, 88
Private nonprofit recreation, 89
Private recreation enterprises, 94
Probationary period, 196
Problems of categorization, 97
Product analysis, 265
Profit and loss statement, 202, 203, 250
Promotion, 271
Providers, 85
  private, 85
  public, 85
  quasi-public, 85
Psychocentric/locals-passivees, 33
Psychology of travel, 26
Public attitude, 289
Publicity, 280
Public recreation, 56, 58
Public versus private, 55

Railroad, 8, 45
Reasons for increased travel, 45–53
Recreation, 317
  education, 311
  enterprises, 92, 94
  private, 57
  resources, 313
  services, 313
Recreation activities, 20, 60, 61, 65, 66, 67, 68, 70, 74, 91, 95, 302, 305
  indoor, most popular, 71
  private, 68
Recreation enterprises, 92
Recruitment, 192

Safety, 214
Safety records, 48
Secondary income, 221
Selling, 254
Service, 188, 255
Shopping mall, 304
Small Business Administration, 216, 221
Social welfare program, 56
Societies, Greek, 1
  leisure, 1
  Roman, 1, 7
Soil Conservation Service, 93, 216, 221
Southern Travel Directors Council, 326
Span of control, 186
Staffing, 185
Staff morale, 197
Standard Industrial-Classification System
  (SIC), 96
State, highway department, 236
  lands, 87
  recreation areas, 86
  tourism departments, 284
Supply, 85–184
  manpower, 327
Supply and demand, 229

Tax considerations, 210
Tax records, 202
Technology, 14
Television, 42, 60
Tertiary zone, 235
Theft, procedures for reducing, 208
Tourism, 3, 314
  associations, 281
  attractions, 7
  education, 327
  industry, 3
  services, 4
Tourist, activities, 20
  attractions, 20
Track record, 330
Trade journals, 23, 24, 117, 124, 129, 134,
    144, 148, 153, 157, 160, 163, 167,
    171, 173, 174, 177, 180
Transient, 239
Transportation, 6, 55
Travel, 3, 5, 8, 9, 42

air, 9
automobile, 9
barriers to, 42, 43
benefits of, 26
bus, 9
cultural motives for, 28
educational motives for, 28
increase in, 45
  reasons for, 11
motivation studies, 34, 35, 36
motives for, 28
phychology of, 26
rail, 9
reasons for, 30, 43
social significance of, 41
water, 9
Travel agencies, 283
Travel agent, 10
Travel and tourism, components of, 4, 21, 35
  expenditures, 257
  history of, 7, 21
  industry, 3, 4
Travel industry, 3
Travel motivation studies, 34–41
Tresspasser, 213
TWA, 21

U.S. Office of Education, 312
U.S. Travel Bureau, 302
Urbanization, 13, 41
User behavior, 262

Vacation homes, 71
Vandalism, 212, 215
Variable costs, 244

Why People Travel, 26–53, 257
Wisconsin one-write system, 206
Work alienation, 42
Work ethic, 291
Work incentives, 197
Work week, 1, 14

Year round leisure, 41
Young adults, 15, 50

Zone penetration, 234, 235

Date Due